PARIS

1965-1971

MW01075000

Books by Janet Flanner

PARIS JOURNAL

VOLUME II 1965-1971

JANET FLANNER (GENÊT)

Edited by William Shawn

A Harvest Book

Harcourt Brace Jovanovich
New York and London

Copyright © 1965, 1966, 1967, 1968, 1969, 1970 by
The New Yorker Magazine, Inc.
Copyright © 1971 by The New Yorker Magazine, Inc.

All rights reserved. No part of this publication may be
reproduced or transmitted in any form or by any means,
electronic or mechanical, including photocopy, recording, or
any information storage and retrieval system, without
permission in writing from the publisher.

Printed in the United States of America

Harvest edition published by arrangement with
The New Yorker Magazine, Inc.

Library of Congress Cataloging in Publication Data

Flanner, Janet, 1892–
Paris Journal.

(A Harvest book ; HB 359–360)
Reprint of the ed. published by Atheneum, New York.
Includes index.
CONTENTS: [v. 1] 1944–1965.—v. 2. 1965–1971.
1. Paris—History—1944–   2. France—Politics and
government—1945–   3. Paris—Intellectual life.
I. Title.
DC737.F55 1977   944'.361'082   76-45462
ISBN 0-15-670950-3 (v. 1)
0-15-670951-1 (v. 2)

First Harvest edition 1977

A B C D E F G H I J

PARIS JOURNAL

1965-1971

1965

December 29, 1964

The record-breaking price of close to seven million francs recently paid to a French collector by the London National Gallery for a large and controversial Cézanne, "Les Grandes Baigneuses," naturally set a new high-water mark in talk in Paris art circles about picture prices vs. aesthetic values, about why collectors collect and what their judgments are worth. Part of this stimulation came from, and some of the answers were discernible in, an unusual husband-and-wife art collection of two hundred items gathered over almost half a century by M. George and Mme. Adèle Besson, which is now on temporary view in the Salle Mollien in the Louvre, because it was recently donated by the couple to the French state. Attention was further attracted to the collection by Mme. Besson's unexpectedly dying the very morning the pictures were put on public view—apparently her first absence from her husband's side in their long art-appreciation career together. They both came from the Jura region (whose chief city, Besançon, is to receive the best part of their pictures for its ill-supplied state museum), where he, a strong Socialist, inherited a small concern that made tobacco pipes. He moved to Paris with his wife in 1904, saw his first modern art, by van Gogh and then by Whistler (he despised the latter), visited the revolutionary Fauve salon of 1905, and, in 1908, ordered his first modern canvas—a portrait of his Adèle by the Fauvist van Dongen. She must have been lovely then, with great black eyes like wine grapes, which the artist stylistically swelled to the size of plums. In 1909, by scrimping,

he was able to order his portrait by Bonnard. Already he was keeping realistic notes: "At this time, Bonnard wore steel pince-nez and
a dark beard. From his upper lip protruded two incisors, which a
dentist twenty years before had filed down—inappropriate to his
frank and astonished expression. As he painted, he was crunching
nut candies, which he pulled from a tiny paper sack." Besson appreciated Bonnard's paintings (he eventually owned six), admiring
him for the same reasons that many French collectors distrusted
him—for his malicious social fantasy, loose painting style, and
bright colors, "which at the end of his life became a frenzy." Soon
after his Bonnard portrait, the Bonnards and the Bessons were dining together weekly. In 1918, Besson ordered a small portrait of
Adèle from Renoir, which the old man dashed off in one morning
while his servant sang "La Madelon." But he was already dying in
his wheelchair, and her face is terra-cotta, colored like the four
other Besson Renoirs, which he could not afford until too late for
them to be very good ones. Among his quartet of Matisses are two
portraits of Besson himself, one still unfinished after fourteen
sociable sittings. Besson's best unit is his half-hundred general
works by Matisse's early, struggling friend (and later Besson's
struggling friend, too) Albert Marquet, so long unappreciated—
truly a poor colorist but a fine painter and aquarellist, whose brilliant, droll, stenographic *encre-de-Chine* street figures are actually
the collection's only internationally known items. Next best are
the two dozen watercolors and drawings by Besson's close friend
Signac. There are three fine Rodin drawings—one really choice—
and less lively and lovely ones by Maillol; a pair of oils by Suzanne
Valadon; and one Dufy drawing, of a wheatfield, and then come
works by Jongkind, Jourdain, Cross, Laprade, Puy, Vallotton, and
even Valtat—those minor, gifted artists and friends who accompany
great art movements like footnotes.

Paris art circles seem to take it for granted that most important
modern art collections were made for the sake of prestige, or sometimes as a refined financial speculation, but only rarely to satisfy
the deep aesthetic passion of a rich man. Being a relatively poor man
with an aesthetic passion, Besson is a real, simon-pure amateur, and
his collection, through its very limitations, possesses a historical
social coherence in personal taste—all true to life and true to art,

all identifiable. The Besson collection is loosely talked of in Paris as being worth (and on a minuscule original investment, mind you) a half, or even a whole, million dollars—but either figure is, for once, beside the point in judging a collection's, or a collector's, worth.

Before the First World War, Besson, who was always didactic, founded a small Paris review, *Les Cahiers d'Aujourd'hui,* in which, over the years, he published his pungent, often slashing personal art critiques. He never favored Cubist art or bought it. Now eighty-three, he is still as implacable an enemy of contemporary abstract art as he was when it first started. In a recent interview, he said that he is still combatting those young Paris art critics "who are all college graduates who majored in philosophy and start everything with Kandinsky and Mondrian." He added, "My late wife and I were simply intoxicated by art."

As the twentieth anniversary of France's liberation from the Germans began coming to a close, the left-wing daily newspaper *Libération,* founded clandestinely in 1941 in the southern Unoccupied Zone of France, came suddenly to its close on November 27th, after twenty-three years of existence. Thus, the list of Paris daily newspapers now adds up to twelve, with about ten slightly different interpretive political identities. The blow fell in *Libération*'s big newsroom (formerly that of the rich, bourgeois *Le Matin,* which collaborated with the Nazis and so lost its postwar right to publication, and even its property, in which *Libération* was presently installed) late on a Thursday afternoon, when the entire collected staff, from editors through reporters and down to the messenger boys, was suddenly informed that tomorrow's edition would be its last. It is significant that the painful announcement was made by Henry Bordage, the editor-in-chief, who represented the Communist Party's interest in the moribund paper. He explained that the Party had made a long financial sacrifice to keep *Libération* going, in the hope that a union of the left would "open political perspectives," which are now certainly not expected in 1965, "or even for a good many years"—a bleak, authoritative statement of national political importance in France, in view of the new year's Presidential election, in which a united left has been hoping to weaken de Gaulle's chances. The manager of the dead newspaper, Emmanuel d'Astier de la Vigerie, is a well-known *rara avis* in French journalism—adventurous, highly intelligent, an aristocrat, a former Navy officer, an intellectual Marxist, but not a Communist. *Libération* was his creation and his contribution to the early French Resistance movement, edited by him and by two companions whom the Nazis caught and executed. It first appeared in Paris on August 19, 1944, on Liberation Day, with a flourishing patriotic circulation of a hundred and fifty thousand but little money. Since no leftist French intelligentsia newspaper ever gets any advertising revenue, by 1948 d'Astier had to seek financial help, either from intelligentsia capitalists—always hard to find—or from the Communists. In 1956, he quarrelled with his Communist backers over Moscow's treatment of Hungary's rebellion, and it was then that the Party put its own man in as editor-in-chief, to keep an eye on him. As dissatisfaction grew, with the paper's circulation down to half of what it had been, d'Astier was even accused of the heresy of "complacence toward Gaullism."

Of *Libération's* dismissed staff of writers, only one had a new post by the next day, at probably twice her *Libération* pay—Mlle. Madeleine Jacob, France's *doyenne* trial and court reporter, whose sardonic, trenchant reports on French justice will now be a feature in *France-Soir,* the most prosperous of all Paris papers, with a circulation of more than a million. However, none of the *Libération* staff has any immediate need to worry, because of the extraordinary protection that must be given dismissed workers (who have not been at fault) by a regulation called the Convention Collective, which governs French employer-and-employee relations, and of which the Communist Party, as the official workers' party, has always been a vociferous advocate; now it is wearing the shoe on the other foot, since its position is that of the employer who did the firing. The Convention's formulations are too complex to go into, but ever since the day of dismissal, the fired *Libération* workers have been returning every working day to the empty newsroom between the hours of five and six, with nothing to do except symbolically fulfill their working contract with the Communist Party—and this will go on through the month of January at full pay. What with one benefit and another, those of the staff who had worked on the paper since 1948, when the Communist Party first began footing the bills, will in some cases receive the equivalent of twenty months' salary. The Party might almost have saved money by paying for *Libération* to stay alive and in print for another year.

Paris is famed for the dramatic and solemn theatricality of its occasional funeral processions for France's great and usually elderly men. Recently, the city witnessed a series of majestic honors offered to the memory and ashes of Jean Moulin, who died young, aged forty-four, in the summer of 1943, tortured to death by the Gestapo in the village of Caluire, near Lyon. Before the war, he had been named Prefect of the department of Eure-et-Loir, with his official residence in the cathedral town of Chartres. There, in 1940, in his first misadventure with the Germans and their torture, he had unsuccessfully tried to kill himself by cutting his throat, on which the scars remained, making him a doubly marked man to the end; not only was he the chief of the Conseil National de la Résistance, which in 1942 he had started organizing for General de Gaulle, then in London, and thus the single omniscient French Resistant, whom the Germans most persistently sought to capture, but he was the man who always had to keep a scarf wrapped high around his throat to hide his identifying scars. Late on Friday afternoon of the week before last, his ashes were first deposited in the court of the crypt called Le Mémorial de la Déportation, behind Notre-Dame, with military honors rendered there to the strains of Chopin's funeral march, and a guard of honor composed of some of his Resistance followers. At nine o'clock that night began the torchlight procession that accompanied his remains to the nearby Panthéon. Passing from the *parvis* of Notre-Dame along by the river with its flaming reflections, and then up the Sorbonne students' Boulevard St.-Michel, the mounted Horse Guards slowly led the way in full dress with their sabres drawn, followed by drums muffled in black cloth to deaden their funeral beat. All the street lights had been turned out on the boulevard, and the boulevard cafés and cinemas followed suit, so no brightness remained to illuminate the way except the torches held aloft by the great crowd following their leader for the last time—men and women who had known and obeyed him in the Resistance, now carrying their associations' flags, and widows and sons and daughters of the Resistance dead, all silently marching, with their torch flames reddening the nocturnal scene. It was a moving and spectacular sight, without sound except for the dull thudding of the drums ahead. At the corner of the Luxembourg Garden, the procession turned toward the Panthéon, ablaze with an effulgent light on its little rise, its domed façade and its pillars cleaned and white, with a waiting tricolor pennant falling from their capitals, the scarlet fold alone being used to shelter his cenotaph for the night, while a tricolor "V" shone up into the night sky from searchlights on the Panthéon's steps.

At noon the next day, the ceremonies were concluded with the government officially present in sheltered tribunes, for the wind was cold. General de Gaulle could be seen in full military attire, with képi and greatcoat, surrounded by his family of Ministers. Minister of Culture André Malraux read aloud his farewell homage, his voice a threnody of melancholy sound accenting his heroic words, largely addressed to the youth of France, most of whom had doubtless never heard before of the long-dead man. The "Chant des Partisans" was sung in a choral arrangement, which perhaps enriched its simple and monotonous tragic tune. With military honors, the remembered courage of Jean Moulin then accompanied his ashes inside the Panthéon.

For several years, there has been in the precincts of Chartres Cathedral an exceptionally appropriate memorial to Jean Moulin, set up on a little triangle of grass against a garden wall. A medallion portrait of him on the wall shows his strong, youthful face in profile, with its sharp features and fervent, full lower lip. The monument itself in the grass triangle consists of a gigantic male hand, as tall as a man, clutching a broken sword.

January 13

The reassuring fact about François Billetdoux as the recently accredited playwright leader of the French avant-garde is that the human material in his latest play is not new, is not even newfangled; is old, is even old-fashioned, realistic, dramatic, emotional, tried and true. It is how he uses this material that makes it fresh. He obtains altitude and breadth—his special dimensions—by showing and telling the audience more than they have been accustomed to see and hear about characters in a crisis on a stage. His "Il Faut Passer par les Nuages" ("Passage Through the Clouds" about sums it up) is the theatrical event of Paris as it is presented at the state-owned Théâtre de France—the old Odéon—by the Madeleine Renaud–Jean-Louis Barrault repertory troupe. In it, Billetdoux has given what might well have been a man's role to a woman, which, of course, changes all the perspectives, though not the facts. She, Claire by name, is a self-made woman with a typical self-made man's past: youthful poverty, an unforgettable first love with a social superior who then disappeared, an illegitimate son, and two more sons by her first marriage, to the town's industrialist, whose factory, on his death, she so reanimates as to make her enormously rich, holding in fief her new, intelligentsia husband, the town's populace, and all her sons—until the early lover's remains are unexpectedly sent back home. This is the audience's first dark view of her—alone in one corner of the stage, with a cemetery tree being pulled aloft to the flies as its scenic use is terminated. Lighted zones of communication are used on the large, bare stage, usually with some temporary identifying morsel of scenery—a mansion door, a chapel dome, a breakfast table—which disappears as the next zone is lighted and more talk begins, between different talkers. This mosaic method affords a scenic speed like that in films. The talk, which is always brief, is a monologue, telling something, or an interview, asking something—in any case, building biographies and information. For more than half the first act, Claire herself never speaks; she is merely talked about or talked to. During this time, her sons are intimately revealed in their little islands of probing light—the eldest, illegitimate one, now a bank president, as a wretched lecher confessing himself (in a daring comic scene) to the family priest; the second son, her favorite, as a weak cuckold; and the third as a French beatnik. Along with the dozen or more related characters, such as her servants and factory hands, all three become identified through gossip, like neighbors in a small-town novel. There also occasionally appears, in a special backstage effulgence, her vision of her first love, in démodé youthful attire, vainly calling to her. Upon her sudden decision that each human being is entitled to his destiny in liberty and love, such as she had missed, Claire dominates the play in speech and well-intentioned active destruction, dividing up her worldly responsibilities among her ill-fitted sons. In Act II, she is rather like King Lear, abandoned by her unloving children and servants, and homeless. In this short act, accompanied only by her little grandson, she talks her heart out in a series of Gallic aphorisms and logical conclusions about modern life generally and about her life specifically—a classic tragic heroine except for her analytical intelligence.

In the role of Claire, Madeleine Renaud is as incomparable in her early long, difficult listening silences as she is in her lengthy final revelatory speeches, which she lets burst forth as if from her own mind, not her trained memory—surely the acme of her stage art. Her husband, Jean-Louis Barrault, has the major invisible role in this play, as director of its complex *mise en scène;* Pierre Bertin, France's subtlest, wittiest, most civilized character actor, deliciously enacts her amoral intelligentsia husband; and Jean Desailly gives probably the richest characterization of his career as the lecher.

"La Bâtarde," the autobiography of the only recently much discussed middle-aged writer Violette Leduc, understandably outsold last month's Prix Goncourt winner ("L'État Sauvage," by Georges Conchon), to which, as to all prize books today, it is the literary superior, its popularity being heightened by its inclusion of several erotic Lesbian experiences. Though Parisians continue their persistent self-destructive Americanization of Paris, there has been no imitation of the recent American phenomenon of erotic books on contemporary life, so Leduc's volume automatically attracted a certain attention as a rarity here. Furthermore, its general remarkable qualities are exceptionally heralded in a magnanimous twelve-page preface by Mlle. Simone de Beauvoir, who, impatient at the long lack of public appreciation of this gifted writer's peculiar talents, energetically reproves the French reading public for its indifference. She says in this preface, "When, in 1945, I began reading a manuscript of Violette Leduc's, I was immediately struck by it—by a temperament, by a style. Genet,

Jouhandeau, Sartre all saluted her as a writer. In her books that followed, her talent was confirmed. Critics not easy to please gave her high praise. But the public would have nothing to do with her. Despite her very considerable *succès d'estime,* Violette Leduc remained obscure." To this Mlle. de Beauvoir adds, "I hope I have persuaded the reader to partake of this book. He will find in it even more than I have promised." In the month before Christmas alone, "The Bastard" sold forty thousand copies, and it and its author were the literary topics of Paris. Its opening paragraph starts, "My case is not unique; I am afraid to die, and I am heartbroken at being on earth. I have not worked, I have not studied. I have wept, I have cried aloud. Tears and crying have taken much of my time—the torture of lost time as soon as one starts reflecting on it! I shall leave as I arrived, intact, burdened with my defects, which have tortured me. I wish I had been born a statue. Virtues, qualities, courage, meditation, culture. Arms folded. Upon these words I have broken myself to bits." She early knew that she was monstrously ugly, and suffered from this human disgrace. Born in the Pas de Calais and now aged fifty-seven, she has the inherited face of a Brueghel peasant woman from those parts, with the long carrot nose drooping below eyes that are slits, a big, thin-lipped, curving mouth, and a thick head of faded hair, like a haystack.

She began writing what eventually became the story of her life, up through her thirty-seventh year, in a Norman village early in the war, when she was sharing a rented peasant cottage with Maurice Sachs, author of "Sabbat" and member of the Bœuf sur le Toit and Cocteau coterie—elegant, snobbish, a self-adulatory brilliant young homosexual, with whom she fell in love, since, as she says of herself, it is her distinction always to desire the impossible. It was he who advised her, when she talked so much of her childhood and youth, to write it down, so he could have some silence, since she suffered from total recall—and, indeed, the reader often suffers from it, too, in this autobiography of nearly five hundred pages. Her mother, a remarkable woman who had been a servant seduced by the son of the house and who taught her daughter to regard men as beasts of prey, later married a shopkeeper with a decorating business and did well, ambitiously offering her daughter an education in good small-town boarding schools. It was in one of their dormitories, divided into cubicles of sheeted privacy, that the adolescent Violette's intimacy with her classmate Isabelle began. This she recounts with delicacy, as if trying to translate the senses into words. Later, there is a long liaison with Hermine, who was a music student in Paris—a relationship of pleasures and pains destroyed largely by Violette's egoistic possessiveness, which made her resent her partner's even going to sleep, since she herself was an insomniac. The events in her life are recounted with an acute sense of balance, in which she always weighs her faults. She was a constant lamenter and complainer, with cause. In this Paris period, in which she worked in a publishing house, wore a bargain suit from Schiaparelli, and led a civilizing life, she had her hideous nose operated on, without any aesthetic improvement. She met and eventually married a semi-impossible, impoverished young Frenchman, aborted a child, and continued that concentrated comprehension of her existence from which she later wrote her five unpopular, lugubriously titled novels—"L'Asphyxie," "L'Affamée," "Ravages" (containing another Lesbian interlude, which Gallimard refused to publish except as a separate special item, called "Thérèse et Isabelle"), "La Vieille Fille et le Mort," and "Trésors à Prendre." Mlle. de Beauvoir and Sartre had used their influence with Gallimard, who was their publisher, to make him publish Leduc as well, and there is a report that at one time he even gave her an ill-paid post as a reader. During the war, in dire poverty in her Norman village, she became a black-marketeer, trundling eggs and fresh meat to Paris. Through this handling of important sums of money and making big profits for the first time in her life, she discovered that she was avaricious. Yet she supplied Sachs with a roll of precious thousands of francs when he perversely set off for Germany under Marshal Pétain's plan for French labor-camp workers, from which he never returned. His departure at dawn in the cold country rain is one of her book's most tragic, deeply felt, and touchingly written emotional sequences. "La Bâtarde" is filled with sudden anguished, tender phrases of sensual beauty, written twenty years ago, that celebrate her loyal, unchanging love of the countryside and of nature—of larks rising "like fireworks" in the early yellow sunlight over the clipped wheat fields, of Normandy's gray skies and flowering apple trees in the

late spring. She says that she always sits to write beneath one particular familiar apple tree, beside that peasant house, which she
has at last been able to purchase as a finally appreciated author.

For years, foreign tourists here have been saying that the
French drive their cars like lunatics. In the past month, a kind of
real madness has been seizing enough of them to make daily headlines in the newspapers, which call these drivers *"les énervés du
volant"*—"the nervous wrecks at the wheel." At the slightest scratch
of a fender or question of who shall pass first at a country road
crossing, the *énervés* leap out and begin hitting each other. One
belligerent *énervé* dropped dead recently in the Rue Richepanse of
a heart attack, although it was on his head that he had been hit by
the other nervous wreck. Two days ago, a Parisian old enough to
be retired from his profession got out and smacked an ambulance
driver, and in the tieup that ensued three people were injured. The
fisticuffs have become so common and violent that a special procedure has just been instituted by the Minister of Justice, by which
motorists who climb out of their cars to hit each other on the street
are arrested, tried within three days, fined, and punished with six-
day jail sentences. The afternoon paper *France-Soir* has been running a "campaign against violence," which features a sticker to
paste on your rear window saying in big letters "NE NOUS FÂCHONS
PAS!"—"LET'S NOT LOSE OUR TEMPERS!" They look disquieting in a
civilized capital city.

January 27

A remarkably intelligent obituary essay on Sir
Winston Churchill appeared on the front page of *Le Monde* the
Tuesday after his death, warmly written by the Fourth Republic
Premier Pierre Mendès-France. More than three thousand words
long and called "L'Homme et Sa Nation," it was an analysis, sum-
ming up, and appreciation, which opened: "The death of no British statesman throughout history has been felt in France like that
of Winston Churchill. . . . Yet no one was more English than he
—in his patriotism, obviously, that burning and permanent pas-

sion, at times going to the length of imperialism, to the length of consecrated egoism, but without the excess or pettiness of vulgar chauvinism or xenophobia, and with no concession to what was merely easy. He was also perfectly English in his profound attachment to the best traditions of political liberty and of law, and, again, in his tastes, his style, his culture, in his impetuous and magnanimous temperament, which in our time seemed happily to bring back the portrait of a high-spirited and loyal baron of Merrie England. No one was more English because, above all, to no one was it vouchsafed to incarnate so completely the magnificent determination of Great Britain faced with a decisive ordeal in its destiny. . . . He said that if one day England had to choose between the United States and Europe, it would always be toward the great West that she would turn, nor is it difficult to comprehend the real sense of his words. True, Churchill did not forget that through his mother some American blood flowed in his veins, but beyond all else he had been intensely conscious during the tragic hours of how much, in the twentieth century, the security of Great Britain was assured only by American solidarity. This he was always to remember. . . . Throughout all the episodes of his life, which was prodigiously filled, animated, and even tumultuous, Churchill was never separate from his nation, nor did he ever try to substitute his own person for it. [As, French readers were to understand, President de Gaulle has.] . . . This is why so many French people today join in the homage being rendered to that purest patriotism which was Churchill's—that which identifies itself always with the liberty and dignity of all men."

Decidedly, the most important national news here was last week's solemn eighteen-hundred-word condemnation of the Fifth Republic government's increasing *dirigisme,* or control, of the country's economy—an attack made by the powerful Conseil National du Patronat Français at its semiannual meeting in Paris. The C.N.P.F. is the equivalent of the American N.A.M., or National Association of Manufacturers, except that, being French, it is considerably more august, démodé, and classically bourgeois. Big-business Frenchmen are worried by the way certain things are going. Granted that the French state is as rich as Midas—is rich enough, it is said, to have honestly balanced the nation's new budget, for the first time since the days of Clemenceau—two major sections of French industry are far poorer than they were a year ago. These are the textile mills in the North, which have been laying men off, and automobile manufacturing. Only Citroën has prospered; in 1964 the business of the nationalized Renault enterprise was down 11.5 per cent. The C.N.P.F. complaint against *dirigisme,* formally titled "A Charter of Liberal Management," was both prolix and specific, and contained fourteen paragraphs, under the heading "Fourteen Fundamental Notions of Economic and Social Progress." Paragraph 2 set the tone—the bourgeoisie's nineteenth-century lais-sez-faire; it declared, "The free creation and free development of business, based on respect for the natural economic laws, are the irreplaceable sources of the betterment of mankind." Paragraph 4 announced, "Profit is one of the essential driving forces of economic growth," and added, "The Marxist economists are now discovering this truth"—the only item in the Charter that the Communist paper *L'Humanité* remained mum about. The Charter also said that authority in business cannot be shared ("All other formulas lead to impotence"), and deplored France's state-established ceiling prices and artificially stabilized currency, which, in the eyes of the C.N.P.F., has encouraged foreign investors (meaning, but not mentioning, Wall Street) to colonialize French industry. And, to increase French production, it urged the Fifth Republic to speed up public services like new schools, hospitals, housing developments, highways, and telephones—a program that would probably also please the modest citizens. Last week's accidental coincidence of the Patronat's complaints about President de Gaulle's economic policies, and the labor unions' agitation, in nationalized industry, against them, at least as far as their own low wages go, was much appreciated by the French press, which treated it like a double bull's-eye. As the dignified *Monde* commented, "Rarely have the railway worker and the corporation president been able to agree so readily about the omnipresence of power." Though President de Gaulle's name was never mentioned, the Charter was the most powerful broadside against his style of governing to have been launched by the moneyed middle and upper classes—who have never approved of him—in the six years he has been in political power.

*   *   *

Five years ago this month, the writer Albert Camus was killed in a speeding car, along with its driver, the nephew of Gaston Gallimard, his publisher. Camus had just turned forty-six, and had, at forty-three, received the Nobel Prize for Literature. The publishing house of Gallimard has now brought out the last remaining fragments of his writings, "Carnets, Janvier 1942–Mars 1951"—a small notebook of private comments that he had kept during the years in which he wrote "L'Étranger," "Le Mythe de Sisyphe," "La Peste," and "L'Homme Révolté," and which constituted his brief literary career as a novelist (except for "La Chute," which is about guilt and justice, came later, was perhaps his best novel, and, for some reason, is hardly mentioned today). Camus has now become the idol of young French readers. In the large provincial town of Montpellier, the university students have just dedicated their undergraduate magazine to his memory. They say that what they desire and obtain from his books is a sense of morality without religion. They are touched by what they identify as his romanticism; that is, his connection with violent situations in modern history. Born in Algeria, brought up in poverty, and later a member of the famous *Combat* Résistance group in Paris, he was a Mediterranean man attached, as a writer, to the myths of ancient Greece, which he reconstructed as contemporary formulas. He used the myth of Sisyphus, eternally rolling his stone uphill, only to have it slide back, as an example of the absurd—that modern definition of emptied fate. There are more references to Nietzsche and Gide in the notebook than there are to Lenin or Sartre. It is as though Camus learned to be part of his time painstakingly late. Sometimes, in the "Carnets," he defines the meaning of a work in progress. He jotted down, "The absurd is tragic mankind in front of a mirror," "I have tried with all my force, knowing my weaknesses, to be a man of morality. Morality kills," "For the Christians the revelation is at the beginning of the history. For the Marxists it is at the end. Two religions," "Great souls interest me, they alone, but I myself am not a great soul." "Tragedy is not a solution," he wrote pessimistically. "Can I be only a witness [to history]? In other words, have I a right to be only an artist?"

Silenced through the pain caused him by France's Algerian War, he had nothing consequential to say or write in his last few years. It was supposed by his friends that it was not too late for him finally to write a great, mature novel. His Nobel Prize was regarded here as an investiture for the future, for what he might write more than for what he had already written—had he only lived.

February 11

General de Gaulle's recent press conference under the crystal chandeliers of the Palais de l'Élysée—where, in continuance of his stately custom, even at the age of seventy-four, he recited an hour-and-a-quarter speech from memory—seemed in many ways the most stimulating lecture he has given us on yesterday's European history. It was a talk on French policy in which, for once, as French journalists noted, he spoke *"avec sérénité."* He seemed to function with ease, knowing himself to be unique in his protean faculties and in his protean position as the only global-minded statesman now still both alive and in office, and as the only professional historian who is also a President, and vice versa. Certainly the imprint of history was visible even in the date he chose for the press meeting, which was February 4th, the twentieth anniversary of the opening of the conference in the Yusupov Palace, at Yalta, where the map of Europe was in part redrawn by the Big Three, all non-Europeans—Stalin, Roosevelt, and Churchill. The national leaders of the period are all dead now, except the uninvited de Gaulle. For him, with his historiographical brain and his Gallic heart, which so acutely recalls all its past bitternesses, February 4th, as it was passed in that remote, unseen palace, must represent the blackest, blankest day in his career. In last week's *Nouvel Observateur,* the opening article, called "Ce Qui Obsède de Gaulle," states that though the General has changed his mind "a hundred, a thousand" times about Indo-China, Germany, Algeria, China, the French Empire, and even Europe since Yalta, his continuing, unalterable "obsession [is] to return to France its 'rank.' This rank is at the head of a Europe become 'one of three planetary powers and, if necessary one day, the arbitrator between the Soviet and the Anglo-Saxon camps.'"

De Gaulle's press-conference reference to Europe as "the mother of modern civilization" and to the United States as "her daughter" sounded somewhat coolly unpaternal to *Le Monde's* editor, who commented, of the United States, "She is a big girl now, who has succeeded in life. It would seem quite difficult to call upon her only in case of grave danger to the ancestral home"—as, after all, France has done twice when attacked by Germany. Nor does all the French press agree with de Gaulle's conclusion that since the problem of a reunited Germany is the dominant problem of Europe, the decision of whether or not to have a single Germany in the future should be made by the Europeans themselves, without any aid from the so-called Anglo-Saxons. For, it is argued, both the American Anglo-Saxons and the English ones, as signers of the Potsdam Agreement, are surely entitled to say their own little word on the reuniting of Germany—such as yes or no.

The reaction to the press conference showed that the proposed reëstablishment of the gold standard was far more interesting to the French public than a possible reunification of Germany, all of which seemed perfectly normal, the word "gold" always having its own magic. General de Gaulle's press-conference attack on the gold-exchange standard, by means of which the dollar, the pound, and gold are freely convertible for the settlement of international debts, was immediately recognized here, in London, in Washington, and all over Europe as the biggest monetary challenge since the war. His paean to gold, inspired by the often expressed convictions of his orthodox economist Jacques Rueff, of the Académie Française, who is also a member of the Institut, was indeed a burst of glittering oratory. The General said, "This is the truth. There is no real criterion except gold. *Ah, oui,* the nature of gold does not change. It can be used equally well in ingots, bars, and coins. It has no nationality. It is eternally and universally accepted as the unalterable fiduciary value par excellence." According to a financial authority writing in *Le Monde,* "it is not only these positive virtues and the economic puritanism of the gold standard that please de Gaulle. A return to the practices employed before the war of 1914 would also reduce the present so-called imperialism of the dollar and the aggressiveness of American businessmen, who are investing at a great rate in Europe"—a simple, rather anti-American statement that was perfectly comprehensible to French adults. But the explanation of the gold-exchange standard given by the Academician Rueff baffled most adults. He said that its principle was the same as that of children playing marbles, who at the end of each game give back to the losers the marbles they staked as their bets.

As for further international money matters, there is news here this week of a possible synthetic new reserve currency, to be known as C.R.U.—the initials of something that has been baptized in advance the Collective Reserve Unit. So far, nobody knows what it really is—only that it will be invisible.

Parisians are deeply concerned about the American war in Vietnam, which Washington does not call a war but euphemistically calls something else. By many French, worried and experienced, it is called *"une sale petite guerre coloniale qui pourrait tourner mal, comme Dien-Bien-Phu."* At an Anglo-American Press Club luncheon last week, the former Premier Edgar Faure, just back from an official tour of the Middle East, said over coffee that if he were in President Johnson's shoes he would ask President de Gaulle's advice, which every journalist present knew would be "Negotiate!" An important editorial in *Le Monde* said, in part, "The question that everyone is asking about the recent raid by United States and South Vietnamese bombers to the north of the Seventeenth Parallel is: Where will the policy of 'a blow for a blow' lead? One wonders unhappily whether the Americans can give the answer. Morality and reality, which Americans like to believe are the same thing, must give them something to cogitate about right now." *Le Monde* continued bitterly, obviously recalling France's men and prestige lost in both places, "The experiences of civil war in Indo-China and Algeria clearly show that you cannot squash insects with a steam hammer"—the insects being native guerrilla fighters. "American policy would be comprehensible if it were accompanied by a willingness to negotiate. But to strike without hope of winning, or of making peace, either, is a very surprising strategy."

A new book by Elsa Triolet has a double importance in Paris, because of her long association with Louis Aragon, whose volumes of poetry have so loyally evoked "Les Yeux d'Elsa" (which are a handsome blue) that their literary relations seem merely a printed version of their actual union. Aside from Aragon's acknowledged great gifts as a writer, he has for years been the intellectual *éminence grise* of the French Communist Party, while on her side, as a Russian-born émigré intellectual whose sister, in Moscow, was the companion of the Party playwright Mayakovsky, her role has been the counterpart of his. For years, Mme. Triolet and Aragon have been the most notable legendary couple among the intelligentsia of Paris, a distinction now broadened to include the recently fabled younger pair, Jean-Paul Sartre and Mlle. Simone de Beauvoir—the four of them, diverse rather than intimate, adding up to the most famous, formidable, cerebral literary quartet on earth. Mme. Triolet's new book has just been published with a publicity band referring to "Elsa's eyes," which gives it the customary Aragon imprimatur. It is called "Le Grand Jamais"—an idiomatic negating phrase that resists exact translation but means something like "Never in the World." It is a most unusual novel, often funny enough to make the reader laugh out loud. It oddly begins with a dead husband in his marital bed, discoursing to himself in an appropriate interior monologue on his first and second wives, his sisters, his past work as a modest *lycée* history professor, and his favorite pupils, sociably introducing his coterie to the reader en route to his grave. The Triolet novel thus starts backward, with the hero's end. What it goes on to relate is how, after his death, his life is transformed into something it never was and something far superior—a brilliant, if risky, comic technical device. As a pleasant, unimportant Parisian historian, skeptical and romantic, the Triolet hero, outlandishly named Régis Lalande, had in his forties entertained himself and his young, delightful, unfaithful wife Madeleine by privately writing falsified histories of Russia's Catherine the Great and Ludwig II of Bavaria—Wagner's mad royal friend —supplying their lives with improvements he thought they merited, shifting facts as a poet might shift the metre of his verse, and upholding his premise that history was not fixed but optional. After his death, enough of these lyric daft manuscripts come to light to cause a literary sensation. The only savage touch in the Triolet book is her depiction of the gullibility of her Paris literary set, which swallows Lalande's hoax whole as an inspired new historical interpretation, posthumously making him a hitherto unsuspected literary genius. Lectures are given on him, a foundation is set up for the exegesis of his scarce manuscript pages. All this is riotously laughable. Madeleine's discarded first lover, his favorite pupil, becomes the leading Lalande authority. Her current lover, a virile sculptor, grudgingly accompanies her on a grotesque travelogue through the Bavarian *Schlösser* of Ludwig, and, on his return to Paris, creates a peculiar plastic Lalande public monument, containing a gyroscopic spiral that revolves, to the inaugural cheers of the intelligentsia, whenever the Paris sun very occasionally strikes it. During this triumph, Madeleine walks off, abandoning both her husband's fame and her lover, and this is the abrupt end of this odd book. It is occasionally marred by Mme. Triolet's interruptive comments to the reader, such as her long statement that her aim has been to write "a classic novel." This she has not done, because she has chosen light comedy, not heavy tragedy, as her medium. Like all French books lately, hers is very long, but it is also, on the whole, very droll.

Urban French radio fans who never take the trouble to listen at seven o'clock in the morning to a ten-minute program on village affairs called "Bonjour, Monsieur le Maire" are missing something unusual in this day and age. It is something not made up but true, and right out of the horse's mouth—a brief matinal vignette of rural life, and the real voice of provincial French towns, talking about people's problems, hopes, frustrations, and needs, about village plans and local ambitions and authorities. It is like paragraphs from Balzac. Sponsored by Butagaz, it is intelligently, conscientiously organized. Travelling reporters interview mayors of country communes all over France, asking the mayors for their local news, good or bad, and tape-recording what the mayors say. In their various regional accents, most mayors make the same complaint—that the young folks flee country life for city pleasures, more money, and less drudgery—and voice the same aspiration, which is to attract tourists, the motorized bonanza of modern times. They lovingly describe their local châteaux, inns, special foods, panoramas, and commerce, and, when possible, their proud prosperity. On a recent program were to be heard the mayor of the Basque village of Saint-Jean-le-Vieux and its family of bellmakers, who for centuries have made bells for the cattle, goats, and sheep that are the town's wealth. They played the bells for the recording—deep bells for cows, sensible medium ones for sheep, tinkling ones for goats. The village makes such good sheep cheese that it is sold as Roquefort, the mayor said proudly. The mayor of Les Alliés, near the Swiss border, had a sadder report. Once the village was so prosperous, owing to smugglers' bringing in contraband Swiss alcoholic spirits, that it supported eleven families of customs officers. Now the only commerce is in cows' milk sent to local cities—a great comedown, the mayor felt. The well-educated mayor of Sainte-Lunaise, near Bourges, told a typical story of depopulation —of a dying village of only forty-five inhabitants. "We are rich," he said. "We have everything—even our own village scales for weighing our fine cattle. We make our own wine." But they have a scarcity of young people to marry and raise families. The mayor owns a little eleventh-century church, sold, like many others, during the atheistic Revolution, in which he once stored his hay, and which he has now finally cleared out and uses part of as his mayoral office. He sounded like a freethinker himself. The mayor of Quincié-en-Beaujolais said that his villagers had been vintners for the last thousand years. His village was rich. The mayor of a little town near Bordeaux was aided in his report by his village curate, a *prêtre-ouvrier,* or worker-priest (now frowned on by the Church), who was also chief of the fire department, which had valiantly extinguished several forest fires last summer. One mayor in Brittany said that he was a water diviner by profession, and was now searching for oil. The ninety-year-old mayor of some little place could give no account of anything but sang a couple of old songs in a cracked voice. Hopes for new roads, running water, extended electricity and telephones, better schools, and better communications are the mayors' recurrent themes. As one mayor thoughtfully stated, "To conquer isolation is the aim of most villages."

March 10

At six o'clock last Saturday morning, a line was already forming on the steps of the Opéra, composed of optimists hoping to buy tickets to next Saturday night's seventh, and final, performance of "Tosca" by Mme. Maria Callas—the end of her present *tournée* here. There was such a crowd and such violent scuffling when the Opéra ticket offices finally opened that some of the *guichet* windows were broken. To keep the peace, a supplemental eighth "Tosca" was sandwiched in for this Wednesday. These "Tosca"s have been triumphs for Callas. Her voice sounds healthier than it did a year ago in her "Norma" series, being devoid of frightening outcries and occasionally marked only by a vibrato, like worn velvet that has lost the evenness of its texture. Her tragic top notes, sung *mi-voix,* as if to herself, are loudly covered by the orchestra, but the middle and lower registers are unique in their physical loveliness and in their ministrations to her genius for emotive acting—for magnificently incarnating the musical melodrama in which Sardou and Puccini perfectly met on the same desperate, passionate human level. In her duality as actress and singer, Callas has seemed doubly unrivalled. In the opening act, in the church, when, thin and agitated, she enters in full voice and in full love, one does not know which complete concentration of the senses to offer her—whether of the ears or of the eyes—so prodigious is her performance. (Clarendon, *Figaro's* well-seasoned music critic, opened his Callas review by saying, "I have the impression of having seen 'Tosca' for the first time in my life.") In the fatal scene with Scarpia (handsomely sung by Tito Gobbi), she—or perhaps the stage director, Franco Zeffirelli—has created a new long moment of dramatic tension. As she stands by Scarpia's supper table and sees a knife, there comes slowly into her face the look of decision. The knife is in her hand as the amorous tyrant impatiently throws himself upon her and upon its mortal thrust—far better melodrama than the customary womanly rush across the stage and the bare, uplifted soprano arm with its brandished weapon. The first act's precise reproduction of the transept of Rome's Sant' Andrea della Valle Church, lent, as were all the sets, by Covent Garden, seemed to please all the theatrical realists, though it was so crowded with realism that the bishop's procession could hardly squeeze through. The London set for the Castel Sant' Angelo was architecturally a confusing disappointment—a kind of deep well with a steep staircase leading up to the crenellated roof. After all that Floria Tosca

has been through in the past twenty hours, it seems a petty addition
for her to have to run full tilt upstairs like a woman frantically
hunting something—such as a place for a leap to her death, which
is not shown.

"Goldfinger," which has opened in the original English version at the Bonaparte, on the Left Bank, and at the Marignan, just
off the Champs-Élysées, is such a hysterical hit with the French that
it has become lethal, like SMERSH, annihilating all the other first-
run movies in town. When the huge sidewalk queues of waiting
Parisians fail to get in to see it, they don't simply go to another
movie across the street as a substitute; they go home, discouraged.
There has never been anything in Paris like its uninhibited appeal,
or like its sartorial influence, not on adolescents but on grown-up
Frenchmen. There are now James Bond boutiques at the Galeries
Lafayette and the Printemps, selling trenchcoats with secret pockets, cufflinks marked "007," key rings of the nude gilded girl, and
Doctor No striped pajamas. According to Paris advertising experts,
this is the first time that French industrialists—usually timorous
and conventional—have backed a big promotion scheme built
around a mythical figure (and popular murderer). Because French
textiles in the North had recently slumped and laid off thousands
of workers, which was depressing national news, this week's *Nouvel Observateur* ran a J. B. article of encouraging facts and figures.
It seems that the promotion scheme caught on only when it was
rather cynically accepted by the Boussac group, the biggest textile
people in France and the best-known manufacturers of shirts, rain-
coats, and so on—whom the promoters then reported to the small
fry as "believing in James Bond." This they now certainly do, to
the extent of giving him a big slice of their 1965 advertising budget,
which will include six thousand James Bond-Boussac show windows set up in the French provinces alone.

Because French film critics are on the whole the most intelligent
of any, it was inevitable that what may be the most illuminating
analysis of the Bond phenomenon should come from a French
movie critic. It has just appeared in the *Figaro Littéraire* as the
regular weekly stint of Claude Mauriac, son of the notable Acadé-
micien François Mauriac. It is entitled "James Bond, an Attempted

Explanation," and is extremely interesting. After stating that "Gold-finger" is "a triumph, a fascination, a madness," and a compelling spectacle for both children and their parents, he starts his real theme: "Of all myths, the most ancient is that of the hero. He is one of the archetypes that Jung discovered in the collective un-conscious—the strong man, the all-powerful one who triumphs over evil incarnate in the shape of dragons and monsters. 'There are no tribes, no races, no peoples where one cannot find traces of his presence'—'Modern Man in Search of a Soul,' page 296," Mauriac adds in careful identification, as he does with all his quotations from books by Jung, who seems to be his mainstay. "The novelty in science fiction, the comic strips, and the movies," Mauriac goes on to say, "is that the monsters have changed shape, have become modernized—that man has recreated them in the image of what menaces him. The apocalypse to come is not confined to the heav-ens. That is why there is such an accumulation of atrocious gadgets in 'Goldfinger,' which go even farther into power and terror. To-day, we comprehend the pressure of the fictitious on our souls. We await obscurely the image of all that since the beginning of time we have faced in our innermost beings. Dragons no longer affright us, but the bomb does—and, from now on, the Chinese more than the Russians. The racism, sadism, and wickedness of which James Bond gives us so many examples doubtless derive, as Jung indicates, from the fact that no heroes struggle victoriously against their de-mons except by assimilating certain of their attributes. We meet the dragon in various human or material forms in 'Goldfinger.' And the hero, the enigmatic Sean Connery, is more a robot than a statue, since marble seems insufficient today to celebrate the god-mortals—Hercules, Roland, Superman, Tarzan, and James Bond. Everything is improbable in 'Goldfinger,' and yet nothing in it astonishes us. The cinema has become our mythology, and films our most personal dreams."

Metropolitan France and its overseas *départements* of Gua-deloupe, Martinique, Guiana, and Réunion are holding their mu-nicipal elections this coming Sunday and, in some cases, the Sun-day after, the latter being to obtain plurality votes where a majority vote was not won on the first balloting. It is the most complicated method that any republic has yet managed to devise for merely electing a mayor. And rare are the French citizens who can explain it to you clearly, although twenty-eight million of them—nearly two million more of them female than male—will cast their votes this weekend. It is the French male's passion for multiple political parties, started in the Third Republic, long before women had suffrage here, that makes most of the confusion today, there still being nine parties different enough to count. There are the Communists, the largest-voting French party; the Union de la Nouvelle République, who are the Gaullists; the S.F.I.O., or Section Française de l'Internationale Ouvrière; the Union Démocratique du Travail, a pro-Gaullist Socialist splinter; the Parti Socialiste Unifié, which is several united Socialist splinters; the Mouvement Républicain Populaire, Georges Bidault's Catholic reform party (from which he has been ejected), founded after the Second World War; the Radical Socialists, who were the original middle-class, anticlerical bourgeois party of the Third Republic; the Indépendants, an anti-left, middle-of-the-road group; and a brand-new party called P.A.R.I.S., the initials standing for Pour l'Aménagement et le Renouveau Institutionel et Social. This is a party created for the extreme right by Jean-Louis Tixier-Vignancour, the lawyer who defended the O.A.S. officers now in prison for life for their rebellion against de Gaulle in Algiers; Tixier-Vignancour is not only anti-Gaullist but still pro-Pétainist. To facilitate being voted for, these nine parties have formed coalitions among themselves, joining with parties of vaguely similar political coloring and presenting combined slates of candidates for each French commune. These slates are made public on what is called an Official Electoral List, and it is for this electoral list, not for individual candidates, that the voters vote. Furthermore, each electoral list, once formed, starts operating in the campaign under a special campaign name. You will find it easier to believe all this by reading the four major electoral-list titles for Paris, with the parties they stand for. There is the Union Démocratique list, which represents a coalition of the Communists, the S.F.I.O. Socialists, and the P.S.U. Socialists, and should have been called the Front Populaire list. Second, there is the Union pour le Renouveau de Paris list, which is mostly Gaullists, with hangers-on. Third is the Liberté de Paris list, composed of center parties, such as the Indépendants and the M.R.P. Then there is the P.A.R.I.S. list, mostly patronized by extremists of the right and by the Tixier wild men.

Now comes the part that is most difficult of all to believe. Before the municipal elections are held, each group of coalition parties cooks up what the French call its "political cuisine." That is to say, in a private caucus these parties divvy up among themselves, according to the political strength of each, the municipal-councillor posts—which are, after all, the reason for election, since the municipal councillors subsequently elect a mayor from among themselves. Furthermore, the candidate they agree in caucus to put at the head of their coalition list is the lucky fellow who they decide before the election is the one their municipal councillors will vote for after they are elected, if they are elected. Well, that is the way the French citizens nowadays elect a new major or reëlect an old one. There are nearly thirty-eight thousand communes in France, and each commune is entitled to its mayor. As a guide to whether national politics are running for or against the Gaullist party, Marseille is called "the lighthouse of the elections" because it is the second-biggest city of France and, above all, because the Socialist Gaston Defferre, the present mayor, who is running for reëlection, is so far the only important candidate to announce that he will run against the General in this autumn's Presidential election. (Tixier has also tossed his hat into the ring, but no one gives him a chance of winning.) In Marseille, Defferre's greatest rival is Dr. Joseph Comiti, a Gaullist and the president of the local medical association —a powerful post. Comiti claims that Marseille under Defferre— himself generally adjudged a perfectly honest man—has been eaten alive by municipal corruption. The favored Comiti poster shows a mouse running around inside a fat cheese, with the warning "To Avoid This, Vote for Professor Comiti's Rénovation de Marseille List of Candidates."

Until late in February, de Gaulle chose to dissuade those of his Ministers who, feeling closer than he to the town sidewalks and the country grass roots, wanted to run in the municipal elections so as to extend the Gaullist party's national solidarity for the presidential election and for the parliamentary elections that will follow, on both of which their present political careers depend. Now de

Gaulle has done a sudden *volte-face* and is pushing his Ministers
into the municipal candidacies. If one can believe certain Paris
political reports, Michel Maurice-Bokanowski, the Minister of Industry, is to run in Asnières; Minister of Public Works Marc Jac-
quet will run at Barbizon; the Minister of Justice will run in a
little town in the Maine-et-Loire; three Secretaries of State will be
running at Chambéry, Libourne, and Broglie; and the Secretary-
General of the Merchant Marine will run in Angers—at least a big
town. Also, four Ministers will run in Paris itself—the Minister of
the Interior, the Minister of Postal Affairs, the Minister of Veterans'
Affairs, and the Secretary of State for Foreign Affairs.

There is, of course, a great deal of overt and covert resentment
on the part of many French over this entry into local political
affairs of candidates of such overweening national calibre. The
peppery little anti-Gaullist morning paper *Combat* had its say on
its Monday front page in an editorial titled "Charles XI, Emperor
of the French"—meaning de Gaulle, of course, the mythical suc-
cesor, in *Combat*'s opinion, of Charles X, the unpopular diehard
anti-libertarian King of France who was pushed off the throne by
the revolution of 1830. "The intervention of the government in the
present electoral campaign daily becomes more cynical and indecent," *Combat* declared. "The prefects have to act, willy-nilly, as
recruiting agents for the U.N.R. election lists, and the television
openly backs the Gaullist candidates. There is nothing for the
citizens here to do but to acclaim de Gaulle as Charles XI, Emperor
of the French."

What the French are obviously tensely interested in knowing
is what de Gaulle's chances are of being merely the continuing President of France after the national election in the fall. The reason
for the recent exceptionally heated talk and writing about the
municipal elections, of course, is that the humble municipal elections are being regarded as a dry run for the big election next fall.

March 24

Franz Kafka's unfinished first novel, "Amerika,"
has with difficulty been turned into a play without a proper end-

ing, and is now being valorously given by an enormous cast as part of the repertory of the Théâtre de France-Odéon after mixed but mostly damning reviews. It was called boring, incomprehensible, lugubrious, and morbid, and a punishment for the theatregoer to sit through. Yet the play is well attended, especially in the modest-priced balconies, by the young French. As a magical theatre man, Jean-Louis Barrault, who adapted the Kafka opus for its world première here, has (with the help of Antoine Bourseiller, who furnished the *mise en scène*) borrowed everything he could think of to gay it up—a full orchestra, inserts of harsh, brassy recorded music, monologues sung by any actress who can carry a tune (a device criticized as an imitation of Brecht, and even foolishly compared to "Les Parapluies de Cherbourg"), plus occasional cinematographic parades across the stage of dozens of speechless waltzers in evening clothes, whirling under spotlights. To many adults in the audience, these were vain virtuosities of the so-called "total-theatre" type, which failed to animate Kafka's simple theme. His theme is that of petty human injustice—pathetically true, but monotonous and essentially undramatic in this play. The only wonder about "L'Amérique" is why Barrault, a theatrical expert on Kafka material, deemed it worth this elaborate effort. In 1947, with the collaboration of André Gide, Barrault triumphantly produced the first stage version ever given of Kafka's "The Trial," now a modern theatre classic. In 1958, he was the first to stage "The Castle." These two were the initial representations and the popularizers of the character K. "L'Amérique" is Barrault's third version of K., and the earliest version by Kafka himself. In it, K. is a sixteen-year-old German youth named Karl Rossmann who seems unable to understand even how a wily servant girl has made him a father, after which his impoverished, shocked parents ship him to New York to make a new start, the only stage décor for this scene being an ironic representation of the Statue of Liberty. (Kafka never saw America; the closest he came was seeing in Hamburg a ship bound for the United States.)

After Karl's arrival, there follow the novel's lengthy incidents, which are almost like long nightmare short stories on injustice: that about the ship's stoker, that about the émigré New York uncle who turns out to be rich but disowns the nephew as disloyal, that about the Occidental Hotel, where K. is a martyrized bellboy, loved and protected only by the old female chief cook and by a tender blond stenographer—a young foreign failure followed wherever he goes by two bloodsucking Yankee crooks, who form his nemesis. A mixture of candor, indiscretion, kindness, and greenhorn optimism, young K. seems a natural magnet for the plain hard luck he constantly runs into—at least as played, without much charm, by the actor Michel Creton. The play is brought to an artificial end by an apotheosis presumably staged at the mythical Theatre of Oklahoma, where K. is a stagehand among winged angels (including his erstwhile love, the pretty stenographer) perched atop tall ladders, with a mysterious kind of barrier behind the footlights, which apparently indicates that K. is to continue to stay in the United States under some sort of claustrophobic injustice for the rest of his days. For many adults theatregoers, "L' Amérique" is probably an elaborate failure. But it is haunted by Kafka himself.

On March 17th, six days after her sixty-ninth birthday, Nancy Cunard died here suddenly in the Hôpital Cochin. Both in Paris and earlier in London, she was one of the most astonishing personalities of her generation. During the First World War, she, Lady Diana Manners, and Iris Tree formed an inseparable trio of beauties—a kind of Mayfair troika of friendship, elegance, intelligence, and daring as leaders of the new generation of débutantes, who in evening clothes watched the Zeppelins from the roofs of the great town mansions and voted Labour in the opening peace. She passed her childhood at Nevill Holt, a vast, plain Georgian castle that covers considerably more ground space than the New York Public Library. At the tea hour in the great drawing rooms, where as a little girl she was occasionally permitted an appearance, she obtained remarkable, enduring visions of certain final remnants of Edwardian society, for her mother, the California-born Lady Maude Cunard, was a famous hostess with a compelling wit. Her father, Sir Bache Cunard, of the shipping family, was quieter and took up silversmithing and ironwork as a hobby. He made by hand a number of pony-size horseshoes, which he affixed to the castle's backgarden gate in such a way as to spell "Come into the garden, Maude," which infuriated Her Ladyship—one of Nancy Cunard's favorite family stories. She was a remarkably vivid and noted conversationalist and *raconteuse;* her vocabulary in both French and English was vast, precise as a dictionary when it suited the subject, and punctuated by racy slang—and, above all, by her own laughter—when she was telling something funny. Her laughter was like a descending octave; those who knew her well could recognize it anywhere and thus know that she was unexpectedly on the scene—in Venice, Vienna, Madrid, Florence, or Harlem, for she was a driven traveller, locomoting restlessly on her indomitable energy, slender though she was. She was famous, too, for what is called in French *son regard*—for her intense manner of looking at you, of seeing you and seizing you with her large jade-green eyes, always heavily outlined, top and bottom, with black makeup below her thick, ash-colored hair. From her childhood, which was lonely, she was an interminable reader and a book lover. She became a kind of general Egeria to the postwar London literary generation, knew everybody, was known by everybody. Aldous Huxley used her as the main female character, Marjorie Carling, in "Point Counter Point," and she was Iris March of Michael Arlen's "The Green Hat." She was a contributing member of London's *Blast* group for new writing and art forms, and its Wyndham Lewis drew some excellent Cubist portraits of her.

In the early twenties, she began living in Paris, in an Île-Saint-Louis flat. There she became connected with the just-beginning Surrealist group and with one of its founders, Louis Aragon. Now that she was freed of her English background (or so she hoped), her personal radical convictions and tastes soon took their decisive shape. Associated through Aragon with Communism, she herself was probably only a poetic anarchist, and certainly was against any government you could mention, being impassioned for her own liberty, for everybody's liberties. In 1934, her ardor for the cause of equality for Negroes, which dominated the rest of her life, resulted (after four years' documentation, museum studies, and travels in North and South America) in a gigantic, eight-hundred-and-fifty-five-page anthology called "Negro," of which the *New Statesman* said, "No review can do justice to such a volume." It was the first book of such scope—of such unlimited immediate hopes for the

Negroes—and it had an unusual list of distinguished contributors. It contained translations by Samuel Beckett, articles by her friends Ezra Pound, Harold Acton, and Norman Douglas, by Raymond Michelet, René Crevel, William Plomer, George Antheil, Alfred Kreymborg, Langston Hughes, Countee Cullen, and so on and on, with dozens of photographs of African tribal artwork. From then on, she was speeded up by history itself—by the Spanish war, which she attended on the side of the Loyalists, and then by the Second World War, in which her country house in Normandy (she was in London, working for the Free French) was occupied by the Nazis. They threw her fine collection of rare modern books, some of which she had published, and her Negro sculpture and masks into the well, along with a sheep's carcass. After the war, she concentrated on publishing, and on her Hours Press, in Normandy, about which she recently wrote a book, to be brought out this autumn by the University of Southern Illinois Press and in London. Over its pre- and postwar years, the Hours published short works—original or reprints, often in de-luxe format—by George Moore, Norman Douglas, Richard Aldington, and Robert Graves and Laura Riding. In 1930, there appeared the first one-volume edition of Pound's "A Draft of XXX Cantos"—a major undertaking—and also "Whoroscope," by Samuel Beckett, his first separately published work. She had never heard of him until he won her Hours' prize of ten pounds for a poem on "Time," his being free verse on Descartes. In the middle fifties, London publishers brought out two memoirs she had written—a word portrait of Norman Douglas called "Grand Man" and "G. M.: Memories of George Moore," a great friend of Lady Cunard's whom Nancy Cunard had known since childhood. This last was a first-class veracious study—a penetrating atmospheric picture of Moore as a *fin-de-siècle* Edwardian Irishman. Years earlier, in the twenties, this correspondent, on a visit to London, had been taken by Nancy Cunard to have tea with him in his house in Ebury Street, with its Monets and Manets on the staircase wall and G. M. in his study upstairs, already deep in his bread and butter and first cup of tea. At once, as Nancy drank hers, she asked him why, since he had accepted French Impressionist painting when it was new in Paris, did he refuse the new art of the École de Paris? First he answered that he had been young in Paris then, and no man could be young twice about new art; then he added, with distaste, "I have seen a canvas by your Cézanne —a portrait of a peasant by a peasant." Laughing but persistent, for she always enjoyed the struggle of discussion, she asked him whether he had read James Joyce's novel of genius, "Ulysses." He had read it, G. M. said, "But it is not a novel. There is not a tree in it."

Over the last two years, she had been writing an endless poem against war called "Visions Experienced by the Bards of the Middle Ages." In 1925, when she was twenty-nine, her friends Virginia and Leonard Woolf themselves set the type at the Hogarth Press for a long poem of hers because they so admired and relished it. It was called "Parallax," has been out of print ever since, and is so nearly forgotten that it is like a new poem today. Its subject is apparently a young male poet. This is the third stanza:

> Come music,
> In a clear vernal month
> Outside the window sighing in a lane,
> With trysts by appletrees—
> Moths drift in the room,
> Measure with running feet the book he reads.
> The month is golden to all ripening seeds;
> Long dawns, suspended twilight by a sea
> Of slow transition, halting at full ebb;
> Midnight, aurora, daytime, all in one key—
> The whispering hour before a storm, the treacherous hour
> Breaking—
> So wake, wind's fever, branches delirious
> Against a riven sky.
> All houses are too small now,
> A thought outgrows a brain—
> Open the doors, the skeleton must pass
> Into the night.

Stanza eight continues:

> Think now how friends grow old—
> Their diverse brains, hearts, faces, modify;
> Each candle wasting at both ends, the sly
> Disguise of its treacherous flame. . . .
> Am I the same?

Or a vagrant, of other breed, gone further, lost—
I am most surely at the beginning yet.
If so, contemporaries, what have you done?

The popularity of Euripides' tragedy "The Trojan Women"
in a modern-worded translation by Jean-Paul Sartre has made it
the most difficult play in Paris to get seats for, although it is given
in one of the city's biggest theatres, the state-supported Théâtre
National Populaire. Were these woes of the conquered Trojan
women offered in the noble French strophes of those Racinian
Greek classics popular at the court of Louis XIV, the T.N.P. would
be empty. What attracts today's French public is the salty Sartrian
language, his known anti-war frame of reference, and the skill
with which he reanimates the old text by his contemporary vocabulary and his implications, so that in the imagination of the audience
the Trojan War is an early filthy colonial struggle like that of
France in Algeria, and the deporting of Hecuba and Cassandra and
all the female chorus to Greece is like the Nazi deportation of the
Jews to the slave camps. Behind all these identifiable references in
the Sartre play is that woeful background sense of "imbecile man's"
historical rise to civilization through its destruction in wars, which
has been going on steadily over the thousands and hundreds of
years past, including the twenty years in the middle of the fifth
century B.C. when Euripides vainly wrote his great warning plays.
To Hecuba, fallen Queen of Troy, Sartre gives the only lines
fashioned with the poetry of bitter female grief, such as "Weep? I
have no more tears. I must throw my body upon the earth so it
may mourn silently, tossing from side to side like a bark in a
tempest." To the flippant Helen in her reconciliation scene with
her *cocu magnifique,* the cuckolded Menelaus, he gives rather faded
gag lines, such as "I am all alone in the world. Nobody understands me," which make the T.N.P. gallery guffaw with joy. The
chorus, commenting on her going scot-free despite her bloody
crime in starting the war by adulterously eloping with handsome
young Paris, keeps repeating the up-to-date maxim "Crime pays!
Crime pays!" Cassandra has one fine scalding speech on international morality, saying, "Glory to those who defend their country!
But those others, the conquerors—those who wage a filthy war and

die of it—their death is even stupider than their lives." However, it is to Andromache, Hector's widow, that there falls the speech of most explicit modern insult, obtained by Sartre's probably permissible use of today's geographical names rather than those of Euripides' time. She says in excoriation, "Men of Europe, you despise Africa and Asia and call us barbarians, I believe. But when vainglory and cupidity throw you upon us, you pillage, you torture, you massacre. Which are the barbarians then? And you, you Greeks, so proud of your humanities, where are you?" Poseidon speaks the tragedy's great, terrifying tag line: "Make war, mortal imbeciles! Ravage the fields and the cities, and torture the conquered. You will all die of it." Sartre's text, on sale for only one franc fifty, or thirty cents, in accordance with the T.N.P.'s popular policy, is possibly best appreciated after the performance, when you can read it undisturbed in your own room. Declaiming in the stentorian outdoor fashion of the Euripideans, the T.N.P. cast shouts and groans, and the choruses chant and countermarch in their multicolored togas like sound-equipped, dressed-up, animated statuary on the move. There always tends to be something collegiate about even professional actors dressed like archaics.

April 22

As was quite natural, Easter here was not what it used to be, since each year it grows less so. Even a decade ago, it was still largely a church-and-family fête, with everybody attending High Mass while steeple bells rang overhead in jubilant holy clamor, followed by the post-Lenten gastronomic feast at the home table, building up to the succulent innocence of milk-fed lamb, roasted. Today, the Paris Easter is increasingly celebrated *in absentia,* it being the opening major vacation date on the seasonal calendar. It is also the spring festival of the automobile, which this year reached its peak on Maundy Thursday, when about a million and a half Parisians left town by car. The deserted city looked bare, humanized. The curbs of the narrow Paris streets, beside which thousands of French cars of various ages sleep freely night and day, somnolently clogging the traffic, were mostly untenanted. Even the leafy alleys of the Bois de Boulogne, where Parisians have been desperately parking their cars long distance, were nearly as empty as the bridle paths.

It must be supposed that the particularly acute parking problem of Paris was intelligently calculated by the municipality to be coming to a crisis this year, because the city fathers have finally done something gigantic about it, which is costing a king's ransom. This is the underground Parking des Champs-Élysées, beneath the Avenue George V, which will be the only six-story subterranean car park in Europe—or in the world, the French say—of which the top story has just been finished. The newly repaved Avenue George V, closed to traffic for the past half year, was thus opened again last Thursday—the precise day promised by La Société des Grands Travaux de Marseille, builders of this complex steel-and-cement parking labyrinth for twelve hundred cars, who have promised that the two top stories will be fit for use by June 15th, and that all six stories, with stairs, elevators, and spiral ramps, will be completed and ready for customers by January 15, 1966. The roof over the top story was, naturally, the most important item of construction, since it had to be strong enough to support its portion of the annual July 14th French Army parade, including hundred-ton tanks, along the Avenue George V.

The Marseille outfit seems rather remarkable. One of its young chiefs here, Roger Exbrayat, forty-two years old and a graduate engineer from the Conservatoire des Arts et Métiers, worked on the Aswan Dam, in Egypt, at the age of twenty. This Marseille team, by ripping out the Avenue George V and trucking it away, along with Paris clay and limestone to a depth of two stories, was able to begin its job in what the French call the *ciel ouvert,* but the team is now using the opposite, *sous-œuvre* system, since it is progressively building from Story 3 down to Story 6. The two top stories are each destined to hold four hundred cars parked by the hour, at two francs (about forty cents) an hour. Story 3 will be reserved for parking by the month, at about forty dollars per car. Story 4 is intended for parking by the year, and Stories 5 and 6 will be equipped with private garages, to be leased, according to the size of the vehicle, for the equivalent of between a hundred and fifteen to a hundred and thirty-five dollars a year, for a term of thirty years. The Conseil Municipal de Paris has entered into a contract with La Société des Parkings des Champs-Élysées, according to which the Société will pay the City of Paris three per cent of its receipts over the next thirty years. Billions upon billions of francs will be involved in this subsoil sextuple parking lot and what follows, because as a prototype it will be repeated *grosso modo* elsewhere—under the Rue de Harlay, behind the Palais de Justice (280 cars); under the Rue Vivienne (800 cars); under the Boulevard Haussmann (2,000); and under the Avenue Foch (3,000). And after all this expense only 7,280 cars will have been taken off the Paris streets and put out of everybody's way, at the owners' constant cost. This will still leave thousands and thousands of them sitting by the curbstone for nothing, as usual—a habit that the economical French now have and greatly prefer. An incredible number of modest Parisians bought their cars as status symbols, which they can rarely operate. With French gasoline the most costly in Europe (almost a dollar a gallon), they can afford to use them only on fine weekends or over big holidays, such as Easter or the Feast of the Assumption, in mid-August.

Because Paris theatres are grousing more than usual about slim audiences, and because it is almost impossible to capture a taxi between eight and nine at night, the major theatre-ticket agencies have just had a bright idea, if theatregoers can afford it. Beginning this week, for an additional six francs (about a dollar-twenty) on top of the ticket price and the twenty-per-cent agency fee, they will give a coupon that guarantees a nearby parking place for the theatregoer's private car, usable at fifteen midtown theatres, including the Opéra.

It is good news, and bad news, too, that for more than a year now the French automobile industry has been operating in what the French financial journals call "semi-apathy." It is bad news in that the auto workers' overtime hours and pay, which alone permitted them to buy their part of France's new standard of modern living, may now be cancelled. However, it is good news in that the feverish annual overproduction of French cars will be sharply diminished this year, with fewer cars made, and fewer sold under the hypnotism of the autumn Salon de l'Auto, to add to those inert, senile leftovers from other years parked by the thousand in the streets.

There is also one sad, even sentimental, automobile-news item.

Panhard, the oldest French motorcar concern, which in 1891 manufactured "the first vehicle set in action by a gasoline motor"—a fantastic, almost frightening French invention then—will this month disappear from the automotive scene. It has been absorbed— or eaten up, if you choose—by Citroën.

The Louvre's Salon Carré was temporarily stripped of its famous permanent paintings recently to make way for a Caravaggio exhibition, and now that it is over, one may frankly say that the Caravaggio canvases shown were hardly worth the trouble. Expected loans of his fine paintings evidently failed to materialize. In most of those displayed, his famed dark backgrounds had, with the action of time, become black, *hélas!* The Musée Jacquemar-André exhibition of "Cocteau et Son Temps" was another error, but one that is still going on. What Cocteau and his time consisted of cannot be laid out in showcases or framed under glass on walls. He created an epoch and inhabited it as both progenitor and follower. A demi-genius, he was lavishly endowed with taste and a sense of style, which he prodigally lent for half a century to the French and to foreigners in crowds. He was a unique influence, creator, and fabricator, with an instantaneous appreciation of what was new, which at his leisure he bred with what was antique, creating his own artistic hybrids. The paltry Cocteau items displayed in the present exhibition are like old empty envelopes that once contained coveted invitations to immediate pleasures.

Amid the endless and usual spring exhibitions of modern nonfigurative art, which continues to indicate, without form, what is going on inside the artists' imaginations and psyches, there has been a welcome interruption by reality in the Bibliothèque Nationale's retrospective of the works of the great nineteenth-century portraitist Nadar, the most ubiquitous Paris photographer of his time. What a satisfaction! How satisfying to gaze at the physically concrete, the accurate, the personal, the whole human phizzes of people famed for their talents, or even their mere importance, a hundred and fifty years ago—to see their true visages and what they actually looked like: nose, eyes, hair, and forehead, with the brains sometimes seeming visibly to bulge behind it, like the swollen, splendid forehead of Baudelaire in what was probably Nadar's most famous portrait of genius. Nadar had met him in the Luxembourg Gardens in 1844, which must have been affecting, for later the poet wrote the photographer that he was "happy in the friendship—I am little accustomed to tenderness." Fortunately, Nadar—the nickname he was professionally known by, his real name being Félix Tournachon—was a prodigious gossip and garrulous besides. He kept a notebook of what he said and thought about his sitters, for example mentioning as important Baudelaire's "glabrous face, his nose with its odd finial curly tip, his head rising from the collar of his greatcoat, invariably turned high"—a photo that Manet later tried to make an engraving of, as his own portrait of that dark soul. Nadar had trouble photographing George Sand in 1863, she being unfortunately ultra-feminine in her attire that day, with a vast, loose striped coatee and her hair spread wide in winglike curls. She complained that her friends were scandalized at how ugly he had made her look, compelled him to withdraw the offending photographs from public sale, and tartly advised him to pay more attention to his camera and less to ballooning, aeronautics being something he and his dear friend Jules Verne were fascinated by. In 1856, he took a photo of the young and almost unrecognizable Sarah Bernhardt, leaning against a pillar and englobed in a velvet mantle "to hide her toothpick arms," her face stern, dull, unalight. His photographic portraiture from the mid-century on was the rage in Paris; he exclusively had the most famous public faces, and especially those of the artists, sensitive as they were to this new medium of obtaining a human likeness. Nadar's photo of Corot shows him looking like a handsome elder statesman, with a lean, aquiline face above a black neckcloth. He photographed Courbet (whom he did not like, or his painting "Les Baigneuses," either), and did some wonderful portraits of Delacroix—elegant, aristocratic, with harsh eyes and immaculate goatee, his hand stuck in the bosom of his embroidered waistcoat—and a fine portrait of the handsome Constantin Guys, just back from the Crimean War, in a cutaway jacket. He took fifty photos of Victor Hugo, the lion of Paris, but not one of his mistress, Juliette Drouet. Hugo, who was vain, was pleased with Nadar's results and wrote to thank him, saying, *"Merci, bravo,* you are successful even with an old pate like mine." The most popular photograph of them all, of course, was the one of Hugo on his deathbed, white-bearded and in a white nightshirt, looking like a blanched saint. Nadar photographed the Dumas, father and son; Daudet when young ("Gauche, myopic, timid"); Théophile Gautier; and the snobbish Goncourt brothers, looking self-important. He also did the musicians—Rossini (old but still acute of face), Berlioz, Offenbach (with his ridiculous whiskers awry), and Verdi (splendid at the time of "Traviata"). In the realm of history, he photographed President Thiers, of the new Third Republic, and Ferdinand de Lesseps at the time of "the inauguration of the Suez Isthmus," and also the revolutionary Bakunin, after his flight from Russia, whose "extraordinary prestige came from his gigantic height and his face like a noble, energetic mask, with something in it of both Mirabeau and Danton." Nadar's portraits give us an amazing sense of intimacy with the faces that represented the leading names of Paris. These are his original photos, coming direct from him to us—from his eyes behind his camera to our eyes today.

May 6

A few days before President de Gaulle made his recent address to the nation on television, his Premier, Georges Pompidou, informed certain parliamentarians that "we can hope, think, and believe" that the General will be a candidate for reëlection in December, and that the Tuesday-evening broadcast "could be considered in a sense the starting signal of the campaign, given by the chief of state himself." Yet in all his seventeen-minute memorized monologue, "there was not a word that even in veiled or allusive terms evoked the Presidential election," as *Le Monde* commented in a vexed perplexity, and went on to say, "Some people think the conclusion to be drawn is that the General's plans are impenetrable to everyone, no matter who—even to his own Premier. But why then did he make a speech? Was it out of consideration for his own half-yearly rite of making a declaration? If not, why did he judge it necessary to offer an anthology of the traditional themes of Gaullist foreign policy, without adding anything new? The President of the Republic's discourse has given major dissatisfaction insofar as it seems the expression of a nostalgic dream"—his oneiric notion of France's supreme independence in and of the world—"unincarnated in the realities today of international politics." Minuscule Paul Reynaud, one of the oldest and most experienced republican politicians, and originally the General's devoted admirer, denounced the "sacred egotism" manifest in the political thinking in de Gaulle's speech. One leading editorialist wrote bluntly, "Our national independence, which it pleases de Gaulle to consider his personal creation—and one wonders what it would be like today if the Allied armies had not so powerfully contributed to it—is the motor that animates his politics." The ordinary French populace, which merely talks political comment without writing it, took alarm at the old spectre of isolationism, with France left standing alone proudly "drinking out of her own glass," according to the General. His several disobliging references to the United States being made on the eve of France's fervent celebration of the twentieth anniversary of the end of the war, and at a time when the Soviet Minister of Foreign Affairs chanced to be the only visiting foreign guest, was politically interpreted as "an anti-American festival offered to M. Gromyko" by Sirius, editor-in-chief of *Le Monde,* in one of his rare, puissant columns of comment in his own newspaper.

There was at least one light touch, though—one of the humorous little *"cavalier-seul,"* or "lone-rider," comments that often brighten *Figaro's* front page. Its writer found it impossible to believe that President Johnson had really said that he thought de Gaulle's speech was "good" when so many French political chiefs thought it was bad even before de Gaulle made it. "This is a *good speech* from the American viewpoint?" the paragrapher inquired. "Is President Johnson so dissatisfied with his own policies that he, in his turn, is succumbing to thoughtless anti-Americanism? The idea is unthinkable, as serious thinkers would say; however, if it turns out to be the case, I hope that there are enough pro-American French voices here to bring him to his senses."

The world première of Stravinsky's "Le Sacre du Printemps" was offered to Paris by Sergei Diaghilev at the Théâtre des Champs-Élysées in the spring of 1913—a celebrated date in the history of

unappreciated musical chefs-d'œuvre. The music caused a riot of
hate. The choreography, by Waslaw Nijinsky, was regarded as
painful. In 1920, "Le Sacre" was given at the Champs-Élysées with
milder choreography by Massine, less suited to the music. It was
given in Paris again in 1960, in the Théâtre des Nations season, as
a Belgian production, with choreography by Maurice Béjart, of
Brussels' Théâtre de la Monnaie. It was criticized as offensively
erotic and gross. Two weeks ago, in an extraordinary, humanized
refinement of Béjart's original orgiastic presentation, "Le Sacre"
finally triumphed at the Opéra as a great, memorable, and probably incomparable twentieth-century ballet—the one suitable at
last, after fifty-two years of delay, as the perfect corporeal accompaniment to Stravinsky's earthy, Panic masterpiece. On opening
night here, the audience stood for half an hour applauding, shouting, and cheering.

Béjart's ballet depicts primordial man in a pale, remote Dar-
winian dawn, hopping toadlike with his fellows to the rhythm of
spring; lolling with them in groups shaped like starfish on the
barren strand; then rising, as if on wings, when the offstage sun
draws them in a great rhythmic rushing flight toward its maturing rays. United with light, they thereupon pursue the liturgical
patterns of their expanding primitive dance, violent in its discipline,
its shocks, its aligned leaping bodies with crowds of arms held aloft
embracing the empty spring air, with symmetries like cave frescoes.
The male dancers wear tights, most of them colored like sunburn
but some of them bronzed like the bodies of red men, or nearly
black, like Negroes. The women wear conventional flesh-colored
leotards, and with their appearance the choreography becomes
more amazingly inventive, at an increased, feverish tempo. After
the arrival of the two Elective Affinities (Les Élus), dressed in
marble-white fleshing, so that they look like nude deities, the
ballet reaches its climax, in their prolonged recumbent, static embrace—the crowning act of spring. As the *chef d'orchestre,* vigorous and with a certain amount of poetry, Pierre Boulez, France's
leading dodecaphonic composer, was masterly, conducting with the
security of complete musical knowledge and musicianly rhythm.

The other portions of the Opéra's Stravinsky ballet gala (it
was given only four evenings in succession and will be given this

way again in June) were far less interesting. "Les Noces" was rather like a huge semi-Russian divertissement, with semi-traditional Cossack choreography and with splendid black-and-white costumes and imposing furnishings, perhaps somewhat in the Kremlin style, including two gigantic jewelled icons on the wall. It was followed by "Renard," based on the legend of the fox and the cock, which was originally given here by Diaghilev with the dancers dressed as barnyard creatures. In seeking gaiety, Béjart unfortunately chose to treat it as Pop Art of the Dada period. The reduced orchestra was stationed midstage on a platform supported by old automobile tires, and the quartet of dancers, attired in bathing suits, made their entry in a vintage sports car. It was difficult to hear the Stravinsky music, and it was not worthwhile to watch the dancers, of whom the fox was turned into the character of a beach vamp and the cock into a lifeguard. The backdrop demanded attention but was not rewarding. It was modern Pop Art, which included a rebus consisting of a picture of a hammer followed by a picture of a hundred-lira banknote followed by the printed word "maître." Unscrambled, this added up to "Marteau sans Maître," the title of a poem of that name by René Char. Adjoining the rebus was a copy of the noted early Picasso front-face portrait sketch of Stravinsky, and also the anonymous painting of a red rose that apparently is Béjart's ideogram.

Béjart is the ubiquitous, dominating, and often scandalizing new figure in European ballet. He is now thirty-eight years old —a violent-looking man with pale-blue eyes, a large, intelligent head with a pointed chin like Colette's, and a strong dancer's body. He is French, born in Marseille where his father, Gaston Berger (the son changed the name somewhat to dance under), was director of higher education and wrote books on philosophy. His son majored in philosophy at the university and then, altering his direction, danced first with Roland Petit and afterward for two years in England with the International Ballet. In one place or another in his dancing career, he says, he danced the role of the Prince in "Le Lac des Cygnes" a hundred and thirty times. Since 1959, he has been *maître de ballet* at the Théâtre de la Monnaie, where he founded his Ballet du 20ème Siècle. As a producer of spectacles, he made his début at the Opéra last year with his much discussed pro-

duction of the Berlioz opera "The Damnation of Faust"—aesthetically uneven, occasionally coarse, and very astonishing. In it he
introduced his curious theory of doubling the personalities of the
major characters, using two Fausts and two Marguerites—one pair
danced as human beings, the other pair danced as their accompanying purer psychic selves. After that, he put on a spectacle with
Salvador Dali to Scarlatti music at the Théâtre des Champs-
Élysées, which included sadistic scenes of paralytics and other
horrors, causing the spectators to shout for their money back. His
Brussels production of Beethoven's Ninth Symphony, reportedly
greatly appreciated by the King and Queen of the Belgians as well
as by the Belgian populace, who are very proud of the fuss made
over their Béjart, featured dancers of various races accompanying
the singers in the hymn of joy—a Chinese, a Haitian, and some
other Negroes—to give the impression of universality, one of his
intellectual tics. At this month's Mai Musical, in Bordeaux, Béjart
will present his newest ballet, "Wagner, ou l'Amour Fou." "Le
Sacre" as given here at the Opéra has to date been his greatest
triumph. Béjart says that what he hates above all is economy in
anything. As an eccentric, creative artist, he has certainly been
prodigal of his own talent.

Horror films are never shown on French television, which is
state-owned and strict. Even merely unpleasant televised movies
about the seamy side of life are marked on the weekly printed
government program as *"Reservé aux adultes."* When fed onto the
TV screen for the family drama hour at 9 P.M., they are further
branded with a warning white square in the upper right-hand
corner, above the title, which means *"Déconseillé aux enfants"* and
is tantamount to a signal ordering all good children to clear off
to bed. To satisfy the recent virulent craze, mostly among Left
Bank intellectuals, for old horror films, a kind of unrestricted
popular horror center has been set up in the movie theatre Le
Dragon, in the Rue du Dragon, around the corner from the
Brasserie Lipp, in Saint-Germain des Prés, where a fresh old horror
is being featured daily in a series oddly called Le Premier Congrès
International de l'Abominable. Over the past fortnight, the abominable classics shown have included "Le Masque du Démon," "Le

Baiser du Vampire," "Le Cauchemar de Dracula," "Le Spectre du Chat" and dear old "Frankenstein." "King Kong," made to attract hard cash in 1933, is now appreciated here as pure Surrealist fantasy. The increasingly popular murderous Bette Davis is starring in three movie houses in "Chut . . . Chut, Chére Charlotte." In Montmartre, there is a small horror-film house called Cinéchoc; at the Midi-Minuit movie house on the Boulevard Poissonnière—the old stamping ground for pre-Nazi German films of *Schrecklichkeit* —there is a French-dubbed Italian film, "Danza Macabra," about a haunted château, which must be a honey, since it is forbidden to horror fans under the age of thirteen.

Superior to anything else being shown is a brand-new French terror film, "Le Vampire de Düsseldorf," acted in and directed by an actor-director who has hitherto always been second-rate at each job singly—Robert Hossein. This time, he has hit the double jackpot by his careful study and use of historical documents on the complex, compulsive homicidal monster Peter Kurten, who in 1930 terrorized the Düsseldorf red-light district. As a prelude, Hossein intelligently signals the violent social ambience of the period and its brutal political climate by citing newspaper headlines and newsreels of the Nazi bullies already busy with their dementia, bombing Jewish shops, beating Communists to death, and organizing autos-da-fé of books. By using only small, occasional groups of extras and a mere handful of actors, and by repeatedly using the same locale—the same shabby night club for Kurten's sombre social pleasure, the same deserted park for his seductions and murders, and the same empty midnight streets, where he hurries along before the impoverished dark apartment houses in which sometimes an attic light still burns (is there a girl up there alone?)—M. Hossein achieves a remarkable concentration on, and even amplification of, the brutalized Germanic taint of the city, essential to this film's sinister atmosphere of general criminal alienation and terror. It is almost a silent film, and is thus free for moments at a time to demonstrate what the French admiringly call *le cinéma pur*—those brief, unique scenes of intimate camera drama, which the clumsier theatre cannot capture. There is one such where Kurten, vainly pursued by the police, slips into a church and sits there faintly smiling at the altar. There are special

night-club scenes achieved by his peering through the window at
the pretty little harlot singer whom he really loves, since he does
not kill her, and who loves him. Above all, there are the transformation scenes, when, alone in his decent rented room before his
mirror, he dresses each time for his crime—a clean, quiet working-
man turning himself into a fastidious dandy, with a high wing
collar and with a smart gray hat perched over his immobile face
and its attentive bloodhound eyes.

It has been a chill, depressing, dispiriting spring. In the first
week of March, the meteorological bureau reported as much rain
as was normal for the whole month. From then on, it has rained
pretty continuously for forty-one or forty-two days, by private
count, or a bit more than on Noah. But in suburban gardens the
primroses have held up splendidly, the tulips have taller stems
than they ever had in decent dry, sunny weather, and the wisteria
heads are turning amethyst on the vine despite the inclemency.

June 2

On the whole, this has not been an intellectually
or aesthetically brilliant Paris spring season, but there have been
two major exceptions, and they have been so cerebral as to be over
almost everybody's head, as far as mere public pleasure has been
concerned. Certainly the final concert, at the Salle Pleyel, of the
recent eleventh season of the Domaine Musical, which is devoted
to extreme contemporary music, was an exceptionally recherché
event, even for that rarefied organization. The program concluded
with the presentation, for the first time in France, of "Gruppen
für Drei Orchester," composed in 1957 by Karlheinz Stockhausen,
who himself directed one of the three orchestras that simultaneously
played different and opposing parts of the composition. Combined,
these three bands form the Symphony Orchestra of the West-
deutscher Rundfunk, of Cologne, the West German radio station
that gave the Stockhausen work its première seven years ago and
is the European broadcasting station most noted for its regular
programming of *Musik der Zeit*—music of our time, atonal, far-

out—which young German radio listeners are reportedly crazy about. For this special effort in Paris, two extra platforms for the orchestras were constructed on the main floor of the Pleyel. The one on the left was directed by Stockhausen and the one on the right by Michael Gielen, with the music from both pouring out like discordant cataracts on top of the audience in between and on the third orchestra, which was seated conventionally enough on the stage and was under the baton of Bruno Maderna. Stockhausen, who was the object of all attention, is an extremely handsome blond Nordic, now aged thirty-seven. Of his powers as a composer, the program noted in confused admiration, "How many new ideas and fertile roads are already owed to this great creator, who continually pulverizes the acquired styles and inherited systems of music."

It is true that his three-way stereophonic composition has the impact of a bewildering and semi-exciting pulverization of the sensibilities for any stray ignorant listeners to whom music still means melody and harmony, rather than the computerlike mathematical intricacies of the Stockhausen work. He is the *chef de file* whom the young Continental composers are trying to follow. The program opened with the original 1910 version of Six Pièces pour Grand Orchestre, Opus 6, by the late Anton Webern, whose Viennese expressionism and tonal seductiveness make him the only ultra-modern composer whom old-fashioned musical ignoramuses can enjoy. This was followed by "Le Visage Nuptial" of 1951, composed by Pierre Boulez around the text of a poem of that name by the mystic poet René Char, and featuring choruses singing quarter tones. By ending with Stockhausen, the program intelligently offered a comparison of the changes made over nearly fifty years by three modern composers whom Europeans consider among the most notable.

The Domaine Musical now has something over two hundred and fifty subscribers—an imposing list containing well-known names among avant-garde novelists, painters, musicians, snobs, high-up government officials' wives, art merchants and collectors, writers' widows, wealthy women, and titled aristocrats. In order to satisfy the spatial needs of new music like "Gruppen," Stockhausen envisions a concert hall in spherical form, with the public occupying a platform suspended in the center of the sphere, which will be equipped with banks of loudspeakers and with numerous mobile podiums, permitting all the spatial combinations imaginable. The whole thing sounds easier to imagine in Cologne's Rundfunk than anywhere in Paris.

The other superior seasonal event has been the publication of "La Mise à Mort," by Louis Aragon, a novel (or, at any rate, a fable) of four hundred and twenty-one pages in which the emotion of love is so alive that it is like a character itself—is an entity, an atmosphere, a social conviction, a kind of private government directing the lives of a man and a woman, both late in life, both disguised under a double set of names and personalities. It is a book of such power, of such vital creative ebullience, with such tangents, such poetic outbursts, and such mixtures of mystification with autobiographical and even historical veracities, that its effect on Paris literary circles has been sensational. It is the sixty-fifth volume—large or small, poetry or prose—to be published by Aragon, now in his sixty-eighth year. He has always been a prodigious author and a spectacular Paris personality, whether as a Dadaist, a Surrealist, or a Communist, and in this book his gifts and nature have come to their climax. The book is easy to decipher but not easy to read. The Pirandello problem that Aragon deals with in it is that of the plurality, real or contrived, of the human personality. This plurality he presents in such developed form that at first the reader thinks he is reading about two different men and two different women involved in amorous and jealous rivalry: Anthoine; Alfred; Mme. Ingeborg d'Usher, a famous singer; and Fougère, Anthoine's mistress and the love of Alfred's life. Only later does one surmise, as if partly solving a mystery, that the two men are only facets of a third man, Aragon himself; that Fougère is merely Alfred's private name for the singer Mme. d'Usher; and that she is in reality the writer Elsa Triolet, for whom here in Paris for more than forty years Aragon has been celebrating his devotion, like Dante's for Beatrice. Even after these realistic physical identities have been established and the names of Elsa and Aragon have been occasionally mentioned, like visitors among the quartet of mythical persons, it is the struggles, hopes, jealousies, and tragedies of Anthoine, Alfred, Fougère, and Ingeborg that function as a novel and that shape this audacious, strange book. As one critic paused in the midst of his admiration to declare, "We never know very well where we are in it, or whom we are with." Before it is finished, the labyrinthine volume contains—in a sheer flood of associated ideas, creative imagination, recollections of whole libraries of literature in various languages, and experiences from various travels—three short stories of extraneous lives; recollections of the French Army's 1940 retreat; a journey to Russia, where Malraux came to dinner; Gorky's funeral; Gide in Russia; the First World War as fought in the Alsatian fields; the bitter grief over the way the Spanish war turned out; the bitter questions of Communist conscience as to the guilt of Stalin; Oedipus treated as a comic detective story; digressive scholarly essays on "The Insomnia of Love," on Othello transformed into a murderer by jealousy, on the power of mirrors as passage to new realities for Lewis Carroll's Alice (herself cited in the book as an authority on such experience); the floating, recurrent image of Hamlet. At the end of the book, there is a terrible culminating poetic cry of anguish at the loneliness of love, of man, of identity: "Never will you know—never—what stifles me. The silent novel of myself. This despair of all life. These sobs without sobbing. This abomination of being. And I look behind me to see what follows me, this shadow. There is no one to ask pardon of. I am the bed without sleep, the wine without drunkenness, the voice without an ear to hear."

As a sign that Anthoine's fabled existence is finally diminishing, he loses the ability to see his own image in the mirror. Alfred, when he sees it clear, tries in a jealous rage to kill Anthoine with a blow at the face in the glass, injuring only himself, and gravely. A doctor has the book's final line, when he says to Ingeborg, "Madame, you must understand. He has loved you *to the point of madness.*"

June 16

Marcel Proust died forty-three years ago, and "Le Temps Retrouvé" was posthumously published five years later by his younger brother, the doctor, in 1927. In 1962, the French state acquired for the Bibliothèque Nationale, at a reported cost of almost a quarter of a million dollars, the vast—and obviously invaluable—collection of original manuscripts and memorabilia that had been preserved by the novelist's niece and only heir, Mme. Suzy Mante-Proust. During that long *lapsus* in documentation, Proust had early become the most studied, written-about, and scrutinized European novelist of this century. With these new acquisitions—sixty general notebooks and twenty *cahiers* containing the entire handwritten finished text of "À la Recherche du Temps Perdu"—plus added memorabilia from half a hundred French Proust collectors, mostly aristocratic, the first complete and richly intimate exhibition ever organized around the life and works of Proust has now opened at the Bibliothèque. It is to be on view all summer. As the sapient catalogue preface states, "This exhibition restores the features and memories of the personages and the society" that furnished the material of his novels. And there, indeed, the personages all are, in their original portraits or cabinet photographs. There is the Laszlo portrait of the Comtesse Henri Greffulhe, with bared shoulders and bold, fashionable face, whom Proust first saw at a costume ball dressed as a mauve Cattleya orchid—the queen of Paris society and one of Proust's sources for the Princesse de Guermantes. There is the photograph of the disdainful, beautiful Comtesse Adhéaume de Chevigné, basis for the Duchesse de Guermantes, who had spoken slightingly of the first volume of "À la Recherche," and to whom Proust ambiguously wrote, "Madame, I am not writing to you, but I am writing only of you"—referring to "Le Côté de Guermantes," which began his exacerbation with the same aristocrats who had earlier fascinated him, like a special human race. There is a colored likeness of the kindly, top-hatted Charles Haas, who later became the tormented Swann. There is a dramatic photograph of Marie de Benardaky; she and Proust were both fifteen when they fell in love in their way, she being later preserved by him as the provocative adolescent Gilberte. She wears in the photo the fur toque that Gilberte wore when she kept her lover waiting so long that wintry day. There is a Boldini portrait of the Comte Robert de Montesquiou, the decadent, notorious poet and Greffulhe cousin who was the corrupt Baron de Charlus in Proust's re-creation; with the same secret vice as Proust himself, the Comte accepted Proust's as if it were a reliable password, so as to let the ambitious bourgeois young literary genius enter the sacred precincts of the highest heraldic society, who thereafter gilded, darkened, created, and furnished his lifework. There is one curious, rather ludicrous snapshot of de Montesquiou standing before the rotunda of his Neuilly mansion, which he called the Pavillon des Muses, and where he gave amazing fêtes, attended by Proust. In the snapshot, he is shown in a perfectly tailored dark suit holding an enormous long-stemmed hothouse rose in each white-kid-gloved hand—a handsome, lush poseur. He was the hinge in Proust's opening literary career, permitting the writer's entry onto the scenes and among the characters he was to remember on paper and turn into literature. The earlier, more innocent epoch of Proust's youth is represented in the exhibition by material from his holidays at the village of Illiers, which became Combray, hawthorns in bloom, and Swann's Way. There are family pictures of his mother and of Tante Léonie's Illiers garden, and an old postcard of the village square where the Prousts had been ensconced as tradesmen since the time of Louis XIII and where Marcel's Grandfather Proust kept a modest, money-making shop.

The most fascinating part of the exhibit is, naturally, Proust's manuscripts—the pages of his genius, written and written over, like embroidery in ink, with his stitchlike, pointed, hasty calligraphy as he felt that time was growing short. There is on display the page from "Du Côté de Chez Swann" that contains (though one can hardly discover it for the overscribbling) the most famous phrase he ever wrote, about his cup of tea and the madeleine: *"Tout Combray et ses environs . . . est sortie, ville et jardins, de ma tasse de thé."* Later, in the years of reclusion after his mother's death, when he was so hypersensitively ill that he was living in a cork-lined room, he nevertheless wrote the multiple last notebooks, which began with "Sodome et Gomorrhe." As the catalogue preface remarks, "That a man of sickly nature, more and more ill, most of the time in bed, had the force to cover so many pages is hardly believable." In order to make room for his repeated corrections and ultimate inspirations in writing "La Prisonnière," he pasted additional manuscript pages together, attaching the first sheet to his notebook page; in one instance, he arrived at a pasted-up insertion two and a half metres in length—a long yellowed scroll hanging inertly in one of the exhibition's showcases. There is also on view—and most touching of all—the last page of his work and of his life. At the bottom of his final page of "Le Temps Retrouvé," of which only two lines toward the end stand uncorrected, he wrote his last words, "*. . . dans le Temps,*" and below them scrawled *"Fin."* The next day, he died.

June 28

In the five days between Wednesday, June 30th, and Sunday, July 4th, two million Parisians, adult and juvenile, are expected to leave the city, in the first exodus of the new national staggered-summer-vacation plan, the aim being to break French workers' and employees' habit of all wanting to enjoy their month's paid holiday the same month—preferably August. In this they were aided in the past by many French factories' and shops' habit of closing from the end of July to the beginning of September. This year, thousands of factories and shops are closing for July. Slightly more than a million of the departing vacationers are leaving in their own cars—a tremendous proof of the buyer's market and the affluence that the Fifth Republic has been enjoying, until lately. This year, the French automobile industry—literally the wheels on which prosperous France runs—is suffering from what is tactfully called *un malaise persistant,* or slump, brought on in part by foreseeable consumer saturation and in part by the alarming and still mounting prices of food and general French living. New-car licenses, which naturally reflect new-car sales, have declined nearly twelve per cent from this time last year. On the production side, only Citröen has announced a feeble rise—of one per cent. Renault production is down fourteen per cent; Peugeot, which had labor troubles in the spring, has slipped nineteen; and the once popular Simca, now owned by Chrysler as a result of one of those so-called United States investment colonizations of France, which President de Gaulle so bitterly resents, has dropped twenty-five per cent, which he may resent even more. These facts and figures are taken from a recent issue of the Communist daily *Humanité,* the Paris workman's newspaper, which is always in the know about capitalist France's factory news, especially if it is gloomy.

For the eight hundred and fifty thousand vacationists who are leaving Paris by rail, the admirably managed state-owned French railways are supplying fourteen hundred and fifteen main-line trains, nearly three hundred of them extras put on for the peak day of July 1st, which will be bedlam, as usual, in the six major Paris stations. The worst will be the Gare de Lyon, where trains leave for the Midi, earlier afflicted by a devastating rain shortage, which the waterlogged Parisians, after three months of umbrellas, are doubtless praying can be relied on again. Because of the disgraceful shortage of Paris taxis and the unpredictable traffic jams on the Paris streets, travellers have been advised to check their luggage two days in advance and, in order to make sure they don't miss their trains, to go to the station by Métro, which even well-off Parisians are being forced to use more and more as the only rapid, uninterrupted transportation for getting approximately where they want to go.

With two million Parisians out of town and on holiday, Paris itself will take on its own special, entrancing, rather somnolent vacation visage, looking years younger—looking perhaps almost 1900—with half-emptied streets to stroll on beneath its opaline day sky, which, after sunset, clears and hardens into a kind of crystal twilight. These charms will be difficult to appreciate this summer, with the city torn up in mid-town as it has not been since Baron Haussmann ripped it apart in its previous great modernization, during the Second Empire. On the Cours la Reine, trees are down, and bulldozers, cranes, and giant dirt diggers are busy extending the Right Bank riverside express route from the new underpass at the Place de l'Alma down toward the Concorde, which it will duck under; then, after running along at river level again and passing beneath three bridges, it will emerge at house level once more at the Rue du Louvre. The work must be finished by the end of 1976, and to pay for it and all kinds of other new urbanisms the City of Paris has just launched a bond issue of four hundred million francs, paying interest of five and three-quarters per cent, which is very good indeed. Furthermore, there is a hurly-burly going on on the rim of Paris as the thirty-six-kilometre peripheral boulevard that will link up all the old Paris toll gates—Sèvres, Italie, Maillot, Saint-Cloud, and so on—is built. All the above works are, of course, in honor of the automobile.

This last week, we learned from Premier Pompidou what has to be constructed within a distance of about sixty kilometers outside Paris in time for the new century, according to a project officially called Paris en l'An 2000—Paris in the Year 2000. Eight new satellite towns are to be built around eight charming old ones in the still lovely agricultural Seine Valley, in order that Paris may expand to a population of fourteen million thirty-five years from now. To the west and south of Paris, there will be five new towns, starting on the west with the medieval town of Mantes-la-Jolie (it contains a huge, handsome Gothic church built in the twelfth and thirteenth centuries) and ending on the south with Tigery-Lieu-saint, surrounded by moated fortress farms in the richest arable land in the district. The three satellites on the east and north of Paris will start with Bry-Noisy-le-Grand and end to the north at Pontoise, an ancient, picturesque little regatta town on the River Oise. (Cézanne used to go there to paint with his friends.) The satellites will be not just dormitory towns but autonomous small cities containing imposing new intellectual cores, for which Paris has need but no room. These will include two university centers, a center for advanced nuclear study and another for the study of the theories of propulsion, as well as relocations of other important schools, such as the Institut National Agronomique, the École Poly-technique, the Collège des Techniques Avancées, and an extension of the Faculté des Sciences, at Orsay. There will also be a Cité de la Télévision; a Parc de Culture, named for Minister of Culture André Malraux and furnished with museums and art libraries; a new airport, which will supplant Le Bourget; dozens of planned green spaces—and to the south, like the inevitable fly in the ointment, what is called "a vast industrial zone."

Paris en l'An 2000 was worked out by the planning authorities of the District de la Région de Paris, but until now the plans were kept secret from the public, mainly to try to head off real-estate speculation, and also consternation, in the Seine Valley. As for the new population, it is now limited on paper, and in theory, to only sixty or eighty human beings per hectare (two and a half acres). However, there will also be two hundred and sixty kilometres of express tracks to tie the body of Paris to what are now wheat and cauliflower fields, pear orchards, and woodlands like the ancient Forêt de Sénart, famous for its stag hunts, which will all disappear, along with the sparse farming population—far less than sixty men and a few boys to a two-and-a-half-acre plot. There will also be new traffic arteries connecting every place with every other place at a hundred and fifty kilometres an hour across that rich Île-de-France landscape, which today is still semi-rural and peopled by farmers with duckponds. As a project for the future, Paris en l'An 2000 seems to be the most ambitious, elaborate example of modern capital-city suburban planning and countryside invasion yet devised by metropolitan men.

July 28

Adlai Stevenson was highly appreciated by the French as a phenomenon, as something very special, made in America and not mass-produced but unique—a pure United States mentality that was also sensitive and idealistic, a Midwestern apostle of unreconstructed liberalism, although the latter is a political philosophy that the English are more familiar with than the French, especially right now. As a candidate in the 1956 election, he was France's favorite by a wide margin over General Eisenhower. *Le Monde*'s obituary spoke of him as "a man who played a great role in the history of the American political imagination without ever having been able to find his just place on the political scene." It added, "The tragedy of Dallas assured to John F. Kennedy a posthumous radiance that memories of Stevenson will doubtless never know. Yet Stevenson during his lifetime was no less an influence than the assassinated President—at least before his assassination. He was, indeed, even more—a sort of indestructible image of liberalism. Without doubt, Stevenson's integrity and intelligence were loftier than those of even the élite of American political personalities. American liberalism, which today enjoys popularity, lacking neither advocates nor spectacular converts, now no longer has a leading figure or even a mentor. To its last breath, it will be devoted to two representatives of the older generation—Mme. Eleanor Roosevelt and Adlai Stevenson himself. The first has been absent for some years, and the second had his hands tied by his post at the United Nations. Yet even while defending in Manhattan the most indefensible American interventions, he continued to incarnate a certain progressive conscience, a certain ideal, which developed, as it were, in his shadow, and even in his silences, before rewarding him with the funeral of a national hero."

It is strange that Paris, with its ever-fresh pride in its master political caricaturist Daumier, should today have no cartoonist with anything at all of Daumier's cruel critical art. It was the weekly *Express*'s Polish-born caricaturist Tim who supplied Paris with its only graphic interpretation of Stevenson's death. In an almost exaggerated refinement of his hallucinatory linear style, he showed Stevenson as if at the moment of dying on one of London's sidewalks, his body tilting backward in pain, his hands clasped in supplication over his heart, his mouth agape in horror at the public menace just over his head—two falling bombs, one labelled "Vietnam," the other "Santo Domingo."

The semi-official rumor that de Gaulle will at present neither affirm nor deny his December candidacy (deduced from the cancellation of his expected summer press conference, now put off until September, when surely he will have to say "Yes, I will run" or "No, I won't") has given his political enemies, which means all the parties of France except his own, a welcome respite—or so you might think—in which to catch their breath and pull their wits together to discover what candidates, if any, they can devise to run against the General. They have done nothing of the sort. They still seem to have no idea at all who their certain-to-lose martyr candidates are going to be. The only possible candidate of national dimensions who could also interest the intellectual young voters— very touchy and important here—would be the ill-starred, brilliant Mendès-France. Unfortunately, he is personally opposed to the principle of the Presidential-election system that de Gaulle has set up. As one commentator here has just remarked, "It would be highly illogical of him to say, 'Vote for me, so that if I am elected I can suppress the type of election that has put me in power.'" The total collapse last month of Gaston Defferre's impossibly intelligent pragmatic federation plan, which involved the three left-of-center parties—Socialists, Radicals, and the Mouvement Républicain Populaire—temporarily swept their cupboards bare of any surviving electoral material. At the last minute, the federation's surface quarrel was about sheer nomenclature—about whether it was to be called La Fédération Démocrate Socialiste or La Fédération Socialiste des Démocrates, a bitter semantic squabble such as French leftist politicians are theoretically ready to die for, by killing their parties' chances of a unified success. But what actually wrecked the federation was the late-nineteenth-century reef of *la laïcité*—the lay conviction against permitting the modern French state to furnish any public-education funds to Catholic schools. This is a vital, permanent part of the bitter quarrel that accompanied the separation of Church and State at the turn of the century. As political Catholics, the M.R.P. refused to disavow its belief in such school help; as anticlericals, the Radicals backed the Socialists, who deliberately brought up *la question de la laïcité* in order to wreck the federation—or so Defferre himself said—since the trio had agreed on all other national political problems. The collapse of Defferre as a nationally known new leader and of his federating idea is regarded now in Paris as the inevitable catastrophe that awaited French leftist bigots, who, in their vociferous planned electoral fight against President de Gaulle, could not afford to risk losing one iota of their manpower or their political drive and now have lost it all.

These disputants have been invaluable, though, in demonstrating once more to themselves and to the world how de Gaulle came to power over France in the first place, and looks as though he would remain in it in the second, to the end of his strength. For he will win, hot or cold, in December—hot if he has the health to run, cold if his heir apparent, Premier Pompidou, runs in his place, or if, after de Gaulle's election to the seven-year Presidential term, Pompidou, by a referendum, becomes Vice-President, which will set up the machinery for the de Gaulle succession and dynasty for surely the last time, to end in 1972. (De Gaulle, if he runs this December, will probably lose the 7th, 16th, and 17th Paris *arrondissements,* the strongholds of the rich, the remnants of the aristocracy, and the big French industrialists, who will vote en bloc against him and for the extreme right—for Jean-Louis Tixier-Vignancour, an intelligent, theatrical lawyer with wiliness, brains, and a deep bass voice.) However, the only aid being given to de Gaulle's dauphin at present is that of Arthème Fayard, the publisher, insofar as he has just brought out a book that is very easy to read during the vacation sloth, or even to skip through, and is surely bound to be some kind of best-seller. Titled "Le Destin Secret de Georges Pompidou," it is by the popular political writer Merry Bromberger and is the first Pompidou biography to be printed; its outside back cover disarmingly and shrewdly states that at first glance the Pompidou career resembles *"un conte de fées"*—a fairy story. It goes on, "Head of his class on leaving the Normale Supérieure, he did not tarry long in the teaching ranks, and after the Liberation he entered de Gaulle's Cabinet. He next became a Conseiller d'État without ever having been a jurist. Later, he became a bank director [for the Rothschilds] without having had any special banking training. In today's technological epoch, this man of cultivated tastes, as interested in art as a Florentine, cuts a superior figure, despite his peasant ancestry. His life was made up of surprises until the day in 1962 when he became a Premier without ever having even been a Deputy. Whatever he has already accomplished, his future will contain more than his past." His future could contain only one important thing more, though this thing would surprise no one, except that, for once, he is being carefully trained for it—his eventual residence in the Palais de l'Élysée.

August 10

In response to Washington's appeal to American travellers to spend their touring money at home this summer, so as to cut part of our annual dollar drain abroad, an estimated million and a half of our compatriots—a record number—nevertheless elected to come abroad. On the other hand, and for the first time, more than a quarter of a million Europeans chose to go to the United States for their holiday. This includes thousands of tourists from France—a rare and recent event in French history. During the

French Revolution, some aristocrats crossed to London to keep their heads on their shoulders, and in this last war certain French who had reason to know they would be on the Nazi proscription lists gratefully sought haven in New York. In times past, only to save their lives did the French leave their own land, and of late only to save money—the second vital Gallic consideration. During the prosperities, inflations, and high prices of the Fourth and Fifth Republics, the French discovered that it was cheaper to vacation in Spain than to stay at home on their own beaches; next, they went to Portugal, Elba, the Greek islands, and Corsica, following the sun and the latest international discoveries in low prices until their age-old inherited *noli-me-tangere* nationalism was shredded and they stepped forth, suitcase in hand, as modern tourists and travellers. William Taylor, the only American travel agent here who specializes in French clients, says that in 1961 he booked three hundred French tourists to go see America; this year he expects the figure to be five thousand. Born into an international-minded family, and nephew of the late Francis Taylor, director of New York's Metropolitan Museum, Taylor grew up in Paris, is natively bilingual, and knows the French mentality as well as he knows the modern French novel. He says that his French travellers, on returning, report that they found American food edible but tasteless (as they expected), our renowned gargantuan beefsteaks handsome to look at but without flavor to chew, our soda-fountain sweet milk drinks insipid, and our strawberry shortcake no equal to a French strawberry tart; in general, in all ways they found that America emphasized quantity rather than quality, and excess rather than discrimination. Their severest criticism, though, according to Taylor, was of the total lack of organization to take care of French visitors, whom America had advertised for, and hugely, in French newspapers. In most of the official tourist centers they visited, the French travellers were given as sightseeing help nothing but an occasional map, handed out by an employee who spoke nothing but American. To the French who went to New York by ship, our piers seemed shockingly barbaric—no place to sit down except on their luggage, no plumbing, no café amenities, and their welcoming friends, if any, kept at a distance like prisoners behind barricades.

What the returning French did like was our motels, our fabulously functioning plumbing, like a new law of life, our well-equipped transcontinental buses for surface travel, so that they could stare out windows and really see those United States, and our eight-lane highways for speed, in cases where they bought a second-hand jalopy and drove off across the New World on their own. They loved the tidy New England villages, our modern architecture, the exciting sense of space, and the easy friendliness of the people. Since the war, America, more than any other country, has influenced Paris particularly; snack bars, hamburgers, *franglais,* novels in translation, blue jeans on both sexes, *yé-yé* sports clothes, like the clothes of American teen-agers, and American mores learned from American movies were all familiar in advance, especially to the tourists from Paris. Yet, faced with the originals—with our crowds, our stretching geography—the French tourists, to their surprise, found the real United States a foreign country. What they profoundly appreciated, and few missed seeing, were our national parks, our earthly natural marvels like the Grand Canyon, the spectacular and uninhabitable vastness of our landscapes, such as the European continent did not inherit in its creation. Over the last few years, the cowboy West has been more popular, more of an ocular excitement, than ever in the Paris movie houses, where Western films, with their cinematographic hills and horizons and the sartorial stimulus of the cowboy dressed fit to kill, furnished the original propaganda that eventually led the French to go to the United States to see how much was true.

The average French tourists try to cram the whole United States into two weeks, at five hundred dollars a week, excluding food but including transatlantic and local transportation on a planned trip; if the tourists move as a group, a French-speaking guide is thrown in. For youngish French businessmen, the trip to the States is considered in and very important, they being the generation most intelligently dissatisfied with *les vieilles peaux,* the so-called old skins, who invariably rule gerontocratic France. This year, many of this under-forty age group included in their trip a swing into the Southern states to observe the black-and-white situation for themselves; a group of sixteen French tourists—both men and women—actually took part in the Selma march. Forty-eight young men in the French retail-clothing business—the project started with a pair of them, who drummed up the others so as to obtain special professional treatment from their American opposite numbers—recently flew to Manhattan, Washington, a Carolina textile town, Buffalo, Chicago, and then back to New York to try to find out why Americans make more money selling men's clothes than they did in France. One informative sight they saw was Seventh Avenue cutting machines slicing out a hundred or more pant legs at a time. Next year, they are going to go again, to see more, including the Grand Canyon, and to learn more about how to make more money. A thirty-year-old French pomologist and his wife, from near Bordeaux, this summer took an educational tour, visiting American apple-growers to find out if they grow anything finer than the French *calville.* They don't, the pomologist told Taylor.

Never has the French weather been talked about so much by the French as it has been this summer, and never has it been so constantly cursed by farmers and fishermen, and by vacationers from the provinces come to Paris for an August treat. Newspaper headlines unite in calling it *"l'été pourri"*—the rotten summer. With New York suffering from heat and a water shortage, Paris has been inundated by rainstorms and is cold besides. Last Saturday in Paris, it rained without letup from ten in the morning until eleven at night, when it hailed. Almost two and a half inches of water fell, the thermometer dropped to fifty-seven, and the Seine rose nearly six feet above its normal height—unheard of in midsummer.

It has been so cold in Brittany that the chilly Atlantic waters have driven most of the sardines south. At the little port of Quiberon, the most important sardine center in all France, the fishermen last month caught in their pale-blue nets only a few more than five hundred tons of this delectable fish—a third of normal. This year, sardines seem to be abandoning France, not even stopping offshore down at Royan, where grilled fresh sardines are customarily a welcome daily fish in the vacation-colony *pensions.* According to figures just released by the French canning industry, the sardine catch from the whole French Atlantic littoral is at present less than four thousand tons, as against fourteen thousand tons in a good piscatorial summer. The Quiberon sardine canners, many of them women, who are on piecework wages, have been earning only a few hundred francs a month, and the fishermen—often their husbands —in the three months that the sardines have supposedly been running have averaged only a thousand francs. The situation is so bad that the mayor of Quiberon has asked the government for immediate emergency aid.

There is also bad trouble, but for the opposite reason, in the peach regions of the Rhône-Alpes area, France's main peach orchards. This crisis is provoked by there being too many peaches, both white and yellow—twenty per cent more than last year, and exceptionally large, too. The glut can be blamed on the cursed weather—on a chilly June, which delayed the ripening of the early crop, and on a belatedly hot July, in which both early and late fruit ripened at the same time, in competition. The white-peach crop of two thousand tons in the Rhône Valley alone could not find buyers. (In Paris, the chilled Parisians did not fancy eating peaches, so bought nearly none.) Competition from Italian peach growers practically cut off exports of French fruit to Federal Germany. The Ministry of Finance in Paris has just received the president of the Comité Économique Fruits et Légumes de la Région Rhône-Alpes, who requested government help, just like the sardine mayor. Normally, the French government provides financial aid to farmers' committees when the committees represent at least twenty-five per cent of the area's producers. Since only twenty per cent were represented on the Rhône-Alpes committee, its request was refused. Its president promptly went back home to his peach farm and resigned.

To publicize their really wretched situation and the gastronomic perfection of their fruits, the growers in the Département du Drôme last week organized giveaways on the roads to passing motorists, so their lovely fruit would not rot untasted. They chose Route National No. 7, between Valence and Montélimar, and on it gave away eighteen tons of their best. They put five or six fine peaches in a little basket, which was offered by local pretty girls to the astonished motoring vacationists at traffic intersections when the lights turned red and the cars stopped. Over the village streets, banners had been hung up saying "Rhône Valley—Cradle of Peaches" or "Unsold Fine Peaches—Help Yourself." Some peaches were wrapped in a bit of paper carrying a protest to the Minister of Finance or were accompanied by a tract giving facts and figures on the peach crisis. "For the kilo of peaches that the city housewife pays two francs for, the farmer-producer is being paid thirty centimes. That doesn't even pay us for the gathering, the packing. We are being ruined! This is a catastrophe!" is what the tract made clear, ending politely with "Pleasant Journey!"

As the French phrase goes, "There isn't a cat in Paris," meaning it is empty—is emptied utterly by the holiday. The August holiday here is like a mild sleeping sickness; the city seems drowsy, somnolent, recumbent. It is no time to be hungry for fine food, because the restaurants are mostly closed; no time to have a toothache, because your dentist is on his Normandy farm; no time to be ill, because your doctor has gone to Norway; no time to twist your sacroiliac, because your osteopath is climbing mountains in Switzerland. A vacation is a time for resting. The capital of France itself seems to be resting, sprawling indolently beside the Seine.

August 25

It was Louis Philippe, otherwise a monarch with little enough aesthetic sense, who in 1830 saved Versailles by turning it, at his own expense, into "a museum consecrated to all the French glories." A few years later, this was translated, without losing much of its exalted implication, into the simpler title of Musée National d'Histoire de France, which it still officially bears today. Already in Louis Philippe's time there was talk of making Versailles a military hospital or a college; Napoleon had considered tearing it down and building something in his own style; and the bourgeois businessmen of the eighteen-thirties wanted to get their hands on the vast Versailles gardens and cut them up into attractive building lots. Until this year, the interior of the château mostly retained its uninhabited, museum appearance, except for special apartments, astonishing to the tourist eye with their rich remnants of furnishings, such as the overloaded, remarkable Clock Room. This summer, Versailles has been changed by the opening of fifty rooms authentically restored to the times and styles of Louis XIV, XV, and XVI, with the seventeenth century installed in the north wing of the château and the eighteenth century in the central section. These fifty *salles,* which had lain empty and dilapidating for a century and a half, their *boiseries* accumulating decades of dust, and sacking, covering what had been their silk-hung walls, today afford visible connections with Versailles' past as the Bourbon family's château and home (nineteen royal infants were born there, of whom few lived long, possibly owing to the famously malodorous palace sanitation), from the glorious, stilted long reign of the Sun King to the murderous edge of the Revolution. What today's visitor looks at are magnificent, if not numerous, authentic period furnishings beneath a population of royal-family portraits, including mistresses, on the silk walls—luxurious damask seats, gilded beds, facial likenesses, and dress and wig styles of two centuries of uninterrupted opulent, dominant, and spendthrift French history. And this year's Bourbon presentations are only the beginning. M. Gérard Van der Kemp, the director of Versailles, plans next year to open some twenty rooms in the South Attic, which will be devoted to Napoleon Bonaparte's Empire and style; the following year, the North Attic will be consecrated to the Bourbon Restoration period, the July Monarchy, and Napoleon III's Second Empire. This will make Versailles the most explicitly historical grand château of all Europe.

As has been pointed out in museum circles here, M. Van der Kemp's exceptional suitability for his post lies in his fresh museological ideas and his invaluable social relations with French and foreign multi-millionaires who love art and Versailles. The funds that Versailles receives from the state for purchasing new acquisitions are derisory, the equivalent of only three hundred and forty thousand dollars being annually provided for this purpose for all the museums in France. The reliable generosity of Mr. David Rockefeller furnished a unique treasure to the recent Versailles refurbishings (after he had first had a copy of his gift made for himself). It is a large gros-point carpet of dark brown strewn with small flowers, which Marie Antoinette and her sister-in-law Mme. Elizabeth worked on at Versailles, and which the two wretched ladies had time to finish in the Temple Prison before being beheaded. (A border that someone later attached to the carpet states these facts in embroidery.) The restoration of the Queen's apartment contains certain furnishings that she actually lived with, such as her fancy marble chimneypiece, a commode, some salon furniture, and the silk cover from her bed, patterned with garlands of pansies. This last article recently turned up in a New York antique shop and was presented to Versailles by an anonymous American admirer. Princesse Doan de Champassak (the former Barbara Hutton) gave the Queen's exquisite pale Savonnerie carpet. In its prime, Versailles was so overstuffed with furniture that the sale of its contents by the Garde Mobilière continued for two or three years after the Revolution, and it is doubtless from those sales that odd, invaluable pieces still turn up. Another American donor to Versailles is Mrs. Florence Gould, who gave a Louis XV commode made of tôle—the only one ever heard of—which was probably gold-washed for His Majesty but is now a faded copper color. No relics of his dauphin's bedroom could be found, so superb equivalents from the period were donated by Comte Guy de Boisrouvray, including a Polish-style gilded bed that was once the property of the Marquise du Châtelet, the famous young female mathematician who was also the mistress of the elderly Voltaire. However, the most glittering reconstitution of any is that of the room in which for years the mechanics of all French power resided—La Chambre du Roi, restored in part as the spectacle that Louis XIV himself looked on. The restoration is a wall covering of blazingly scarlet-patterned gold-and-silver cloth, its overpowering color and glitter interspersed with woven representations of green marble pillars—the chilling formal touch suitable to this monarch "whose presence, in any place, imposed a silence that was almost a sort of terror," according to the memoirs of the watchful little Duc de Saint-Simon. The pattern of this silk, salvaged from fragments still in storage, is of such complexity that only one weaver today in the Lyon silk establishment was competent to repeat it and train the necessary helpers. The silk that has been put up so far is the gift of the late Arturo Lopez-Willshaw; a new Maecenas is needed to pay for what should still go on the looms to complete the King's Chamber.

In the eighteenth-century rooms, the most interesting elements are the Académie Royale collection of portraits of themselves and each other by the epoch's painters, and portraits of King Louis XV's personal favorites, including that great member of the amoral intelligentsia Mme. de Pompadour. Also fine is Nattier's gallery of portraits of the King, his Queen, and his children, the best of Nattier being available only at Versailles. In the final room is the last portrait of Louis XVI, already helplessly wearing a tricolor cockade on his hat, for the Revolution was close. Its approach is apparent in David's astonishing, enormous sketch of the Jeu de Paume Convention leaders, also in the room. Like certain other classicist painters, he first drew in his figures stark naked, then dressed them—magnificent, cold-lined males with the occasional tracing of a shoe on a bare foot or the vague indication of breeches soon to cover thighs. At the right of the sketch, painted in color, are the heads and faces of some of those fighters for a people's constitution. The room is hung with a copy of a cotton print of the Revolutionary Phrygian bonnet, in tricolor, and this, together with David's great unfinished canvas, gives terrific effect to what followed the French kings of the other rooms.

This may well seem a very lengthy report on what intelligent tourists who can survive three hours' peering and walking can now see in Versailles. So far, there is no catalogue of the fifty new rooms' contents, adding the fatigue of close inspection of identification cards to the weariness of the visitor's poor feet. Still, it is a remarkable, rare, and artistic French history lesson, produced by the reigning inhabitants of the château, and now illustrated, in part, for the first time.

September 8

General de Gaulle is always his own oracle. No one can prophesy for him in advance, no one is ever his surrogate, because no one can know precisely what he has on his mind. As chief of a modern state, he has risen to a pinnacle and remained there on his gift for words, a leader whose policies are established by his voice and vocabulary, usually announced by him semi-annually in his speeches to his nation—to the world, really. For the

French, there is no knowing what he is going to say to them about their country or about their way of leading their lives until they see and hear him saying it on television—a direct form of communication of which he has the official art, looking his millions of compatriot listeners right in the eye, treating them to even his parenthetical thoughts with a professional wave of his large, pale hand. He is to speak tomorrow, Thursday, in the gilt ballroom of the Élysée Palace, talking in theory to his countrymen but physically addressing his words to the assembled international press, always favored on these occasions by being admitted to the intimacy of his presence, which descends upon them directly and uniquely, as it never does on his senate or assembly—a strange system by which the journalists, the movie cameras, and his microphone are delegated to receive his decisions viva voce, to hear and see him as he really is. This Thursday, the journalists' eyes will have an extra burden of discernment. If, as is hoped, he refers even ambiguously during his speech to his possible candidacy for reëlection as President, will they be able to see in his elderly face the strength needed for seven more years of leadership—a continuing portrait of him, as it were?

If he does run again, who runs against him is still unimportant. It is taken for granted that he will prove unbeatable, though doubtless achieving a smaller majority than will satisfy his sense of the grandeur of the France he has revived. If he does not run, the chaotic condition of France, again rampant with multiple party candidates, struggling for power, like hungry, waterlogged sailors climbing aboard a raft, is even in imagination so confusing (and so realistic) a picture that it is supposed that de Gaulle not only will but must run again, if only salvationally, to prepare France for its post-de Gaulle period. It is this future that everyone hopes he will outline tomorrow, and consequently the suspense before this press conference has been unusually nerve-racking for the chancelleries here. NATO and SHAPE will doubtless undergo the drastic changes he envisions as necessary in order to assure France the freedom from American pressure and integration that he reportedly feels she will need as the smaller and less powerful country she will unquestionably be when he no longer leads her. It will be the difference of only one Frenchman less among forty-eight million, but by his absence from power, as even the anti-Gaullists appreciate, he will shrink the whole country.

The official homage of France was nocturnally rendered last Wednesday by a torchlight procession that accompanied the lying in state of the famed modernist architect Charles Le Corbusier, held in the Louvre's Renaissance chef-d'œuvre, the Cour Carrée. A simulated green lawn had been specially laid down against the court's east wall, and on it rested his bare, undraped wooden coffin, alone in its harsh contemporary simplicity amid all the kingly decoration. A half-dozen Gardes Républicains in dress uniform stood near with sabres drawn, and in the court's west portico was massed a military band, whose brief portions from Beethoven's and Chopin's funeral marches echoed contrapuntally within the floodlit court walls on the chilly night air. This was the second such open-air homage to a celebrated French art figure (the first was to Georges Braque), both created as imposing ceremonies by M. André Malraux, Minister of Cultural Affairs, to stress France's interest in her major artists—very belated indeed in the case of Le Corbusier, as Malraux's stirring, elegiac speech boldly stated. To the crowd of perhaps four thousand, including ambassadors and other notables, he said that no one "had ever been so long, so patiently insulted" as Le Corbusier, the revolutionary-minded architectural genius and urbanist, Swiss-born but become French by naturalization and choice. His theories finally made him famous around the world, but, as he complained to the end, little of the praise ever came from France.

Although Le Corbusier had fanatic admirers among the French intelligentsia, he early alarmed French businessmen, municipalities, and the bigoted *beaux-arts* Establishment. In 1925, at the Exposition des Arts Décoratifs, he presented his astounding Voisin plan for modernizing central Paris, in which, through a kind of reformer's genius, he had interested the automobile-manufacturing firm of Voisin (both Peugeot and Citroën had turned him down) by explaining that since its motorcars were helping create the horrible urban traffic problem, it might well finance an exploration of possible ways and means to a solution. The extravagant plan proposed by Corbu (his name was so long that this became his nickname) was to raze all the buildings between the

Châtelet and the Louvre, replacing them with a few skyscrapers (then a Paris novelty, though now no more); to raze Les Halles also (now part of the present Paris municipal plan); and to pierce the city with an east-west automobile throughway (now being finished on both sides of the Seine)—all of which solutions were then regarded as too costly or too crazy. Throughout his career, Corbu made a fetish of sunlight, declaring that building permits should not be issued to construct apartment houses in which any room could not have contact with the sun. His insistence on the privilege of sunlight is being largely followed nowadays in those domino-like low-rent apartment houses that you see all over France. Utopian, arrogant, an agitator, and an intransigent positivist in his combative style, because he had had few chances when young to build what he believed in and perforce could only write about it in such books as "The City of Tomorrow," he became Europe's personal symbol of urban humanism, the exponent of "the stupendous building beauty of reinforced concrete," and famed for his axiom "A house is a machine for living in." Frank Lloyd Wright, also an intransigent architectural master, dismissed Corbu as "a box builder."

In the mid-nineteen-twenties, Corbu began building concrete suburban houses near Paris for avant-garde home lovers. They were suspended on concrete columns and were designed to the mathematical formula of what the French call *la section d'or*—the golden mean. One of the most celebrated, built in 1926, was at Garches, and another, built in 1931 and called Villa Savoye, was in the river town of Poissy. A London expert has just said that their construction "excited interest and discussion throughout the world," and that "it is doubtful if any houses of the century have won greater fame." According to long-standing Poissy village gossip, the Villa Savoye was commissioned by a mysterious rich American, who then abandoned it; derelict and seized for unpaid taxes by the town a few years ago, it was to be torn down and the site used for a school until Malraux, outraged, declared it an untouchable *monument historique*. In 1930, Corbu built what is regarded as the first completely modern building in Paris, ordered by the Swiss. This was the Swiss Pavilion, still part of the international Cité Universitaire and still notable for its flat surfaces, steel-set windows, and exactly balanced proportions. The next year, he went to Moscow and built the Ministry of Light Industry, still regarded as Russia's most modernist construction. The year after, he won a competition for the design of a U.S.S.R. government building to be called the Palace of the Soviets and met Stalin, but the Soviet thaw in favor of modernism had passed and the conformist freeze had set in again, which meant that Corbu was bypassed. His output in France was small and rather late. In 1952, he built what he felt was his greatest innovation, and it caused the greatest scandal of his career. This was La Cité Radieuse—the City of Light—which he declared was "a town of sixteen hundred living under one roof." Set up on *pilotis,* or stilts (an eccentricity that became a Corbu trademark), it was a big apartment house just outside Marseille, with community facilities such as a small hospital, clubrooms, restaurants, and shops —with every comfort, indeed, except local popularity and resident satisfactions. The city authorities refused to run a bus line out to it, and for years it was not completely inhabited. "Let them bark," Corbu said coldly of his Marseille critics, as if they were dogs. He built another Cité Radieuse at Nantes, without scandal; a delightful, popular little rural church, "shaped like a crab-shell," at Ronchamp, in the center of France, to replace a bombed-out chapel; and a dour cement Dominican monastery near Lyon, though he was himself an agnostic.

After the First World War, Le Corbusier was embittered by losing the promised commission to build the Geneva palace for the League of Nations, to which he was inclined because of his pacifism. He hoped to have his revenge, as he called it, through his appointment as a consultant on the designing of New York's glassbox United Nations Building, also built to preserve peace, but following its completion he more or less disavowed the whole East River project. Actually, his greatest glory, and also his unique dealing with what is still called beauty, lay in his recent designing of the main buildings for Chandigarh, the new capital city of Punjab. On his Indian project more than on any other he ever created he left his most unusual individual mark, such as the graceful serpentine walls of the Governor's Palace and the handsomely decorative "claustra," composed of gigantic open squares, that shield the High Court Building from the sun—a new problem for him who spent his European career searching to put sunlight inside his walls.

Because Le Corbusier was the world's greatest modern architect, or so the French now call him as a form of respect, his death was treated as a major Paris news event, with reams about him and his career in the press, and lengthy commentaries on the state radio—complimentary treatment such as he had not received during his life here. The fulsome press flattery made sad reading.

September 21

Mme. Françoise Sagan's popularity as a writer does not wane. "La Chamade" ("Beating a Retreat"), which is her sixth novel, is the best-seller on the autumn fiction list. All her novels have been best-sellers, and all are really more or less the same novel, except her first, "Bonjour Tristesse," which was like nothing she has written since. It was a single, perfect chance shot, fired by a very young, unknown girl with a steady, intelligent, precocious eye, and when it hit the mark in dead center, it loosed a treasure-trove of wealth, of international fame, and of pleasures, which fell on top of her like the premature dénouement of a fairy tale. Her aim has never again been so exact except in her comedy "Château en Suède," a chef-d'œuvre of a comic fantasy theatre piece. Thus, in her eleven-year career she has produced a pair of small modern classics, sexually amoral, that deal in a civilized, devious way with murder. Each time a new Sagan novel is announced, the invidious *tout-Paris* advance news is that it will be a failure, which it never is financially. The treasure-trove's contents publicly placed Mme. Sagan in a Parisian libertarian ambience, among the city's pleasure-loving inhabitants—a climate and characters so well suited to her temperament and talent that she has used and reused them ever since as material for her novels, doubtless her only known economy. In "La Chamade," she has written with lucidity, good taste, civilized cynicism, and familiarity about a little coterie of up-to-date Parisians, old and young, whose enjoyments, pangs, peace of mind, and day-and-night life, along with the moralities they can afford to omit, are all basic luxuries, dependent upon their having or needing quite a lot of money. They sit up late in night clubs drinking whiskey, dine out, and have lovers, and also have good upper-bourgeois French manners, since the emancipated bourgeoisie is what they are. Two of the lovers are paid for—the thirty-year-old heroine, Lucile (Sagan usually keeps her heroine in her own age group), who lives in luxury with, and is kept with more generosity than passionate pressure by, the fifty-year-old millionaire, Charles; and the handsome maverick, Antoine, semi-kept by forty-year-old Diane, and a bargain he is, too. The scenes of Lucile's and Antoine's love affair are the most believable parts of the book. Sagan's literary gift is for the heat of the emotions and for the ardent enigma of love. Forced by Antoine to come live openly and honestly with him, and, worst of all, even to take an ill-paid job, since his job, in a publishing house, is like that, too, Lucile refuses to go to a cheap abortionist—their only solution in her revolt against having a child in uncomfortable poverty. So he takes her to a costly Geneva clinic on the complacent Charles's money. In one of those final chapters the length of a postscript which are typical of Sagan, the reader learns the novel's happy ending—that two years later Charles and Lucile get married. In other words, Lucile beats a retreat, as the book's title makes clear. "We are not made for legality, you and I," she had said to Antoine in a moment of clarity and revolt, nonconformism being her version of liberty. She wanted the responsibility of possessing nothing—neither a child (Mme. Sagan has a little son, now three years old) nor a husband nor a house nor an occupation. She wanted only to be furnished with the elements of life, as if her soul were like a modern furnished apartment in which she lived but owned nothing. She is the full-length portrait of a lucid, superior cocotte, such as no other contemporary novelist has created, painted almost entirely on the surface.

"La Chamade" will probably arouse a certain amount of disapproval even in Paris, because of Mme. Sagan's importance and her popularity with women readers in France, because of the lack of conventional hypocrisy that her characters show in leading their own lives, and because of her presenting them as if they were acting normally in the Fifth Republic. There will be talk in Church circles against the leading role she has given to *une société pourrie* —a rotten society. One literary critic has already referred to *la dolce vita* and to "the demimonde in which Mme. Sagan has lived." Another critic, more wisely referring merely to her technique as a writer, has said, "Her surest instrument remains her mirror."

Jean-Paul Sartre's brief, always alarming and impressive play about Hell, "Huis Clos," first produced during the last days of the German Occupation, was revived for a month or so during the summer-holiday vacuum. Now there is a revival of his 1959 full-length drama "Les Séquestrés d'Altona," at the Théâtre de l'Athénée, which should go through the winter. Though the text has not been altered, Sartre has changed, it seems, its application in his own mind. Despite the fact that (as you may well know) the drama revolves around the voluntary self-confinement for long years of a former Nazi officer, Franz, sequestered upstairs in his father's country mansion and cut off from all communication with the world except the last world he knew—that of his guilt for crimes committed on orders during the war—Sartre now claims that his intention in this play was to stigmatize the French Army for the tortures it practiced in the recent Algerian war. Certainly they needed stigmatizing, even at this late date, but to one's eyes and ears in the Théâtre de l'Athénée his present revived Nazi play is still about self-torturing Franz recollecting Nazi crimes. Because of more decisive acting, the play seems more comprehensible this time than it did before, though perhaps we are simply more familiar in memory with its strange material. Claude Dauphin seems more vital as the heroic father, and Serge Reggiani, as Franz, is clearer in projecting the ex-soldier's hallucinations—the self-criticism he has delivered to his tape recorder, the aberrant confessions he has made to an audience of imagined monsters, mostly crabs, as if he were at the bottom of the sea. The importance of his sister, who is his incestuous mistress in his sequestration, is, however, mostly lost by Mme. Evelyne Rey, who mumbles her lines so they can hardly be heard, let alone their import understood. It is still a powerful play—a double play, with the Germanic evil of a whole past war condensed into the vaporing inside one soldier's head, so that there are two evils: what he did and what he has become. The play lasts three and a half hours. They are long, horrifying, thoughtful hours to sit through.

October 5

An exhibition of a hundred and two French paintings that the French may never have laid eyes on, unless they saw them in Russia, has been drawn from the Hermitage State Museum, in Leningrad, and the Pushkin Museum of Fine Arts, in Moscow; was displayed all summer in Bordeaux; and will now be on view in the Louvre until January, constituting the greatest art exchange ever organized between Russia and France. (It is rather a lopsided exchange, since France sent only fifty-two canvases to Russia, or merely half as many, and not all French, at that.) What the Russians sent back here on loan amounts to an aesthetic historic rainbow that stretched for almost a hundred and fifty years from Paris to St. Petersburg—a colored bridge of French art that began under Empress Catherine the Great, when she started buying it in huge quantities and at long distance in the early seventeen-seventies, and that ended in 1917 under Lenin, when the Russian Revolution prevented the bourgeois industrialist collector Sergei Shchukin from making his annual trip to Paris to buy further alarming modern art by Matisse and Picasso. One of the Empress's chief art advisers in Paris was the encyclopedist Diderot. (A true philosopher, in 1773 he undertook the rigorous trip to St. Petersburg to visit her, "arriving more dead than alive," he complained, and said of her, "She has the soul of Brutus and the charms of Cleopatra.") On his say-so, the Empress bought at one fell swoop the famous four-hundred-item collection of Pierre Crozat, one of Louis XIV's tax collectors. It was mainly from this hoard that there came this exhibition's sixteenth- and seventeenth-century treasures—Louis Le Nain's "Visit to the Grandmother," and the sumptuous Poussin "Tancrède et Herminie," who are in company with the most beautiful white horse of European art. Then comes a weaker selection from the eighteenth century—an exquisite, uncharacteristic Boucher landscape with figures, illustrating La Fontaine's fable "The Hermit;" one of Lancret's several versions of "La Camargo," the Belgian dancer, which hung in Catherine's apartment in the Winter Palace; Chardin's flawless canvas "The Washerwoman" (an odd art property for an empress); and Hubert Robert's "Terrace of Marly," depicting one of the two famed "Horses of the Sun" (now decorating the Place de la Concorde) and painted with such superb light that the Empress invited him to visit her. (He declined.) Among the Watteaus is one so small as to rank as a Crozat gem—"The Coquettes Returning from the Ball" in company with a little blackamoor.

The subsequent Czars not being collectors, the mid-nineteenth French century in this exhibition is nearly empty. But toward its end come the masterpieces that then spread into our modern time —almost forty of those shown having been collected by Shchukin or, on a lesser scale, by the Morozov brothers, Mikhail and Ivan. They start with Impressionism and elegant Renoirs, and move into Expressionism, including one great Gauguin of sunflowers on a chair—but where are Shchukin's thirteen other Gauguins? He owned seven Rousseaus, of which only one is shown—"Walk in the Luxembourg Garden." There are four of the same collector's Cézannes, painted at the height of his genius and including the celebrated portrait of, presumably, his wife in a pale-blue tailor-made suit with a flowered hat and a masterpiece bouquet of rumpled flowers. There are also Shchukin's unequalled Fauve and Cubist masterpieces—the early Matisse "Dancers Among the Nasturtiums," his "Nymph and Satyr," which is like a dream of motion, and his superb "Riffian," or native chief. There are seven Picassos painted around 1908, all famed and rare, such as the proto-Cubist "Woman with Fan" and, even more strange, like a female from a newly composed race, "The Nude Woman in the Forest," with closed eyes. These early Matisse and Picasso canvases are at the height of each painter's creative invention, are high-tide canvases of modern art. Shchukin had been frightened by "Les Demoiselles d'Avignon" but later purchased their significant art elements and the style of their bodies in these canvases. Miss Alice Toklas said that he always bought his Picassos somewhat stale—a year or so after he got used to their fresh, terrifying novelty. Picasso's early mistress, Fernande Olivier, said in her memoirs that the Russian looked like a pale pig and stammered so horribly that it made art conversation with Picasso difficult when the foreigner came to make his welcome purchases. Shchukin was buying Picassos when even the Spaniard's Paris painter friends thought he was crazy—so mad, Derain said, that "one day we will find him hanged behind one of his own canvases." The Russian bought Matisse and Picasso when the French considered them untouchable, anarchistic, and decadent. And when his vast, invaluable collection of modern art, then the greatest in the world, was nationalized (or seized) by the Revolution, the Communists thought the Matisse and Picasso paintings servile, bourgeois, and thus, again, decadent, and stowed them away out of sight. It was not until 1954 that the world knew where they were—in The Hermitage attic, the unframed canvases hung on racks like laundry stretched to dry. By that time, Shchukin had long since died in straitened circumstances in Paris, to which he had somehow successfully fled.

A strange, mixed aura hangs over the Russian loan show at the Louvre. There is the surface glamour that anything from Russia (even if it was originally from France) has for people here in the West. Then, there is the notorious personality of the great sensuous, adulterous Catherine, intelligently importing civilizing art into her foreign wintry fastness to show to her court and her lovers—art that we now also can see, as if our sight mingled with hers and theirs. There is also a retrospective sense of alarm in looking at the Fauve and Cubist pictures, which were like dangerous, cursed fetishes to those who had aesthetic faith in them when their government still did not believe.

The great question here in all the newspapers and private conversations, whatever the class or qualification, is *"Oui ou non?"* Will the General run again for President or will he not? This sums up the entire national curiosity of France. He is due to give his official answer within the fortnight, on October 15th. Even in anticipation, it is a historic date.

October 20

Now it is St.-Germain des Prés that the French are Americanizing, in the way they perfected on their Champs-Élysées. The second Paris Drugstore will be opened this week on the Boulevard, at the corner of the Rue de Rennes across from the Café des

Deux-Magots, but will be much further out, inside, than its predeces-
sor Drugstore, up near the Arc de Triomphe. Overhead on the wall
above the new Drugstore's circular bar there is a series of astonishing large oval bronze plaques that represent in sculptured *haut-re-
lief* the mouths of six of the most famous women of our time. Even
if the women's names were not inscribed beneath, the mouth of
Brigitte Bardot would be easily recognizable, because her lips are
parted and show her two well-known front teeth. The next most
identifiable is Françoise Sagan's well-shaped, witty mouth. There
are the famous laughing lips of Marilyn Monroe. Jeanne Moreau
is reported to have identified, even from a photograph, her rather
sullen, molded mouth. That of Juliette Greco is *nul* without her
voice coming out from it, and, far sadder, those ravishing lips of
Marlene Dietrich, so celebrated in public mobility for so long a
time, are permanently without meaning in bronze, having neither
charm nor personality. As alternate decorations, there are sculptured
panels of six eyes, each belonging to a famous man of our day, and
each looking practically like all the others, though the choice of
the men is interesting. There is the late Albert Camus and the late
Gérard Philipe, whose romantic glance on the screen or the classic
stage made him the idealized young actor of postwar Paris. The
other eyes belong to Duke Ellington (a nice compliment) and to
Jean-Paul Belmondo, as the new tough-tender movie star; there is
the little bull's eye of Picasso, for whom St.-Germain was a nocturnal conversational field over the years; and, finally, there is the eye
of Dr. Robert Oppenheimer, the physicist. These lip and eye panels
are more entertaining as a historical notion than they could possibly
be as artistic conversation pieces, even after several bourbons, which
is what the young French now drink instead of Scotch, which is
out. The St.-Germain Drugstore will have three official openings
this week, the first on Monday night for diplomats and night-life
notables—black tie and evening gowns de rigueur. On Wednesday
afternoon, in the Drugstore's basement cinema, the world's first
showing will be held of Fellini's latest, already much discussed, if
unseen, new film, called in French "Juliette des Esprits."

Modernization is also charming another corner of the Left
Bank. Straight up the Rue de Rennes, there has been opened the
preliminary entrance of the new Gare Montparnasse, to replace the

old one, which has been in use by Parisians for a hundred and thirteen years, having been a station for horsedrawn suburban *diligences* before railroads were invented. The old red brick station is already being torn down, and the square facing it has been re-named Square 18 Juin—the day in 1940 when General de Gaulle made his famous broadcast appeal from London. On the site of the old station will arise (in 1967) the highest skyscraper now planned for all Europe—the Tour Montparnasse hotel, of fifty stories (if its five basements are counted), to contain five hundred de-luxe rooms, as well as shops, a conference auditorium, a swimming pool, a cinema, a roof-garden restaurant, and so on—the project having been officially approved only this last week by Premier Pompidou. There was violent opposition to the scheme, led principally by the conservative Deputy Frédéric-Dupont, who apparently lives nearby and who complained that a spear-shaped edifice of such altitude would ruin the historic south skyline of Paris—which, of course, nobody of imagination could deny. The Deputy also said that the Tour would particularly destroy the perspective from the Esplanade des Invalides, on which, at long last, a *jardin à la française* was to be planted—one of those delightful gardens of baroque, patterned plants about ten inches high, ill-suited indeed to a distant back-ground skyscraper. At the Observatoire, a few blocks to the south-east, the savants protested that "such a mass in the sky of Paris" would hamper their celestial observations, and that all their noctur-nal calculations would be interfered with by the Tour's high radi-ance of electric light. As is natural in a highly civilized old city that has been enjoying solid prosperity, the architectural future of Paris is already crushing its past.

Certainly the new Montparnasse hotel accommodations are a capital-city necessity. The still unfinished Paris Hilton, behind the Tour Eiffel, is said to be the first big new Paris hotel in thirty-three years, and during the Salon de l'Automobile last week, there were not enough empty beds to be found in town for the visitors and the motor trade. The news from the Salon is good and bad. Sales of new cars at the Salon were from twenty to fifty per cent higher than last year—awful news for people who live in overmotorized Paris and must now face an influx of thousands of redundant new cars, but good news for the automobile workers, who had a lean, jobless spell earlier this year. Perhaps in anticipation, the Champs-Élysées suddenly looks naked. This last weekend, all parking of cars by the curb was forbidden, and it is rumored that double parking—and maybe parking of any sort—under the trees beside the broad sidewalk will also be outlawed, apparently to force sou-pinching car owners to cease parking by the year in public for nothing and to use instead, at two francs an hour, the new neighborhood subterranean Avenue George V municipal garage, which still has plenty of empty space.

November 2

It has been supposed from the first that the present French Presidential electoral campaign would be rather bizarre, if only because General de Gaulle has aloofly refused to say whether he will run in it or not. Even now, forty-eight hours before he makes his official TV announcement, three of his Ministers think he will, or might, say no, and several million French people think, or hope, he will say yes. The situation unexpectedly became almost ludicrous this past week when public attention, dramatically concentrated, as if at a theatre, on whether the great national star, still sitting in his dressing room considering his major Thespian lines, "To be or not to be," would make his reappearance or not upon the world stage, was suddenly and completely distracted by the political intrusion of birth control, like a catch phrase shouted from the cheaper seats in the gallery. It is the first time in French political history that the basic, intimate issue of family planning has dominated an election—the first time, indeed, that the doctrine of contraception has ever been argued and reported on, and in an explicit vocabulary, for any reason whatever, on the front pages of the entire Paris press. The birth-control issue was raised almost accidentally by the anti-Gaullist left, immediately turning into a brilliant chance political maneuver of enormous possible influence on women voters—a majority (fifty-four per cent) of the electorate.

It was a week ago this last Sunday that Deputy François Mitterrand, Presidential candidate of the now exceptionally united, and thus powerful, French left (composed of the Socialists, Radical Socialists, Independent Socialists, and Communists), said *à l'improviste,* in an electioneering speech on his own home ground at Nevers, "Women should have the right to have one, two, three, four, or five children if they so desire, or to have none at all." He afterward declared that he said this because he thinks it, but with no notion that he was kindling a vital political issue. Immediately, voting for Mitterrand was envisioned as voting for a birth-control government, whereas a vote for de Gaulle would be for a government that has quite correctly upheld (with no expressed thought of abrogating or reforming it) the French law forbidding *"la propagande anticonceptionnelle,"* passed back in 1920 as a Parliamentary effort to fill French cradles left empty by the absence of husbands, or their deaths, in the First World War. On Thursday, the afternoon *Paris-Presse* carried the headline "LA 'PILULE' MISE À L'ÉTUDE EN FRANCE," meaning that the contraceptive pill was being investigated by the French government. In Parliament the day before, de Gaulle's Minister of Public Health, Raymond Marcellin, hurriedly discussed the pill (in his budget report), saying, "The government has no intention of avoiding the problem of planned parenthood. It expects to define its position after a study of all its aspects—medical, demographic, juridical, moral." He said that he and the Minister of Justice had been studying claims in the medical press that "the pill is not proved to be without danger" and that three recent cases of vascular thrombosis had resulted from certain preventives, and added that the whole contraception problem, in his personal opinion, was "a very delicate affair." Since M. Marcellin never once spoke up in favor of birth control, the Parliamentarians of the left said that he talked like an ostrich with its head still in the sand. He was also sharply questioned in the Chamber by the rich, energetic feminist deputy Mme. Jacqueline Thome-Patenôtre, who demanded of him that the 1920 law be modified so as to permit family planning as it exists in "evolved countries so unlike France." She added that it was high time for the French to drop their hypocrisy about their abortions, which, as she has already told Parliament, have lately reached a million a year—just like French births.

Because all the minor candidates felt that they should step into the political mainstream of birth control, Maître Jean-Louis Tixier-Vignancour, the brainy, rather showoff, extremely reactionary lawyer running against de Gaulle, asked for repeal of the 1920 law because, as he cynically said, it had morally never worked in private any better than prohibition had worked in the United States. The new candidate of the center, M. Jean Lecanuet—who oddly presents himself as representing the deceived former Gaullist devotees, of which he was one, and who is now running, he says, for a Gaullism "the size of a normal man, not a superman like de Gaulle"—made some sort of faint anti-left statement about even Christian groups' having lately been preoccupied with family planning. Apparently, this has been true, under cover, for several years, but it took the present political importance of the issue to bring the details to light. It seems that the first family-planning center was opened in Grenoble in 1961, and shortly afterward one opened in Paris; now about seventy centers nationally serve what is called, in Franglais, Le Mouvement Français pour le Planning Familial, with five hundred doctors willing to work with them. (Actually, as the law of 1920 stands, French doctors can be stricken from the medical register for disseminating birth-control information.) To all these activities the government chose to close its eyes. As a result, in the past six months three Paris city hospitals—the Necker, the Bichat, and the Broca—have quietly opened consultative services on family planning. It would now seem that no matter which political side wins in December—whether it is the left or de Gaulle himself or merely his candidate—permissive birth-control laws will be the eventual major result of this extraordinary Presidential election.

Each of the five candidates for the seven-year term (counting de Gaulle as No. 1) will be entitled to two hours' speaking time on both radio and TV, and will not have to pay a sou to the state network. Last week, Premier Georges Pompidou set up the national commission whose duty it will be to see that the campaign material used—especially on TV—is of "a dignified tone." It is already known that a biting little undignified film that Tixier-Vignancour has had made will certainly not be shown on the screen. It is a takeoff on the fairy story of Snow White, who in Tixier's skit has been turned into Marianne, the girl in sabots and Phrygian cap who represents the French Republic. She is looking at herself in her pocket mirror when suddenly her face fades out and de Gaulle's face fades in. At this, in fright, she drops her mirror, which breaks as she cries, *"Zut!* Another seven years of bad luck!" The difficulty of knowing what a dignified tone would be in a personal, political TV polemic against de Gaulle and his regime is already worrying politicians. A law of 1881 protects him, as chief of state, against what is called "any offense." But in the election will he be running as chief of state or just as a candidate? Politicians fear that he will be running as both, and that on TV especially—though this is their most valuable electioneering mass medium—they had better watch their "p"s and "q"s. French political emotions can be violent, and the dignified *grand Charlie* is known to be hyper-sensitive. In a recent trial here in Paris, the novelist Jacques Laurent, author of the Caroline Chérie series of frothy novels, but also the author of "Mauriac sous de Gaulle," which is the book that made his trouble, was fined the equivalent of twelve hundred dollars and ordered to delete twenty-five pages from his book. He had accused the chief of state of being "a man of blood," "a man who does not keep his word," and "a fomenter of civil war"—all considered legally offensive. His lawyer pointed out in court that Laurent's case was the hundred-and-first such trial in the past six years of Gaullism, whereas there were only six trials for insulting state chiefs in the Third and Fourth Republics combined. They, however, were much smaller chiefs.

December 1

Until this weekend, it was not thought that the small crowd of five other candidates for the Presidency of General de Gaulle's Fifth Republic could impede de Gaulle himself from coming in with a dominant majority of about sixty per cent of the votes. His total is now calculated as down to fifty-one per cent, which would be safe but humiliating, considering the semi-royal standard of his personal expectations. At fifty per cent he will have to submit—though would he?—to the disgrace of a runoff with the rival who has the next-greatest load of votes. The leading rival in personality, and as a public discovery, is the Kennedyesque, pleasing young moderate politician Jean Lecanuet, who will probably come in only third—an obscure senatorial nobody, known only in Demo-Christian Mouvement Républicain Populaire circles until two weeks ago, when, for the first time, he stepped in front of the state TV cameras, where for seven years de Gaulle had been the nation's great politico-historical star. The biggest irony is that de Gaulle, who introduced and perfected this mass medium here, founding his Fifth Republic on his well-articulated words and holding his government together by his transmitted voice and the photogenic image of his strangely Gothic visage, should now be faced by an election from which he is bound to emerge damaged by these TV electoral beginners, who for a fortnight have been stealing his show and his votes. Shops that rent out TV sets report a three-hundred-per-cent jump in their business during this Presidential contest. Until last week, de Gaulle seemed to be the only Frenchman in France uninterested in the campaign. He was like an elderly giant standing on his own private hill, viewing from afar the landscape with figures. It seems incredible that he planned to use only the final eight minutes of the two hours of TV time allotted to each candidate, until his worried Ministers and Premier Pompidou dared to harass him. They were deeply alarmed for him and for themselves by the headway made by his rivals, and by French citizens' habit of listening on some six million TV sets in fashionable salons, in bourgeois parlors, and on modest kitchen tables to the evening's attacks on the General and his government, like a new kind of cynical night-club entertainment brought into the home. He has now turned to his election duties belatedly. With the election itself due on Sunday and the campaign ending on Friday, he will talk twice during these next few days on the radio, and will appear twice on TV, where all six candidates will say their final say (separated by seven-minute "musical interludes"), with the last word going to the lucky Lecanuet (their positions on this program were drawn by lot), preceded by de Gaulle, like a runner-up on what has always been his own political show.

In many ways, everything has been strangely changed in this last week, as if the cork had blown out of a bottle of soured wine.

A stream of criticism, dissatisfaction, candor, resentment, and even abuse of de Gaulle has flowed out into the public French air. The dignified, tactful critiques that the French press has in the past given him, often in full measure, have suddenly become a kind of turgid flood, draining angry, pent-up emotions away. For example, the cover of a recent copy of the weekly *L'Express*—noted, it is true, for its career of candid anti-Gaullism—bore as its opening campaign contribution a handsome colored photograph of de Gaulle in evening regalia, with the carved Élysée entry gate pictured just behind him, like a small stone coat of arms. Beside his photo was printed in large letters *"De Gaulle—à Vie?"* ("De Gaulle for Life?"). Inside, the editor, Jean-Jacques Servan-Schreiber, in his personal political column, gave the following terse, harsh answer to his own query: "May General de Gaulle live as long as God wishes, but what the country needs is his political death."

The famous satirical weekly *Le Canard Enchaîné,* its wicked humor always blisteringly against any government or establishment, has for two years been running a brilliant takeoff of the Duc de Saint-Simon's court memoirs of Louis XIV, with de Gaulle referred to as Le Roi and the weekly Élysée events inscribed in pastiche ducal style. Following de Gaulle's November 4th warning on what would happen to France if he were not reëlected to guide it on December 5th—a warning in which he stated, "No one could doubt that France would immediately collapse and undergo a disintegration without reprieve," which unpleasantly recalled to the French of today Louis XV's prophecy *"Après moi le déluge"*—the *Canard* gave the following vicious portrait of what de Gaulle had looked like giving that speech on the TV screen: "On that contentious face—quarrelsome, grating, plastered by makeup so as to meet the public gaze—old age had already established its opening ruins. The eyes set within the overripe circles launched sparks. Holding his long, plucked neck far forward, as if to bay his phrases louder and nearer, and as if in a windy tempest, he let fly his harangue in a heated voice. In proportion as he sought to snare his listeners, there seemed visible, twisting in the vipers' nest of his seventy-five-year-old passion, his unbearable haughtiness, the dizzied mind, his pride, the violent ambition to labor at the absolute deification of his omnipotence, the bitter thirst to reign, the folly of believing that were he to perish all would be wiped away—the low and crass appetite to disparage all that is not he himself."

After de Gaulle's Tuesday-night TV speech, his first but so belated, and generally called his speech of riposte to his rival candidates and critics on all sides, it was astonishing to read the enfeebled comment in the next morning's *Figaro* editorial. "One would have wished," it said, "that the President of the Republic, whose eviction on Sunday . . . will not fail to plunge France into confusion, had made up his mind to let us know what his plans are for choosing his successor." Thus *Figaro* spoke as if the fight were already over. "Instead of this implacable battle between the holder of power and those who at any price want to dislodge him," *Figaro* continued, "we could have wished to hear from both sides propositions of a nature to give us confidence in our tomorrows." The theme of chaos was one of the more telling familiar threats that had dotted de Gaulle's speech of the night before—by no means one of his great ones, even at this critical moment—when he said of his five rival candidates, "Their mutual contradictions, their irreconcilable followers, and their divergent combinations demonstrate clearly that the accession of no matter which one of them to the supreme governmental post would infallibly mark a return to the odious confusion in which the French state formerly dragged itself along, to the misfortune of France."

The five candidates running against de Gaulle are certainly a mixed group, yet characteristic, in their non-similarity, of France's inevitable, classic mélange—rich, bourgeois, and revolutionary, like a bag containing scraps of colored stuffs left from the past. Vaguely under the third heading comes the most touching candidate, who turned up just a half hour before the candidacy list was closed. He is a fifty-eight-year-old suburban watch repairer named Marcel Barbu, who announced himself to the Conseil Constitutionnel in the Palais-Royal by saying, "I represent the Association Immobilière of Sannois"—a modest little section a few kilometres to the northwest of Paris—"of which I am the head. I do not expect to be elected President. My only aim is to profit from the Presidential campaign by laying bare on TV my difficulties with the government in matters of building and rentals. To pay the ten-thousand-franc candidate's deposit"—put up by some loyal friends—"seems cheap for the privilege of talking to fifty million French people about our troubles." Were he ever President of France, he says, he would at once appoint a Ministry for the Rights of Man. His family was "poor and atheist." After marriage, he and his wife founded work centers for the making of watchcases. When the war came, he took what money they had and, on the theory that all men are brothers, divided it with his workmen. He was himself in the famous Vercors Maquis, was early arrested and sent to Buchenwald, but survived, and on liberation in 1945 he was able to find his wife and family, which now consists of twelve children. The next year, he was elected Communist deputy from the Drôme Department, but refused to sit with the Communists, finding them too conventional, he said. So he sat on a stool to the left of the Party parliamentary benches, and later resigned. A few years later, already disgusted with the French government, he staged a hunger strike for eight days, during which he lived in an old automobile. In his TV speeches, he perspired a great deal from nervousness but stuck to his points and his criticism of de Gaulle, talking shrewd, truthful, idealistic common sense.

The other candidates are more experienced and ordinary. Pierre Marcilhacy is the candidate of the liberals. Formerly an Independent, he was so independent that he resigned from the party. Nearly two inches taller than de Gaulle and well to do, with a nice Paris town house and a country place, made from a mill, in the Charente, where he is a senator, he is married to a former mannequin from Vera Borea. Her family were Dutch Army people. He himself, the son and grandson of lawyers, is a lawyer who is now attached to the Conseil d'État—a high connection indeed. During the German Occupation, he defended some of the French *résistants* in the special courts. He thinks the General's shapeless financial policies, and those of his Finance Minister, have dilapidated "the fortunes of Papa"—the French phrase for sound family investments.

Jean-Louis Tixier-Vignancour, aged fifty-eight, candidate of the extreme right, is a very different kind of lawyer. He defended ex-General Salan, of the plastic-bomb-throwing Secret Army Organization, and saved Salan's head; before that he was Chief of Information for Pétain in the Vichy government. His hobby is playing with lead soldiers. A brilliant, bass-voiced, melodramatic law-court performer, he is a deputy himself and the grandson of one. His electioneering speeches have been witty and class-conscious, and his enemies say that the number of votes cast for him will indicate how many Vichyites and Fascists are still alive in France.

The leading candidate in terms of political importance is François Mitterrand, standing for the united left, including the Communists and all sorts of Socialists. Aged forty-nine, he is the son of a railroad worker who was also a reader of Latin and Greek. Mitterrand is a university man and a lawyer, and met his wife when both were in the Resistance, for which brave work she received the Croix de Guerre. He entered Liberation politics, was a Minister for the first time at the age of thirty-one, and has served in Parliament as an expert on African affairs. He is a solid, political-brained man and talker, who says he believes that Socialism will increasingly model the society of tomorrow, and that new Socialists must be ready to take part in business expansion, as the basis of the prosperity that Europe must have for that new society. Mitterrand is not an easy or a popular man, being intelligent and obstinate. From the first, it has been supposed that he will be de Gaulle's most important vote-getting rival, since he has the entire Communist Party behind him, ordered to vote for his name. This is the first time since 1936 and that year's famous Front Populaire, under Léon Blum, that the entire French left, dropping its internal squabbles as to which way leads best to Marxism, has united to make itself felt against the right and the middle.

As for Lecanuet, he says that he became a candidate to try to change the way things have been going. During the war, as a youth, he was in the Resistance as an exploder of plastic bombs on railroad tracks, majored in philosophy, became rather a pet of Simone de Beauvoir and Sartre as a student. Now forty-five, he is an exceptionally fine brand-new TV performer—handsome, and with clear, orderly ideas for bettering France. "One can see that France has been the last in production growth for the last seven years, last in housing, and last in salaries and income to keep up living standards, especially for farmers," he said on TV. "On the other hand, it has been the first in high prices and in taxes per capita. I am fighting against solitary power—power that is absolute, consular, without dialogue, without control, without any counter-weight." He is pro-European and pro-Common Market, and was an M.R.P. Christian Democrat, "but not a clerical," when he resigned to run against de Gaulle. He is the youngest candidate to enter the lists and the only previously unknown one who, it is thought, will be heard of again before his political career is much older. He is the discovery of 1965.

December 9

Never in the electoral history of France have the French voted as heavily as they did last Sunday—eighty-five per cent of the enrolled voters. Yet they gave President de Gaulle so light and insufficient a tally (just under forty-four per cent) that he will have to stand on a runoff second ballot the Sunday after next, and obtain from it at least a fifty-one-per-cent dominance over his Communist-supported rival, Deputy François Mitterrand, who won just over thirty-two per cent of last Sunday's votes—a high victory for the left. In the last fortnight, de Gaulle's reputation has been shaken like a statue loosened on its pedestal by time and weathering. It may be that a seven-year Presidential term is too long for France, where a third of the voters are thirty-five years old or less; to them seven years seems a long political mortgage on their future, rather than an enticing investment for tomorrow and tomorrow. It may be that de Gaulle at seventy-five is too aged to have competed easily against the TV surprise of the campaign—Jean Lecanuet, thirty years his junior, young enough to be his son, with pro-European ideas that are appropriate to his generation and are anathema to the General, who saved France with his chauvinistic nationalism.

The unexpected outcome of last Sunday's election astonished France, shook it, and delighted de Gaulle's bourgeois French enemies—at least until they began worrying about Mitterrand, with his third of the nation's vote. For he turned the long-sought *ouverture à gauche,* or opening to the left, into reality by coming in on the cardiac side of the French body politic—the emotional, physical side, which is still a residue of the French Revolution, being composed of the French workers and masses and poor. It is taken for granted that in the December 19th runoff de Gaulle will obtain far more than the needed absolute majority, owing to the repentant bourgeoisie's voting loyally for him this time (instead of for Lecanuet, of the Demo-Christian M.R.P. Party), through fear of Mitterrand and his left—both of which, ironically, will be de Gaulle's aids in victory. It is now figured that de Gaulle was defeated Sunday not by the left's voting against him but by the right's failing to vote for him. It was all along taken for granted that de Gaulle would face up to the humiliating second vote, rather than retire once more to his country house at Colombey-les-Deux-Églises to brood and continue writing his memoirs instead of living them, like an unpleasant postscript. The vote for the office of President by direct suffrage, which de Gaulle must have thought would aid in perpetuating his Gaullist system, was his unique democratic creation for modern France, and for him not to have abided by its statutes would have seemed *lâche,* or cowardly, as the French said, and would have been the suicide of his myth and of his claims to honorable glory.

The voting for President seemed to the French like a political picnic, as if, after seven years, they had finally been invited to step out-of-doors and decide which path they would walk down next, and with whom. Only three of the six candidates were consequential enough to be worth voting seriously for—de Gaulle, Mitterrand, and Lecanuet, who now plans to found a centrist pro-European party of his own, to be called Le Centre Démocrate. Tixier-Vignancour, the extreme-right ex-Vichy candidate, who received only a handful of votes, mostly from the refugee *pieds noirs,* or white Algerian newcomers of O.A.S. persuasion, has offered to transfer his votes to Mitterrand, in a last effort to injure de Gaulle. "My only aim was to put de Gaulle into the runoff vote," he has just said with coarse candor. "And there he is! I am delighted. If he runs, I shall do everything to assure his defeat. The French have shown their hostility to his regime—that's the main thing." The eccentric suburban candidate, Marcel Barbu, gave most of his precious last-minute TV speech to explaining how de Gaulle had refused to receive him at the Élysée for a private talk when he wanted to tell the General about the bad housing for the French poor—Barbu's special political concern. Of all the six candidates on that final pre-election TV show, de Gaulle included, Barbu seemed the only pure spirit, without worldly ambition except for others.

It must be noted that this election was influenced by de Gaulle's seven long years of contempt for France's multi-party political system, surely the curse of republican France. In the election, the parties for once played a subsidiary role. It was less the M.R.P. Party that supported Lecanuet than it was a segment of public opinion that, like him, felt the Common Market must not be allowed to fail. True, the Communist Party obediently supported Mitterrand, though with many defections, but the Socialists voted for him not as Socialist Party doctrinaires but as individuals sharing Mitterrand's Socialist views.

Le Monde's front-page editorial on Wednesday, three nights after the election, was entitled "Un Choc." In part, it said, "Rarely has an election result so surprised international opinion. Whether one liked him or not, General de Gaulle was deemed to hold such authority over the French people that it seemed unimaginable that the majority of them could have inflicted on him what is difficult to interpret otherwise than as a disavowal. The reasons are multiple, and even contradictory, but it was a disavowal just the same. Democracy is not so widespread around the globe that there exist many countries where the people can offer themselves the luxury of forcing into a run-off vote a chief of state who is in the image of a national hero. . . . In fact, there are many people, who are moved to a moment's compassion for this new blow in the evening of his life, inflicted on him by destiny."

December 22

In a way—a very definite way—the extraordinary Fifth Republic of General de Gaulle ended when he failed to be reëlected its President two weeks ago, on December 5th. The hiatus cut short the historical continuity, marking the finish of a singular epoch. In the eyes of many of the discerning, the runoff second election last Sunday, which restored him as President of France, was merely the first act of the post-Gaullist period. Things have radically changed in this last fortnight, when de Gaulle's uninterrupted power suddenly declined, like a famous public fountain losing its soaring strength and controlled display. The first election showed that five per cent less than half of the nation's voters had voted for him; the second showed that five per cent more than half of France's voters had, literally on second thought, cast their ballots in his favor—a grudging, middling medium in both cases, little like the flow of emotional extremes of anger and enthusiasm that he had formerly tapped during his seven historic years. The third, and decisive, election will be upon him fifteen months from now—the legislative elections to be held in the spring of 1967 and already the dominant new political topic. It would be more than a miracle of survival if the General's Gaullist party should again win a majority of the incoming deputies, it being more likely that they will be eaten alive in the power-hungry fray and demolished as a political force. Without his majority, de Gaulle's extended Fifth Republic could not survive, even as a postscript to itself, and it certainly could not carry on with an Assembly inimical to him as chief of state. "With a hostile Assembly in place, a head-on collision between it and General de Gaulle looms up," observed London's *Sunday Times* with longsighted neighborly prophetic candor, adding, "Since the Gaullists' constitution is no better than any South American republic's in providing ways out of the dilemma, the country would be in danger of being ungovernable." This is just where de Gaulle came in as President seven years ago, because France *was* ungovernable. If she perhaps becomes ungovernable again in 1967, the Gaullist circle and cycle can be supposed to have been completed. There can no longer be any curiosity as to who his successor may be, or how he can be dynastically inserted into a republic's Presidential regime. De Gaulle's successor, it is now clear, will be the new and certainly hostile French Parliament fifteen months from now.

Not only de Gaulle's position and entity changed in the past fortnight but also the faces and forces on the public scene—new ones that aided his opening demi-defeat without themselves being victorious, though big winners. In the second-round election, the

left-wing candidate François Mitterrand, who at the last held in
his hand all the disparate leftist and anti-Gaullist votes—so artificially composed a hand that it was like one made up by a
gambler—increased his share of the vote from thirty-two per
cent to forty-five, which was better than de Gaulle's rate of gain.
Mitterrand received ten and a half million votes—a signal slice of a
changed and changing France. The day before the election, *Figaro's*
brief front-page editorial peremptorily declared, "We must now
envision the future! Starting tomorrow, there must be created in
the newly restored calm a great centrist and European political
party, competent to bring together in the face of the neo-Fascist
Popular Front"—a diametric confusion of terms that only *Figaro,*
in its bourgeois terror of anything left of the right, could have
thought up—"all the men of good will and reasonableness, no matter
to which spiritual family they belong." Young Jean Lecanuet, the
popular centrist newcomer in the elections, has already founded
his promised Centre Démocratique, which could be a rallying
point for pro-Europeans like him and for obstinate believers in the
Common Market. Unfortunately, being a tyro, Lecanuet offended
many pro-European middle-of-the-road types by urging his followers, when he came in only third in the election, to cast their votes
in the runoff election for Mitterrand, who, though certainly pro-
European, was also certainly pro-Communist by association. Dis-
obedient and balking at Communism, they gave at least half their
votes to the anti-European de Gaulle, which came in very handy.
The confusion and lack of doctrinal strictness or hairsplitting
among the leftist parties—Communists, Socialists of various sorts,
Radicals, and even left-wing Demo-Christians, all bundled together
in supposed coöperation for the election and thus getting their
doctrinal sharp corners chipped off or blunted in their unusual intimacy—constituted another new election feature and a healthy, up-
to-date political novelty for France. If France is really going to try
to find a vaguely common ground for its multi-party political system to function on after the 1967 elections, some political commentators think it should indeed start planning right now, as *Figaro*
advised, and before French politicians forget the habit of enforced
stability, almost like a coma, which the citizenry has partly enjoyed
in the Fifth Republic. The Paris Bourse rose violently last midweek

on the public pollsters' prediction that de Gaulle would surely get in on Sunday, if neither illustriously nor triumphantly.

This second electioneering period was even more entertaining than the first, and far more dramatic. Television (aside from de Gaulle's own stately performances over the years) was an absolute political novelty to the French in the campaign, the way President Roosevelt's fireside talks on radio were to us twenty-five years ago, when the whole nation listened, fascinated by the intimacy. But in this second electioneering period the French met on TV a new de Gaulle, who must have been given explicit hints to be more *bon-homme,* or folksy, and who turned out at moments to be a born entertainer (as reports from top circles had always said he was, though until now it was difficult for millions of the French nation to believe it). He talked politics on the screen as confidentially and as maliciously as tycoons talk office gossip, along with all the facts and figures, in a series of interviews with another Gaullist, the young editor of the weekly *Figaro Littéraire,* who asked obviously prearranged questions—in reality, electioneering debates held *in absentia* with Mitterrand, who was interviewed at a later hour by his own specialist. De Gaulle was interviewed at home—that is to say, sitting in a probably priceless eighteenth-century *fauteuil* in a drawing room of the Palais d'Élysée. He was the perfect seated giant, long legs at ease, face alert, eyelids lifting with vision or malice, proboscis flaring as the whole elderly visage was suddenly illuminated with ready opinion and knowledge, the voice breaking with eagerness into the once familiar high *tessitura,* as in the early TV days, before he was professionally coached. He was questioned about, and gave explanations of, nearly all the things that anti-Gaullists consider the sore points of his administration—its high prices, poor telephone service, inadequate schools, discontented farmers (who, he says, will be the first in his Nouvelle République plans for 1966 to receive bigger profit awards). His flow of facts and figures was, as usual, amazing—if not always accurate, his critics said. Above all, he talked about France as if she were some beautiful, superior orphan maiden he was personally protecting against neighbors whom he did not trust. He used neither his abstruse similes nor any classical literary allusions nor his trumpeting official voice; he talked and seemed to think quite simply in the vernacular, and was jocular. The humble people all over France who heard him must have comprehended him completely. To make clear his contempt for the multiple political parties he fights as the disorder of nationalist France, he mentioned *"les partis"* twenty-four times, with increasing vindictiveness, in a single dialogue. He never mentioned Mitterrand by name but declared that this "regime of parties" had its candidate, whom he contemptuously, and oddly, described as "a floating envelope filled with the parties' intrigues and schisms." To describe the ruin that the parties could bring, he likened France to a home where the housewife is distressed that her husband *"s'en aille bambocher de toute part"* ("gets drunk all over town"), that the boys put their feet on the table, and that the girls don't come home at night—all this with a jocularity that set male Paris listeners roaring with laughter and complicity. It was a comparison that *Le Monde* objected to as de Gaulle's "coarse banter." The most popular political cartoon, reprinted all over France and Europe, was by Jacques Faizant and was originally printed in both *Paris-Presse* and *France-Soir* the same afternoon. It showed little Mlle. Marianne, symbol of the Republic, with her suitcase all packed to leave but sitting affectionately on de Gaulle's lap with her arms around his neck and slangily saying, "Well, you see, you dear old booby—why didn't you talk to me like that earlier?" The most quoted portion of his final dialogue he spoke quietly, touchingly: "La Nouvelle République has its President. It is I. Here I am, as I am. I don't say that I am perfect, or that my age is not what it is. I don't claim in any way to know everything or to be able to do everything."

One thing that the much criticized French state TV is going to have to do is to continue to show opposing political figures on its screen as a form of fair play—news coverage that it has never practiced in the past, and for which the French public now has a specific taste.

The biggest single event in the Gaullist campaign was its monster mass meeting last Wednesday at the Palais des Sports, out by the Porte de Versailles, where an audience of six thousand was expected but eight thousand managed to squeeze in. The drawing card was the presence, as the main speaker, of Minister of Cultural Affairs André Malraux, still one of the great public characters of Paris, still magnetic to the young as the former youthful revolutionary in China forty years ago and as a kind of permanent intellectual mandarin. While the crowd was packing itself in, the loudspeakers played, fortissimo, the Beethoven "Coriolanus" Overture, in part; a Saint-Saëns concerto; and then parts of Dvořák's "New World" Symphony—all heating music to the ear, and certainly Malraux's own selections and taste, with his flair for planning public performances. As the hall filled (many of us had arrived an hour early, to be sure to have seats down front), there was also the sound of anti-Gaullist factions outside shouting Mitterrand slogans and clamoring to get in, but the crowds of police on the boulevard and the "gorillas," or plainclothesmen, dealt with them, for no nonsense is allowed inside or out at political meetings, which in France too easily turn into riots. The meeting was officially declared open by old François Mauriac, in his faint voice. Deputy Maurice Schumann made a long, excitable, tiptop speech, which frequently had the eight thousand cheering, though a section of young boys booed until the spotlight was turned on them and the gorillas moved near. Malraux was saluted by an uproar of applause and shouts when he rose to speak, starting, as is his habit, in a sombre, vibrant, theatrical voice, then livening it up to suit his stinging insults and phrases as he apostrophized the absent Mitterrand. "Your left is something you have dreamed up," he jeered scornfully, with the ringing authority of a leftist who had fought in both China and Spain, as his listeners well knew. "You think you create a left when you merely talk about it. It is easier to agree with voters on their notion of paradise than to give them the means of going there. The government that Mitterrand promises is history-fiction, just as there is science-fiction." In conclusion, speaking of the left's constant outcry against de Gaulle's exercise of personal power, Malraux shouted, "It is not a question of personal power but of historical power. It is a question of choosing between a man of history who has taken France in charge, and the like of whom France could not find tomorrow, as against politicians, whom one can find anywhere."

* * *

This election seemed a remarkably personal event to Parisians. The TV appearances dominated people's conversation. France has little tradition of dialectic affirmation, excelling instead in negation as a base for criticism. As the campaign grew more intense, the Paris papers ran the names of well-known French people and which side they were going to vote for, and sometimes why. Georges Bidault, once de Gaulle's Resistance chief in Occupied France, said he would "vote for the adversary of General de Gaulle," as did Jacques Soustelle, another former Gaullist in exile. Mendès-France asked those who had confidence in him to vote for Mitterrand, as if it were the same thing. Jean Monnet, the father of a United Europe, obviously listed himself as anti-de Gaulle. Also on the Mitterrand side were the mystical poet René Char, the novelist Jean Giono, the theatre director Jean Vilar, the scientist Jean Rostand, and even Jacques Isorni, Pétain's defense lawyer. Françoise Sagan, who chose de Gaulle, and Marguerite Duras, who chose Mitterrand, had a long tape-recorded argument, which was published in the weekly *Match*—rather good political talk, too. The leftist Catholic weekly *Témoignage Chrétien* came out frankly for Mitterrand by saying that de Gaulle's "authoritarian Republic is in the direct tradition of the Bonapartes," though Cardinal Feltin, of Paris, had distinctly stated that the Church was to leave the voting to the citizen's own conscience.

1966

July 6

Today's single expert on French glories, General Charles de Gaulle, has just enriched the national list of them by the spectacular success of his eleven-day visit to Soviet Russia, which was a Gallic as well as a Gaullist triumph. He was offered a governmental and national welcome such as no visiting foreign head of state had ever before been given in modern times—not even chiefs of Socialist republics. No head of state of any Western republic or democracy having dreamed of proposing himself as a Moscow guest in the first quarter century after the unpopular Bolshevik revolution, and none after this last war, either, for various reasons, General de Gaulle finally arrived the other day as literally a foreign phenomenon, the likes of which the Russian population had never laid eyes on. And there he was—the intelligent, beaked, elderly, outsize, voluble bourgeois national leader, the first ever seen from the outside capitalist world of Western power, which over decades had been so humiliatingly hostile. A professional and practicing historian and a masterly thespian, he did not modestly minimize the éclat of his presence there. "Today, Monsieur le Président," he told the Soviet head of state, Nikolai Podgorny, on their first meeting, "we know, you and I, as the Soviet Union and France know, as our Europe knows and as the world knows, the importance attached to the visit that I have the honor to be paying you." This astounding statement was perfectly true; indeed, the mere fact of his visit was regarded in advance here in Paris as the real event, with little action of equal interest likely to come out of it, or out of the accompanying Franco-Russian conversations, whose most important aspect was that they were to take place at all. However, the London *Times,* usually scanned in Paris by bilingual French during a crisis of curiosity about their own national affairs, had prophetically stated that there were those who looked upon de Gaulle's forthcoming trip "as potentially the most important diplomatic journey of the postwar world." It was not until the visit was well advanced that de Gaulle gave any explanation for it, saying that it had no reason "except the greatest one imaginable today"— the consolidation of peace through *détente,* followed by an entente, "the whole to be set in motion by the Soviet Union and France," without excluding those of good will "whose home is not in Europe"—presumably meaning us Americans. In de Gaulle's intellectualized interpretation, the Russians and the French were designated for this task by history itelf, through their several centuries of sympathy and friendship—which, it seems, have always fascinated him, and on which he is an expert. Nor did any fundamental trouble ever turn them against each other, he said—not even in the time of "War and Peace," he later added in a Kremlin dinner speech, tactfully referring to Tolstoy's novel rather than mention before Muscovites the name of the hated Corsican Napoleon, who tried to capture their city. However, in his final Kremlin speech, made in the famous St. George Room just before his departure, with the cross of this celebrated order set in still twinkling rubies in the ceiling as a relic of Czarist splendor, de Gaulle suddenly delivered himself of his real reason for his visit by stating, "We believe the entire world considers that the period of the Cold War should come to an end, that the equilibrium it seems to maintain is precarious, fallacious, and sterile, and that the deep desire of all peoples is for the establishment of a veritable peace."

Because of his peculiar diplomatic aptitude for transmuting what is visionary within him into motion, and thus into action, his visit was like a European bridge over which an East-West *détente* was invited to take its first steps—a bridge at least open for inspection. The problem of the two Germanys and their differing worth or menace to the East and West remained between the Russians and the Frenchman an unsolved riddle. Nor was its solution aided by de Gaulle's declaring that East Germany was simply a *"création artificielle de l'U.R.S.S."* The projects for future Soviet-French cultural, technical, and trade relations (the last having been especially disappointing so far, since the Italian Fiat received more favorable treatment than the French Renault in the plan for automobile factories to be set up in Russia) were mere welcome window dressing, almost on the consular level, for the opposing sides to talk about, though the two countries' exchanges of exhibitions of great art over the recent years have certainly been appreciated in both Moscow and Paris, and it was agreed that they should be continued. However, the greatest addition to this atmosphere was the impact of de Gaulle himself on Russia and on the Russians lining the streets shouting *"Druzhba!,"* meaning *"Amitié!,"* and waving little government-supplied flags, red on one side for the Bolshevik revolution and tricolor on the other side for what remains of *la révolution française.* It is figured that in the provincial cities alone at least a million Russians saw de Gaulle. The impact he made on the higher government circles was that of his intelligent French presence and mind and of his combination of experience and freshness of perception on the dogma of the Cold War, which, in his seventy-sixth year, he could regard as démodé for a world to be renewed —an impact that also impressed the Continent of Europe, and especially his own French hexagon of it, making of his expedition "a remarkable journey," as he himself said upon reaching Paris.

Of the two sights that were of the greatest interest to de Gaulle as a military man, one occurred in the last part of his visit to Leningrad, capriciously founded by Peter the Great on a marsh and elevated in the eighteenth century to become the intellectual, Europeanized center of all vast Russia. To the notables of today who received him there, de Gaulle said in his speech (one of the nineteen he made in less than a dozen days), "Your founder desired that from this place your country should be in direct and permanent contact with the exterior world," St. Petersburg having served as what that monarch famously called "a window to Europe." Thus, it was meant to serve today as a contact between East and West, which, on a graceful propaganda note, de Gaulle said he hoped would continue "for the good of both sides." Nor did he omit an appropriate, necessary allusion to Communism, since it was in that city that Lenin, arriving from exile in Switzerland, first took command of the revolution. As de Gaulle said, with consummate diplomacy, "It was here that there took place the most important event, without doubt, of your inner national history. I mean to say those important changes accomplished within your country beginning in 1917"—with the Bolshevik revolution, which shook the world, and which de Gaulle, as a young officer volunteering for foreign service, fought against in Poland. He ended his speech by reciting a brief verse on the beauties of old St. Petersburg by the poet Pushkin, speaking it with careful diction in Russian, learned by heart for the occasion. Then began his visit to Piskaryovskoye, the enormous cemetery of Leningrad, which, as he well knew in advance, was literally a city of the dead—of the estimated nine hundred thousand Leningrad inhabitants who died of famine or the cold in the terrible eight hundred and eighty-two days, from August 21, 1941, to January 20, 1944, of assault and siege by Hitler's armies. All that is known of de Gaulle's visit by us outsiders is that he tersely signed the golden book for visitors with the phrase *"Aux morts de Leningrad—France amie,"* as if he and she were one.

The other peak event for him was more animated—his visit as a military man to the battlefield of Volgograd, formerly known in glory as Stalingrad. There de Gaulle's personal guide was the great, obstinate Marshal Nikolai Voronov, his coeval, who led the Soviet troops to their final victory. Through interpreters, Voronov himself described to the listening French general the battle as it had been fought and how he had fought it. On that battlefield, after six and a half months of fighting—from August 12, 1942, to January 31, 1943—the Nazi Field Marshal Friedrich Paulus surrendered to the Russians, along with forty other German generals and a hundred thousand officers and men, all brought to a standstill. It was the Wehrmacht's first great defeat, and it changed the course of the war. The mayor of Volgograd then gave de Gaulle a memento of his visit and of the past—a small *coffre* containing Stalingrad earth mixed with the blood of Soviet defenders. The box bears an inscription that says, in translation, "May this souvenir recall to our people that it is indispensable to take measures to avoid the renewal of such a tragedy." In a roundabout way, this, indeed, was the object and meaning of de Gaulle's Russian visit.

Visitors who arrived here toward the tail end of the June season were lucky to be so tardy, for they could see a few curiously
interesting and unusual productions in the line of entertainment,
some of which had arrived belatedly. (They could also miss the
earlier half of the year's stage offerings, which were mostly of lesser
importance, like those in New York.) The main event here has
been Eugène Ionesco's first long three-act play, "La Soif et la Faim,"
which was honored by being given its first production at the Comédie-Française, the major French theatre Establishment and the
goal of every living playwright in the French language, since all
the accepted talents, from Molière on, are perpetuated in its repertory. For Ionesco, who started here ten years ago as an unknown,
penniless Rumanian in the avant-garde little theatres, to be seen at
the Comédie has been a special extension of his fame. "La Soif et
la Faim" is oneiric in form, which is to say that it consists of three
separate dreams (turning into nightmares), representing three ep-
ochs in the existence of its protagonist, named Jean. In Dream No.
1, or Act I, he is young, handsome, married, and a father, a man
deformed only by his sensibilities and his aspirations toward perfection in both love and life. These hopes and feelings become the
hunger and thirst of the play's title, and apparently end in Jean's
starvation when he applies them, as his last resources, to what men
have made of freedom of thought and religion. It must be said at
once that the performance of the Comédie's Robert Hirsch—now
its bravura star—as Jean is what makes this strange, obscure play
comprehensible. With great physical *élan* he shows the youth, leaping in the air with desires; then the touching romantic paralysis of
the middle-aged, lonely male; and, finally, the alarmed, homeless
older man, sitting aloft above the stage on a kind of throne of decision, where he visualizes in terror the caged conclusion of his
own lost hopes for righteous clarity. It is so peculiar and fascinating
a play that it demands Hirsch's brilliant, synthesizing performance
to seem united. In Act I, Jean has returned with his loving young
wife and babe to their former apartment, which he now imagines
infested with decay, added to by the impromptu visit of his mad
old aunt and her insane yearning for the imagined fine life she
should have had. In Act II, there is a remarkable scene between

Jean and two absolutely identical uniformed and mustachioed museum guards, one on each side of a set that represents nothing but space, who keep reiterating that the museum (of what treasures is never stated) is closing soon, while he keeps insisting that a lady he cannot even clearly describe will soon arrive to keep a rendezvous —the best and most imaginative scene in the play. The last act is, however, the oddest. Now an aging wanderer, Jean falls in weariness into a kind of bogus monks' abbey, where, as part of his own ultimate captivity, they set him first to judge the antics of two clowns, confined in golden cages, who in a long debate on both deism and Communism must finally accept each other's pro- or anti-deist convictions before being fed a beaker of soup. Is the author's aim to show the sadism of simple Fascism, or merely the brainwashing that ideologies can impose? Early in the play's run at the Comédie, its Tuesday-night season-ticket subscribers (in evening clothes, which are de rigueur for such affairs) raised a scandal themselves by shouting *"Quel scandale!"* when one of the caged clowns was forced to recite the Lord's Prayer. "Hunger and Thirst" is the most stimulating, if addling (and also too long), metaphysical play that Paris has lately seen, and it either provides an important up-to-date shock in the Comédie's repertory or should not be there at all.

The anti-Vietnam war sentiment here is now freely expressed in various ways. The most biting has been the large cartoons that appeared recently in the famous satirical weekly *Le Canard Enchaîné,* notorious for the violence of its pacifism, its wit, and its anarchism. The cover of a special Vietnam supplement showed in the background the Statue of Liberty wearing a gas mask and holding aloft a napalm torch. Below was President Johnson in an eight-star general's combat helmet, his tunic covered with medals shaped like crosses, which ran back to become crosses in a Vietnam cemetery. An inside-page cartoon showed a G.I. watching the self-immolation of four Buddhists and remarking, "No doubt about it —their firepower is superior to ours." The whole back page was given over to a drawing that showed a Vietnamese mother fleeing over a native landscape with her child in her arms as the bombs fell. The caption—a pun of the sort that this weekly affects—read "Pentagonizer."

July 19

Last week's traditional Bastille Day military parade was generally satisfying to the Paris populace and unexpectedly informative to the foreign diplomatic corps, also present. As a lucky dispensation in this chilly, stormy French summer, General de Gaulle was favored by what is called "de Gaulle weather," meaning unexpected fine sunshine, which drew big crowds to the Champs-Élysées sidewalks, with the avenue itself topped by the monumental white bulk of the newly cleaned Arc de Triomphe. Near the reviewing stand, where the General-President stood firm for ninety minutes taking the salute, sat his personally invited guests, the chorus of the Soviet Navy—all this adding up to a perfect *mise en scène* for what this parade in the sky and on the asphalt was obviously aimed to be: the initial display of France's semi-self-sufficient military power since de Gaulle divorced her from NATO in such matters. As the parade's official program over-elegantly stated, "To render dissuasion credible, France must have a coherent ensemble of nuclear force." The opening flyover of the *force de frappe* above the avenue treetops was deafeningly led by fifteen of France's most modern strategic bombers, the Mirage IVs —"principal instrument of dissuasion"—which could carry an atomic bomb to an altitude of sixty thousand feet. What was brand-new, however, and viewed by French and foreign observers for the first time, was the Aéronavale's Bréguet Atlantic anti-submarine plane. There were also Crusader fighter planes, purchased by the Aéronavale from the United States, and, on trucks, a pair of Yankee tactical missiles—a Hawk and an Honest John (both fancifully repainted virgin white by the French), dating from NATO days and the latter still without its nuclear warhead, which Washington held back on. To the watchful diplomatic corps and military experts, the ensuing long, unpicturesque parade of French armor, some new and some merely renovated—all of it except the giant tanks rather dull for the sidewalk crowds, who would rather have seen and heard more regimental bands playing "Auprès de Ma Blonde," featured only by one of them—was of absorbing interest. It denoted, a British expert said, "an extensive degree of standardization."

Some new bright-red Paris fire engines and rigs—plus a rescue canoe, complete with a live frogman-fireman in diving costume inside, for saving Parisians who fall into the Seine—were the only part of the procession that aroused both handclapping and comfortable laughter on the sidewalks. Of the ten thousand parading men, the marchers who drew the loudest applause were the two old favorite fighting units that had been the most suspect five years ago. One was the colonial paratroopers, who, as punishment for their participation in the Algiers *Putsch* against de Gaulle's Algerian policy, had lost the privilege of wearing their unique dark-red berets, which (believe it or not) de Gaulle, by Presidential decree, restored in time for them to wear them again, as proud as Lucifers, in the parade. The other unit, even more loudly cheered, consisted of three companies from the notorious 1st Regiment of the Foreign Legion, a regiment that not only actively backed the abortive mutiny of the generals against de Gaulle in April, 1961, but even kidnapped the loyal, indignant General Fernand Gambiez, commander-in-chief of the combined Army, Navy, and Air Forces in Algeria; blew up its own quarters at Zéralda, so no other troops could enjoy its property; and pulled out in its trucks theatrically drinking cognac and singing Edith Piaf's then new melodramatic song hit "Je Ne Regrette Rien." As punishment, the regiment was dispersed. Three years ago, elements of it were permitted to march in the July 14th parade, but it was only this last week that three companies of its Légionnaires were on view, as a sign of rehabilitation. Preceded by their engineers, with their bearded *sous-offs* wearing the traditional yellow leather aprons and carrying axes on their shoulders, they were the restored essence of the famous secretive Legion itself, in which every man supposedly serves under an assumed name. With their bronzed, expressionless faces—part of their cachet, like their snow-white *képis* above and their slow, insolent leg-swinging desert gait below, still cadenced, as if walking through sand, to eighty lengthy strides per minute—they were the only troops (of late years, largely German) that aroused the French crowd to a real ovation. To the ordinary, domesticated, modest bourgeois French, the Légionnaires on parade are apparently like fascinating international prodigal sons—favored, forgiven, and loved beyond merit.

* * *

One of the summer surprises for foreign tourists has been the presence in Paris bookshop windows of big portrait photographs of old Maréchal Pétain, usually shown front face and in color, with his scarlet, gold-braided marshal's cap, his still bright-blue eyes even in old age, and his short, crisp white mustache offering the perfect red, white, and blue of the tricolor. Many French say that they were indignant as well as astonished when they first saw his Vichy face on display, until they realized that it was all facile publicity for the stack of new books written about him, ostensibly in commemoration of the fiftieth anniversary of the Battle of Verdun, celebrated last month. Even the unsensational weekly magazine *Match* gave four issues and three cover photos to a life of Pétain and to detailed analysis of his career, in a series entitled "Les Heures Glorieuses et les Heures Noires." One of the covers showed him in the horizon-blue helmet and uniform in which that bloodiest of modern French battles was fought, three-quarters of a million French and Germans falling either wounded or dead. Of this battle, though General Nivelle was put in to replace him, Pétain was justly given the title of victor. It was a battle of such infernal, intimate firepower and such heroic physical endurance that by the early nineteen-twenties, when many of us Americans first sojourned in France, Verdun was already being talked of as a myth of superhuman courage, until gradually (or so it seemed to some of us listeners) the myth paralyzed, rather than inspired, male French youths, draining from them their belligerent strength of patriotism, so that when Hitler's Germans once more went to war, France fell almost undefended, and the elderly hero of Verdun became a Vichy cult. None of the eight or ten popular books on Pétain now on sale —several of which are, naturally, apologetics, one being simply and loyally titled "J'Étais l'Ami du Maréchal Pétain"—are worth recommending as consequential works. But, as the critic of *Figaro Littéraire* thoughtfully pointed out, "Their success seems to derive from an honorable motive. There exists today a definite curiosity in the public mind, a desire for some explanation, for some deeper understanding of one of the great political and human dramas of our history." And its question—Was Pétain right or wrong, patriot or traitor?—cut France in two in a passionate, violent division of opinion comparable only to the Dreyfus case.

In his speech at Verdun, General de Gaulle said before a pathetically small crowd, "Pétain possessed, par excellence, the gifts of a leader. If, unhappily, in later times—in the extreme winter of his life and amid overwhelming events—the wear and tear of age led him into weaknesses to be condemned, the glory which twenty-five years earlier he acquired at Verdun, and then maintained in leading the French Army to victory, can be neither contested nor ignored by the nation." It was well known that the Marshal had himself declared that he wished to be buried in the ossuary of Verdun "at the head of my troops"—a wish that was shared devotedly by those innumerable frustrated and embittered French citizens still loyal to him, if only mutely. De Gaulle, toward the end of his Verdun speech, with remarkable diplomacy, even for him, and with such exceptional tact that at first his refusal to grant this wish seemed unapparent, led up to the topic by an elaborate reference to the French Verdun soldier dead, "lying there beneath the earth, *à la face de Dieu,*" and then added, "This is, and, after all, remains, the rule laid down by our wise secular tradition, which consecrates our military cemeteries only to those combatants killed on the battlefield." Pétain, who was tried for his life at the age of ninety and died of old age just four years before his hundredth birthday, lies buried the length of France away from Verdun, in the village cemetery on the little Île d'Yeu. There, during his six years' imprisonment, neither his cell nor the small enclosed garden where he walked once daily nor his guards permitted him to see even the ocean surrounding him and exiling him from France.

The famous, elderly Musée de l'Orangerie, on the riverside Place de la Concorde corner of the Jardin des Tuileries, is again open after having been closed for six years while being rebuilt from the roof down so that it might fittingly and permanently house the hundred and forty-five modern pictures, some splendid, some not, contained in the highly appreciated, if somewhat overestimated, Guillaume-Walter collection. The collection begins with sixteen Cézannes and ends with twenty-two Soutines, and it has now been donated to the Orangerie. It was made separately by Paul Guillaume and Jean Walter, with additions tucked into it by the handsome lady, still alive, who was first the wife of Guillaume, when he was one of the most discerning young Paris merchant-collectors, and then the wife of Walter, the multimillionaire owner of the rich Zellidja iron mines in Morocco. She is now the very wealthy widow of both of them, and donor to the Orangerie of this undeniably welcome and in many ways important collection. An exaggeration of its aesthetic worth was unfortunately created by the catalogue itself, which on its opening page refers to "the profound gratitude of France in welcoming one of the most prestigious collections it has ever received"—the perfect hyperbole of thanks. It took the sharp, informed eye of M. Georges Bernier, editor of *L'Œil,* the most intelligent and professional Paris art monthly, to look the Orangerie gift horse in the mouth and report what he saw there, and also say something about Paul Guillaume, an extraordinary personality who died in 1934 and of whom the catalogue makes absolutely no biographical mention.

Guillaume was a merchant out of the ordinary who saved for his own collection the pictures he most loved and sold the others, many of them to the irascible Dr. Barnes, of Philadelphia, who became a Soutine enthusiast and buyer and helped lift the wretched artist from poverty to fame. Guillaume's Soutines constitute the museum's most nearly complete unity, comprising all his peculiar subjects—raw beef carcasses, deplumed fowl, choirboys, men-servants, delirious landscapes, and distorted sycamore trees. As a collector, Guillaume also especially favored Matisse, Picasso, and Modigliani, whose last portrait of him now hangs here, showing him as rather haughty, in felt hat, business suit, and gloves, but lovingly dedicated at the top and bottom (in Italian) to "Star of the Sea" and "The New Pilot," which Modigliani thought he was, in guiding young artists and new art. Of Guillaume's great Matisses, only one that is major is now included—"The Three Sisters"—and his Picasso holdings also have shrunk to a dozen, two of them thrilling: a proto-Cubist "Nude Against Red Background," of 1906, and a nude Iberian-type "Woman with a Comb." Of the sixteen Cézannes, two are magnificent, both being portraits of the artist's wife, one in blue and pink. The other Cézannes—nudes, forests and landscapes, and a couple of exquisite flower studies—make a chronology of his works, which Mme. Guillaume-Walter aimed at, with practical common sense. But what happened to her first husband's known and listed collection of many outstanding modern-art canvases, absent here—whether he sold them, whether she did after his death, which new ones she bought, which ones her second husband bought under her direction—is never indicated in the Orangerie catalogue, which is of the type given to noting all the authorities' squabbles about the dates when the pictures were painted. As the Orangerie collection also includes quantities of Renoirs, Utrillos, and Derains, a Van Dongen, some Marie Laurencins, one Gauguin, a Monet and a Sisley, and some fine Douanier Rousseaus, there are a great many dates to squabble over. Cézanne, though, remains the pivotal painter, because he often took three or four years to paint a picture, which gives the Orangerie cataloguists a lot of leeway on his sixteen canvases.

The Orangerie was so extensively rebuilt that it ranks in official circles as the first new Paris museum to be constructed in the past thirty years. Its collection will be on show until early September. Afterward, Mme. Walter, who enjoys its use during her lifetime, will supposedly pack it up and take it home, and the Orangerie will turn to a big exhibition of Vermeer.

August 3

As with any great capital city, Paris is in its most inert month. The city has a certain hallucinatory quality in August—a mixture of the true and the unreal. It is neither full nor emptied, being still crammed with cars but empty of entertainment, as if the taxis were going nowhere important and the people inside had lost the good addresses they thought would produce pleasures.

Beginning in July, an estimated two million Paris inhabitants who work for their living, whether in high financial brackets or low, left the city for their yearly four weeks of *congés payés*, or paid vacation. Now more than two million others have left in the August exodus, this month being always slightly preferred as possibly supplying a drier, sunnier, and surer French holiday climate—

hardly dreamed of this summer amid the winds and downpours. The law establishing these paid holidays was voted just three decades ago, in the summer of 1936, so this is its thirtieth anniversary, dilated on at length by all the Paris papers. For these vacations, more than any other vital novelty, have modernized the once deep-rooted, immobile French citizens and altered the habits of the nation. Via these holidays, the French finally learned to travel like everyone else—to the Costa Brava, Madrid, Portugal, and now Greece, adding to the new pleasure of voyaging that of holiday-making in countries cheaper than France. These vacations were the unplanned and astonishing finale of what in 1936 was called "the explosion of the Front Populaire"—the left-wing government bloc led by Socialist Léon Blum, France's first Jewish Premier. The main social demands of his program were a forty-hour week and collective bargaining, plus, as a Socialist ideal, the reform of the Banque de France, bulwark of the notoriously rich Two Hundred Families, all these reforms being then bold innovations. Thirty years ago, France was operating in many ways as if still in the nineteenth century, with brutal wage cuts for workers during the financial crisis, rising living costs and unemployment, and an old-fashioned, powerful owner class functioning as France's economic masters in the country's oligarchic Third Republic, when the state itself lacked the right to say "Boo!" as a form of intervention. In that May's parliamentary elections, the new Front Populaire, for once combined instead of doctrinally quarrelling, had won nearly twice as many seats as the conservative, rich right, which thus created a new political atmosphere to breathe in. All over France, as if smelling a new chance suddenly, the laboring class spontaneously entered into highly organized sitdown strikes, which started in a factory in Le Havre and soon reached the point where strikers were installing themselves almost like block parties in the Citroën factory; in the big Paris department stores, such as the Printemps and the Galeries Lafayette; in Heudebert's enormous Paris bakery, famous for its boxes of sweet wafers; in Marseille's great ship-works; in Lorraine steel mills; in Lyon printing plants—in practically every kind of establishment. Ultimately, a million and a half workers had locked themselves into their struck factories, where, with their own guards at the door, the men slept on the floor at night, by day ate the food their families brought, played their accordions, danced with their wives and girls, kept the premises clean, and, if there was machinery, kept it polished. It was, in a way, a dream strike, especially for France. There was no violence, no sabotage, no bloodshed, nothing but disciplined patience, with the strikers each morning refusing to decamp unless their boss yielded to their demand for a shorter work week and a twelve-percent pay increase—the eventual basis for the historic Accord Matignon.

The late Simone Weil, Catholic convert extraordinary and philosophy student, visited one of these struck factories and wrote of the strange euphoria of the strikers, who, *"bien sur,* knew that the hard life of a worker would have to be faced again." She went on, "But they did not think about that. They were like soldiers on leave during a war. What was unlimited was their present happiness." Some of the strikers who could sing or do tricks emerged from their locked-in privacy to make publicity for their cause, giving shows on midtown street corners. Memorable was a group that assembled each afternoon on the bank of the Seine beside the Pont Royal, from which we passersby watched one slim young worker especially, who, with a fishing pole for balance, walked a heavy tightrope he had set up almost at eye level with us, while his comrades below, in clown makeup, blew trumpets at us, juggled, and passed their workmen's caps up on a stick, so we could give them money as well as applause. The sitdown strikes had a peculiar popularity with the ordinary Paris public, maybe because the locked-in workers seemed dramatic, and maybe because there was a certain contagion of hope and good cheer that spread from the strikers' belief that better times were coming. In a way, this was the sentiment even of a few of the more intelligent capitalist leaders, who realized that time had caught up with them and that Blum's Matignon Accord "preserved the country, saving it from riots that might have turned into civil war," or so the head of the Comité des Forges, France's steel trust, candidly admitted, adding, "In signing this accord, we certainly saved our social regime." Their regime weathered the approaching difficulties better than Blum's Popular Front, on which, with his characteristic political probity, he had not imposed his full Socialistic views, since neither his radical colleagues nor even the Communist Comrades shared them. He merely tried to copy Franklin Roosevelt in dealing with a capitalist impasse. By September, retail prices had risen six per cent, so that half the workers' new wage gain was already lost. The unexpected paid-holiday plan had already become law at the end of June, rushed through with enthusiasm, like a quick miracle, and now in September the capitalists began having some revenge, for devaluation became a government necessity, hastening the end of the Front Populaire regime. However, France's political climate had changed, influenced by outside European events. The Spanish Civil War had broken out that summer and divided the French left as with a bayonet, some leftists being against aid to the Republican fighters, who for them ranked merely as anarchists and Communists. Blum and his Front Populaire, before their inevitable fall, had together founded a new basis for contemporary France, on which, in part, it still functions—a reformed Banque de France; *congés payés;* a guaranteed minimum wage; nationalized railways, mines, gas, and electricity; and a greatly strengthened working class, which, according to last week's government wage report, is now earning seven per cent more than it did in 1965.

August 16

Up to a dozen years ago, the Grand Trianon, that perfect small one-story pleasure pavilion of pink and pale-green marble, built in 1687 for Louis XIV so that he could get away from the vast formalities of nearby Versailles, was so widely appreciated for what the French for almost three centuries called its *charme mélancolique* that it was permitted to fall almost into ruin by 1953, and the roof leaked. Three years ago, under the inspiration of M. André Malraux, Minister of Cultural Affairs, the Grand Trianon began undergoing not only salvation but a triple transformation. From these it emerged on view this summer as a museum with historic furnishings, such as royal beds for tourists to stare at by day and for the Fifth Republic's most honored guests eventually to sleep in. For now the Trianon is to function as a guesthouse for visiting heads of state and their suites, plus—its third use—serving as the suburban Presidential residence of General and Mme. de Gaulle, where they may personally offer hospitality to distinguished visitors. The de Gaulles' apartment (not on view to the public but early photographed in all its intimate colors by the weekly magazine *Match,* for every eye) occupies a two-story section of the palace, at the rear, where "the trees almost enter my windows," pleasantly wrote the King's daughter-in-law the Princess Palatine, whose scandalous letters home usually concentrated on Versailles's malodorous drains, which outraged her German sense of cleanliness. The de Gaulles' bedroom contains narrow twin beds (certainly the first ever introduced into so notable a pleasure haunt) covered by cherry-colored *toile d'Aix,* specially woven from an old design. Their bathrooms are two of the four de-luxe *chef-d'état* plumbing installations—the twenty-one regular guest bathrooms being merely of mahogany and white marble, with ivory handles for the faucets. Casings of burled ash enclose the lavabos and bathtubs, the General's outsize and rare tub having been bought secondhand and then completely reënamelled. The pavilion's *boiseries* are among the best remaining of the Louis XIV epoch, and many of the bibelots and furnishings are Louis XVI, but a significant amount is early Napoleon, such as the salon's Consulat chairs, ornamented with bronze Sphinxes after his victorious Egyptian battles. Like all the better Trianon furnishings, they have mostly come from the Mobilier National, that replete state warehouse of dynastic second-hand furniture left from the destructions of French history.

It being well known that after the French Revolution the Trianon furniture was sold dirt cheap, presumably as royal rubbish, it seems captious even of the always argumentative Parisians to complain that the glorious Louis XIV Trianon is today furnished largely by the upstart Napoleon Bonaparte. For, after all, it was he who in 1805, as Emperor, fitted out the empty little palace anew, and naturally in his own untutored meridional, semi-Egyptian, often loud-colored historical style, and gave it to his mother, Madame Mère (who did not like it and rarely used it). His Tuileries bed, now in the finest of the Trianon's state guest chambers (former bedroom of the Sun King himself), probably serves as a kind of key to the transmutations among France's rulers—usually old and never very young—surrounded by the power struggles of their mistresses or cast-off wives, by the crowds of royal relatives, and by the inbred atmosphere and the frequent political dramas, which, all together, made the Trianon such a fantastic, famous royal picnic ground, when it was not a damp bore near a canal. It was down this canal that the Versailles intimates en route to the Trianon were rowed for perhaps an hour in great painted galleys (or else they were coached down through the fountained parks), usually returning to Versailles at night. The key Bonaparte bed is gilded, and when it was in the Tuileries it bore his double-eagled coat of arms. After St. Helena, it passed to the next ruler, once more of royal blood—Louis XVIII, who died in it. This so alarmed his successor, Charles X, grandson of Louis XV, that he never slept in it at all, in his brief career passing only one night in the Trianon, where he paused while fleeing toward exile after the angry, small 1830 revolution that his anti-liberalism had provoked. This unrest brought in his kinsman Louis-Philippe as the liberal citizen-king, who had his own coat of arms carved on Napoleon's bed and slept in it domestically, being the father of nine children. It was he who donated the famous Bonaparte bed to the Trianon, which he loved and partly rehabilitated. He built a new chapel in Louis XIV's old billiard room and transferred the lovely *boiseries* from the Versailles apartment of the late, headless Marie-Antoinette to his own salon in the dainty pleasure palace. But his pro-English policies led to the little 1848 revolution against him, and to his abdication. En route to admirable England, like Charles X, he, too, paused, even in his haste, to sleep at the Trianon for the last time, and probably in his and Napoleon's own bed.

The Trianon was less sinful than Versailles. At the age of sixty, Louis XIV moved from the Trianon's left wing to its right to be closer to pious Mme. de Maintenon, who, though he had secretly married her, still held to the enviable, more powerful public position of *Maîtresse en Titre*. Things were somewhat livelier when his great-grandson Louis XV grew up. He gave the Trianon to his Queen but took it back to give it to his extraordinary, intelligent mistress Mme. de Pompadour, with whom he openly shared Mme. de Maintenon's former apartment, made over, and there entertained Czar Peter the Great.

The Trianon is still a great novelty to visit and look at, even on the inevitable guided tour. There are twenty-six rooms to see, of varying interest. Some of them remain exquisite in themselves, such as Louis XIV's long, narrow banqueting hall, its tall garden windows alternating with tall panel pictures by Jean Cotelle, ordered from him by the King himself and depicting the Versailles and Trianon gardens, fountains, cascades, and tended perspectives. Napoleon's exiguous private bedroom is fascinating, almost feminine, decorated according to his own design in chamois-colored moiré silk polka-dotted with minuscule brown stars. His bathroom carpet imitates a leopard skin. His Salon des Malachites features this violent exotic green stone (given him by Czar Alexander I after Tilsit), used as a candelabra pedestal, a tabletop, and so on. In Louis-Philippe's Grand Salon, for typical family utility, there is a mahogany table (made by the celebrated *ébéniste* Alphonse Jacob) equipped with numbered drawers, one for each of the princesses to keep her crochet work in, and what are listed as "two big, comfortable armchairs, Restoration style," presumably for the parents, with some less comfortable small matching chairs placed in a circle for the children. The Salon des Glaces is a powerful sight, with its alternating rectangular and arched mirrors reflecting its massive gold and white furniture, its bronze torch holders (some of them originals), designed by the famed metalworker Thomire, and its vivid blue curtains in the "Four Corners of the World" pattern, earlier woven for Marie-Antoinette and never used, which Napoleon's mother insisted on buying, giving them a raison d'être at last.

The Trianon's famous gardens deserve a final word. They were first planted by Lenôtre himself, then a veteran Royal Gardener in his seventies. He said that his gardens were composed of flowers "in millions of pots," changed every day, to be freshly in bloom. His tuberoses were so splendid that Mme. de Maintenon complained of them, declaring that their excessive perfume at dusk drove everyone indoors. This summer's Trianon parterre garden was in Lenôtre's passementerie style: low mixed pink and scarlet begonias, knotted occasionally by a clump of blue ageratum, and threaded here and there by yellow calceolaria—quite like floral embroidery patterning the ground.

The declaration published in last week's *Nouvel Observateur,*
the leading leftist independent intelligentsia weekly, by former
Premier Mendès-France, was a brief consolidation of the general
French opinion (not always the case with his ideas) on the Vietnam
conflict—something the French think he can be an authority on,
since he stopped their apparently endless hemorrhagic war in Indo-
China in 1954. His declaration started by his saying that the escalation of violence grows worse day by day. "It risks spreading the
fire that blazes in Southeast Asia to other nations and continents.
It revolts all those attached to peace and who respect the dignity of
man. For a quarter century, the Vietnamese people have endured
their Calvary with courage and pride . . . and each new ordeal
stiffens them still more in their interminable combat for their
liberty. . . . The reëstablishment of peace will come not through
the inhuman intensification of suffering and mourning for the
dead but through negotiation with the true representatives of the
Vietnamese people"—a reference to the Vietcong, most of the
French press thought. Then he asked, "How many more atrocities
are needed for these obvious truths to be recognized and accepted
as the basis of the necessary and urgent negotiations?"

August 30

As chief of state, President de Gaulle is an aerial
phenomenon. The luggage of his seventy-five years seems not a
bit overweight for him to carry on his present nineteen-day journey, of fifty-six flight hours, to four of the classic five parts of the
world—Africa, Asia, Oceania, and America (in its French island
of Guadeloupe)—a tour in the sky of forty-three thousand five
hundred kilometres, or a little more than the length of the equator.
As has been pointed out here, in his vast circling of the globe from
west to east he gains an extra day on the calendar by using it twice,
arriving in Tahiti on September 7th from Nouméa, which he will
have left the day before—also September 7th. As devotees of Jules
Verne, the French have been quick to recognize that Phileas Fogg,
in "Around the World in 80 Days," unexpectedly won his bet on

just such a duplicate day, which he had forgotten to count on. General de Gaulle's takeoff from Orly on this long and obviously significant diplomatic journey, for once important to others besides himself and France, was reportedly quite an affair. His waiting plane was flying his personal pennant of the French colors with his Croix de Lorraine on its white band; the airport's Grand Salon, reserved for V.I.P.s, was decorated with a great tricolor bouquet of white gladiolas, blue iris, and scarlet dahlias; and his full Cabinet of Ministers, headed by Premier Pompidou, plus the Military Governor of Paris, were all punctiliously assembled to bid him a formal bon voyage. To his Ministers he said, "Messieurs, I am sorry you may not all take part in this journey. And, to tell you the truth, I am a little sad to leave you for so long." (Among members of his entourage, de Gaulle is noted for his small truths' being often lightened by a little humor, and vice versa.) A military guard of honor presented arms while the band played the "Marseillaise," and de Gaulle, in summer uniform, stood rigidly at the salute; then it played the "Marche Lorraine" as he strode up the steps into the Presidential DC-8 jet. (Mme. de Gaulle, accompanied by her maid, had earlier been quietly escorted into the plane, dressed in a well-cut gray travelling costume and toque.) For once, there was no chartered press plane, only three Paris publications having been willing to pay the equivalent of two thousand dollars for a reporter's round-trip ticket, since it will be cheaper for the press to fly in reporters from eastern offices to cover the widely scattered points on de Gaulle's route.

According to the government *porte-parole,* "the President of the Republic himself traced the journey he will make," of which the natural finale is to be his visit to France's nuclear-experiment station near Papeete, where a bomb will be exploded in his honor. En route, he wanted to look in on Djibouti, on the coast of French Somaliland—France's only remaining African holding, which a few years ago chose the semi-independent status of a French territory. This visit, said the *porte-parole,* was to "see the population for himself and hear how things were going locally." As the newspapers have since reported, what he saw and heard locally was a violent mob of Djibouti natives shouting *"Vive de Gaulle!"* and also *"Vive l'Indépendance Totale!,"* which was not as illogical as it sounds, because it was de Gaulle himself who earlier parcelled out decolonization to most of France's subject peoples—a leader from whom the Somali nationalists now perhaps aspired to draw further freedoms. His chilly response to the rioters on the Place Rimbaud, named for the poet, was contained in his statement in the Territorial Assembly that waving pro-independence placards, "which I have read," cannot decide the destiny of a nation. He then added, "I am a man who has lived through a great deal, who has seen a great many varied events. Nothing astonishes me, nothing will astonish me. Whatever happens, I shall continue to serve France." However, his final words there had to do with his next port of call, Phnom Penh. "In Cambodia," he said, "I shall have something to say on the war in Vietnam and on the dangers it presents to the world." Already, the Western world's chancelleries are deeply curious to hear what he may say, prophetically.

In a way, French newspaper readers get twice as much news on the Vietnam war as do readers in the United States. Here in Paris, the papers, of course, carry the regular dispatches from Saigon on the American armed forces and their war against North Vietnam. But in Paris we also receive news that United States readers do not get—two different kinds of it, really, both from Hanoi—about the North Vietnamese war against the American forces. One of these reports is featured in *L'Humanité,* the French Communist Party's daily Paris paper, and comes irregularly from its Hanoi correspondent, always with a heavy Soviet slant of often considerable interest, since we all want to know more about the depth of Moscow's relations with North Vietnam. The other Hanoi news source is the regular daily professional dispatch from the correspondent there for the non-political Agence France-Presse, the big French national and international news service. (The A.F.-P. also distributes South Vietnam dispatches from its Saigon office, since dispensing news to its clients—among them the state radio here and the government itself—is its business.) But these two journalists working out of Hanoi are literally the only permanent Western correspondents accredited to the press service of the North Vietnamese Ministry of Foreign Affairs. Press visas for Hanoi are hard to come by, whereas for Saigon they must come easy, to judge by the reported presence there of about three hundred correspondents, living and working in something like organized comfort. And Hanoi cable rates are high; a thousand words sent to Paris costs about three hundred dollars—considerably dearer than the rate from Peking.

The A.F.-P. correspondent, Jean Rafaelli, sent out to Hanoi in the spring to do daily dispatches, is now returning to Paris after a stint of three months of work in such difficult and fatiguing conditions that his successor will be limited to the same period. According to what he has written to his friends in the A.F.-P. Paris office, on the Place de la Bourse, there are no baths or public transportation or taxis in Hanoi. To spare him walking an average ten kilometres a day to collect information, his office here vainly tried to ship him a small motorcycle. Food is scarce, and his seat in a restaurant has to be booked a week in advance; the foreigners live in a restricted quarter, so conversations with native personalities are difficult; he has to have a permit to leave the city to visit local villages for news and another permit to get back in. A thick administrative fog apparently hangs over the city, plus a special Oriental evasiveness. Officials never say no to a request but "I shall advise you later," and never do. The North Vietnamese imitate as well as they are able a system that Moscow once reserved for foreign correspondents—semi-isolation, frustration, bafflement. The best thing about Hanoi for a correspondent is that there is no censor.

Among important news events announced first in Rafaelli's dispatches was the secret visit to Moscow of the North Vietnamese Premier Pham Van Dong to discuss Soviet aid, and the parading by the North Vietnamese authorities of the wretched American aviator prisoners. Early in August, he wrote about the evacuation of the Hanoi and Haiphong urban population to the mountains and jungles as an answer to Washington's escalation of the bombing attacks, and about the removal of the cities' factories and their reconstruction elsewhere. In one piece, he wrote of the bombing of a village near Hanoi in which the attack lasted only thirty seconds and killed forty villagers. In connection with Hanoi's preparations for celebrating its twenty-first anniversary of independence, on September 2nd, he wrote of what the government there called "the American underestimation of the will to resist of the North

Vietnamese—a people who have behind them the experience in survival of twenty-two years of almost uninterrupted war," and who will, they say, continue fighting "in the *maquis* if the Americans bomb all their cities flat." This American minimizing of their resistance was viewed by the North Vietnamese government as "a fundamental tactical error." Much of what Rafaelli reports is tragic and terrible, because he is writing about the people on the poorer, frugal side of the conflict against a rich foreign force. In addition to the dominant Paris papers like *Le Figaro, Le Monde, Paris Presse,* and *France-Soir,* his reports are carried in such powerful provincial papers as *Sud-Ouest,* of Bordeaux, and *Le Progrès,* of Lyon. They can be published in popular French papers because France is officially neutral in the war. However, the French people, on the whole, are not, being convinced that as a repetition of history it is a frightful, frightening mistake, which no victory can solve. Part of their pessimism lies in their memory of their own Indo-Chinese war (which Washington at that time thought was frightful)—an eight-year destructive French colonial struggle that ended in the four-month-long battle of the little plain of Dien Bien Phu in North Vietnam.

In our memory, Paris has never looked so shabby, so dishevelled, so torn up by Algerian workmen laboring underground among the city's very intestines—its sewers, heating pipes, electric cables, natural-gas conduits, and so on—aided by noisy, bright-orange digging machines, some of which go clanking on into the night. A new traffic tunnel is being constructed under the Place de la Concorde, and so is a Seine-side expressway down below the Louvre. Kindred mutilating improvements are taking place all over town, in practically every quarter, including underground garages to house the Paris share of what the French government estimates as France's ten million automobiles. For them and their needs, Paris is being torn apart as it never was for its citizens.

September 22

The autumn theatre season has begun at the fusty, overdecorated, elderly Gymnase, today nearly a hundred and fifty years old but still holding up on the now shabby lower-boulevard frontier of Montmartre, where Mme. Françoise Sagan's new comedy, "Le Cheval Évanoui," or "The Fainting Horse," is the major social and theatrical Paris event. According to the opening-night reaction, it is the best play she has written since her first, "Château en Suède," and it is an undoubted hit, which should run three years, or a thousand and one performances, and bring her in another fortune, estimated in advance at two million francs. Part of its instantaneous success certainly lies in its having been directed to a pitch of unusual expert, useful speed by Jacques Charon, of the Comédie-Française. Set amid the sporting high life of county England, where animal lovers reign (the cast even contains a stuffed pug dog mounted on rollers—a sentimental ornament of a splendid drawing room that has been identified as a replica of the famous salon in the Rothschild country house at Ferrières), the play is about money and love and the difficulty of getting both for nothing, especially in upper-class circles. It contains two solid characters with whom Sagan has become familiar in her career. One is the inevitable older man, of forty, who since her late teens has never been absent from her personnel—in this case, he is Mr. Henry James Chesterfield, the witty, tactfully unfaithful, penniless husband of a rich wife, who gladly bought him, like a civilized conjugal bibelot, when both were young. The other is the attractive, no longer virginal, though still unmarried, youngish Frenchwoman, in this case named Coralie, who is Sagan's *porte-parole* and interpreter. There also turns up among the Chesterfields' house guests a brutish, loutish young Frenchman, the violent lover of the non-virgin, whom he plans to marry as soon as he can first marry and then be divorced from the silly, rich Chesterfield schoolgirl daughter, to whom he has managed to become engaged and on whose *dot* he plans ultimately to live in idle, amorous sloth with his Coralie. To establish the faint flavor of incest that Sagan often uses to spice her social scene, the French lover and Coralie pass themselves off as brother and sister—a piece of flummery that Henry James sees through as soon as his concupiscent, cynical eye first lights on Coralie's answering gaze. As usual, the dominant psychology of Sagan's play lies in her endowing the two major characters with a capacity for real passion, as something rare, important, and costly in private life, and there are scenes of embraces accompanied by vivid, always fresh-sounding ardent dialogue that invariably has an indubitable quality of personal Saganesque wisdom, commentary, and experience. These scenes are played to perfection by Jacques François, who has made of his pastiche Briton Chesterfield a remarkably subtle, intelligent, disabused, and complicated new boulevard character, and, in a well-paced, charming performance, by the blond, sensuous Nicole Courcel (whom you may recall from that notable film "Sundays and Cybèle"). In the end, Henry James settles things by buying a pair of airplane tickets to fly somewhere— anywhere—that Coralie will go, either because he can no longer endure what he is at home or maybe so that she can use them to fly back to France with her penniless French brute, in order to make him take a job and let them both lead a decent life in which neither money nor love will come easy or free. The rest of the play's characters are mere window dressing—and how sumptuous they look! Only on a Paris stage would you see actresses dressed with such chic, their clothes having been designed for them by Marc Bohan, of the late Christian Dior's *maison de couture*. Mrs. Chesterfield's first-act informal, non-décolleté floating dinner gown of some pale-blue gold-flecked fabric garbs her in beauty like a rich British piece of pallid sunset sky, cut to fit perfectly over her narrow, defrauded wifely shoulders. Nicole Courcel wears one especially enchanting short scarlet silk frock in which *diamants* are concealed in the rare pleats, to flicker under movement like hidden information.

In all her plays since "Château en Suède," a modern French classic in lunatic fantasy, rich characterizations, amorality, tight technique, and hard, civilized French hearts, Mme. Sagan has vainly competed against herself as her own superior, with whom she never seems able to catch up—a curious professional destiny in which she seems always to lose because she has already won so decisively.

The greatest surprise of Jean Genet's play "Les Paravents" ("The Screens"), appearing in revival at the Odéon-Théâtre de France after its tempestuous spring performances, which called out the riot police in answer to screams of protest from members of the audience, is that it is now popular. It seems humorous as well as rationally tragic, being a rich, sprawling, tumultuous report on man's fate; seems feministic (odd indeed, considering the author's professional preference for men); seems an enrichment to the listening imagination of the beholder, instead of an insult to it; and is certainly an extraordinary, inventive, stylistic spectacle in color—all brought to a final focus in what must be regarded as an oddly resurrectional happy ending, since the main characters are now dead and glad to be. In an epilogue, the dead sit in gossiping critical judgment on their past erroneous lives. The door to death is represented by a paper-filled frame from which each human being, on crashing through, salutes eternity with the same commonplace astonished lines: "Well, what do you know? And they make such a fuss about it!" This is the only instance where Genet seems to minimize his poetic sense of human fate. The cast is enormous, with some sixty speaking parts. Time is condensed by having actions in group pantomime serve as backgrounds to conversations by individuals on entirely different affairs. The stage technique aims at making everything visible, even what characters are thinking. "Les Paravents" was written in 1959, but no French producer could risk producing it during the Algerian war, since its main male character, Saïd the Arab, in a typical Genet paradox, was a half local hero, half traitor who sold out to the French.

Jean-Louis Barrault, the producer, and Roger Blin, the director (who gave Beckett's "Waiting for Godot" its first showing here), have created a theatrical miracle in uniting the meanders of Genet's scope, which contains four affiliated stories. There is that of the hero-traitor Saïd's marriage to the ugliest woman of the next village—all he could afford to purchase. There is the growing Algerian insurrection. There are the careers of Saïd's mother (played with screaming laughter by Maria Casarès) and her friend Warda, owner of the local bordello (played by Madeleine Renaud in such a splendor of gold-and-silver panelled skirts and tautly elevated pale-blue wig as to be on a level with the superiority of her diction in tossing off gutter talk). And there is the homosexual love story of the handsomest soldier in the French company and his handsome lieutenant, with its scatological ending—part of the smashing caricatures of sacrosanct patriotism that at first so offended Parisians (now calmed by the suppression onstage of the French flag). What is so amazing is that in all these village developments it is the women who, in their cackling and screaming, arrive at wisdom and common sense, while the men continue to goad themselves and their neighbors by their follies committed as divine right—the right to be superior and wrong. One of the most striking roles is played by Barrault himself as a putrescent, greenish cadaver who still has something to say about life and death.

The brilliance of the play's complete theatricality—with the beggar's rainbow rags of the finest frayed, multicolored chiffon; with its screens, which Genet declared should represent "the walls of corruption and fear, which prevent men from seeing the truth," suddenly moving forward or upward on silent rollers until they sink to final invisibility to make way for the epilogue by the dead —can be comprehended only by seeing it all. With Genet's dramatic, errant text, it constitutes the most stimulating, triumphant achievement of the French theatre since the end of the Second World War.

If "Fahrenheit 451" had been given a prize at the recent XXVII Venice Film Festival (and a pity this was not the case), it would have won it as a British film, though it was made in the English language (from the American Ray Bradbury's best-known old science-fiction novel of that name) in a London studio, backed there by American money, and entered in the Venetian lists as a proper British production in color—which it is, all right, except that it was directed by François Truffaut, which automatically turns it into a completely French movie. Truffaut's fame started when he was twenty-seven with "Les Quatre Cents Coups," and this new production is merely the fifth film in his sparse ten-year directing career, since he is a special, finical, and fitful worker. He also, it seems, has a particular passion for books. This last is what led him to make "Fahrenheit 451," which not only is about books but in its title indicates the degree of heat at which paper ignites. For book burning is what the new film is about, as practiced in some up-to-date, only slightly imaginary country, where the national firemen's job is not to put out fires but to kindle them in libraries, creating autos-da-fé of the printed word like those the Nazis organized, as did the Spanish Inquisitors—both warming their bigotries before the same kind of infernal flames. Truffaut's fantasy movie is close to a chef-d'œuvre, especially in its final intellectual, tender scenes. Being an artist, he has made it strictly apolitical. He has also avoided the claptrap of mechanical gadgetry that afflicts most sci-fi celluloid creations, except for one excellent grotesque moment when the firemen, on a hurry call to raid a bibliophile's cache of hidden volumes, float down from the sky, their trousers filled by the wind like funnelled sails. He has also evaded sadism. The fat, elderly female book lover who is burned along with her books seems a minor sad figure in Truffaut's eyes compared to the authors and books involved in the holocaust—Dostoevski, Sartre, Balzac, Henry Miller, Henry James, even Hitler with his "Mein Kampf," Cervantes, Proust, Shakespeare, Gide, a Spanish crossword-puzzle book, and so on—many of the greatest names in inherited literature kindled in a heap, as if mankind's recorded ideas, and even its pastimes, could literally go up in smoke and thus be destroyed forever.

The society that Truffaut caricatures is only a little more perilously advanced than ours today on its collective diet of television, on the dwindling ability of its human beings to communicate with each other, on its beatifically prosperous push-button civilization, seated in comfort amid the increasing dangers of uncontrollable progress. Truffaut's protagonists are a leading junior fireman named Montag, played with just the right amount of leftover Austrian accent by Oskar Werner, and two versions of the new star Julie Christie: one long-haired, as Montag's conservative, docile wife, who later denounces him, and the other short-haired, as the modern rebel who leads him into literacy, secret reading, and his downfall—a role in which Miss Christie looks like only the top or facial portion of a Carnaby Street mannequin, so devoid of human expression as to seem to lack any vital organs, such as a heart, below. Truffaut's film has a humorous, happy, fantastic ending, filled with his personal emotion about books, which is his special gift to the viewer and warming to any bookworm's soul. Montag flees to the forest (with his short-haired mistress), where all the book lovers live in exile while learning by heart the text of some favorite great book, which they will thus save for a time for posterity, such as the memoirs of the Duc de Saint-Simon—a jocose touch, since they run in any good memorizable edition to a punishing number of volumes. There is a pair of male twins who should be female working together at memorizing "Pride and Prejudice," there is an old public-library reader type memorizing Stendhal's "Vie de Henri Brulard," and there is a threadbare scholar who is becoming the conserver of Machiavelli's "The Prince"—all refugees strolling around with portions, at least, of the world's greatest literature in various languages printed through memory inside their heads.

September 29

Europe's finest summer art show in many seasons, called "Dans la Lumière de Vermeer," patiently assembled for the splendid recent celebration in The Hague of the Mauritshuis' hundred-and-fiftieth anniversary, is now installed in honor at the Orangerie, with twelve glowing proofs of Vermeer's special Dutch genius, so mysteriously ignored until a century ago. In the middle eighteen-sixties, a young French traveller and art critic, Théophile Thoré-Bürger, published the first source book on Vermeer, inspired to curiosity about this then obscure painter by the Mauritshuis' single proof of his greatness—the "View of Delft." In a way, Vermeer was later rediscovered by another Frenchman, Marcel Proust, and emotionally revalued in "À la Recherche du Temps Perdu." Actually, Hippolyte Taine, the old French art philosopher, had mentioned Vermeer, and the two gossiping Goncourt Brothers in their 1861 diary had remarked that Vermeer was *"diantrement original,"* or deucedly unusual, so Paris literary circles were already talking about him. There was then, as now, little to know except that he was baptized in 1632 in Delft; lived his life and died there at the age of forty-three; was acting president of the Delft painters' guild at thirty; and was a married man and the father of eight living children, for whose daily bread he owed the baker so big a bill that his widow paid it by giving the baker two of his pictures.

In the glorious, exceptional autumnal Paris sunshine, one carries the sun's radiance from the Tuileries gardens into the Orangerie itself, where it becomes part of the emotion of light that animates the Vermeer canvases. Among the twelve are the two from today's

Mauritshuis that have become world-famous, the first being "Young Girl in a Turban," of that special Chinese blue—clearer than Delft blue—that he favored, in combination with the Chinese yellow of her turban's ponytail drapery, intensified by the bright, innocent white of her eyes, which matches the professional white of her large pendant-pearl earring. The other universal favorite is his "View of Delft," a triumph of light, painted like a vision on the River Schie's mirroring water and in the far shore's airy brightness, which picks out the city's gabled tan façades—a panorama of truth and affectionate familiarity. The greatest masculine portrait in the exhibition is "The Astronomer," from the Paris Rothschild collection, with his scientist's sensitive hand stretched to lie on the astral globe of the heavens. Vienna sent the other big picturesque male figure, in "The Artist in His Studio" (not included in the Hague exhibition), with the seated painter seen only from the back and supposed to be Vermeer himself—precisely because he thus avoided portraying his own face, he having significantly left no self-portrait. There is the "Woman with Water Jug," from New York. There is the "Lady Standing at the Virginals," from London, and "The Letter-Writer," from the Beit collection, in Ireland. The Vermeer pictures in the Orangerie are exceptionally accompanied by pictures by other artists, ranging from Cézanne on back through Caravaggio to Giorgione and his masterpiece "Le Concert Champêtre," brought across from the Louvre—a family of painters over the centuries who are related to Vermeer as painters of light or as a clan of genre artists who, like him, reported in paint on people quietly living their lives indoors: making lace, making music, studying the stars, or literately reading their correspondence.

In 1921, Marcel Proust saw the "View of Delft" at the Jeu de Paume in a Netherlands exhibition. He had already used Vermeer like a bystander in the love affair between Swann and Odette, just as he used the Sonate de Vinteuil for its musical accompaniment. As Proust grew more ill himself, he brought Vermeer into "Le Temps Perdu" like a witness to the approaching death of the writer Bergote, who was struck down by apoplexy precisely while staring at the "View of Delft": "His giddiness increased; he fixed his eyes, like a child upon a yellow butterfly which it is trying to catch, upon the precious little patch of wall"—presumably that patch of wall, in yellow, on the lower right side of the canvas, just behind the town gate's left pepperpot tower. " 'That is how I ought to have written,' he said. 'My last books are too dry; I ought to have gone over them with several coats of paint, made my language exquisite in itself, like this little patch of yellow wall.' Meanwhile he was not unconscious of the gravity of his condition"—for he was dying. Vermeer was the only painter from the past whom Proust seemed repeatedly to consult and rely upon, like an occasional mentor of the emotions among his book's characters.

Premier Pompidou was interviewed on the state television on Monday evening and said, among other things, that after the elections next March he could, if necessary, envision governing without a majority—"though this is only my personal opinion," he added with a smile, in his well-articulated, unruffled fashion of speaking. He went on, "I believe that the political policy we have been conducting until now, which the country approved when it last reëlected General de Gaulle, should continue. I would form a government based on the possibility of modifications"—a euphemism for Gaullist losses—"in the National Assembly. Such modifications are normal; this is a democratic regime. It is what we have left of a Parliamentary regime, since it is basically half Presidential, half Parliamentary." This was a definition at last of the Fifth Republic's present format, and one that by its candor aroused astonishment among some of the French—until they thought it over carefully. The Gaullists' main adversary in the electoral campaign (and Pompidou was equally frank about this) will be young Jean Lecanuet, unheard of until he made his rocketlike rise through television last year as a new type of screen politician, with a good smile and teeth, and fresh conventional ideas. Of the Assembly itself Pompidou in his TV talk gave an unfamiliar new picture, with a Parliamentary majority no longer being necessary for a government to remain in place, and with Parliament's important function being to furnish Ministers from among its deputies. According to critics of what the Premier said—and they were numerous—the concept of a majority, on which the Gaullist regime founded the last two legislatures, has now lost much of its force. It seems to be giving way to a concept of empiricism, which might not be alien to the Premier's nature and philosophy, now adjusted to looking forward to the Gaullists' no longer having to win overpoweringly, as de Gaulle always demanded, with passion, of his voters. As one critic said, never had Pompidou given his TV listeners so little to hang on to. What he said was as smooth and shapely as an egg.

The most remarkable small personal element in the most dramatic fortnight of the Second World War's early French history disappeared last week with the death at the American Hospital in Neuilly of eighty-eight-year-old Paul Reynaud, the littlest Premier France had ever seen—stretched to his full dapper height, he measured five feet three inches—on whom, as the final head of the amoral, shiftless Third Republic, fell the crushing weight in mid-June, 1940, of that hasty French defeat and debacle without precedent. Ironically, over years as a parliamentarian he had been almost a lone right-wing warning voice on the Nazis' war intentions, on Marshal Pétain's weak Army, and, at the last, on Pétain's molelike blind faith in the underground defense of the Maginot Line. He had been the early discoverer of a certain Lieutenant Colonel Charles de Gaulle and his plan for Europe's first mechanized army of tanks, proposed to the Chamber by Reynaud and rejected by the politicians and the *état-major* as inglorious garage-type arms, with which by 1940 the Nazi copyists were flattening northern France. After Dunkirk, when all seemed lost, Reynaud appointed Brigadier General de Gaulle his Under-Secretary of War and sent him to London to explore the possibility of continuing the fight in France's African empire, and as the feverish hope simply for an armistice weakened his Ministers, the Army, and much of the French nation, he advised the Third Republic's President, Albert Lebrun, to let the government's more popular new member, Pétain, take over. This only Lebrun had the constitutional power to decide on, though in the panicky politicians' collective memories Reynaud unjustly served for the rest of his life as the guilty scapegoat. After his tottering government's rejection of Winston Churchill's gallantly proposed Anglo-French Union, which only Reynaud favored, the clairvoyant little leader was replaced by Pétain as Premier. Vichy first put Reynaud under house arrest, then imprisoned him in the Pyrenees fortress of Portalet, where eventually it delivered him over to the

Nazis. That is his brief Second World War history: a few anguished months as Premier, for the first time in his long political life, and nearly five years in prison for having been right, in advance—for having seen and, like a Cassandra, early prophesied in Parliament that Germany would make war and that France's Army had been left too weak to resist by Marshal Pétain and by political maneuvers. At his funeral service last week in the Basilica of Ste. Clotilde, close behind Parliament, his funeral elegy was read by a Notre-Dame priest, Father Carré, who by chance had also been imprisoned as an anti-Vichy Frenchman in Portalet, at the same time as the deceased.

There was something alert and mouselike in Reynaud's intelligent miniature face, with his arched eyebrows and slanting, watchful, bright eyes. Graduated with *brio* from the Paris bar, he was a member of a Parliamentary family from the southern Basses-Alpes. From the beginning of his long Chamber career, which took place scenically over all three of the last republics, he was noted as a phenomenal, brilliant speaker who in Chamber debate filled the hemicycle and the visitors' loges with listeners hanging upon his words—rather than upon his progressive, pro-European ideas. He lacked the large, mirroring magnetism of a great political leader, and was repeatedly only a Cabinet Minister. In his closely applied French intelligence, he was an early believer in European collective security, and vainly favored sanctions against Italy after Mussolini took Abyssinia, vainly endorsed military movement against Germany when Hitler occupied the Rhineland, and logically disbelieved in Chamberlain's Munich. His personal standard of patriotism was never popular in France, because it always entailed independent action.

Though Reynaud was nearly seventy years old when released from captivity, on being elected deputy to the new Constituent Assembly in 1946 he again became France's most brilliant debater. At seventy-nine, he begot his last child (the last Mme. Reynaud was considerably taller and younger than her husband), and following the Algiers *Putsch* of 1958, though nominally a right-wing independent, he voted loyally for de Gaulle's investiture. But in 1960 there began the autumn of his disbelief in de Gaulle's republicanism, his disapproval of the General's exalted, waxing antiparliamentarianism and his balancing authoritarianism. Republican to the bone by breeding and long second-rank political exercise, Reynaud was a leader of a group of deputies listed to vote "no" against de Gaulle in the October, 1962, referendum. In consequence, he lost his Assembly seat in the November national elections. Although eighty-four years old, he vigorously continued to attack the General in pamphlets and newspaper interviews for his slack backing of the Common Market, for his hostile attitude toward England and the United States, for his narrow Gallic anti-European conceptions. Last year, Reynaud began slowly dying.

In connection with the news of his death last week, *Le Figaro*, which had never admired him, paradoxically was given the privilege of publishing a rare communication sent in from the late Sir Winston's editor and friend Mr. Emery Reves, describing from memory the last talk between Churchill and Reynaud, which took place in Reves' Midi house in 1959—a talk in which the great Churchillian sense of fair play must finally have healed Reynaud's wound of injustice, still left from 1940. "You were unlucky because a large part of the French people did not want to continue the war, and the most eminent of the French generals and admirals were defeatists and demanded capitulation," Sir Winston reportedly declared candidly to Reynaud. "I felt great pity for you during those tragic days. If *my* generals had adopted that attitude, if the English people had been as demoralized as the French, I could never have saved England! I was lucky, so my name was associated with victory. Yours was associated with defeat, which was unjust. But history will recognize that you knew the truth and that nobody in your place could have done any better." For many Parisians, it was as if the great dead Sir Winston had somehow sent a laurel wreath to honor the burial of the small, brilliant dead Frenchman.

October 12

Last Thursday was an ideal day for the transport strike here, with beautiful, sunny weather that was not too warm for pleasant walking—except for those thousands of office workers living in the suburbs who, with both the Métro and the bus lines struck, had to walk one or two hours to get to their midtown jobs, where many arrived steaming with fatigue and exasperation. It was a very unpopular strike, especially as regards the Métro, being the fifth this year. It coincided—obviously by intent, so as to insure a maximum of public discomfort—with the opening of the Salon de l'Automobile, which always produces special traffic jams of cars from the provinces, adding to the by now regular bottlenecks caused by the Paris street excavations, barricades, and giant digging machines, scattered like impediments over the Concorde and other centers. Also, as the Communist daily *Humanité* grandly stated, "In Thursday's absence of traditional transportation, the workers took their cars to go to the factories." This was the first time anyone could recall the Communist press having front-paged the news that French workers are paid enough to do anything about cars except assemble them in the Simca or Renault works. By noon, the melee on the Concorde looked like a gigantic Cubist picture. The strike was not total, owing to dissensions over strike psychology among the three labor unions, which often enough split the unity of French labor sentiment—the powerful, Communist-dominated Confédération Générale du Travail, the smaller Demo-Christian Confédération Française Démocratique du Travail, and the little Socialist Force Ouvrière, which alone refused to back the bus strike. Ranked as only a quasi-total success—after all, half the autobus lines were operative, and perhaps a dozen of the five hundred subway trains—the strike was principally aimed by the transport workers at obtaining two consecutive days off out of every seven, instead of only one day, as now, while retaining the same pay. The combined, nationalized Paris Métro and bus system, for years run at a deficit, is by now well known in labor circles for giving its workers cruel schedules, based on a split working day of seven and a half hours' actual work, which, by being staggered to take in the idle hours of slack traffic, adds up to thirteen hours out of twenty-four. Its workers, in rotation, get one Sunday every seven weeks with their families, and have had Christmas with the children only three or four times over the past fifteen years.

The unions have now written M. Edgar Pisani, the Minister of Equipment, asking him for some immediate proposal to ameliorate the Paris transport problem. Otherwise, one week from now they will all three confer among themselves about future action. It seems that the C.G.T. favors strikes of limited length frequently repeated, so as to constitute a "rhythm of agitation"; the C.F.D.T. wants hard and total single strikes; and the Socialist group inclines to surprise strikes with no advance warning and of at least three days' duration. By now, all three unions are apparently agreed that in Paris a one-day transport strike, even when repeated five times in ten months, nets nothing but five isolated days of urban disorder and quintupled unpopularity for the strikers—with whom, also, this last strike was not popular. French workers have had the legal right to strike since 1864, and by long tradition the workers seem to know better than their union leaders when the public wind is in their favor or is blowing against them.

Apropos of this last week's strike, the resolute small morning paper *Combat* (of which Albert Camus was an early editor) pointed out that in the Fifth Republic's centralization of power France's labor unions, except in a crisis, are given little or no part in the development of labor measures. "It should be noted that a real lassitude weighs on all the partners in our social and economic life," it said. "Technocracy, though a good thing administratively speaking, is bad on the democratic level. Today the French are both tranquil and dissatisfied." Then it added, with one of its customary anti-Gaullist flourishes, "General de Gaulle incarnates these two contradictory sentiments."

Apparently, the fantasy word *"surréaliste"* first appeared in Paris literary circles when the Polish-born French-language poet Guillaume Apollinaire used it to describe a text he had composed. This he showed to two precocious, admiring young writers, André Breton and Philippe Soupault, who had become acquainted at Apollinaire's bedside in the hospital where he shortly afterward died, on the first night of peace after the end of the First World War. As the beginning of what became a long friendship between the two young writers (which ended only a fortnight ago with Breton's death), they soon collaborated in writing a strange work called "Les Champs Magnétiques," which dealt with *l'onirocritie,* or the ancient study of dreams. Apollinaire's text had rather indicated this interesting direction for them to embark on, and in homage to him they referred to what they wrote as "surrealist," like the baptism of something. It was Breton, of course, who soon realized that their pages were indeed basic to what he later called the Surrealist Revolution, but which he had first to measure. He was a medical student who had become interested in psychiatry and occultism, and in his teens, a pursuit of complete liberty of mind, he had admired, among French writers, Mallarmé, Huysmans, and Barrès (though on him he later recanted). At the age of seventeen, he entered into a literary correspondence with Paul Valéry. He also wrote admirable poems in the Mallarmé manner (as a preliminary to becoming one of the very great modern French poets). In 1916, as a medic in the French Army, he worked in Nantes in the neurological center and discovered Freud. In 1919, in Paris, he discovered Dada, brought from Switzerland by the Rumanian intellectual Tristan Tzara; with Soupault and the brilliant writer Louis Aragon he founded the review called *Littérature,* in which "Les Champs Magnétiques" was published, along with a Valéry contribution. By 1922, Dada had disintegrated, and Breton went to Vienna to talk with Freud. Back in Paris, he moved in permanence to a flat in Montmartre, on the Rue Fontaine, near the hedonistic, nocturnally always brightly blazing Place Blanche, of which he poetically said, "Nights here do not exist, except in legend." In this apartment he lived for the rest of his life, like a part of his famous ethnological collection, which included one of the finest known groups of African masks and statues of gods. That year, after meeting Freud, he began the psychic and oneiric studies he made with, and on, such friends as Paul Éluard and Robert Desnos and Max Ernst and Francis Picabia, since obedience to his ideologies was the price he exacted for not being exiled from the cult. There were also experiments in hypnotic sleep, especially with the young novelist René Crevel (the only gay spirit of all those pre-Surrealists, and eventually a suicide), who finally complained that all the other writers present at these séances were taking notes to use from his imagination when it was at its very best, during induced slumber, from which he could never profit. In 1924, Breton published the "Manifeste du Surréalisme." His definition of Surrealism was "pure psychic automatism by which expression is proposed—either verbally or in writing or in any other manner—of the real functioning of thought, in an absence of all control set up by reason, and outside any aesthetic or moral consideration." A French encyclopedia's definition, in quoting Breton, is "Surrealism (philosophy): It rests on the belief in the superior reality of certain forms of association neglected until now, on the dominant power of dreams, and on free movement of thought. It tends definitely to tear down all other psychic mechanisms and to substitute for them in resolving the main problems of life." This first and more important "Manifeste" (there was a second one later, rather like a New Testament) is a small red paperback booklet, now a bibliophilic item. It had an immediate incendiary reaction in Paris literary circles, and in moral circles as well, condemning, as it did, French traditional logic, and postulating, in the interests of superior man himself, the primacy of the unconscious, of the dream, of a new invisible reality, as well as the uses even of folly and certainly of eroticism. Breton, who had created Surrealism, became its magic chief. He denounced the family, patriotism, religion. His definition of God went beyond and below atheism. He temporarily joined the Communist Party, though he later became a Trotzky follower and eventually visited the lost leader in Mexico. The bitter political quarrel between Breton and Aragon, who was Surrealism's only great fiction writer and who became the professional intellectual leader of the French Communist Party, split the Surrealists like a catastrophe from on high, and consumed the two men's friendship. It was through Breton's painters— Duchamp, Ernst, Picabia, Miró, Magritte, Matta (and, for a brief period in the nineteen-thirties, even Picasso was disturbed by the Surrealistic style), and, at first above all, Dali (until he was read out of the group)—that the Western world recognized, enjoyed, and was educated into Surrealism's extensions for the eye and its surmises. It is highly probable that the collapse of the old-fashioned French novel and the final emergence of *nouvelle-vague* writing are due to Surrealism. Breton himself ranked as the finest stylistic writer in contemporary French letters. His revolution was bloodless but not painless for the bourgeoisie.

October 25

Suddenly—that is to say, forty-six years after the passage of the French law forbidding diffusion of any means or propaganda relative to birth control—Parliament will be hastily offered, just before the end of its present session, a bill to legalize what is called in Franglais *le planning familial,* which shows how foreign the whole idea has been in France. Under the Ministry of Health, an ad-hoc Parliamentary Commission was assembled this summer to study the delicate problem. It included five of the eight women deputies, plus consultant doctors, cancer specialists, demographic experts, sociologists, dermatologists, pharmacists, two Nobel Prize biologists, a rabbi, and a Protestant clergyman. (The expected Catholic prelate, perhaps significantly, failed to materialize.) To the surprise of the nation, the bill is being brought in by a Gaullist deputy, M. Lucien Neuwirth, of the Loire *département.* The taboo subject was first mentioned impromptu by the leftist political leader François Mitterrand nearly a year ago in an unimportant small electioneering speech. It was seized upon by French women of the leftist parties with a grip of gratitude that only incalculable numbers of other women could understand. French men are understanding it better now, since a public-opinion poll has just shown that ninety per cent of French female voters between the ages of twenty-five and thirty-four want legal means for "the voluntary limitation of children"—a politico-gynecological electoral bloc of an importance that cannot be ignored by either the right or the left, with elections coming up in March. What the French government had wanted of women (and men) in 1920 was precisely what so many couples do not want today and live together in fear of—quantities of babies. The 1920 law was passed in favor of fecundity because France had in four years of war lost so many of its young males and fathers-to-be in the trenches. Times and ideas have changed, but the law remains.

In the last fortnight, literally every Paris newspaper and important weekly magazine has run articles on some aspect of *les naissances contrôlées.* Because the United States approved use of the contraceptive pill six years ago, most of the articles have featured the American version of what is called here *la pilule,* this being what France has heard of and does not possess, and what French law still forbids concocting. *Le Monde* has run an impressive series, signed by a distinguished medico, on the medical formulas used for contraceptives in various countries, such as Sweden, as well as the United States, since France "must turn to foreign countries," as *Le Monde* says, "to gather disinterested practical information." *France-Soir,* the only French daily with a national circulation of a million, has been running a series on the pill that tends to wind up next to the black sporting pages on autumn horse racing. Gossip columnists report that the young pro-pill generation jeers at its opponents as *"les lapinistes,"* or the rabbit clan, devoted to sheer fertility. The leading Paris leftist intellectual weekly, *Le Nouvel Observateur,* has over several months been running highly intelligent articles on what it has just called "the final settlement that touches the secret mainsprings of the morals of our society and the direct future of millions of couples." In this week's number, the *Observateur* cover carries in red letters the announcement "Opération Pilule," and in the text, which gives both sides of the arguments, it cites a second Gaullist deputy, the Abbé Laudrin, from deeply Catholic Brittany, who declares that it is a scandalous act, "shocking to Catholic consciences," for Parliament to presume to vote on birth control "before the Vatican has made its pronouncement." Michel Debré, Economics Minister, who is all for governmental penny-pinching and is always shown in cartoons carrying a piggy bank, has, the *Observateur* claims, already seen to it that the national Social Security list of pharmaceutical products, on which the French get an eighty-per-cent price reimbursement if ordered by their doctor, will not include the pill in any future form, which will prejudice the poorer class of women against it. Premier Pompidou has said nothing official except that he wants further scientific backing in the matter. He has certainly not received it so far from the Ordre des Médecins (the French doctors' professional association), which merely declared that it considered birth control "an extra-medical matter," or none of its business. A representative of the Ordre Légal, a Maître Mouquin, recently contributed an article to the society's professional bulletin that went as far as to make a scandal. Denouncing family planning, "which comes to us from America, like racketeers and kidnapping," he ended his diatribe by hoping "not to be here to see what happens when the people, stuffed with pills and ravaged by contraception, find themselves facing millions of the yellow race swarming over their continent." If the bill on birth control is readied for presentation to Parliament before this session ends, it will be the first time in French history that the family bed and cradle have been seen in so glaringly bright a political spotlight.

November 8

Twice a year, President de Gaulle tells his nation and the world what he thinks about things—a pair of seasonal confidences that customarily take place in the autumn and the spring, recited without fault from memory at his semiannual press conferences in the Palais de l'Élysée's ballroom, of which, on Friday of last week, he held the fourteenth since assuming the Presidency. Whereas in our country there is a constant official flow of White House information, like a form of national publicity, plus streams of printed revelatory Washington gossip, radio newscasts, and often TV specials about our President, so that our citizens know several times a day what is on his mind or what problems he is dealing with, President de Gaulle regularly functions in a majestic protocol of silence and curtained reserve, which are part of his character and power. During the year, he ordinarily talks extensively only when he is away from home and travelling, as recently when in Russia, Phnom Penh, and Djibouti. The cabled reports of what the General has said someplace on the other side of the world are always hot news in the French press. In the regular Paris governmental routine, his name appears in newspapers so sparingly that it always catches the reader's eye, even if it is only in a Friday announcement that he is weekending with Mme. de Gaulle at Colombey-les-Deux-Églises—though with what Sunday-noon dinner guests, which might give a hint as to the after-coffee political topics of conversation, is almost never printed. The French know what is going on in the government week by week through the press reports from the Conseil des Ministres, and twice a year they hear about the top level from de Gaulle himself. What he offers then is something almost ocular—his personal view as if he were like the mythical two-visaged Janus, endowed with the ability to look in two directions at once. After giving his view of what has happened of importance, good or bad, in the six months gone by, he then takes a penetrating look at what may be coming up in the near future.

This recent press conference was the only dull one among all the fourteen he has held, and he and France are to be congratulated, for nothing in French affairs has gone very wrong over this last half year. As he warned his auditors in his opening sentence, "We have nothing dramatic to say today. In contrast to the past, France right now is not living in any drama." As for the continuing American war in Vietnam, he seemed like a teacher of history lecturing dryly on the present actions of others and forgetting the chapters on his own former national involvement, especially when he said that he found it "absolutely detestable that a little people should be bombed by a very big people"—which France certainly was (if already waning) thirteen years ago, when she vainly bombed the Vietnamese before the downfall of French imperial power in Indo-China at Dien Bien Phu. However, like a history adept who could offer a footnote from France's more recent war against a little people in Algeria, he said, with the harsh pride of experience, that if he spoke so definitely of the American necessity to create peace in Vietnam (a peace that de Gaulle said cannot be merely won), it was because in Algeria the French had finally, in 1962, taken that task of deliberate peacemaking on themselves. "And, believe us, it was meritorious," de Gaulle added, it being a peace he himself had made. The attachés of the European chancelleries at the press talk were impressed by his personal warning that "the Americans must recognize that in Asia no important treaty will be valid without the participation of China" and that the United States must draw the obvious conclusions about recognizing "this great state and the position due to it in the United Nations." De Gaulle said little that was new. Yet he himself, in a way, seemed like a new international character, possibly more vexatious than usual and more openly at outs with his former allies both in Washington and in Bonn, but equipped with a new set of international intimates. For instance, his Embassy in Peking is the most influential of any of the Western representations there. In Europe, the General is now acting as an elderly new friend to the fringe of small Communized states—Rumania, Poland, Yugoslavia, Czechoslovakia, Hungary—and is soon to dispense official

Paris hospitality to top visitors from the Kremlin itself, first to Soviet Premier Aleksei Kosygin in December and then, in the spring, to President Nikolai Podgorny and Party chief Leonid Brezhnev, in a fanfare visit. De Gaulle has come a long way from his early days as head of France's Provisional Government, when he called the French Communists "the separatists."

What Parisians discussed most about de Gaulle's press speech was what he omitted from it—any reference to the Ben Barka murder scandal and its trial, which, until interrupted last week by the voluntary surrender here of King Hassan's chief of secret police, was the most gossiped-about, shocking Franco-Arab event of this past half year. Mehdi Ben Barka, a rarely liberal young Moroccan leader, was kidnapped last autumn in front of the new Drugstore in St.-Germain-des-Prés and then presumably done to death, in a sordid underworld crime, by French and Moroccan police stooges and crooks, whose trial, now to be started all over again, has already smelled to high heaven.

The brighter news for France's future, which de Gaulle did indeed mention, is the proposed Vallon Amendment—an opening segment of the association between capital and labor that de Gaulle first talked of nearly twenty years ago. By this amendment, industrial workers will become, in a way, minor shareholders in companies that profit from capital gains. French factory labor, now riding high in full employment, would rather have ever-higher wages than shares. The best Paris cartoon on the matter shows a capitalist boss cheerfully telling an unenthusiastic worker, "Now you'll be able to own your own monkey wrench!"

Jean Genet's controversial play "Les Paravents" ("The Screens"), whose revival surprisingly achieved great popular success here, finally closed a few days ago at the Barrault-Renaud subsidized Théâtre de France with another attack, on the next-to-last night, by right-wing students, who threw stench bombs on the audience, and, on the last night, with a brief visit of official approval by André Malraux, Minister of Cultural Affairs, who had just succeeded in getting Parliament to refuse to cut the theatre's state appropriation. His personal intervention in the Assembly was rare good theatre in itself. The incident arose out of his presentation to Parliament of his annual cultural budget, when the Centre Democratique deputy M. Christian Bonnet, from the Brittany town of Morbihan, insisted on reading aloud to the Chamber the most scurrilous passage from Genet's play—a passage he called "a real exploitation of rottenness"—because he feared that many of the deputies probably did not understand what the subsidy quarrel was actually about. With extreme moderation, Deputy Bonnet then asked only for the deduction from the Théâtre de France subsidy of the exact sum that "The Screens" had cost to produce, because, he said, it is Parliament's duty to know where, how, and on what the taxpayers' money is being spent in such public projects. Whereupon Malraux, who had already been speaking from the rostrum about his budget with such ardor and volubility that the Chamber could hardly follow his words, tossed aside the sheets of paper he had been carrying in disorder, removed his spectacles, and, with a punctuating gesture of his right hand aloft, began the scintillating harangue that Parliament and its visitors' gallery had been waiting for. "Liberty does not always have clean hands," he explosively began. "You must look twice before throwing liberty out of the window. You say that this play is anti-French; it is anti-human—indeed, anti-everything. And so was Goya, as you can see in his Caprichos etchings. You have mentioned rottenness. Be careful—with quotations you can damn anything. What do you say to 'La Charogne,' by Baudelaire? I certainly don't pretend that Genet is Baudelaire. What I want to say is that if anything wounds your sensibilities, it is unreasonable for you to forbid it. What is reasonable is for you to look at something else. We don't authorize 'Les Paravents' so that it can be objected to, perhaps legitimately; we authorize it despite that, because, after all, we admire Baudelaire for the end of his poem, not for his description of the rotting carcass." (A ripple of applause came from numerous Gaullist benches.)

Deputy Bonnet then interrupted to say stolidly, "I never heard that Baudelaire was published at state expense. Or that Goya's paintings were made with the help of the Spanish state."

"Come, come!" Malraux riposted. "Goya's most famous portraits are those of the Royal Family."

"It is not that my sensibilities have been offended," protested honest Deputy Bonnet. "When all is said and done, as everybody says, no one is forced to buy a ticket for the Théâtre de France. But the taxpayer is forced to pay his taxes"—which has meant paying willy-nilly for the subsidy for Genet's play. "I hate intolerance, I am against censorship," Bonnet went on obstinately. "But you cannot ask the state for three hundred million Old Francs— that is to say, more than the theatre's entire receipts—and at the same time refuse to such public authorities as Parliament all right to take a look at what the theatre may be doing."

"Careful!" warned Malraux. "Baudelaire was not published at the expense of Napoleon III, but just the same you have put yourself in the position of those who condemned the poet. Neither you nor I know where poetry finds its roots," he said in final fulguration.

It was one of those rare, up-to-date intellectual debates, and at its end the stalwart provincial deputy gave way before the Paris inclination toward libertinism, which Genet has helped make a certain fashion here.

November 22

There has never been in any place or at any time in our present world so vast and inclusive a retrospective showing of art by one living artist as the "Hommage à Pablo Picasso," now opened here, without him, to celebrate his recent eighty-fifth birthday. Basically, it is an exchange of gifts. The gift that Paris offers to him is that of the highest degree of official honor that it can manifest for a functioning, astonishing octogenarian and for his work, plus profound gratitude (and pride) that in youth he chose not to live in Barcelona and Spain but to start his career in Paris and continue it in France, on both of which his Iberian genius has enormously shed its lustre. The gift that Picasso offers in return is more complicated. It is that of being the accepted aesthetic phenomenon of the present century, who, more than any other artist, has created and illustrated it—the foreign artist living in France who added to the troubled nineteen-hundreds by his dynamic gifts for destruction, creation, re-creation, metamorphosis, and reanimated mythologies; who has painted love, hate, and loveliness; who has sometimes revised classicism; and who has often invested horrors in ugliness that balance the glories to be found in his manual gift for perfect composition, which ranks as beauty. He has been the dominant, inventive Cubist, whose geometries on canvas were portraits catching the fleeting likeness of the "space-time continuum" theory; the anti-segregationist who borrowed from Negro art; the technician whose brush was like a scalpel operating on facial flesh, altering the relations of noses and eyes and profiles. He has been the master painter and artificer of the Western world, a thousand of whose creations, made by him over the past seventy-one years, are now on view in the Grand and the Petit Palais and in the gallery of the Bibliothèque Nationale.

His pictures in the Grand Palais represent the major part of his autobiography. During a few days before the exhibition officially opened, when the press had the luck to stroll about in freedom while the carpenters were still at work with hammer and saw, making frames, it was like walking through his past life, with time to stop and stare. It seems no secret that all the Grand Palais canvases that are framed in unpainted fresh wood belong to Picasso himself—something over a hundred of them, sent unframed to Paris at the last minute. These are his own pictures, saved by him over the years for his own historical or personal reasons, many never seen before in public, and identified in the catalogue only by the fact that they are given no ownership at all, he having an unexpectedly strong sense of privacy. The first two pictures on the Grand Palais list, both newly framed and dated 1895, are "L'Homme à la Casquette" (a bearded workman in a cap) and "Fillette aux Pieds Nus" (a gypsy-looking barefoot girl)—both classic realistic nineteenth-century paintings by a fourteen-year-old prodigy, and technically so adult as to furnish a mature base for his coming career, from which he could extend himself, when he was ready, into stylistic destructions without self-destruction. Most of these early canvases are signed "P," or else "Pablo Ruiz Picasso," Ruiz being his father's name and Picasso his mother's—prettier and rarer—which he soon took as his signature. This was a second downgrading of his unfortunate father, a minimal art professor and painter of floral bouquets for dining-room decoration, who in abnegation had literally handed over his paints and brushes to his son when he saw that at thirteen he "could paint like Raphael." Picture No. 8 on the Grand Palais list is another small canvas from his personal archives. Called "Évocation" and dated 1901, it looks like a colorful sketch for a Christian Assumption. It depicts the burial of his painter friend Carlos Casagemas, who had come with him to Paris in 1900 and later killed himself over an unhappy love affair. Another portrait of him from memory is the male figure in "La Vie," of the melancholy Blue Period (lent by the Cleveland Museum of Art). From this dark-spirited epoch, the most impressive large canvas (from Picasso's collection) is the rarely exhibited self-portrait, painted at the age of twenty, depicting a thick-lipped Spanish youth with straggling beard and glowing, hungry black eyes, his torso wrapped in his overcoat against the cold air of Paris and poverty, in which (he later said) he burned his drawings to keep warm and ate slightly rotted sausages, which were cheap. Among the other Blues, there is the well-known portrait of "La Célestine," the matron with the opaque, strabismic eye. The other outstanding historic Blue portrait is of Jaime Sabartés with a beer mug in his hand, which gives the picture its usual title of "Le Bock" (exceptionally lent by Moscow's Pushkin Museum). It is a portrait like this that gives the exhibition its persistent rich autobiographical flavor. The writer Sabartés, who knew Picasso from their youth together, was for more than half a century his intermittent Spanish secretary, often living with him at close range, and his eventually published memoirs furnished a Picassoan psychological inventory that art appreciators still carry with them in their memories, like a handy, accurate list of what is to be seen or found again in any new Picasso exhibition, always as a result of what Picasso himself is like. Sabartés once described Picasso as having a brain like *"un incendie cérébral,"* and added that his is an intelligence in a constant state of susceptibility. He attaches himself only to what is essential; what is minor will follow. He never loses his strength by diluting himself, is the sworn enemy of any and all systems. He has more curiosity than a thousand women put together. He is interested in everything, and completely absorbed by some things. Discovery is what he deeply cares for.

What fascinated Picasso by 1904 was happiness, which he

found in his long, well-known liaison with Fernande Olivier, a handsome, almond-eyed, intelligent model (she had been educated to become a schoolteacher), who lived with him in the Montmartre tenement that was known as Le Bateau-Lavoir because it looked like a Seine laundry barge. His second fascination was the Montmartre circus, where he and she went to see the acrobats and equestrians when they could afford it. In her recollections (everyone with experience of him has always written about him) of the seven years she spent with him, called "Picasso et Ses Amis," she recalls one period when they were so poor that she had no shoes and had to stay indoors, and the many times they did not have enough to eat. Considering the popularity of Picasso's circus paintings and how many of them he painted, the Grand Palais circus section seems lacking, there being only four examples—three small ones from his own collection and one large, handsome "Acrobat's Family" of father, mother, and child, like a pastiche of a Holy Family, with the seated observant monkey that he often included as a pagan witness. The exhibition also shows only one early Fernande portrait (also from his private archives), titled "Fernande à la Mantilla." However, the new Rose Period, as it was called in its healthy opposition to the melancholy Blue (and because Picasso used certain new brick-red tones), and which further developed in their 1906 summer together in Gosol, in Andorra, produced one of his first great classic pictures, of major value in the "Hommage." Called "La Toilette," it shows a splendid young nude of great beauty and delicate proportions (supposedly Fernande) standing and dressing her hair before a small, square mirror held aslant by a handmaiden robed in blue—a pair of serene demigoddesses in the Greek manner. During the Gosol summer, he also painted "Woman with Loaves of Bread" balanced on her kerchiefed head —a distinct advance toward what was to be his new, severer personal style, en route to his great revolution in modern art.

By 1905, Picasso had started being moderately successful. That is to say, the sagacious, celebrated art merchant Ambroise Vollard had paid him the equivalent of four hundred dollars for thirty canvases—about thirteen dollars apiece—which financed the Gosol trip. He had also been discovered by two discerning American tyro art collectors with little money—Miss Gertrude Stein and her brother Leo. In the winter of 1905–06, Miss Stein sat eighty times for her portrait by Picasso, while Fernande, who had a lovely voice, read aloud all of La Fontaine's "Fables" to her. Claiming that he "could not see her anymore" (in artists' parlance), he wiped out her face before departing for Gosol, and, on returning to Paris in the autumn, repainted it without having her pose again. The new face, seeming masklike, with thickened eyelids and lips, as if made of clay, was an accentuation of the Gosol style, influenced (Picasso said years later) by the ancient Spanish pre-Roman discoveries that had been displayed at the Louvre and had enormously impressed him. The latest version, rather dull, of Miss Stein's opinion of the portrait has at least the full force of her repetitive style: "For me it is me. It is the only reproduction of me which will always be me." Now known to Parisians as part of the Picasso legend, her portrait was what the French crowds, in their melee, pushed forward to try to look at among all the portraits to be seen at the Grand Palais opening last Saturday afternoon. (It was lent by New York's Metropolitan Museum, to which she appropriately bequeathed it as a transatlantic modern classic.) According to art critics, it was the ultimate exaggeration of the Stein portrait's Iberian tendencies that led Picasso, after long inspirational labors, trials, and tentative sketches during 1906 and into 1907, to his concentration of them all in his formidable revolutionary proto-Cubist picture "Les Demoiselles d'Avignon," which marked a new epoch in the history of modern art. Paris is now calling it "the picture of the century." It is certainly the climax of the Picassos at the Grand Palais. After the First World War, it was André Breton who persuaded Jacques Doucet, the former Paris dressmaker, to buy it for his eclectic private museum, and just before this last war it was bought by the New York Museum of Modern Art. Picasso's other climactic masterpiece, the anti-Fascist Surrealist "Guernica," which he has lent to the same museum, was deemed too fragile to send over for the "Hommage." In the autumn of 1906, when Picasso first conceived the "Demoiselles," he had just turned twenty-five.

By 1908, he was busy exploring Cubism in Paris (as was Georges Braque in Estaque, on the Mediterranean, though neither knew what the other was up to, nor was either sure enough of what Cubism consisted of to be able to define it). When Miss Stein, with her hearty appetite for explanations, asked Picasso to put into words what Cubism was, he told her, with enigmatic clarity, "You paint not what you see but what you know is there." The Picasso Cubist display at the Grand Palais is one of its richest features. In a kind of bay, as if to accommodate groups of immobile, fascinated admirers, and as side accompaniments to the "Demoiselles" and Miss Stein, there is a quartet of analytical-Cubist portraits of highest autobiographical significance. There is Fernande, painted in 1909 and unfortunately looking plump, and, dated over the next two years, his portraits of Ambroise Vollard (lent by Moscow), of the German critic Wilhelm Uhde, with his strangely pinched mouth (from the London collection of Roland and Lee Penrose), and of the heroic first Cubist art merchant, Daniel-Henry Kahnweiler (from the Chicago Art Institute). From Picasso's own collection of Cubist canvases there is the "Man with the Mandolin," and there are dozens from other sources, such as "Le Violon," as his analytical Cubism began flattening itself out into synthetic Cubism's clearer small charms, shown in the exquisite "Still-Life with Fruit, Glass, Knife, and Newspaper." Then in 1921 came the magical, majestic rectilinear Fontainebleau Cubist compositions, with noble strong colors, like painted carpentry, such as "The Three Musicians," the example at the Grand Palais being the musicians from the Philadelphia Museum of Art. Beyond the portraits of Olga Koklova, the Russian dancer who was his first wife, there is a long gallery in the Palais that seems given over almost exclusively to portraits of the various other women he has loved, with or without the children he has fathered. As though skillfully mixing oil with water, he has retained their likenesses, in many cases, while deforming their features. The most resistant beauty in this contingent remains the elegant Yugoslav Dora Maar, as is proved in two splendid portraits depicting her beauty and in a third, significantly called "Weeping Woman," which is a map of facial grief. Energetically devoted to women, he uses their faces in his paintings as mirrors in which he reflects his patterns of physical distortion—carving the nose and the lips apart in such a way that these two features seem to be seen in profile and head on. He gives them nostrils like the ends of trumpets, mouths like tubes. His distortion of the female face by which it is seen from two directions united is a kind of artist's pun that amounts to metamorphosis. To this he often adds grotesqueries, ferocities, and the full liberty of sheer ugliness, like forms of social anger against the world for its physical cruelties, which he has confined to color and canvas.

Twelve thousand people have fought their way into the Grand Palais since the exhibition opened. At the Orangerie Museum, the Vermeer exhibition, now about to close, still has queues forming in the rain under the Tuileries trees. Aside from the big "Hommage à Picasso," there are remarkably choice small Picasso shows in art galleries all over the city. It is as if Paris were intoxicated with art and still could not satisfy its thirst.

December 21

The political campaign has started here in preparation for the March elections, which will be vital, or else fatal, to the future of de Gaulle's Fifth Republic. His majority party has already started pasting up its propaganda and emblems, giving France its new intellectualized slang name of "Le Hexagon"—which it is, on the map, though no one has ever talked about its shape before. The Gaullist emblem stylizes France's desire to expand its influence—"for France is not closed within any narrow nationalism," the Gaullist party patiently explains. In the center of the hexagon can be printed the candidates' slogans, such as "Peace, Independence, Progress" or "Security First of All." (The recent visit here by the Russian leader Aleksei Kosygin was coolly received by the French Communists, who thought he might have waited to visit until after the elections, since his obviously friendly relations with de Gaulle will surely cost the Communists a slice of what might have been automatic anti-de Gaulle votes.) Another of the election posters guarantees "Five Years of Stability, from 1967 to 1972," if the Fifth Republic Gaullists win. Yet another poster accents the Gaullists' governmental stability, inviting the electorate to choose between this regime, which has had only two governments in nine years, and the others, who set up and let fall twenty-two governments in thirteen years. With the warnings from Communist China about possibly lending a helping hand to the

Vietcong, with the impassioned pleas for peace by the Pope, with the strict, non-indulgent attitude of the United Nations' severe Asian chief U Thant toward repeated escalation of the war, there is no question but that the most popular election appeal of the Gaullists will be, as usual, the brains of General de Gaulle himself, who more than a year ago freed France of her NATO military relations so she might not be pulled into any war not to her own liking.

1967

January 3

The photographs of Henri Cartier-Bresson have been the only ones ever given a one-man show in the Pavillon de Marsan, in the Musée des Arts Décoratifs of the Louvre, and a second exhibition of them will be on view there until the end of this month. His status here is that of an artist, with the rank of master photographer of his time. His Leica is his third eye, which in an instant can make permanent what it sees. These two hundred prints are the result of ten years of journeying over the world and of looking—of obtaining from life itself and from its human or animal inhabitants his magical, perfect compositions. His subjects range from Japanese girls weeping in Tokyo at the funeral of a Kabuki actor to an elderly Virginia lady and her ancient bull terrier at rest on her wrought-iron porch; to a group of hard-faced, aproned French village housewives listening without faith to a broadcast speech by de Gaulle; to a large white horse nibbling from a hedge in Ireland, like a hungry phantom equine; to a fat kerchiefed Yugoslav female selling her field daisies on a city sidewalk; to a caped French priest crossing an antique donkeyback bridge; to three West Berlin men perched on top of a box before the Berlin Wall and the East Berlin apartment houses, where, if a curtain twitches in certain of the windows, it means that they have been seen and thanked by some East Berliners for their speechless visit. There are portraits of the Daughters of the Confederacy and of the gifted Sapphic novelist Violette Leduc, of Academician François Mauriac, of women drying their saris in India, of nuns staring at the Matisse dancing nudes

in the New York Museum of Modern Art, of melancholy Gia-
cometti, of the famous Mme. Marie-Louise Bousquet, hands clasped
like a bird's wing below her face, openmouthed as if crowing with
delight. It is a great exhibition of Cartier-Bresson's subtleties and
clarities, of which a duplicate show is now travelling around
Japan and will be in New York in 1968.

When young, Cartier-Bresson broke with his stiff, well-to-do
Norman family, was a hunter on the Ivory Coast for a year, then
in Paris studied to be a painter for two years with André Lhote,
became the photographer he is, and now once again has broken
with the moneyed aspect of existence—with commercial photography. On the Pavillon de Marsan's entry wall is displayed his
recent dictum on that subject, printed in French, which in English
would read, "The profound transformations in the world have affected our profession. I am referring in particular to the unbalanced
situation that exists between the necessities of merchandising and
advertising in our consumer society and the personal report of a
photographer who has been out in the field"—who has reported on
life with his camera, not on goods for sale. "This affects all photographers, especially the younger generation, tending to estrange them
from what is for me the world and mankind. Fortunately, there
are still publications that encourage individuality and give one the
confirmation that other people, too, accept life and say 'yes, yes,
yes' "—to life and to photography practiced not mainly for Madi-
son Avenue but as a modern art.

January 18

During this past week, the coming parliamentary
election unexpectedly developed a mild comic side, which will certainly be lacking in the intemperate March struggle at the polls for
the continuing survival or the final defeat of General de Gaulle's
personal Fifth Republic. The humor was unconsciously furnished
by the solemn, technocratic Valéry Giscard d'Estaing, de Gaulle's
young former Minister of Finance, now an important contender
for post-de Gaulle power and leader of the Parti Républicain Indépendant, the new revisionist Gaullist splinter group he has just

launched, which is already a thorn in the elderly General's side. For more than a fortnight, Giscard has been treating his eighty-three Indépendant candidates as so-called *députés élèves,* or student deputies, and himself as their schoolmaster, holding classes (at first attended in curiosity by the astonished Paris press) to edify and ripen them politically for the electoral campaign—an education that last week reached the calisthenic stage in order to train them to stay both relaxed and hardy during the gruelling speechmaking period lying just ahead. To this special séance, held in a dining room of the Left Bank Hôtel Lutétia, press photographers were also invited, and since Giscard is a thorough planner, the eight physical exercises prescribed for the candidates were presented by a doctor who is a *spécialiste de décontraction,* attached to France's national ski team. The published photographs showed about a dozen decontracted candidates (from Chartres, Pontoise, Puy-de-Dôme, and so on) in their shirtsleeves and suspenders, with collars unbuttoned, all leaning back in their chairs with heads high and eyes closed, as in a faint. There was also a photo showing them exercising while seated, trying to touch their foreheads to their knees, which the plumper candidates failed to manage—a gymnastic spectacle of humped backs and bulging shirttails fit to throw prospective voters into snickers. Last week, Giscard said that he and his Indépendants were "yes, but" Gaullist candidates. The following morning, at the weekly Conseil des Ministres, which de Gaulle attends, often like a statue, he reportedly burst forth suddenly, with brutal wisdom, "One does not govern with 'but,'" showing what was uppermost in his mind.

De Gaulle's anger is credited to the fact that Giscard, who was given preferential government treatment while Finance Minister because of his youthful professional brilliance as a technocrat, now seems fractionally disloyal, which to de Gaulle is unpardonable. Nevertheless, Giscard's Indépendants are a vital part of the Gaullist majority. Without the thirty-five parliamentary seats they have been sitting on—in disguise, as it were—the Gaullist U.N.R. party would have been only a minority. Giscard's personal pitch for his Indépendant group in the coming election is his slogan *"Jeunesse et Avenir,"* featuring his own youth, he being only thirty-seven, and the vastly important new political balance, which is tipping toward the mass of young French voting for the first time in their lives this year—citizens now matured from that vast crop of French babies born in 1946 from the conjugal reunions at the end of the war. There are also about a hundred dissident mature Gaullists newly organized for candidacies under the title of Centre National pour la Cinquième République, which actually includes some former U.N.R. deputies who claim they are still Gaullists but against Premier Georges Pompidou, and are probably only liberal reformers. More alarming for de Gaulle's real candidates is the Fédération Nationale des Gaullistes Indépendants of seventy members, now being reportedly put together by Gaullists still completely attached to the person of the General but not to his present policies, especially in party affairs. There is also a floating dozen or more far less serious unofficial Gaullist candidates, unaccepted by the U.N.R. committee, who are now like bastard Gaullists, unrecognized by the dynastic family but still clinging to the use of the family name.

This is the first time since de Gaulle took office in January, 1959, as the first President of the new Fifth Republic that Gaullism has broken into such splinter factions—not to mention a rival Gaullist party (without de Gaulle, of course), which is what Giscard's group actually amounts to. It was such fragmentations of the big old political formations, which originally had stood as strong, intact, and differentiated as oak trees, that wrecked the parliamentary system of the semi-antique Third Republic, then wrecked the up-to-date Fourth. The Fifth Republic's Gaullism has now also begun to lose the signs of its strict singularity. In the past at election time, there were propaganda outpourings of special fervor and intelligence from the brains and inspiration of the top figures around the tall leader. In the old days, the aesthete André Malraux created memorable, handsome Gaullist publicity posters from the nation's art archives, featuring the reproduction, for instance, of a little-known statue by the sculptor Rude and one by Rodin. For this present election, the publicity for the legitimate Gaullist party was placed in the professional hands of a Paris outfit modelled on the American plan and called Services et Méthodes. It was apparently this firm that, for the publicity badges and wall posters, conjured up the hexagon symbol of France (though without mentioning that France had already been so identified in some early drawings by the architect Le Corbusier). It seems that it also conducted the advertising for young Jean Lecanuet in the Presidential campaign a year ago, when he was de Gaulle's rival and lost. The company was extremely successful, however, in an earlier campaign to popularize the character and figure of James Bond—a movie job in which it plastered haberdashery windows all over France with James Bond white button-down shirts, James Bond leather jackets, and whatever else constituted a complete James Bond outfit. The U.N.R. Gaullists should probably be grateful that nothing more *outré* appears on their Services et Méthodes electoral publicity than Le Corbusier's impersonal hexagon, even though it has actually been quite mystifying to the rural electors, unaware that they live in such a geometrically shaped France. They do, however, know Charles de Gaulle's double-barred Cross of Lorraine, which is stamped upon it, by heart.

February 1

The distinguished, unusual novelist Mme. Nathalie Sarraute recently agreed to write two experimental one-act scripts for some West German radio network, on second thought withdrew them, and then, on third thought, let them be successfully produced. They are now being presented as a pair of short plays by the Barrault-Renaud company at their new Petit-Odéon. This minuscule hundred-seat theatre, which has been squeezed in, like an upstairs broom closet, above the regular Odéon auditorium, makes for a type of social intimacy between actors and audience that is perfectly suited to the Sarraute pieces, "Le Silence" and "Le Mensonge" ("The Lie"). The same uncertainty that she herself first felt about them as radio scripts has pursued them here as plays, and they have had a mixed reception. Some intelligent theatregoers have listened to them with unfaltering, wide-eyed interest, while others have been put to sleep. In the plays' development Mme. Sarraute has followed her subtle psychological system of what she defines as *"les tropismes"*—actually, a botanical term normally applied to plants, rather than to people, except here in Paris, where she has made it an accepted literary term. In vegetal life, plants unaffectedly show their tropism in response to exterior stimuli by growing toward or away from them, and Mme. Sarraute finds that human beings do so, too—in small, immediate moves, that is, and not in great dramatic, passionate pushes such as might lead to murder or marriage. In "Le Silence," half a dozen acquaintances at a small party show their tropism by shrinking away from the man who merely says nothing at all until it is nearly too late while another man, who finally flies into a fury, has been interesting them all with his long account of a journey or some exploit he has just concluded. In the tiny theatre, one listens with rising alarm to Mme. Sarraute's terribly lifelike, undramatic conversation (though some people are bored by its naturalness, by its growing irascibilities and partisanships), as one thinks to oneself: How true it sounds—just like all of us. It's just like nations, even. How awful! Madeleine Renaud, a very great actress, dominates the scene merely by half closing her eyes, by smiling with patience, by quickly turning her profile, as if to ward off a direct verbal blow; her face, by its perfected pantomime of expressions, furnishes the complete vocabulary of what she hardly bothers to say. "Le Mensonge" passes by a tropism into moral conflict, since it deals with a woman who has just palpably lied to her friends in belatedly stating that she did not flee to safety in Switzerland during the war—a falsehood so powerfully influential on them all, especially on one man, that it freezes and destroys the verdant affections they had all enjoyed with her and, in a way, with each other.

Paris has lately seen installed several new pocket theatres, which open at odd hours (like the Petit-Odéon, where the curtain rises at nine-fifteen) and, by offering late-afternoon or late-after-dinner intimate or intellectual entertainment, aid the several theatres' main box offices to survive, this being, as usual, an unbrilliant Paris theatre season.

As far off as China is around the world from France, Mao Tse-tung's "thoughts" and recent Red Guard upheavals have reached the French political left and divided it into two unequal parts; have cut off most of the young intellectual Communists in the Paris universities from the French Communist Party's experienced officials and its solid working class; have, indeed, set up the same dividing line in Paris as the one that separates Peking from Moscow. L'Union des Étudiants Communistes, the big postwar national student union, with an office next to the Sorbonne, has lately lost its power, its student heads, and many of its members, who have chosen Peking as their ideological political center. About eighty per cent of the student organizations have now become pro-Chinese. Calling themselves L'Union des Jeunesses Communistes (Marxiste-Léniniste), they are drawn together by a devotion to Stalin as the only true practicing Marxist that Russia produced after Lenin. Their adherents in the Sorbonne and the École Normale Supérieure would number about a thousand. It is their conviction that revisionism in Russia since Khrushchev's famous speech against Stalin's cult of personal power at Moscow's 20th Party Congress has weakened Marx's doctrine in the way that water weakens strong wine; that the French Communist Party, which held out for nearly two years against Khrushchevism, has now succumbed to what the young purists call parliamentarianism; that French political practices have democratized Communism and turned its thinking into something non-revolutionary. In December, L'Union des Jeunesses Communistes (Marxist-Léniniste) held its first big meeting, in the Salles des Horticulteurs, in the Rue de Grenelle, to which the angered French Communist Party sent what are called its stalwarts—mature men, trained over years in street fighting against the French police—and they beat up the rebel youths terribly, shouting that they were the *vendus de Pékin;* that is, bought out by Peking. Actually, Peking has indeed sent funds to pay for some of the young group's propaganda publications, called "Cahiers Marxistes-Léninistes" and containing cultural articles of various sorts, such as "The Peasants of Balzac" and reprints from early Stalin texts. Peking also sends these French university students small pamphlets on "La Grande Révolution Culturelle Socialiste en Chine" and a well-edited weekly called *Information Pékin,* which is also available in English, Spanish, German, and Japanese. This and other Mao propaganda can be subscribed to in several Paris bookshops.

The principal intellectual master of the pro-Chinese university students is Professor Louis Althusser, professor of philosophy at the École Normale Supérieure, a man now forty-five years old and considered the first outstanding lecturer, writer, and exponent of Marxism since the war. Who would have thought before the war that the powerful French Communist Party would now be treated by French intellectual youth as passé?

Oliver Messiaen and a concert featuring four of his modern symphonic styles were accorded a popular triumph Monday night in the vast Théâtre National Populaire, where he was given a half-hour ovation and his name was shouted when he finally appeared on the stage—a big, modest man with tousled gray hair who looks like a mild country schoolmaster but is ranked by musicians as next to Boulez in his gifts. Through Messiaen's concert, French contemporary music, which is usually confined to circles of the initiate, received the widest acclaim by *le grand public* that it has ever known in Paris. The considerably enlarged symphony orchestra of Radio-diffusion Télévision Française played under its regular, rigorous conductor, Charles Bruck, and was supplemented by the Percussion de Strasbourg group, specialists in experimental music. The stage was crowded with regular and exceptional musical instruments, since Messiaen's instrumentation is always elaborate, and even the conventional instruments are placed by him in odd arrangements to obtain original acoustical effects. The first number on the program, "J'Attends la Résurrection des Morts," on Biblical texts, was commissioned by André Malraux, Minister of Cultural Affairs, in memory of the French dead of both wars and was first performed in 1965 at the Sainte-Chapelle in Paris and then in the Cathedral of Chartres for a solemn commemoration attended by General de Gaulle. It is its sound effects that are the most astonishing; musically, they seem Eastern rather than of liturgical inspiration. There was one great, almost deafening gong, and smaller gongs; the percussion, hung from tall racks, sounded like the Indonesian *gamelan*. The score demands a huge wind ensemble, both wood and brass, in stage center, and the general musical effect is of tragic grandeur. The second number was "Les Offrandes Oubliées," composed in 1930, when Messiaen was only twenty-two; it is excitingly melodic, personal, and original, despite its reminiscences of Stravinsky's "Apollo Musagetes" and the second movement of

Debussy's "La Mer." In its third part, the entire group of first violins plays *unisono* while half the second fiddles and the violas play
divisi within the group, with no cellos or basses at all, producing
an amazing airy, exquisite concoction of floating sound. The third
number was Messiaen's famous "Oiseaux Exotiques," he having a
passion for exotic birds. The piano part must be fiendishly difficult,
is wildly exciting, and was played like a storm, and from memory
only, by Mme. Yvonne Loriod, Messiaen's wife, now the ranking
woman pianist of France. She wore an elaborate cherry-colored
gown, with her black hair piled high, and her eyes (behind her
gold-rimmed glasses) gleamed with attention as she gazed unre-
lentingly up and down the piano keys—a magnificent performance
that brought down the house. The program terminated with the
third, fourth, and fifth movements of "Turangalila" (the entire
opus takes two hours to play)—a Sanskrit word that Messiaen
chooses to translate as "A Hymn to Superior Supreme Joy." It is
written for one of the largest orchestral formations on record—almost as large as that for Mahler's Eighth Symphony—and features
the use of the electronic Ondes Martenot, played by Jeanne Loriod
(in elaborate pale blue), the composer's sister-in-law. This work
was commissioned by the late Serge Koussevitzky for the Boston
Symphony Orchestra, which gave it its first performance in 1949,
under Leonard Bernstein. It contains leitmotifs that aid the ear to
follow the tumultuous music. As for the Ondes Martenot, like a
sound from outer space it dominated the entire orchestra as no
human voice could ever do.

The single complete copy of Mozart's invaluable autograph
manuscript of "Don Giovanni"—the opera's five hundred and
eighty-eight pages in his own hand and as he composed it in fountains of bright or dark melody back in Prague in 1787—now exists
only in the first facsimile edition ever printed from it. Providen-
tially appearing in Paris during this very week when parts of the
manuscript were reported missing or stolen from the Bibliothèque
Nationale, it was published by *La Revue Musicale* and the master
printer André-Gabriel Maisonneuve. Ironically, it was in order to
do some last-minute rephotographing of certain Act I passages that
the guarded strongroom of the Bibliothèque's music division was
opened, about three weeks ago, and four bound fascicles, or note-

books, including three from the first act, were removed. On their being returned about eight days later, discovery was made of the mysterious, scandalous, and still inexplicable disappearance of the opera's famous overture, two fascicles of Act II, and the separate notebook containing "Il mio tesoro," the star aria of Don Ottavio. Also missing was the romantic arborvitae chest that the manuscript's former owner, the celebrated diva Pauline Viardot, had had made to hold it, and in which it had safely reposed for more than a hundred years. A source close to the director of the Bibliothèque's music department has just said that the missing part of the Mozart manuscript is "definitely less than one half of the library's total possession," of which there still remain the three fascicles of Act I and one of Act II, as well as the four-page aria for Don Ottavio, "Dalla sua pace," which Mozart wrote the following year for "Don Giovanni's" Vienna production and that city's then reigning, now forgotten, tenor. Mozart hoped thus to win more favor from the captious Viennese than they had vouchsafed his earlier "Figaro." Unhappily, they declared "Don Giovanni" to be "tasteless, insipid," and its music marked by "caprice, fantasy, and pride but no heart." It was Vienna that gave young Mozart the traumatic fear that grew upon him until his lonely death there four years later—the fear that none of his music would live.

Since Mozart died, his manuscript has had four owners. His widow, Constanze, in 1800 sold his papers to a German publisher, Johann-Anton André, on whose demise, in 1842, they passed to his daughter, married to the well-known Austrian piano maker Johann Baptist Streicher. He unsuccessfully tried to sell them to the royal libraries of Berlin and Vienna, to the British Museum, and, finally, even to Queen Victoria. In 1855, Streicher asked a relative, the pianist Ernst Pauer, to lend a hand. In the July 15th *Revue et Gazette Musicale de Paris,* Pauer ran this announcement: "The pianist Pauer, now giving concerts in London, offers the manuscript of the score of 'Don Juan,' from the hand of the composer, for two hundred pounds sterling." In London, the celebrated soprano Pauline Viardot, sister of the singer Maria Malibran—both famous daughters of Manuel Garcia, the noted Spanish voice teacher—was performing in Meyerbeer's recent success "Le Prophète." She immediately purchased the manuscript—getting a small rebate of twenty pounds—with the sacrifice of about five thousand francs' worth of her diamonds. In her little Paris mansion on the Rue Douai, she displayed the manuscript to Gounod, Liszt, Saint-Saëns, and Rossini, who fell to his knees and wept as he kissed the pages, crying "He was God himself." In 1889, she decided to will it to the library of the Paris Conservatoire, but three years later she felt so well that she preferred to present it personally—nor did she die until 1910, aged almost ninety. In 1911, the Conservatoire moved from the Faubourg Poissonnière to the Rue de Madrid, and the Mozart opus went with it. In those careless old days, admirers were free to handle the manuscript for their pleasure or instruction. In 1964, it was moved with the other Conservatoire treasures to the new, up-to-date Bibliothèque Nationale music room, with its electric alarm system, air-conditioned safe, and constant security service by guards—from which nearly half of it has just vanished into thin air.

The new facsimile edition is accompanied by a brochure that features a fascinating report by M. François Lesure, director of the Bibliothèque's music department, on what Mozart's notation looks like and why. He says that "Don Giovanni" contains remarkably few erasures or corrections, though there is slanting, uncertain notation and hesitation in the initial phrase of Donna Anna's first aria and there are numerous scratchings out toward the end of Act II. He used different strengths of ink, which acted as his instrumental guide—in the opening of Act I the ink is blackest in the parts for the violins and the bass, and in the vocal parts. He first jotted down his main musical themes and their major developments and then furnished the orchestration, sometimes as an insert; the farther he went in the manuscript, the surer he was in his complete rush of creation, the opera's final pages being written in upright clear notes, erect with his full genius.

The *editio princeps* of the new facsimile publication by *La Revue Musicale* and M. Maisonneuve is limited to fifteen hundred numbered copies, priced at the equivalent of ninety dollars and weighing nearly ten pounds. It is boxed, and its eight fascicles are bound, in handsome dark-red paper that resembles the dark morocco-leather binding supplied by Mme. Viardot, and its pages are about thirteen by ten inches in size, as were the sheets of cigh-

teenth-century yellowish paper on which Mozart wrote his now
half-lost masterpiece.

February 14

France has few flies in her ointment as she awaits
her coming elections. She sits prosperous and proud amid her own
high prices. Her past seems to have dropped into oblivion. Her
fairly recent colonial anguish in Algeria lies buried, like soldiers'
bones, under the sand. In her progressively new entity and at peace,
she has watched her paper franc accumulate the strength to raid
both the gold dollar and the sterling pound. As the leading European power, she—or, rather, he, for de Gaulle has summed up
France exclusively over the past eight years—has again just
thwarted England's tentative gesture toward entering the Common
Market. In the English colony here, a recent caustic cartoon on that
subject by Papas in the *Guardian* gave great satisfaction. The artist
showed de Gaulle as Chanticleer, with his gigantic nose and wat-
tled, elderly cheeks serving as the cock's haughty likeness, and the
words "British Entry"—meaning to the Common Market—scribbled across a rising sun, to which celestial body the French farmyard leader addresses his irate warning "Down, damn you! I
haven't crowed yet." In de Gaulle's rather meagre preëlection TV
speech to his nation last week, he alerted his listeners to the danger
that would attend a defeat of the Fifth Republic at the polls—
France's loss of her independence vis-à-vis "the American hegemony," which of late has become his classic bugbear phrase. It was
refreshing to read the next morning in *Figaro*—often the only
French friend in print that we Americans still have here—the
spirited outcry in its editorial column. "It will surprise no one," the
editorial concluded, "that we energetically regret in the Chief of
State's TV speech the fresh and useless allusion to the American
hegemony. It seems as if General de Gaulle were determined to
defoliate friendship from those widening avenues that are leading
to his solitude."

The election campaign officially opened for the dominant
Candidats de la Majorité—meaning the U.N.R. Gaullists, who

were the party in power during this last Parliament—in a monster meeting held early last week at the Palais des Sports. It featured refinements of political publicity and psychology such as no French election in history ever dreamed of, French election campaigns having until now always maintained a certain village or neighborhood character, which seemed to give them their authentic republican, belligerent, and personal quality. The Palais des Sports' main attraction was a regular production—a fantastic ceremony called "La Présentation des Candidats." It consisted of almost all of the close to five hundred majority candidates, drawn from their bailiwicks all over France, and even from the overseas constituencies—candidates come by car, train, plane, and boat to be seated that special Tuesday night on the Palais des Sports stage, waiting quietly behind the curtain, like so many actors, until it lifted (about a half hour late), and there they all were, laughing with self-consciousness and excitement, the men who hoped by the magic of the vote to become the people's choice, suddenly revealed in physical and political union to the crowd of eight thousand spectators, who in that first moment of companionship and recognition were aroused to frenzied bedlam. In the front row on the stage sat ruddy-faced Premier Georges Pompidou, flanked by his government colleagues —Debré, Chaban-Delmas, Joxe, Faure, Malraux, and all the rest— with lesser dignitaries and Party committeemen seated behind, and the rows of candidates craning their necks to stare at the agitated crowd. Three dozen so-called hostesses dressed in turquoise blue— nice-looking nieces or cousins of the government—had already distributed to the crowd the Party badges, key rings, gadgets, and brochures, and soon a dozen loudspeakers began playing Stravinsky's "Sacre du Printemps." (Malraux always chooses the appropriate rousing music for these great Gaullist rallies, which in the past was usually Beethoven.) Over the Russian musical upheaval came the announcements, on a giant movie screen, of "Les Réussites de la France" ("The Successes of France"), a newsreel jumble and ballyhoo of the French individuals and creations that won fame this past year under the Fifth Republic. They included the champion athlete Michel Jazy, the beautiful modernist bridge at Oléron, the submarine Gymnote, and France's four Nobel Prize winners. (All four of them soon signed a round-robin signalling their interest in the Grenoble campaign of the intellectual *chef de l'opposition* to the Gaullist party—the brilliant reconstructed Socialist Pierre Mendès-France, who, after twelve years in the political wilderness, has come back to the election arena.) Finally came the speeches—solid rather than stimulating, except for a flashing definition furnished by Malraux, who pointed out, "The Fifth Republic is *not* the Fourth Republic plus General de Gaulle."

The truth is that this is a dull but very important election. De Gaulle himself has ambiguously said, "It is an election to preserve the institutions of the Fifth Republic." Actually, it is an election that, perhaps for the last time in his political life, he trusts will once more give his followers what he has just called "a coherent and constant" parliamentary majority. Against him will be his natural enemies the Communists and Socialists, that traditional French pair of the left, who usually rally about forty-five per cent of the national vote and are now in alliance with the left-wing odds and ends in the new Fédération de la Gauche, a tripartite combination recently banded together for electoral strength like a mock Front Populaire. If de Gaulle fails in his majority, those against him this time might have enough seats in Parliament to overthrow his government and his France's proud position—the regular habit in the volatile Fourth Republic, during whose twelve years of existence twenty-two governments fell flat. In his TV speech, the General declared that "for the first time in almost a hundred years" France possesses a majority party. It is, of course, his.

As for the Fifth Republic's institutions that de Gaulle wants preserved, it has been his special and exceptional mélange of extremely personal power and abstract Presidential privileges that over the past eight years has kept France's government functioning without his ever once falling, not even when he changed Premiers in midstream. Who else (some of the more realistic French voters are now asking themselves, in a kind of last-minute *examen de conscience*), and aided by exactly what institutions, could have been so deft a government gyroscope as he, balancing between speeches and referendums and visions for France, with his aging, pawky body, his weighty personality, and his alert, compressed, brilliant, and educated mind and memory? It would seem that de Gaulle himself as a tireless, if fatiguing, phenomenon has been the singular unique institution of the Fifth Republic.

It is expected—though, of course, it is not sure—that his majority party will be continued in office in March, mostly because the great quantity of French people of all classes who do not want his regime still ardently want the flourishing contemporary France that it and he have created.

March 1

The latest big theatrical hit in Paris was first produced here three hundred and two years ago, and is now going unusually strong. It is Molière's "Dom Juan, or The Feast of the Statue," which was created in February, 1665, under Louis XIV, and is playing today in what was Molière's theatre, La Comédie-Française. The legend of the libertine seducer cast down into Hell by the graveyard image of the Commander whom he himself murdered had long been played in Paris in various popular semi-comic versions, taken from the Spanish, from the Italian, and even from the Portuguese. "Dom," Lisbon's equivalent of "Don," was adopted by Molière when he hastily created, in his new version of the old play, his novel type of villain—*"un grand seigneur, méchant homme,"* the nobleman who was, humanly, a bad man. Though Molière lacked our precise term, he made his Dom Juan what we would call an anti-hero—an erotomaniac, an anarchist, an ungrateful and cruel son, an egotistical rebel against the Establishment, a psychological sadist who enjoyed the tears of others, a pathological liar, and an intellectual atheist in an amoral court society dominated by hypocritical *dévots* and churchmen. Molière's so-called comedy, in which he himself played Sganarelle, the credulous, conservative buffoon valet, was such a scandal and such a success in that February of 1665 that by the end of March it had been withdrawn, probably under pious official pressure. A violent, provocative, sensual play, philosophical, socially critical, and sobering—or so it seems today—"Dom Juan" has never before been popular in modern times; for a century and a half it was not played in Paris at all, and since the war it has enjoyed only one great revival—twenty years ago at the Théâtre de l'Athénée, where Louis Jouvet splendidly played the hidalgo libertine, in two memorable, magnificent identical embroidered costumes—white on black for Act I, and black on white for Act II, white being traditional for the supper scene—which were designed, as was the fantastic baroque décor, by Christian Bérard.

It is partly the rush to see something old and rare that has made the Comédie-Française spectacle so popular, but its basic interest for serious theatregoers lies in its direction, by Antoine Bourseiller, France's most creative avant-garde director, who was recently named head of Le Centre Dramatique, in Aix-en-Provence, the Mecca in the recrudescence of French provincial theatres. For his first act, he uses a morbid forest of what appear to be copper-plated trees. Dom Juan is dressed in what looks like a greenish-silver leather dinner jacket and matching modern narrow trousers, his only seventeenth-century touch being a dangling gilt rapier. Sganarelle is less well tailored in a bluish-silver leather jerkin, Donna Elvira wears the proper sapphire velvet, and the ghostly Commander is in a Roman toga. Bourseiller, in his direction of the two halves of that classic male couple, the master and the servant, gives the dominance to the role of Sganarelle, which was doubtless Molière's intention, since he wrote the part for himself. At the Comédie-Française, it is certainly played by the superior actor, Jacques Charon, in a masterly comic, nimble performance of a lovable knave, stuffed with Christian principles, hypocrisies, pathos, and low-class humanity—the age-old ignorant and superstitious poltroon. Contrasted with him is the educated nonbeliever, Dom Juan, recklessly tracing his path from one desire to another—tracing it literally, in diagonal movements across the Comédie's large stage, like a man on some invisible angular personal journey of the passions. The blond handsomeness and pallid personality of Georges Descrières, playing the anti-hero, seemed feeble for a man strong enough to have given so much pain—feeble even when he was reciting his great definition of his rationalistic disbelief, a famous Molière speech and very nearly the shortest: "I believe that two and two are four, Sganarelle, and that four and four are eight." At the end of the play, when the statue says the fatal words "Give me your hand," the descent of the soul of the sinner into Hell also seemed theatrically weak, for it was accompanied by too few flames and too little thunder for such a major damnation. But Sganarelle's final cry over the body of his cursed and lost master reached the power of tragic grief as Charon sobbed, "Oh, my wages! My wages!"

"Dom Juan" is the only truly serious play now on in Paris. Through Molière's voice, it asks two questions of its twentieth-century French audiences in the capital of this still Catholic land: "Do you believe in God?" and "Do you believe in the Last Judgment?"

The parliamentary elections that will take place at the end of this week have assumed an extraordinary animation, thanks to the electorate's staying at home during the campaign and watching its TV. Five years ago, in the previous such contest, the Fifth Republic did not concentrate so intensely on the home screen in so many kitchens and little salons as to make it what this election is—France's first election campaign dominated by television. This explains the furious outcry that arose from all the political parties that are fighting the Gaullist candidates when President de Gaulle suddenly announced, a few days ago, that he would give an extra televised national talk this Saturday night at eight o'clock, though the electoral campaign legally ends at midnight Friday. This Saturday-night extension would grant him the privilege of having the last word spoken in the campaign, and left echoing on the air, before the voting starts Sunday morning, with the opposition candidates almost powerless to refute anything he might advise the nation's voters to do or not to do, because it is improbable that any Sunday newspaper in France would print their protests. In the meantime, the press all over France has been harshly critical of de Gaulle's decision to speak, and the words "cheating" and "scandalous" have been freely printed to describe his conduct—for the first time in his long, austere career. The idea of the Saturday-night broadcast is so unpopular that the opposition is quite cheered up, for it looks as if the Gaullist party could lose many much-needed votes, which might be withheld as a way of punishing de Gaulle for this ineptitude.

It has been noticed that Giscard d'Estaing, the leader of the Independent Republican Gaullists, refused to comment on the

Saturday-night talk—a sure sign that he disapproves of it. The editor of the Communist paper *L'Humanité* violently called de Gaulle's project "a characteristic rape" of election practices, and extreme-right leader Jean-Louis Tixier-Vignancour has urged the technical crew of the state TV to strike on Saturday, so as to kill *le Grand Charles's* broadcast. François Mitterrand, the leader of the Federated Leftists, accused de Gaulle of acting more like the chief of a personal party than a chief of state. Jean Lecanuet, the Democratic Center Movement leader, said, "De Gaulle's intervention in his own favor is contrary to all custom and is inadmissible." Socialist Mayor Gaston Deferre, of Marseille, no longer a young politician, said sadly, "Need one remind him that this way of working risks doing himself a disservice? It is a sign of old age in a man accustomed to not making mistakes." And the chief of the intelligentsia Socialist opposition, Pierre Mendès-France, interrupted his all-important debate with Premier Georges Pompidou in Grenoble Monday night—to which Paris was listening over the radio, as the major campaign event—harshly to say of de Gaulle's projected extra broadcast, "This is an unexpected and illegal decision. It is the first time the General has gone this far. . . . I see only one explanation—for the first time he is afraid."

Mendès, who ordinarily lives in Paris, has been given half a large apartment in Grenoble by an antique dealer who is an admirer. (The dealer first cleared it of its fine furniture, so Mendès could use it as an office.) Mendès made the apartment his campaign headquarters, because he is standing for election in Grenoble, and the national debate was held in that handsome provincial city, in the local ice-skating rink, where the audience sat for nearly four hours in all, its chilly feet on planks set over the ice, to hear a debate of less than an hour. One could not always hear it clearly here in Paris, for the excited partisans became rampageous at times, but it got a complete full-page report in most Paris papers the next day, so Parisians could read what the pair had said. The essence of their confrontation—*le face à face,* as the French call this kind of argument, which has proved an electrifying political novelty—was about what de Gaulle had called his Fifth Republic's institutions, which he wants preserved, though they are essentially mixed and confusing, his regime being in part Presidential, like the one in

Washington, and in part parliamentary, as is usual in Paris. The bone of contention between the two speakers was how would the Gaullist anti-left govern with a left-wing parliamentary majority. The answer of Mendès, who himself was a Premier back in 1954, but was less far to the left than he is today, was that "the people have the right to change their minds and demand that the President of the Republic change his government policy to suit theirs" —that "the majority has the right to demand governing powers, *à la français.*" Pompidou saw the affair the other way, in the more up-to-date political style. He claimed that since 1965, when the President of the Republic, by universal suffrage, had been given his new constitutional right to govern, his position was "that of captain," as it were—Parliament existed to control governing power but not to exercise it (rather like the American Congress). To Mendès' theory, Pompidou said, "You show you are a man of the over-and-done-with Third Republic, and I regret this." To which Mendès replied, with equal political *esprit,* "Listening to you, I have the impression you are a man of the Second Empire." Both men appeared to be speaking the truth, unfortunately for France.

Down on the modest neighborhood female political level, this writer attended a meeting called "Avec les Femmes," which was held, appropriately, in a girls' public grade school in the Fifteenth Arrondissement—a drab district on the Left Bank—and was attended by small-bourgeois and white-collar workers. The main speaker was Mme. Gisèle Halimi, who is a Federated Leftist campaigning under the slogan "A Woman of Our Time for a Modern France," and she was well worth the taxi ride across town to listen to. A born good speaker, and good-looking, she is, according to her throw-away biographical sheet, a lawyer, thirty-nine years old, the mother of three children, and a member of the Commission Juridique du Tribunal International, which was founded by Bertrand Russell; and she is also the author, in collaboration with Mme. Simone de Beauvoir, of "Djamila Boupacha," that painful book about the horribly tortured Algerian girl of that name accused of being a spy against the French Army, whose soldiers did the torturing. It was one of the infamous torture cases that occurred during the Algerian war and against which the French intellectuals loyally but vainly lifted their pens.

Mme. Halimi's political program was also printed on a throw-away. On it she says that her future and that of her children should not be decided by only one man, aged seventy-six, "a regular president-monarch from another century." She is against the atomic bomb and the *force de frappe,* and against the spending of any state money on this kind of death. She is for "modern intelligence" and for peace. She is also for a population limit, and at the meeting she talked intelligently and statistically about the anti-conception pill. (This is the first French election in which the pill has had a political position.) It seems, she explained, that the law of 1920, drawn up when France needed extra babies to replace the dead of the First World War, which made birth control illegal has never been annulled, because of churchly and professional pressures, including pressure from the French medical profession, which has been "extremely reticent in backing family planning." What has been done to circumvent the 1920 law is the granting of legal permission to doctors to give the pills to their patients if the doctor sees fit and if the patient can afford to pay for them. During her speech, Mme. Halimi was attentively watched and listened to by a handsome and very mannerly little boy in the front row, who was referred to by her friends as her "gorilla"—the slang name for any of the burly guards who accompany de Gaulle when he speaks in public. Her gorilla was her son, aged about ten.

March 14

The French parliamentary election, which was prophesied to be dull but vital for the preservation of de Gaulle's institutions, turned out to be sensational, and left his Fifth Republic party barely balanced on what looked like a dangerous chasm of possible defeat. Amid real political excitement, the de Gaulle party obtained at the last moment what Paris calls the minority of a majority—exactly the necessary two hundred and forty-four Chamber seats to sit on without immediate danger. The turnout of eighty per cent of the electorate was among the largest that modern France has known since the Front Populaire vote of 1936, which, in one way, this election resembled, because this one, too, was a

great national upheaval from the left. But this time everything was
simplified. The Gaullist slogan was the familiar brief one of "Progress, Independence, and Peace." The slogan of the left was brand-
new and succinct: "The End of Personal Power," meaning an end
to de Gaulle's indubitably very successful method of idiosyncratic
governing of France over the past eight years. To achieve this aim,
the Communists and the important new Federation of the Left (of
Socialists, Radicals, and various non-Communists) joined in a
powerful, disciplined attack, which they carried through with unexpected brilliance and sobriety, and, in some instances, even self-
sacrifice. Together, they so damaged the prestige of the de Gaulle
regime that it would seem he cannot go on being himself as he was.

The result of this election, which has encouraged, shocked,
alarmed, and astonished France as well as Europe, indicates to
many observers that the French nation now seems better balanced
democratically—all parts of the Republic's body politic being visibly
present, with the left hand operative, and with the brainy governmental head still in place, at least for the moment, on its shoulders
—then at any time since the war. To many here, the post-election
picture, which few had dreamed of, looks healthy and encouraging. If the Communist-Federation pact was one man's creation, it
was probably that of the Federation's chief, François Mitterrand.
In any case, it has given him a popularity and admiration that he
has never known before in his very shifting political reincarna-
tions, and he is now being given credit for the brilliant tactical
triumph of the whole anti-de Gaulle maneuver, with Waldeck
Rochet, chief of the Communists, more quietly overseeing his
party's obedience to Communist discipline.

It must be understood that France's election consisted, as usual,
of two Sunday elections a week apart, of which the first, on March
5th, was naïvely important, because it gave the true picture of
which candidates and parties the French citizens chose voluntarily,
before pressure was put on some candidates to disappear from the
lists and some voters were ordered to vote for a different man and
party in the decisive runoff election. These perfectly licit election
machinations must, by law, take place before midnight on the
Tuesday following the first Sunday election. What is set up on
Tuesday is the alliances between politically sympathetic parties,

which can spectacularly shape a French election. The dominant maneuver is what are called *les désistements,* or withdrawals, first practiced in 1876, in the early, difficult days of the Third Republic, with the aim of narrowing the voting results. Arranging the *désistements* is a logical, cynical, carefully figured-out way of providing for the survival of the fittest, and, like all French political maneuvers, the process is complicated. In it, candidates drop from sight, go home, and give up dreams of being a deputy in Parliament. Voters are informed whom to vote for in the new alliances by party leaders, or, nowadays, even by TV announcements. A few Communist Party voters who disobeyed in this election have been expelled from the Party, which, for a Communist, is political suicide or assassination. In the Federation of the Left, those who were recalcitrant have been threatened with milder party discipline later. *Désistements* rely on an electorate that accepts guidance after having voted. The Communists are so obedient to Party orders—or thus the joke goes—that if told to vote for de Gaulle they would all do so. These *désistements* are so conventional and familiar here that in this election the morning paper *Figaro* ran its report of them on page 2, usually given over to accidents and crime—the special emotional touch being supplied by those candidates, cut down like martyrs, who were called *"les sacrifiés."* In the careful planning of this election, the Communists and the Federation of the Left arranged things so that between them they had only one candidate in each runoff race, perfectly and economically fixed, if possible, to beat the Gaullist. An example of how the system works was provided last week by the case of Pierre Mendès-France, running from Grenoble (the one Frenchman of the left "to whom rivals and colleagues would accord the stature of statesman and not politician"), who had been out of the governmental radius for twelve years and was badly needed as a chief of the opposition. In the first voting, his rival, the Gaullist Jean Vanier, was the winner, with around twenty-four thousand votes to Mendès' twenty-one thousand and the Communist Giard's thirteen thousand. By Giard's *désistement,* Mendès' vote in the second round topped the Gaullist's, and certainly the better brain—Mendès—was elected for the service of France.

What the two parties of the left can agree on, after at least shaking the Gaullist party like a somewhat worn velvet banner, is demands for better schools, hospitals, pensions, and universities, all of which have interested de Gaulle less than the inflation of *la grandeur de la France.* His real interest has been the costly *force de frappe.* The interest of the young French voters—whether left or independent Gaullist—born from the family reunions at the end of the Second World War, is better housing, plumbing, and education so they, too, can get married and without worry. On the physical, even social, level of improvement for *le peuple,* the modest little French, the General's vision has largely been in the clouds, too presbyopic to see things close to home. This has been an election of the highest consequence for France, possibly for the Common Market, possibly for Russian-American relations, perhaps even for better relations between Paris and Washington. The French left is no longer anti-Yankee, that being part of the Gaullist ideology.

Through the election, the Gaullist party itself has taken on a certain new shape. The junior Gaullist party—those independents headed by the ambitious former Gaullist Minister of Finance Giscard d'Estaing—has come through very well, and five years from now it and he might be the post-de Gaulle Gaullists of France. Young Jean Lecanuet, whose agreeable center, democratic, liberal appeal was quite successful during the Presidential campaign two years ago, was, on the whole, shattered in the parliamentary election, probably because he was trying to look in two political directions at once. But all this is unimportant compared to the probable governmental alterations—with or without the faithful Premier Pompidou—that de Gaulle now faces, and to the probability that the two parties of the left, because successful in this recent alliance, can remain politically neighborly and not lose sight of each other in animosities, as they did after the Front Populaire. The injury to the Gaullists' prestige has resulted at least in an increased social stability for France generally. This may sound sententious, but it has suddenly become hopeful and true, it would seem.

Miss Alice B. Toklas, who died last week in Paris, would have been ninety in April. Her relations with life had been impaired a few years ago by a bad fall, which confined her to her room, and with time her eyesight had become diminished. But there was little she wanted to read with her magnifying glass, and not a great deal she still wanted to hear, except what she herself said when she talked about Miss Gertrude Stein. Even at her age, she had an astonishing memory—as exact as a silver engraving—of all that Miss Stein had said on any subject they had discussed in their long friendship together. In company with this memory, Miss Toklas had her own creative, critical mind, still of rare validity, which had continued to function since Miss Stein's death in 1946, nearly a quarter of a century ago. If at some time in the past year or so a visitor to Miss Toklas's alien modern apartment out on the Rue de la Convention asked what Miss Stein had thought about this artist or that writer or that former mutual friend, Miss Toklas, as if on a rapid impulse, would start recollecting what she herself had thought at the time, until she would suddenly cease, as if with a sense of heresy or as if she were contributing to apocrypha, and, in shock, would fall silent. It was in those long silent moments that she miraculously reflected both herself and Miss Stein, complete and complemented.

The unique collection of early Picassos that Miss Stein started when nearly no one yet wanted what he painted (and for which she paid so little, since she was not rich, that Picasso said, with generous humor, that it would be almost cheaper for them both if he gave them to her for nothing) was famous by the time the two ladies moved, with these pictures to their last flat together, in the Rue Christine. It will be recalled that because Miss Toklas, in ill health and by then alone in the world, went to Rome in 1960 for the better part of a year—"My first infidelity to Paris," she said, and certainly it was the most costly—the Tribunal de la Seine, on a demand made in the interests of the ultimate heirs of Miss Stein, authorized seizure of the picture collection, on the ground that it had been left without a resident guardian (and other irregularities). The sequestration of the collection in the vaults of the Paris branch of the Chase Manhattan Bank prevented Miss Toklas's further enjoyment of the terms of Miss Stein's will, which permitted her the sale of a canvas if she should be in need. With the death of Miss Toklas, the pictures now pass to the heirs, who are the three offspring of Miss Stein's early-deceased nephew Allan Stein—that rather unattractive little boy with a tennis racket in an early portrait by Picasso. The heirs are Mr. Daniel Stein, of California, now in his thirties, son of Allan Stein's first marriage, and, by a second marriage, a girl and a boy, Mlle. Gabrielle and M. Michael Stein, brought up modestly in Paris and now in their twenties. It has been stated by a friend that the wish of the two younger heirs is to maintain the collection as a memorial to Gertrude Stein, whom they could hardly ever have laid eyes on. The pictures are now valued by art authorities (who have not seen them for years) at about two and a half million dollars. On Miss Stein's death, an official inventory listed twenty-two Picasso oil paintings. First on the list was the large "Femme Nue sur Fond Rose," which hung against the fireplace mirror in the Rue Christine salon, unlike anything else Picasso ever painted, and Miss Stein's favorite. Then came "Jeune Fille aux Fleurs," the famous nude girl holding a basket of flowers—her first purchase, with her brother Leo. Miss Stein thought the figure's legs badly painted, so the Montmartre art merchant said, "Oh, cut them off if you don't like them—the artist won't mind anything if you'll only buy." Perhaps finest on the list were the inestimably valuable small male heads—two rose and one green—of proto-Cubist type, painted during Picasso's composition of "Les Demoiselles d'Avignon." The collecton is like no other, because of the great representational early paintings from those fresh, fertile years of Picasso. It is a collection associated with sadness, on the whole—with its former owners gone and only Picasso still alive, at eighty-five.

A new French five-franc note, of a rather ugly blue green, has now been put into circulation, and it is one of the most diverting and informative pieces of printed money ever issued by the Banque de France. It honors the universally best known of all French chemists, Louis Pasteur (1822–95), whose portrait it bears—showing his affectionate eyes, gray beard, and domed, intellectual forehead—and, nearby, the modest brick building that was the original Institut Pasteur, where he carried on his researches, so beneficial to man and beast. Both men and beasts are pictured on the note, which carries nearly a dozen pictorial references to Pasteur's works. On the obverse, up in the border, are chickens and sheep, which recall his prevention of chicken cholera and of anthrax among sheep and cattle—at that time ruining French farmers. He also eliminated a plague among silkworms (creatures difficult to portray decoratively), which was bankrupting the French silk industry—a triumph indicated on the banknote merely by scrolls of mulberry leaves such as the silkworms were fed when in good health. There are, furthermore, trellises of grapes and vine leaves, representing his success in the problems of controlling fermentation in wine, which led, in turn, to his research into germs, the resultant pasteurization of milk, and, eventually, to asepsis applied to surgical instruments, which revolutionized the practice of surgery. From his work with wine, Pasteur concluded that "wine is the healthiest liquid man can drink," a theory in which the alcoholically inclined French people and the great French winegrowers have gladly concurred. His most noted discovery, of course, was the cure for rabies. The largest configuration on the five-franc note shows a statue of a dog biting a barefoot shepherd boy whose name was Jupille—famous in French medical history as the second human being to be spared by Pasteur's method the horrors of death from rabies. The only really important identification lacking on the Pasteur note is Pasteur's name, which money portraits never carry in France, the theory being that a face so honored needs no nominal identification. This is not necessarily the case with Pasteur, since his name is known all over the Western world but not what he looked like.

April 5

Not in recent memory has the National Assembly been as crowded as it was for the opening, on Monday, of the third legislative session of de Gaulle's Fifth Republic, predictably more of a risk for him and for France than the two preceding. Every able-bodied deputy—those newly elected last month and those who are old Parliamentary hands—turned up to sit in the hemicycle (helter-skelter, rather than grouped according to political parties) to see with his own eyes how this extremely important election of the President of the Chamber would turn out, and above all to try to tilt the election for or against de Gaulle's candidate, de Gaulle himself always seeming present like an aura around any candidate connected with his Fifth Republic. The visitors' loges were crammed with the international diplomatic corps and with brightly dressed women, the *rentrée* always being a politico-social event. The inadequate, minuscule press balcony, next to the ceiling, was packed with correspondents in two tiers, like a layer cake. This focal Parliamentary meeting took place in a France that had no government that day—in fact, still has none. As a prudent maneuver, de Gaulle's government had resigned Saturday, so that its twenty-two Ministers could vote as mere deputies. It was rather like hitching one's race horses to a plow for an afternoon's hard pull. The Cabinet's resignation would also make it easier for de Gaulle to discard permanently those members of it whom he might not contemplate inviting to turn into Ministers again later this week.

Monday's reëlection of M. Jacques Chaban-Delmas, who was de Gaulle's President of the Chamber for the past eight years, was the first sign of Gaullist political luck since the close-to-disastrous March elections. The President of the Chamber, whose authoritative position resembles that of the Speaker in Britain's Parliament, sits on a splendid brass-trimmed chair, decorated with lions and caryatids, that occupies the little tribune facing and overlooking the deputies. His entry into the Chamber takes place between a hedge of saluting Gardes Républicains and is accompanied by a rolling drumbeat. In the state hierarchy, he ranks as the fourth-most-important personage, the first being the President of the Republic, the second the President of the Senate (who may nevertheless soon be wiped out, along with the superannuated Senate itself), and the third the Premier. Then comes Chaban-Delmas once more, a politically highly intelligent dandy in cutaway and striped trousers by day, in tails and a white tie the size of a big butterfly at night sessions. He lives in state-bestowed furnished quarters behind the Chamber—the sumptuous Hôtel de Lassay, equipped at the state's expense with silver, servants, chauffeurs, linen, china, and car. What is more important right now is that with de Gaulle's government faced for the first time by a strong, brainy, semi-united opposition of the left, Chaban-Delmas has the power to control a great deal of that opposition at its parliamentary source—to intervene in the debates, to interpret texts, to cut short awkward discussions, to forbid the reading of certain troublesome speeches, to curtail oppositional interference with the de Gaulle government's plans to govern.

At the moment, the Gaullists' prospects are not gay. The French industrial picture is rather melancholy, with a plague of strikes at Saint-Nazaire, Lyon, and Besançon, and with angry demonstrations by wine-growing farmers in the south, whose bishops in Carcassonne, Perpignan, Nîmes, and Montpellier have raised their voices in the farmers' behalf, saying that not for sixty years has there been a comparable upheaval in the wine-growing industry. The farmers accuse the government of keeping substantial quantities of their French wines off the market in order to make easier the sale of Tunisian wines—on top of the Algerian wines already flooding the southern market. The country's social services are in the red by three billion francs, and there is a six-billion-franc deficit in the nationalized industries. France's prosperity and pride of two years ago have suffered by having had a reef taken in them; government money is short for all the social reforms that have not been made and are now piling high. Prices constantly rise, food is dear, and working-class discontent is politically expensive. The psychological shock of having almost lost the March elections has also cost a fortune in that precious public investment, political faith. These are some of the reasons that this third legislative session of de Gaulle's Fifth Republic carries its special hazards as it enters French current events.

On Thursday a week ago, two days before General de Gaulle's deadline for all Allied military installations to leave the soil of France, the semicircle of multicolored NATO flags was hauled down at SHAPE, in the modest-looking rural center of Rocquencourt, near the Forest of Marly, outside Paris, and after sixteen years Supreme Headquarters Allied Powers Europe came to its end in this Gallic part of the Continent. The military music that accompanied the brief ceremony was supplied by a British band from the Royal Armoured Corps, and after the flags were lowered it unexpectedly struck up "Charlie Is My Darling"—the wittiest, most sarcastic musical rebuke possible to the absent President de Gaulle at this farewell meeting of France's fourteen NATO military allies. In the consistent Gaullist climate of anti-Americanism that

hangs over the Fifth Republic like a very long spell of bad transatlantic weather, there were no bright flashes of gratitude expressed
in the Paris papers for the departing SHAPE group, headed for
its new quarters in Belgium, except for one long, lively contribution written by the Academician André François-Poncet, formerly
French Ambassador to West Germany. It was titled, with academic
precision, "Amica America," and it was published on the front
page of the well-regarded *Figaro,* doubtless the only Paris paper
that could have enjoyed printing it. It consisted of an illuminating
dialogue between L'Un and L'Autre, or This One and That One—
This One being anti-American and pro-Gaullist, and That One
being pro-American and not very fond of de Gaulle, and speaking
pretty clearly for the ex-Ambassador himself. The pro-American
slant in M. François-Poncet's dialogue was a rare treat for us American readers here. The article ran as follows, in part:

> THIS ONE: The ceremonies that marked the definite rup-
> ture between France and NATO were highly dignified. Allied
> headquarters at Rocquencourt closed its doors. Handshakes
> and courteous military salutes. General de Gaulle had already
> given the Grand Cross of the Legion of Honor to the Ameri-
> can General Lemnitzer and kissed him on both cheeks. No
> bitter words. Everything went off very nicely.
>
> THAT ONE: That's official propaganda. In reality, the
> Americans left shocked and embittered. They are still asking
> themselves what they did to be thrown out of a country that,
> essentially, they helped liberate and in which the graves of
> their soldiers killed in our cause can be counted by the thou-
> sand.
>
> THIS ONE: Just the same, the Americans are foreigners,
> and it's not normal for a foreign power to maintain a military
> garrison in a country not its own.
>
> THAT ONE: The Americans installed their military base
> here because we asked them to, as friends, in the defense of a
> free world.
>
> THIS ONE: In relation to America, we were living in a
> state of dependence. De Gaulle has restored French independ-
> ence.
>
> THAT ONE: Now you've said a mouthful! Just what the
> Gaullists said during their election campaign! But they never
> told us what this dependence consisted of. When the Ameri-

cans gave us the Marshall Plan, did they demand any humiliating exchanges for it?

THIS ONE: You forget that it took them two years to come to our aid in both World Wars. They left us on the shelf at Yalta and were flatly against us at Suez.

THAT ONE: There's both truth and falsehood in what you say. They were against any intervention, yet their Army crossed the Atlantic and was ready to fight with a will as soon as it landed. As for Yalta, what did France look like then? Whom was she following? Pétain, de Gaulle, Giraud, or the Communists? Only Churchill had faith in us. It's true that Suez was a hard blow. It's odd that whenever this subject comes up you insist more on the American responsibility for it than on the Soviet veto, though that was accompanied by an explicit threat of war. However well-founded your criticisms of America may be, they will never free us of the debt we owe the country that saved our lives. In the range of human sentiments, individual or collective, loyalty ranks highest, ingratitude lowest. It is painful that our country places itself on this lowest level. What good has it done us to carry on this remorseless, systematic anti-American campaign?

THIS ONE: You say we have destroyed America's friendship for us. If the Americans were as offended as you say, General Lemnitzer would not have accepted being decorated and embraced by General de Gaulle.

THAT ONE: A ribbon of honor on the breast does not erase the mark of a kick on the backside. The Americans accepted because they did not want to worsen things by making a scandal. They happen to think that General de Gaulle and Gaullism are not eternal. Until things change, they are determined not to deepen between the two countries a chasm that they hope one day will no longer exist. May that day come soon! This is my wish and the wish of thousands of Frenchmen.

That One's fervent closing words are probably true, too.

April 20

Twenty-five coastal villages in two major Brittany departments—Côtes du Nord and Finistère—have been officially declared devastated areas, because of the destruction they have suffered

from what the seafaring population there has called *la marée noire,*
meaning the floating sheets of oil from the wrecked carcass of the
Torrey Canyon. One of these oily shrouds, fifty kilometres long,
has been reported by naval air observers to have, fortunately, set
out Saturday evening for the Atlantic, propelled by heaven-sent
northeast winds. "A means of dealing with these navigating masses
of oil has not yet been discovered," General de Gaulle's new Minister of Information confessed. He added that the new government
will make a declaration on the subject, to be followed by a debate
on April 25th—which does not seem too soon, considering that fifty
Breton deputies are now demanding that what has happened to
their coast be considered a national catastrophe. At least, the nation
will be asked, through Parliament, to help pay for it by voting
credits to owners of oyster beds and mussel and clam farms ruined
by the oil, to fishermen who cannot sell their catches, and to the
Breton hotelkeepers, if their beaches—some of which have sands a
foot deep in oil—and the picturesque pink granite rocks, like those
near Paimpol, cannot be cleared of their thick, glutinous black coat-
ing before the holiday season begins. Probably only Nature herself,
with fog and rains, can really cleanse the rocks, over the years. The
damage was done in four days, during which the government
dawdled parsimoniously while trying to decide whether to mobilize
the Army (always a costly move) and even whether to set aside
fifteen million francs for equipment—though at first someone forgot to include rubber boots for the soldiers on the filthy beaches.
Now the long stretches of Brittany sands look like what one reporter
called "a nightmare beach picnic," with local men and women and
the bigger children, and the soldiers—five or six thousand of them,
the infantry armed with shovels, the engineers from the École
Nationale des Ponts et Chaussées with their trucks, and even the
sapeurs-pompiers with their high-powered fire hoses—all darkly
smeared on their faces and hands with the stinking, petrol-per-
fumed unguent, gathering up the oil, inch by inch and mile by
mile, into pails and hauling it away to wreck nearby quarries. Of
all the press photographs of laborious courage, the most affecting
was of an old Breton woman, wearing steel spectacles, trousers, a
kitchen apron, and rubber boots, with a scarf tied over her meagre
skull, scooping up the black muck in a frying pan as if it were the

makings of some hellish omelette.

The beds of the Belon oysters, the most costly and refined in Europe, have apparently been saved. Otherwise, the losses are generally heavy. For example, nearly three thousand acres of excellent, more ordinary oysters are reported ruined in the estuary of the little Jaudy River. But the greatest loss is the loss of faith created by the bitterness of the Bretons because the Paris government waited until beyond the last minute to start saving them from what the Cornwall fishermen had warned three weeks earlier might happen to the Cherbourg peninsula. Brittany is a poorly populated region, which gets its livelihood from the ocean and summer visitors, and without government aid many Breton families now face ruin. They are ranked as the most pious population of France, and on a Sunday their small, ancient Romanesque gray stone churches in fishing villages are filled with women dressed in black Sabbatical mourning below their varied medieval white starched headgear—widows, mostly, since the Breton men depend on the sea for their living and habitually perish there. The older Breton villagers in Finistère still speak no French at all, and around the cottages all the generations even today still speak Breton together. Proud of their Celtic race and language, they have always been the least assimilated of French provincials. Just before the war, there was a revival of the fanatical autonomy movement called, in Breton, Breiz Atao, meaning Brittany Forever, whose goal was actually secession from France and an independent Breton state. During the war, the Germans even offered to send Breton war prisoners back home as liberated non-Frenchmen if they would renounce their French citizenship. In the present disaster, the old Celtic feeling of being outsiders in France has risen again like bile, because of the government's delay in fighting the oil. Reporters have quoted graffiti scrawled on Finistère seawalls saying, "Paris doesn't give a fig about what happens to Brittany"—expressed more coarsely, as might be expected.

The real lost ones up there are the seabirds, of value only to the balance of nature. An estimated twenty-five thousand of them perished last week—rendered flightless by the oil on their feathers and waterlogged, drowned, starved, poisoned, or chilled to death. They were almost the entire population of the largest bird sanctuary in this part of Europe—on the Île Rouzic, offshore from Perros-Guirec, near Lannion. The present loss also stretches into the future, since this is the sanctuary nesting season for the cormorants, guillemots, and penguins, and for the only colony in France of the rare puffins, now feared completely wiped out. Local ornithologists calculate that all the birds of the sanctuary are probably doomed, though an *hôpital des oiseaux* has been set up on the pier at Perros-Guirec by the Ligue Française de Protection des Oiseaux. There the birds that the children have picked up inert but still alive are brought for salvation. This includes first putting an elastic band around their beaks, so they don't nip a thumb off their saviors, then cramming them with dead fish (which they don't like, since at liberty they skim living food from the waves), and giving them salt water to drink and milk as a detoxicant against the oil they have swallowed. They are cleaned feather by feather with a fine paintbrush and covered with talcum, the while being handled with great care, since their bones break easily when touched, as they do not under gale winds. The birds are kept warm at a temperature of about a hundred degrees, since all that is really known of such sacrificial birds is that at a body temperature of eighty-five degrees they die of chill. Only one bird in ten brought alive to the bird hospital survives.

Though last Tuesday's first new parliamentary session of the Gaullist government was thought by some visionaries to constitute a certain premature portrait of post-Gaullism, in this Tuesday's National Assembly the verbal violence and belligerence of the new Opposition, led by François Mitterrand, chief of the Federation of the Left, looked back rather than forward, as if parliamentary history were seeing and listening to over its shoulder what it so often saw and heard and was mauled by, thirty or forty years ago, in the bellicose Assembly practices of the Third Republic. "He was excellent," some of the old parliamentary gossips said of Mitterrand afterward, exactly as if they were speaking of a leading débutant actor in a new spectacle, which in a way this was. Mitterrand's quick talent for composing and speaking his explosive lines, the melodramatic atmosphere of a single attacker against a roster of established power furnished the mixed excitement of drama and reality, and also announced the presence of a third element—a complete change in the atmosphere of the Chamber. How long the new anti-government aspirations can last at such a pitch, how often Mitterrand can repeat his success with his polemics, and even how long polemics can wear well as political weapons in a France that over nearly nine years has become trained to a government of stately intellectualized political practices, in which only one highly intelligent, academic voice and one inspired mind, projected by de Gaulle, have established their rarefied influence—these are questions so insolubly French that only time will supply, even for Parisians, any notion of what the answers may be.

After Premier Pompidou made his opening policy speech, clearly restricted more or less to what he had said for five years, though with social reforms included that would certainly be new—a limited Premier, since the choice, new Fifth Republic creations, whatever they may be, must be left for de Gaulle's announcing, in his coming press conference—Mitterrand, on the speaker's tribune, leaned forward to the attack, a nervous, incisive speaker, lean-jawed, with quick, watchful eyes and, for a Frenchman, very quiet hands, making few gestures. In his first sentence, he defended the people's protest against "personal power" and against "a majority that since the shock of the recent elections, on the night of the twelfth and thirteenth of March, seemed stricken with amnesia to such a point as to have forgotten that it had lost its strength and its hopes." He added, "You are a government in *résidence surveillée*" —meaning captive under lock and key, the key being held by de Gaulle. Mitterrand's sharp, bold insults in well-chosen clichés aroused his partisans in the Opposition to gusts of laughter and applause. His speech soon became an open attack on General de Gaulle himself. Mitterrand inquired if de Gaulle had had the right, as chief of a political party that his constitution does not recognize, to intervene in the electoral campaign by exceeding the legal privileges, this being a reference to his having talked on TV the night after the polls closed on Friday, an infringement still so ill received by many that the question raised a murmur over many of the Parliament benches. "And what did it lead to? A majority that has to count on its fingers to be sure it really is a majority." He then openly accused the government of electoral frauds in Martinique and Guadeloupe, from which helpful votes came in belatedly. "The strikes over the last fifty days prove that for the past five years you have had no answer ready for the French workers. We are living already in the post-Gaullist era," he said, in final accusation, to Premier Pompidou, sitting without visible reaction on the government front bench. "Your policy speech at no point included a definition of national solidarity or of international security, or of justice or progress. But the country knows that justice and progress are not to be expected—from your government." From his Federation of the Left, the Communists, and even some of the center group now called Progress and Democracy, though its majority supposedly affords the Gaullists the extra voting aid they vitally need, Mitterand received an ovation, which carried him from the speaker's tribune down to his party seat in the hemicycle.

This is the first bareknuckle verbal attack that the de Gaulle government has sustained in its close to nine years of grave, undisputed, and relatively calm power. As *Le Monde* said of Mitterrand after his speech, "The man knows how to bite and insult." These abilities were among the political gifts that animated the Third Republic's struggles—the endless, vituperative rising and falling of its governments, its scandals and power battles. Several other newspapers cited the famous retort of President Poincaré to a deputy in Parliament, to whom he said in cold fury, "Monsieur, you are nothing but an abominable scoundrel." If in France's ultimate post-Gaullist era, when the General for one reason or another leaves the scene, France has to proceed toward its Sixth Republic by way of a detour through elements of its Third Republic, it will be an almost incomprehensible step in the wrong direction.

May 3

That General de Gaulle, the Saint-Germain-des-Prés Existentialist Jean-Paul Sartre, the Cambridge University mathematical genius Bertrand Russell, the Swedish government, and the American Army fighting in Vietnam could all be involved with one another to the point of being recently linked in the same international-news paragraphs here in Paris seems one of the more

anomalous minor developments of our war in Asia. The strange
mixture was opened up last week by de Gaulle himself in a private
letter to Sartre as French executive president of the Russell Tribunal—a letter the government made public as if it were a state paper.
In truth, this is what it functioned as, despite its inclusion of de
Gaulle's humorous, caustic reference to the borrowed togas in which
the tribunal members seemed to him theoretically to be draping
themselves in preparation for their opening meeting in France—
which, in the next-to-last paragraph of this now famous letter, de
Gaulle flatly prohibited. Handed out to the press by the Élysée and
published by the newspapers over the length and breadth of France,
the letter was naturally read by the entire nation with special
interest and curiosity, because, for one thing, a personal letter by
de Gaulle in the public domain is a rarity and an item not to miss.
Secondly, its literary involvement, because it was written to Sartre,
gave added esoteric flavor. Furthermore, the letter was highly entertaining, insofar as it made quite clear that de Gaulle and Sartre,
the two most powerful intellectual individualists in the Republic,
were finally at loggerheads—stimulating, titillating, and even promising news to the French public, which over centuries has always
been gluttonously nourished by dissensions and disagreements. The
big note of disappointment in the whole fracas (settled when the
Russell group was unenthusiastically accepted by Stockholm) came
from the tribunal's first choice of a site—Issy-les-Moulineaux, still
recalled by Paris art collectors as the nearby little town where
Matisse lived and painted some of his early great pictures—a town
now grown weighty and politically famed as one of the most Communist of all the Paris working-class suburbs. It had planned a
hearty welcome to the Russell Tribunal, whose view of America's
Vietnam war as a crime against civilization the Issy population already shared, that being the familiar Moscow propaganda line—
and also officially held (or something very close to it) by de Gaulle
himself and his Fifth Republic government, as he candidly pointed
out in that famous letter to *"Mon cher Maître,"* Sartre. "I am only
maître to café waiters, who know I write," Sartre stated categorically
in his answer to de Gaulle, which he did not hand to the press.
Instead, he gave it uniquely to the leading French leftist weekly
Le Nouvel Observateur, which came out last week with photostats

of de Gaulle's letter, titled "Une Lettre de de Gaulle à Sartre," followed by "La Réponse de Sartre à de Gaulle."

Unfortunately, this response was in the form not of a well-written epistle but of what seemed to be a tape-recorded semi-interview—lengthy and rather hit-or-miss but of obvious great interest when Sartre said what was uppermost in his mind, often with slashing, intemperate attacks on de Gaulle. For example, Sartre stated why he thought the Russell Tribunal had suddenly been denied permission to hold its opening meeting in France—permission that, he claimed, had earlier been implicitly accorded. "It is very likely that when Vice-President Humphrey met de Gaulle a fortnight ago, Humphrey insisted on the importance the Americans attached to the tribunal's not being allowed to sit in France," Sartre astonishingly declared. "The American methods of blackmail are numerous, despite France's so-called independence. The French economy is not less and less tied to that of America, as we are made to think, but more and more. For instance, if the Americans ceased leasing their giant computers to France, it would be enough to disorganize our entire economy." Sartre was particularly scathing in his descriptions of what he considered de Gaulle's deforming ideas of justice and political power, and his willful isolation from the country he governs. "According to him, government should not be based on the country but should remain aloof above it," Sartre declared. "His system of criticizing the American policy in Vietnam in what he says while forbidding the French people to demonstrate against the Vietnam war is absolutely anti-democratic . . . . It perfectly illustrates Gaullism itself—the Chief has his own ideas on Vietnam, and occasionally expresses them in his speeches . . . but above all he does not want his views popularized and upheld by the mass of the French people, because that would tie him to the populace, a relation that basically he abhors."

Getting back to the Russell Tribunal, Sartre said that its members' aim in France had been "to see if public opinion felt as the tribunal does about the use of napalm and fragmentation bombs." He added that when de Gaulle invoked *"l'amitié traditionnelle,"* which he declared still ties France to the United States, as a reason for not permitting the Russell Tribunal to meet on French territory, "the real truth is that when it comes to judging from a moral standpoint, governments stick together, there being a concerted effort among them to suppress morality in politics." When asked by his interviewer where the Russell Tribunal would really be welcome to sit today, he said, thinking it over, "Perhaps on a boat anchored outside territorial waters, like the English radio pirates. . . . Paradoxically, it is the difficulties we have met that establish the legitimacy of the tribunal and, furthermore, prove something— that we are *feared*. This does not mean Bertrand Russell himself, who is ninety-four years old, and certainly not me, at the age of sixty-two, or our friends, either. If we were only a handful of intellectual simpletons ridiculously pretending to set ourselves up as judges, they would let us do it and not bother us. So why are they afraid of us? Because," Sartre answered his own question, "we raise a problem that no Western government wants to face—that of the crime of making war, which once more everyone wants preserved, so that he may use it."

For many years, there was a Paris tradition that, for aesthetic reasons, no new building would be permitted by the municipality to be higher than the top of the Arc de Triomphe, already considered extremely tall at a hundred and sixty-five feet when it was completed, in 1836. During the month of April, the Prefecture of the Seine gave a favorable reception to a request for the construction on the Left Bank of the Tour Maine-Montparnasse, which will be fifty-three stories and almost six hundred feet high. It will be in the form of a plain pillar, squarish but with rounded corners— mere bulk and not fancy. This new project has been bitterly debated pro and con for the past ten years, owing to the splendid resistance against it of M. Édouard Frédéric-Dupont, longtime municipal councillor of Paris and deputy from the Seventh Arrondissement, which includes the Invalides, to which he is personally deeply attached as a pure example of pure Louis XIV style, and whose symmetries he has fought to preserve from the contamination of having any *newyorkesque* skyscraper close enough behind it on the horizon to be included in his *vue optique* from the Esplanade. He is, of course, artistically right at a time in modern Paris history when the builders of the whole Maine-Montparnasse complex can afford only to be wrong, since without the tower their investment as a whole will fail to pay. Besides its more than three million square feet of office space, it will contain a de-luxe hotel of two hundred and fifty rooms, perhaps a heliport on the roof, and certainly parking space down below for at least fifteen hundred cars. With good fortune, it will be ready for occupancy in 1971. The only Paris urban expressway, to be named for Vercingetorix (born about 72 B.C. and almost always portrayed on top of a horse), will pass the new building and eventually head west. This is the direction that the new Paris is destined to follow, passing the Rond Point de la Défense and pushing on toward Saint-Germain-en-Laye, toward which the Paris Métro has already, for the past year, been grubbing its way, having just completed three miles of express tracks. Trains will finally rush toward the once campestral Saint-Germain at sixty miles an hour on rubber-tired wheels. Already the Défense community is being rapidly built up with thirty-story skyscrapers for rich industrial companies' offices. All over Paris, minor skyscrapers of twenty stories are pushing up among the still viable, elegant architectural remnants of the Second Empire or the Directoire, and even of the tentative Third Republic, thus bastardizing what is left of the varied but consecutive style and beauty of Paris and its open horizons. The Place de la Concorde is now cleared of the machines that have been working for nearly two years on the underpass that will carry eastbound traffic far beyond the Louvre. But the charming aerial toboggan, as the French call the temporary elevated highway over the diggings, which careers like a roller coaster among the spring-green treetops along the Seine, is still carrying its double lane of oneway traffic, swooping over the bridge entrances en route—the gayest, most eccentric riverine excursion Paris has ever known, which will be long regretted and remembered after it is dismantled this autumn.

May 18

In a well-known ritual in his biannual press conference (or his speech to his nation and to the world), given in the gilded, chandelier-hung Salle des Fêtes in the Presidential Palais de l'Élysée, General de Gaulle always begins by greeting his auditor guests and begging them to be seated; then he invariably asks, as if in a familiar prologue to an amateur playlet, if there are any questions anyone wishes to ask—a cue to three or four selected leading journalists to make a brief inquiry into some important topic that, it is known in advance, the General will speak on in any case. At Tuesday's meeting, an unknown, unchosen questioner hastily rose and for three or four minutes presented a rambling, incoherent series of queries of such lunacy and length that most of them were lost in the audience's uproar of surprised laughter—the first time there has ever been such a comedy interlude. In the unexpected situation, de Gaulle was impeccable. His face relaxing into an attentive smile, he heard the incoherence through to its end and then said, with loud, quick courtesy, "Monsieur, I thank you for your press conference!" The riposte was so pat, the irony and majestic reprimand were such good theatre, that a hum of approval ran through the audience. The rest of the session, in which he himself talked for an hour and twenty minutes—he always recites from the vast, freshly stored resources of his memory—was, on the whole, rather dry with logic, contained flashes of paternal pride in an opening section devoted to France's postwar reconstruction, displayed some academic brilliance on foreign affairs, and then (his oration becoming a little painful and quasi-affectionate) devoted close to a half hour to saying no, or his elaborate version or evasion of that monosyllable, to Great Britain's recent request to be admitted to the Common Market. De Gaulle's advancing age could be heard in his voice, not seen in his face. He looks as he did last year, but the calendar was audible. The vocal sound was a little older, with, at moments, a certain lack, or break, in his famous sostenuto.

The General's opening words significantly made clear the blow to his pride he had received in the poor support his Fifth Republic Party had got from the French voters in the March election, when, for the first time in his presidency, he faced (as he still faces) a dangerously strong opposition in the Federation of the Left. "Had this opposition been able to obtain from Frenchmen a negative majority," de Gaulle said (and heaven knows it came close), "and the submission, or resignation, of the President of the Republic through its legislative obstruction, the government of

France would once again have been merely a kaleidoscopic distribution of portfolios, a constantly changing and powerful combination of rivalries"—this last reference delivered with the passionate contempt he reserves for France's multi-party politics, which brought the country so low that only he was able to save it. "What could the devotees of Moscow and those with a nostalgia for Washington have accomplished?" he asked disparagingly. "To strike down the Fifth Republic by striking its head" (meaning himself) was the common aim of all the opposition, de Gaulle declared bitterly, knowing he spoke the truth. "The Fifth Republic finds a National Assembly where, it would appear, a positive majority exists," he said in an easier tone, using candor almost as a form of humor, which he does on occasion. This reference to the Gaullist majority, which consists of two deputies in the Chamber, made the journalists smile with embarrassment, as if somebody who used to be rich had come down in the world and had publicly drawn attention to his new poverty. His reference to Valéry Giscard d'Estaing and his so-called Independent Republicans (who are really the young technocrat, splinter-group Gaullists) was far more covert and much less genial. De Gaulle said that any effort to weaken this majority made by anyone who had been elected under his banner would "evidently be contrary to the public interest and to public morality"—a very severe slap indeed at young Giscard. In his foreign-affairs references, after congratulating France on maintaining her independence and signalling the fact that in Europe West and East were gradually practicing a relaxation of tension, the General added that "in Asia the scandal of foreign intervention should cease"—meaning, of course, America's Vietnam war.

When the General finally got around to the all-important topic of England and said, "Dear friends, now at long last I am going to answer your question about Britain and the Common Market," his affability instantly tipped off his listeners to the fact that his answer to the island's request to be considered a valid relation of Europe would be no, as expected. "I will start by saying that the movement which seems at present to be leading England to link herself to Europe instead of keeping herself apart [and here he used a poetic, inventive phrase, *au lieu de se tenir au large,* which could be translated, perhaps, as "instead of keeping her distance at sea"] is a movement which can only please France." With strict logic—or so most journalists thought—he then gave the several reasons that make France unable to embrace London's offer "until England has undergone a profound transformation." And on this note his speech came to its close.

Two mornings later, on *Figaro*'s Thursday front page, appeared one of its witty, pertinently impertinent little editorial comments by André Frossard, who said, "England remains an island. I received this news Tuesday at the Élysée with a certain relief. Ever since there has been a question of mooring England to the Continent, I have been seized with retrospective horror at the thought of what would have happened in 1940 if she had been really secured to terra firma to such a point as not to be able to pull herself away in time. The world, in my opinion, needs England just as she is, like a big fine ship floating at a nice good distance from our shores, far enough not to be captured by surprise, close enough to leave us with the hope of eventually climbing on board, capable of what is forbidden to us by the nature of geographic laws, which are what they are. . . . In brief, we need an England that is always in condition to keep her freedom, for the reason that sometimes ours depends on it."

On Wednesday, France underwent the greatest strike by the greatest number of strikers—it really began Tuesday night, at dinnertime—that the country has apparently ever known, and the most peaceful. It may be the only strike in which no Paris policeman was seen to raise a club and no striker was seen to heave a stone or shout an insult. There are an estimated twenty million workers in France, and half of them struck; here in Paris a hundred and fifty thousand paraded for three hours, in a jam from the Place de la Bastille to the Place de la République, carrying placards and streamers saying, "No to government by decree" and "Down with Pompidou." This was not a strike for wages but a purely political strike for purely political reasons. It was a protest strike by the proletariat and many intellectuals against the Government's announced project of legislating financial problems till the end of October by decree, thus bypassing Parliament for the seventh time in seven different years of the Fifth Republic, as de Gaulle himself announced, with calm. The strike was called by the main labor unions, which thus assumed the power of political associations. Paris was paralyzed. Only the sun and the moon continued their movements, and the wretched citizens caught on the streets that afternoon in one of the intemperate downpours that always seem to accompany strikes in which people have no transportation except their legs. Today, the motion of censure against the Pompidou Government will be brought up in Parliament, but neither the Government nor the opposition desires the Government to fall, with the Parliament only newly elected and so much more power to be seized or hoped for or retrieved with reforms by all the newly elected deputies. Tomorrow may prove a preliminary test of strength, because Pierre Mendès-France, standing with the opposition, is making his return to France's political life in a pro-opposition speech, after an exile of nearly a decade. With the strike, France has begun to run a slightly raised political temperature, if only by contagion from the rest of the world, where news from all capitals tends to be alarmingly feverish.

June 1

It seems odd that the most popular among the new books recently published here have assumed less significance than the phenomenon of the old books that are being republished. The Cercle du Bibliophile has just brought out a new edition of the complete works of Stendhal, but its biggest success is with the republishing of Victor Hugo, in forty volumes, and next in popularity is the Club du Livre Français' reissue of Balzac. The most widespread revival has been that of Zola. Four separate editions of his works are now about to come off the presses. The most ambitious and luxurious will be the forty-volume edition of his complete works being brought out in scarlet leather by the Cercle du Bibliophile, each volume containing ten pen-and-ink drawings by the artist who signs himself Tim. They are like black-and-white silhouettes perceived in the dim gaslight of poverty and shadowed by brutality. It will be remembered that Tim also illustrated Kafka's novels. He is almost the only artist now working here as an illustrator of the sort of fine books that were a consistent literary accomplishment in de-luxe French publishing in the old days, examples of which still figure as precious items in auction sales. For instance, from the famous private library of the elderly Dr. A. Roudinesco, to be sold, in part, this week at the Hôtel Drouot, there is a copy of "Parallèlement," by Verlaine, illustrated by Bonnard, then an unknown artist, which the Doctor by chance purchased when he came from Bucharest to Paris as a young medical student. This volume is expected to fetch around three hundred thousand francs, or sixty thousand dollars. Under the imprimatur of Rencontre, another Zola edition is being printed, in twenty-four volumes, and the Cercle du Livre Précieux is publishing his complete works in fifteen volumes, which will include documents of the period, correspondence, and some hitherto unpublished manuscripts. Also, the well-known Bibliothèque de la Pléiade is now finishing its five-volume critics' edition of Zola's famous scandalizing serial novel, "Les Rougon-Macquart," which he bitterly called *l'histoire naturelle et sociale d'une famille sous le Second Empire."* There is also a cheap paperback edition of Zola, in about twenty volumes, which has been extremely popular with young French readers, for whom he has become the favorite nineteenth-century novelist, with Balzac and Hugo left to one side. When one thinks of how shocking and revolting Zola's earnest sociological realism seemed to the bourgeoisie when his novels were first published, and how démodé middle-class French adults find them now, it is extraordinary that the French young read them with passion, like reading terrible true stories of their great-grandfathers' lives and times. The realism of the brutality, drunkenness, and lasciviousness of the Napoleonic Second Empire—so familiar then to the bourgeoisie but considered so scandalous and shocking when Zola put them in print—furnishes raw meat to satisfy youth's appetite today for violence. That both young and old French readers have gone back, at least temporarily, to the nineteenth-century novels of French literary genius certainly indicates a kind of reader rebellion against current French fiction. One of the Paris literary weeklies has just inquired again, in a long article, "Is the French novel of today dead?" Even raising the question so often indicates that it is at least pretty sick.

June 14

Because General de Gaulle founded his career
and the salvation of contemporary France on his gift for the public
spoken word—it will be twenty-seven years this coming Sunday
since that eighteenth of June, 1940, when, as an unknown, he
singularly introduced himself to history by stating over the London
B.B.C., *"Moi, Général de Gaulle, actuellement à Londres, j'invite
les officiers et les soldats français . . ."*—and because, in his unique,
influential verbal style, he has been speaking on the air to millions
of listeners ever since, his silence during the recent alarming six-day
Israeli-Arab war attracted great attention. In the international
confusions, power ploys, and mixed human affections or hatreds felt
for Jews or for Arabs, plus left and right political emotions, all of
which were influential on today's Catholic French mentality, the
French people had to make up their minds for themselves as to
what to think of it all. The only official guidance they received was
slight and very second-hand, passed on by de Gaulle's Minister of
Information after a Conseil des Ministres, presided over by de
Gaulle himself. In the opening sample of this guidance, the Minister prolixly and tautologically divulged to the Paris press, "France
is favorable to a basic settlement that will tend to lead to a true
peace and to a settlement of the Israeli-Arab problems, and not to a
mere sealing off of difficulties that would only delay new ulterior
difficulties from making their appearance"—an idea that de Gaulle
himself would certainly have stated with more enlightening clarity
or else with much richer ambiguity. This official government-
released news was, in the case of *Figaro,* printed not on the front
page but on an inner page under an apparently irrelevant headline
in huge type, "THE GREEN TELEPHONE FUNCTIONED."
And, sure enough, in the scant accompanying text came the news
that the General had "revealed to the Ministerial Council" that he
had been in personal communication with Kosygin on June 5th
and 6th. *Le Monde* reported that "the green phone functioned perfectly," adding, for the benefit of all its readers who happened to
be science-fiction fans, that the instrument was not really a phone

but a teletype that operated on a double circuit, one cable and the other radio. Foolishly asked by the Paris press what Kosygin and de Gaulle had talked about, the Minister discreetly refused to reply but, in a burst of confidence, gave a bloodcurdling revelation that "what seemed rather remarkable was that the great powers"—France, Russia, England, and the United States—"who had more or less refused to make close contacts with each other before the hostilities broke out, spontaneously got in touch as soon as the war became a reality."

An influential source for further confusion and split in the French reaction on the Middle East war lay in the fact that the French Communists, who comprise about a fifth of the most politically minded portion of the population here, loyally followed the Soviet line and were thus pro-Nasser and pro-Arab. The rest of the French, possibly as a belated form of generalized European guilt felt for the fate of the masses of European Jews lost in the horrors of the German crematories, were overwhelmingly pro-Israel, especially after Nasser's insane promise to wipe Israel's two and a half million Jews off the earth of the Holy Land. The Secretary General of the Communist Party, M. Waldeck Rochet, last week gave a speech on the Middle East tension that was reported in his party's daily paper, *Humanité,* in which he said, "In France, a violent anti-Arab campaign has broken out in relation to the State of Israel's right to exist. . . . Our party has always fought racism and anti-Semitism. Thousands of militant Communists in the Nazi concentration camps perished at the side of the thousands and thousands of Jews, also condemned by Hitler. But the fact of recognizing Israel's right to exist and of fighting against anti-Semitism does not oblige us to approve of the anti-Arab policy being dangerously practiced at present by the Israeli government. In fact, we consider that in lending itself to the maneuvers of American capitalism in the hope of imposing its own demands, today's Israeli government has put the security of its own country in a dangerous situation." He concluded with an indignant flourish, as if Washington had been about to launch another unpopular Eastern foreign war for our soldiers to fight in, "It is not merely by chance that today the United States threatens to intervene with force against the United Arab Republic and the Arab peoples' struggle for independence."

On the other hand, the New York *Times* was reported by *Le Monde*'s United Nations correspondent as having stated that "President de Gaulle is apparently willing to throw Israel to the Egyptian sharks." From Tel Aviv itself came the report that the Israelis were "very bitter at the neutrality of the French," with whom they thought they had enjoyed over the years an informal, friendly alliance that was still operative. Were the Egyptians at this moment in any shape to protest about anything at all, Paris Middle East experts suppose that Cairo, too, might well be complaining—in its case, about Moscow's failure to give any important support to the Arab cause during this last fortnight.

Israel's victory has, in spite of everything, been a piece of very good luck indeed for the Gaullist party, and certainly a stroke of good fortune for de Gaulle himself, since foreign affairs are his exclusive concern. And certainly his must have been the decisive voice in the only official statement of government policy made by the Conseil des Ministres, on June 2nd, when the war was about to break—"France is not committed, in any way or on any subject, to any of the states involved." Masses of Gaullists were shocked at what was immediately called his neutralization of France in a time of war between Israel and the Arabs, when the Gaullists felt that France could not, with morality, be neutral about the Jews. There was also the feeling on the part of most of the French that the escaped Jews, having made Israel their abode, should not be betrayed again, and this time by someone they had counted on to stand by them as a friend.

Apparently, the top Gaullist most familiar with de Gaulle's use of neutralism as a doctrinal resource was Premier Pompidou. He had already made a speech about it some time ago, doubtless at de Gaulle's demand and probably so as to put the idea into circulation without anyone's paying much attention to it, because de Gaulle wanted to insert it into history when the right time came. "In this dangerous world," Pompidou said in his speech, "in which the great powers have endless, incalculable strength at their disposal, there must be one voice that can be lifted for the right of nations, no matter how feeble they are, to answer for themselves and say what they want to say about their own destiny"—presumably, whether they get their wish or not. France has, it seems, on de Gaulle's decision, become that single voice, which will naturally give her a unique new importance, if anyone is listening. On de Gaulle's theory of neutralization, an explicit, if puzzling, article with the semi-ironic title "Why de Gaulle Dropped Israel" was published in last week's *Nouvel Observateur,* which analyzes the General's theories, beginning at the beginning: "After having disposed of the Algerian war, after having given independence to the major part of the French empire, de Gaulle's France could claim to have no more colonial or imperialistic ties, and could thus make herself the apostle of coöperation and represent *les petites nations,"* for whom no one normally speaks and who rarely get a chance to speak for themselves. In the world of the little nations, his doctrinaire neutralism seems to de Gaulle to be "the only manner of escape for them—and, indeed, for the entire world—from the blows that are dealt society by the power struggle between the Americans and the Soviet Union," whose "concerted hegemony is a yoke" equally to be resisted, if possible. In his pessimistic wisdom, the article adds, he feels that Russian-American agreements would be almost as dangerous for the world as Russian-American disagreements.

November 1

The big event here in book publishing and reading is the enormous, six-hundred-page volume called "Antimémoires," by André Malraux, General de Gaulle's Minister of Culture. During twenty years of writing, he became the author of what the French now count as six and a half novels. (The Nazis destroyed in manuscript the last half of what would have been the seventh, published as a mutilated fragment.) One of his novels, "Man's Hope," about his experiences as a bomber with the ill-equipped anti-Franco Loyalist aviators, who threw their bombs at the enemy by hand, was made by him into an epic film. He also published several tomes about his complex reasonings on the metamorphoses of art. But it was his celebrity in 1933 as the young author of "Man's Fate" ("La Condition Humaine"), on the Communist revolution starting in China, where he was then living, that made him world famous and gave him his empire over the intelligentsia of French youth. They are now middle-aged yet apparently still susceptible at least to curiosity about his book of so-called non-memoirs, since it has become a best-seller. Today, Malraux, a well-known, multi-sided personality, like repeated portraits of himself incumbent in different offices and stages, still fascinates the French as no other figure. He is thought of as the last romantic. He is recognized as Malraux the young, adventurous art-treasure hunter in the Far East, the early experimental Communist propagandist in Canton, the indomitable warrior for freedoms in Europe, the man of action as a Compagnon de la Libération in France, and the country's most powerful art lover and mover, who presumed to send the Louvre's Venus de Milo to Tokyo.

Malraux's epigraph for his new book is a typically bizarre, humorous, exotic analogy as an explanation of why he ceased to be a writer for so many years. On the first page of his book, he cites a Buddhist text reading, "The elephant is the wisest of all animals, the only one that recalls its earlier lives. Thus it remains quiet for long periods, meditating upon them." From his own meditation Malraux emerges to say in his preface that his non-memoirs contain no confessional materials, since today they would be puerile "compared to the monsters brought forth by psychoanalytical explorations." He also states sombrely, "Man finds the likeness of himself in the questions that he asks. The man you will find in this book is one who agrees with the questions that death asks about the significance of the world." As is well known, death is for Malraux the imagined companion of his mature life, with whom he holds dialogues, more or less, in all his books. A special foreword gives death a positive editorial function in relation to the publication of this new volume, stating that it is only part of an opus that may well include three more volumes, to be published integrally only after the author is dead.

The currently published portion was written as the result of a journey, ironically counselled by Malraux's physicians as a rest cure, two years ago. This took him back to parts of the Orient that he had known in his youth and probably emotionally engendered the present volume, which contains a heterogeneous reassembling of a whole Malraux library of the basic verities. Exceptional in the book are the happy accounts of his repeated visits to the Cairo Museum and the Sphinx, from whom, since the first time he saw her, has flowed an inspiration for his affection for multiple non-Christian gods and antique art, as if she, with her cat paws in the sand (Malraux is a noted cat-lover), represented the stony pet that symbolized art itself for civilized human beings of old, with her immortal answers to questions forever insoluble in the dry desert air.

For American readers of "Antimémoires," the most interesting new elements will be Malraux's great interviews with two of the latest national Eastern leaders—Nehru, now gone, and Mao, now ill. As a writer who has helped make history and is possessed of acute presbyopic political eyesight, which has often enough seen history coming, Malraux, being a novelist, is an incomparable reporter when dealing with heroic historic figures on whom he turns his listening ears and observant eyes. In Nehru's office in New Delhi, the two men of good will, who had last met more than twenty years before, sat at a table of polished precious wood, in which was reflected the rose carried by the gentle chief who governed India. He read Malraux's letter of accreditation from de Gaulle and, with a smile, said, "So now you are a Minister," which Malraux translated from its Hindu background to mean "So now you are in your last incarnation." Along with the rose, Malraux saw reflected in the table Nehru's face, "of which history will save only the mask." Malraux adds, "His was a Roman visage, made a little heavy by the lower lip, which gave his smile the seductiveness that brings to a man of history an imperceptible innocence. I had known him when he had the air of a leader of the Maquis. . . . Now he showed me an ironic benevolence that was also a little weary, covering a firmness that it did not hide. Age had less aged his face than it had given him another face, as happens to many men who once looked like their mothers, and look like their fathers only when growing old. His gestures, formerly quite broad, were now directed toward his body, the fingers almost doubled up. In his gestures I saw the real difference between the Nehru of former days and my present interlocutor. Authority itself is a question of age."

Nehru did not take de Gaulle's Fifth Republic seriously, Malraux reports. But his observations were serious indeed on the decline of England, which he had known for so long as the first of the world's powers. He had watched the decline, too, of Europe, without forgetting that he had also seen Germany and Russia being reborn. Great Britain, Malraux said to him, had conceived its world policy, but not the United States. "It has become the most powerful country on earth without having wanted to be," he continued. "This was not the case with Alexander or Caesar or Tamerlane or Napoleon; their hegemonies were the consequences of conquests. That is perhaps why the United States makes war well and peace poorly." Then they started a discussion of Communism. Nehru thought it less important than formerly. He did not envision a war between Russia and the United States. Of China, he said that each time she became China again she became imperialist again. For Malraux, history over the last forty years had been the upsurge of Communism and the substitution of America for Europe. For Nehru, history had consisted of decolonization and the liberation of Asia. His state Socialism was not tied to the Soviets'. His recent history was that of the liberated underdeveloped countries, "which should change their civilization." He went on, "Science and machines in two hundred years have made a civilization very different from the one that existed at the time of the French and American Revolutions. The India that science and machines will produce in a hundred years will little resemble India today, and maybe not Europe either." For him, the Soviet Union symbolized planning. Would it prove more efficacious against famine than liberal capitalism? The maintenance of independence and the industrialization of India could be founded only on a state. Nehru was conscious of the feebleness of the state he had elaborated, "so I must reinforce it." He believed all revolutions to be inseparable from an ethical will, from a desire for justice. Social justice had proved to be India's most difficult problem. The consciousness of caste was stronger among Indians than that of class. To create modern India, he had been forced to lean indirectly on his people, associating the humblest among them with this great effort. "India must be mobilized by herself, not by government order," he said. But age-old India saw in social injustice a part of the cosmic order, which was necessarily just. He pitied India, knew its misery, but wanted it dedicated to a unique destiny—that of becoming the conscience of the world. Malraux asked him, "Since your independence, what has been your most difficult task?" "To make a just state with just means," Nehru answered in one quick breath.

The interview with Mao Tse-tung took place in 1965 in Peking in the People's Palace at three o'clock in the afternoon. This building had an odd façade of Egyptian columns with red lotuses on their capitals, and a reception room more than three hundred feet long. Among the group awaiting Malraux were Mao and the President of the Chinese Republic, Liu Shao-ch'i, to whom Malraux carried a letter from General de Gaulle. Mao's welcome was cordial, even familiar. "The entire party sat down on rattan chairs with little white doilies on their arms. It was like the waiting room in a tropical railway station," Malraux writes. He made out the face of Mao against the light: "round, smooth, young. The celebrated wart on his chin was like a Buddhist sign. A serenity all the more unexpected, since he was supposed to be a violent man. Behind him his nurse in white." (Malraux knew, although he does not state, that Mao suffers from Parkinson's disease.) The interpreter was a Tonkinese girl who spoke perfect French.

"Once the poor make up their minds to fight, they always beat the rich," Mao began, apparently without preliminaries. "Look at your French Revolution." After the coup by Chiang Kai-shek in Shanghai, which broke the Communists' rise, the Chinese Communists around Mao fell apart. "As you know," he continued, "I decided to go back to my village. In other days, I had known the great famine of Changsha, with the decapitated rebels' heads stuck on high posts, but I had forgotten. Within three kilometres of my village, when I returned, not a piece of bark was left on the trees up to a height of four metres. All had been eaten by those who were hungry. We could make better fighters out of men obliged to eat bark than out of the chauffeurs from Shanghai, or even the coolies."

"Gorky said to me one day in front of Stalin, 'Peasants are the same everywhere,'" Malraux said.

"Neither Gorky, a great vagabond poet, nor Stalin knew the slightest thing about peasants," Mao replied, adding that there was no sense mixing up kulaks with the wretched inhabitants of an underdeveloped country. Around 1919, he said, he had read the "Communist Manifesto" and had helped organize the workers—"and there were more workers than you would think in the Chinese Revolutionary Army." Those who did not go on the Long March made a mistake; Chiang Kai-shek exterminated more than a million of them. "Our people had always hated, distrusted, and feared the soldiery," Mao went on. "They soon saw that our Red Army belonged to them. No class privileges. We all ate the same, wore the same clothes. The soldiers could gather and talk. Above all, the officers hadn't the right to beat or insult them. The troops against us were more numerous, and aided by the Americans, but we often were the victors. You have to learn to make war, but it is simpler than politics. In war, you merely have to have more victories than defeats. In a certain way, the Long March was a retreat, but its result was like a conquest." He spoke bitterly of the Kuomintang and of how those suspected of disloyalty to it were buried alive—peasant women prayed to be born dogs in the next life, so as to be less wretched. "To establish fraternity more than to win liberty was the aim," Mao said. "Revolution is a passionate drama. We did not win the people by appealing to their reason but by developing hope, confidence, fraternity. Faced with famine, the drive for equality takes on a religious character."

During the interview, Mao made no gesture except to carry his cigarette to his mouth or to lay it on the ash receiver. "In his overall immobility, he did not seem a sick man but an emperor of bronze," Malraux says. When Malraux asked whether the opposition was still powerful, Mao replied, "The intellectuals' thoughts are anti-Marxist. Strategically, imperialism is doomed, and with it capitalism, beyond a doubt. Left to itself, humanity would not necessarily reëstablish Communism, but it would reëstablish inequality. You remember that Kosygin said at the Twenty-third Congress, 'Communism is a rise in living standards.' Obviously. And swimming is a way of wearing a bathing suit." He went on, "We are not eating bark, but we are only up to a bowl of rice daily. Revisionism would tear that bowl of rice from our hands. The Soviets' revisionism is an apostasy. It is the death of the revolution. I think that Russia will emerge from its Stalin regime without returning to real capitalism. Just a certain liberalism. I remember the time when you didn't talk politics to your wife. When I heard that the Russians dared make jokes about their government in the Métro, I thought there had not been just a softening of what I had known but a radical transformation." Mao believed that each intervention of the United States made it an object of hate for the poor and revolutionary majority. A new fact, he said, dominated all the political ideologies—a nuclear war would destroy all the nations engaged in it—and he declared that the United States would not use nuclear arms in Vietnam, any more than it had in Korea.

When Malraux said goodbye, Mao "put out a hand that was almost feminine, with rosy palms. To my surprise, he accompanied me, the Tonkinese interpreter between us, a little behind, and his nurse behind him. Mao walks step by step, stiff, as if he did not bend his legs—more the emperor of bronze than ever. He has not been struck down. He has the uncertain equilibrium of the statue of the Commendatore in 'Don Giovanni' and walks like a legendary figure come back from some imperial tomb."

November 15

An inappropriate and unusual modesty marked the front page of *L'Humanité,* the French Communist Party's daily paper, on Tuesday, November 7th, the fiftieth anniversary of the first day of Moscow's ten days that shook the world. Every newspaper or weekly in Paris, left or right, had printed a résumé of what the opening of the October Revolution signified in the contemporary history of the world and of Russia (and eventually of the heavens, too, where Sputnik was the first to shed its artificial pale light), and something special and extra could have been reasonably expected on that Tuesday from *L'Humanité's* outside page. What it offered looked rather like an advertisement—a red rectangle that partially filled its left-hand corner and on which was printed, in white letters considerably smaller than would be used in announcing a sale of workmen's rubber boots, *"1917–1967—Vive le 50° Anniversaire de la Révolution Socialiste d'Octobre!"* There was also a front-page editorial, titled "October in Our Hearts," which was, at first sight, little more than warmed-over milk-and-water Communist sentimentalities, written by one of the Party's minor female figures. However, she did bring up from her recollected travels in the U.S.S.R. two items that were surely news to many readers. In citing the multiple rivers of Russia, she mentioned Siberia's "long river Lena . . . which gave its name to Lenin"—in France, at least, an unfamiliar etymological explanation of how Vladimir Ilyich Ulyanov became the man history knew under a name not his own. She also mentioned the Naryn River, in Kirgizia—a small, violent, rapid stream "in which a staircase of dams was being constructed to irrigate Central Asia when I visited there last spring." She continued, "On the highest of the dams, that of Karakol, the Komsomol workmen had transformed themselves into Alpine climbers so as to cut into the rock the poetry of Mayakovsky to the glory of veritable life, that of Communism. This was their contribution to the coming fiftieth-anniversary celebration."

Page 2 of that Tuesday's *L'Humanité* carried a stenographic report of a pre-anniversary speech delivered Monday night to a packed Communist audience in the Mutualité—the shabby old left-wing hall near the Jardin des Plantes where in earlier days André Gide addressed the P.E.N. Club—by Georges Marchais, a leading member of the Party's Politburo. In it he made a remarkable statement. "Precisely because of the victory of the October Revolution," he said, and because of the recognized existence throughout the world of Socialism as a political system, along with the modifications that have arisen to meet specific situations in France, "it is clearly evident that we [the French] can turn to Socialism through other routes and under other conditions than those of the Russian Communists." On the fortieth, or even the forty-fifth, anniversary of the October Revolution, this would have been denounced as downright heresy by the Paris Communist Party. One of the most important features of the fiftieth anniversary in France seems to be that times have changed.

Since October 1st, the French have had color television—that is to say, a very few French who are very well-to-do and love to spend their money have had it. A French color *récepteur* costs around twelve hundred dollars, which is a great deal more than Germans pay for their color-TV equipment. French color-TV programs are now to be seen twelve hours a week, of which five are on Sunday. The colors are too beautiful—more beautiful than in nature, which is probably a mistake. Reds are as scarlet as in the flowers painted by Odilon Redon, greens are more pastoral than the green willows of Corot, oranges are brighter than any oranges on your breakfast table, being the color painted only by van Gogh. This Sunday just past, there were a color cartoon, color newsreels, a chapter from an American Western serial called "Alamo," with a colorful fight between dark Mexicans and brave white heroes, and, at 8 P.M., a singing dinner show, featuring Johnny Hallyday; his wife, Sylvie Vartan; Régine, the night-club queen; and the pure-voiced, larklike young Mireille Mathieu, who always sounds as if she were singing alone in the middle of a French field.

Radio and television being state monopolies in France, color TV is handled by the government's O.R.T.F.—L'Office de Radio-diffusion-Télévision Française—and only on its second channel, which demands a special antenna. Already, Europe's color TV has been cut into two rival systems, French and German—the result of outside political interference, the French say. Because the Russians sided with the French system, called S.E.C.A.M., the American television people decided to back the German system, P.A.L., until then regarded as an outsider. By the time everything was sorted out at a conference last summer in Oslo, all of Eastern Europe, Russia, and Greece had followed France into S.E.C.A.M., while England, Germany, and most of Western Europe—except France, of course—had joined with P.A.L. Thus, instead of having a hoped-for intelligent, unified international color-TV system from Dublin to Vladivostok, Europe once more has set up a duality of well-entrenched Continental rivals.

Perhaps it should be added that the French color system, unlike American color TV, is practically foolproof, does not have to be fiddled with to keep its colors clear, and is highly resistant to what the French call *les parasites,* or interference and squawking. Furthermore, it is capable of fairly clear transmission at great distances via an artificial satellite. Thus, France and Russia can easily exchange programs.

* * *

Even old-fashioned plain black-and-white TV has been attracting undue attention to itself here. Last week, the government of Charles de Gaulle was defeated by a narrow margin of nine votes in the Parliament. The vote expressed the displeasure that many French feel at the government's plan to introduce brand-name advertising on TV. Actually, the vote by the deputies, which was later negated, refused to authorize O.R.T.F. to collect the annual user's tax, equal to six dollars for a radio and twenty dollars for TV, which makes up ninety per cent of O.R.T.F.'s two-hundred-and-forty-million-dollar budget. Already the Minister of Information has replied that the government will "proceed with its advertising project, without seeking Parliamentary approval, if it can get the Constitutional Council to agree that it is a matter to be decided by regulation, rather than by legislation," which sounds like one of the General's useful old decree devices for simplified governing.

De Gaulle's party has had a majority of exactly one seat since the last elections. It is feared that if he called for Parliament's dissolution and new elections, he might have no majority at all and, *ipso facto,* no government. This brand-name advertising innovation, which he has personally accepted, has proved a plague that has split not only his Gaullist party but also public opinion. His government's reason for accepting it is that with the abolition of the last Common Market tariffs French industry must be permitted television as an advertising medium if it hopes to stand up to its rivals. Of late years, French TV has already accepted "compensated publicity," which urges increased use of various products, such as butter, canned peas, leather, coffee, and carded wool, but mentions no brands. This new, open commercialization of TV, planned to begin next July, has been attacked by practically everybody—naturally, by both the national and the provincial newspaper-owners' associations, which claim that the equivalent of a hundred and fifty million dollars in advertising gained by TV will be lost to the press, and that many little provincial papers, especially, will have to shut down if TV advertising is permitted. Labor is against it, and also former Finance Minister Valéry Giscard d'Estaing, now head of the Gaullist rebel group of forty-two deputies, called the Independent Republicans, whose votes would certainly be needed to pass the advertising measure. Industry is against it, claiming that rich foreign businesses with the habit of TV publicity will swamp most tight-pursed French advertisers. Ordinary little people are against a government monopoly's suddenly enriching itself to such a tune. Nobody has had to mention how French TV viewers are going to feel if, like American viewers, they are to be constantly interrupted by commercials, because this situation will apparently not arise in France. French advertisers will be permitted only to buy time, not create programs, and it may well be that French TV advertising, like that in Italy, will be limited to less than a half hour daily, which seems hardly worth making so much fuss about and risking a government for.

In the face of an autumnal downpour and the beginning of a taxi strike, the new Orchestre de Paris made its début on Tuesday night at the big Théâtre des Champs-Élysées, with listeners packed even in the small birdcage loges hung high (and usually empty) just under the ceiling. It was a French musical event of consequence and hope, both manifest in the spirited directing of the seventy-six-year-old vigorous veteran of the Boston Symphony, Charles Munch, and an event of such importance that the concert was repeated later in the week in the popular Théâtre de l'Est Parisien and at the Sorbonne. It marked the opening of an unprecedented effort in Paris to create a French orchestra that can take its belated place among the world's foremost symphonic groups. According to M. André Malraux, whose energies as France's Minister of Culture are once more responsible for this latest aesthetic test, the aim is "to break out of the musical structures of the nineteenth-century bourgeoisie." The other most quoted dictum in relation to the orchestra is that attributed to Toscanini, who said, "France could have one of the best orchestras in the world if she were willing to spend the money," music not being, according to him, one of the native Gallic passions that could rival the more silent French pleasure of accumulating wealth. A certain theatrical effort was made to dress the Paris Orchestra in a noticeably chic manner, the hundred and ten musicians being garbed by Cardin. For the men, it was midnight-blue evening clothes (with sensible short tails on their tailcoats, so that when seated they did not drag on the floor) with dark-red cummerbunds, frilled shirts, and, unfortunately, black, rather than elegantly white, ties. The four women orchestra members wore straight midnight-blue gowns.

The program consisted of Berlioz' "Symphonie Fantastique," Stravinsky's "Requiem Canticles," and Debussy's "La Mer"—all French, if one considers Stravinsky, as the French seem to, an inhabitant of France. The Berlioz was the chef-d'œuvre in pleasure and performance. Dignified and portly under his full thatch of gray hair, Munch, with the familiarity born of six weeks of rehearsals, rarely altered his podium stance of listener to and observer of what he had with care created—his arms not lifted, his baton barely marking the beat, as the opening delicacies of the woodwinds pursued their melodic punctuation and rhythm, until the sudden interruption of percussion or of the magnificent outcry of Berlioz brass. The texture of the music had a flowing, fresh intelligence, as if it were being written in one's presence, to be listened to with the full attention of perfect surprise. It was a great and disciplined performance by French musicians, rarely so well led that they lose their fractional individuality in the élan of harmonious unity. It was saluted with one of the continuous ovations at which Paris audiences excel, often without cause, the last outburst tending to deteriorate into rhythmic clapping, which is frowned on as bad taste and is heard at every concert of consequence. Part of the intention of this new musical revolution is to raise the threshold of French critical faculties. The Stravinsky aroused only sounds of faint praise and a few impolite whistles. With its choir singing and liturgical quality, it approximated the sounds of orthodox churchliness but without high aspirational content, except in one assembly of splendid single outbursts, each in a different tone, from four trombones, toward the last of the piece. "La Mer" seemed admirable but, for a great sea piece, rather dry.

It is in the composition of the orchestra and the circuit on which it will serve France that the tremendous importance of this initial idea of Malraux's assumes its national quality. For years, Paris has been the Sunday seat of four ill-paid, mostly ill-rehearsed orchestras, which all played at the same matinée hour and often played the same programs. Of the four, the Orchestre du Conservatoire was signally the most able and best rehearsed. Fifty-two of its former players form the marrow and sinews of this new Orchestre de Paris, which was filled out by competitive examination of more than three hundred applicants, French and foreign, with a mere handful being taken from the Opéra orchestra. The services of all its members are exclusive to the Orchestre de Paris, which pays them better than any other players here are paid. They participate in eight full rehearsals for each program, which changes every two weeks. The first three performances, always under Munch, are given in Paris, including the final Saturday-morning dress rehearsal. Then the program is repeated in suburban *maisons de culture* or theatres close to Paris and in big nearby towns such as Rouen. Thus, instead of the fifteen hundred music lovers who might profit from it at one Paris concert, it is heard by perhaps a hundred and fifty thousand on its local circuit. For more than a century, concert music has been centralized in Paris. Now the outcast Sunday orchestras, on small subsidies, are to be drafted for service in the outer provinces, which have for years been bereft even of provincial opera-house troupes such as used to exist. This is why the Berlioz "Symphonie Fantastique" was the most important orchestral performance of the season. It was, in a way, being played for the future and for the ultimate ears of thousands of non-Parisian French.

November 29

This has been Midas week in this part of the world. Seeking the golden touch, men with money have been selling invested values they owned to buy gold itself, temporarily possessed of the mystic quality of super-value. "The fall of the pound sterling, felt across the Channel as a national drama, is not merely a British affair. It concerns the universe," a Paris commentator noted. Certainly a sort of universal gold rush has been the major result. Professional money dealers on the Paris Bourse, in the Zurich and Frankfurt banks, and in London, where the world's great gold market is situated, say that the demand for bullion has been at the highest peak in living memory. "The demand for gold has been enormous, fantastic, gigantic, frantic," *Le Monde* reported, in a style unlike its usual sober writing. The rush reached its international paroxysm on Friday in London, where more than a hundred tons of fine gold were negotiated in that one day, and even in Paris, which ordinarily sells perhaps six hundred and fifty pounds (possibly equal to the weight of sugar needed in one day in the Paris boulevard cafés), the Bourse on Friday sold some ten tons of gold. The coins in demand here were gold napoleons, English gold sovereigns, and American twenty-dollar gold pieces. In General de Gaulle's famous press conference of February, 1965, he spoke with almost medieval appreciation of gold, "which never changes, which can be shaped into ingots, bars, coins, which has no nationality, and which is eternally and universally acceptable as the unalterable fiduciary value par excellence."

The General's disapproval of the present system of backing world finance centers on what he considers its American-dominated fragility, since it depends on the reserve systems of the two English-speaking currencies, the dollar and the pound, rather than exclusively on the value of gold itself. In this he is seconded by M. Jacques Rueff, his Inspector General of Finance, who believes that gold should be given its head and allowed to go to twice its present fixed price of thirty-five dollars an ounce. In this wildest urban gold rush of the century, gold itself has been despoiled of most of its antique dignity, and all its surrounding poetic parlance has been lost in the gibberish of fractional figures describing it on the world's stock exchanges. The crass human emotion inherent in the financial crisis has dominated European newspapers generally, and those of Paris and London especially, so that their headlines are filled with violent money news and their cartoons with disquieting money rumors. An Amsterdam cartoon showed John Bull limping along on a pair of dilapidated crutches in the shape of the British pound sign. In the London *Guardian,* a Papas cartoon represented de Gaulle as an old gravedigger, in a battered French top hat, digging a grave for the dollar next to one already filled with the pound. Tim, of the Paris *Express,* showed Prime Minister Wilson nude, except for his pipe in his mouth, wrestling as a Laocoön against the strangling serpents of the pound. Editorial recriminations against the French government and charges of ambiguity against the French press have emanated from certain English papers and been hurled back across the Channel with Parisian reinterpretations in the next French editions. *Le Monde,* which is the pride of French journalism, was accused by one of the prides of London, the *Observer,* of having contributed to the gold rush when its financial correspondent revealed, in a few lines buried at the bottom of his column, that since last June France had refused to supply any more French bullion to help the international gold pool maintain the price of gold. This weighty item of news fell, ironically and destructively, on the British pound, when Wilson's government was already in a poor way, instead of falling, as was probably intended, on the dollar, which weathered the blow despite a flood of headlines all over this side of the world, such as "DOLLAR UNDER HEAVY PRESSURE," "IS THIS THE TWILIGHT OF THE ALMIGHTY DOLLAR?," and, in the London *Guardian,* "DE GAULLE'S PRIVATE WAR ON THE DOLLAR"—which certain American money experts here thought hit the real nail right on the head. According to this mixed Anglo-American thinking, de Gaulle, who has been highly displeased over the heavy American investments made in Europe, and especially in France, during the past two years, had determined to use gold as an instrument of foreign policy, like a secondary *force de frappe,* in his desire to draw attention to something else that has displeased him—the vulnerability of the dollar reserve system in relation to the large American balance-of-payments deficit. Thus, if the international price of gold suddenly rose under his pressure, it would merely prove that the international price of gold was the only effectual base for a proper international money system, which would also prove that the General had been right in thinking so for years. However, as the *Observer* remarked, by weakening future confidence in the present American reserve system the French government in the past fortnight at least "successfully demystified the obscure science of gold and brought it into the forefront of politics," where, considering all the present confusions of values and definitions, it may well indeed belong.

As an official disclaimer to the English charges of intrigue in France's newspapers and diplomacy, the French Minister of Information, M. Georges Gorse, issued a communiqué this week that spoke of a press campaign's being organized abroad, "particularly in Great Britain," to give "a false and tendentious interpretation to the position adopted by France in the face of recent international events," meaning the monetary melodramas. This communiqué was at once quoted by a leading London daily as one more example of "the curious paranoia afflicting the French in their attitude toward England." The communiqué was repeatedly carried on the French state radio this Sunday, to show how important the government considered it. Its main aim was to deny France's responsibility for troubles external to her, and to emphasize that France had not ceased her warnings against an unhealthy situation in the dollar and pound area, "some of which has now become apparent." The communiqué further declared that the Banque de France had had nothing to do with the devaluation of the British pound, since its decision not to lend further support to the gold pool was made in June and announced to the other central banks (which, as was correct, leaked no news of this disturbingly important event). The communiqué also said that the Banque de France had taken no part in the recent gold rush. The bitterness, candor, dangerous detailed complaints, and mutual accusations recently printed in the French and British papers are regarded in diplomatic circles as historically remarkable and illustrative of the amazingly tough skin that neighboring European nations have developed through experience (and fear) in this last part of the twentieth century. As a commentator in the London *Times* remarked, "If this were the nineteenth century, Britain might well be at war with France by now."

The essential meaning of de Gaulle's Monday-afternoon press conference in the Salles des Fêtes of the Élysée Palace was, oddly enough, completely contained in a cartoon by Jacques Faizant that headed *Figaro*'s front page on Tuesday morning. It showed the General quitting the little stage on which he had spoken and, with an air of supreme satisfaction, saying to himself, *"Qu'est-ce que je ferais si je ne m'avais pas?"*—"What would I do if I didn't have me?" This was the sixteenth of these extraordinary personal spectacles of the French Chief of State talking, without notes or hesitation, for an hour and a half on the policies of his own country in relation to or against other governments or peoples, and it may well have been the most remarkable performance he has ever given. The real question that de Gaulle should have asked himself is what France will do without him, and when this period of widowhood is likely to begin. This was the indelicate question actually put at the press conference by a correspondent, who inquired about "*après Gaullisme*" as part of France's future. "Everything always has an end, and everyone eventually comes to a finish, though for the moment that is not the case," de Gaulle answered, with such an immediate air of having the best of the argument that everyone laughed. "*Après de Gaulle* might begin tonight, or in six months, or even a year," he went on, "or perhaps in five years, that being the term of office that the constitution has fixed for my mandate. However, if I wanted to make some people laugh and others groan, I could say that it might just as likely go on as it is now for ten years, or even fifteen. But, frankly, I don't think so." There was something rather breathtaking in the nimbleness of mind and the defense against mortality still animating this seventy-seven-year-old Frenchman who continues to lead his own country and who energetically offended many other countries and their inhabitants by his Monday speech. He offended the United States, he offended the Queen of England and the non-French Canadians of her Commonwealth, he offended the Labour Government in again refusing England entry into the Common Market, he offended Israel and world Jewry, and he offended President Johnson and his hawks by his reference to the "odious" Vietnam war. Nor could he have pleased the Chinese or the Russian Communists. It was a very remarkable press conference, narrowed to the scope of his own beliefs and dreams—a press conference dedicated not to the minds or ears of the various nationalities present but to one nationality, his own, as if, in extraordinary public intimacy, he were talking exclusively to his France.

1968

January 3

The French painter of nudes who was always respectfully referred to as M. Ingres has come to fame again on the turn of the calendar. He died just one hundred and one years ago, in January, 1867. At the advanced age of eighty-two, he painted his famous canvas "Le Bain Turc," whose theme of two hundred nude Turkish women in a hammam had inspired his senses for nearly half a century—ever since, as a Prix de Rome student, he came across a description of them in an early-eighteenth-century letter of Lady Mary Wortley Montagu, wife of the English Ambassador to the Sublime Porte. "All of them naked," Her Ladyship had written, "yet there was among them all no indecent gesture, no lascivious posture," just the sort of mixed visual eroticism and correct petit-bourgeois conduct that suited the ambiguous, slow-burning genius of the provincial Ingres. Although he was able to crowd into the background of his canvas two dozen or so unclothed houris, the foreground was dominated by one isolated, splendid female nude, seated on a carpet and fully displaying that superb naked, idle, womanly back—that perfectly fleshed view, with averted face, that over time has become Ingres's chaste anatomical trademark, since it is the fourth example he painted in his career, and all four examples have become famous.

"Le Bain Turc" was immediately bought by Prince Napoleon and denounced as scandalously overfull of nudity by his wife, Princess Clotilde, who insisted that the Prince give it back to the painter in exchange for an Ingres self-portrait, showing the stern, fleshy visage behind which all those multiple nudes had been bathing for years in his imagination. Yet when the shocking Turkish-bath canvas was displayed in the Paris Retrospective Salon of 1905, it was suddenly acclaimed and appreciated as an aesthetic revelation—as it was again this winter, in the Petit Palais's remarkably rich and vast Ingres exhibition, which will come to its close at the end of January. This exhibition has attracted the greatest crowds and amount of talk that any recent show has except Picasso's. Painted in 1863 by an elderly hand, the "Bain Turc" has been a pivotal picture twice in its hundred and five years of existence. In fact, the unexpected popularity of the present Ingres exhibition has itself been like a pivot, turning public taste backward in time, manner, and subject matter, in what seems a profound fit of nostalgia.

Artists, art critics, and, above all, art merchants, who in France are regarded as the most acute computers of art values, agree that if this Ingres exhibition had been held ten years ago, it would have had merely a *succès d'estime.* But the past long, lean decade of abstract art has aroused an ocular sensual hunger in the art-loving French public, which the female flesh, the bosoms, the décolletages painted by Ingres, and also the manly, handsome youths with gold watch fobs, and their elders with low white stocks beneath their worldly jowls, have fed. They now give the public just what it has yearned for—normal, visible reality of the kind to be seen in Ingres's impressive oil portraits of the *grande bourgeoisie,* like character illustrations taken alive from Balzac's novels, plus portraits of a few intellectuals, so rare that they figure only in Ingres's special, delicate sketches in pencil.

In analyzing the importance of Ingres's painting, the poet Baudelaire (writing in his "Curiosités Esthétiques") found in his work something bizarre, freakish—a kind of oddness, an almost wanton love for beauty, an almost morbid preoccupation with style. He went on, "This impression, which is hard to define . . . reminds one vaguely and involuntarily of the feelings of faintness induced by the rarefied air, the physical atmosphere, of a chemistry laboratory or by the awareness that one is in the presence of an unearthly order of being; let me say, rather, of an order of being that imitates the unearthly. . . . A man endowed with lofty qualities . . . but quite devoid of that energy of temperament which constitutes the fatality of genius." In a good-natured denunciation of Ingres's shaky anatomical drawings, Baudelaire noted that one could find in an Ingres nude "a navel that has strayed in the direction of the ribs, or a breast that points too much toward the armpit," or "an egregious leg . . . without even a fold at the knee joint." But he failed to rake up the monstrous, fascinating anti-anatomy of the recumbent "Grande Odalisque," begun in 1813, on command, for Caroline Murat, then Queen of Naples, in which Ingres so exaggerated the odalisque's length of spine, in the interest of style, that one critic declared that she had three too many vertebrae and another said, "He is a lucky fellow who can figure out how her leg is attached to her torso." The "Odalisque" is one of the most stared-at canvases in the Petit Palais exhibition. To many of the younger French, it looks like an early Dali. To many of the older art lovers, what Baudelaire wrote about Ingres sounds like certain precepts of Surrealism.

Among the exhibition's finest treasures are the sumptuous oil portraits of women, which Ingres detested painting. For two years, he refused to paint the Baroness James de Rothschild, born Betty de Rothschild, until he saw her and noted how beautiful she was, and even then he took five years to finish her likeness. In it, she sits at ease in silks, with a double elegance of manner inherited from both sides of her privileged family, and in her relaxation as graceful as a hothouse rose beginning to shed its petals. It is a picture rarely seen in public, since it has remained a family possession from the time it left Ingres's easel. Another of the great female portraits is that of Mme. Moitessier, over which he dawdled for twelve years, painting the original, magnificent seated version of this opulent beauty in beflowered white satin, with a mirror at her side repeating her face in profile for good measure, and then painting a standing version of her in black velvet. In the seated version, he had belatedly introduced the figure of her little daughter, who was so fractious that after several sittings he wiped the child off the canvas as not worth the trouble. Considering how ornately Second Empire the Moitessier lady looks, it seems amazing that certain art analysts believe "the monumentality and geometry" of this special Ingres portrait may have influenced a portrait by Picasso painted in 1932, and also a portrait of the first Mme. Picasso, Olga, painted in 1919. During Ingres's maturity, two important new young painters were already observing his style—Manet and Degas. Degas was so fascinated by Ingres's pencil drawings that he made a collection of thirty-three of them.

Ingres's drawings, in their plenitude, are among the great simple treasures at the Petit Palais and have added to the show's popularity not only with the experts but with ordinary visitors, since only a fool could fail to see that here Ingres was dealing almost humbly with the truth about what people he knew looked like. Of all these verities, the most famous is "La Famille Stamaty," for its human richness and for its perfection as the finest portrait Ingres ever made, ranking as one of the gems of modern French art. Constantin Stamaty, a Greek from Constantinople who was a libertarian revolutionary and a friend of Ingres's in Rome, stands noble and bald beside his delicious wife, with a little son leaning against her lap, a tousle-headed teenage son standing behind his mother's chair, and the older daughter—the godchild of the great Chateaubriand—seated at a spinet. Among the intellectual friends whom Ingres sketched was Liszt—handsome, young, long-haired, in Rome with Mme. d'Agoult, who was about to have their third child. Ingres dedicated his Liszt portrait to her, and, in return, when Liszt published his piano transcriptions of Beethoven's Fifth and Sixth Symphonies, he dedicated them to Ingres.

Ingres and his first wife—she wrote to a friend—were at times too poor to buy bread. She had been a hatmaker in a village near his birthplace—Montauban. She was chosen for him by friends who thought he was lonely; it was a marriage of quiet felicity for thirty-five years, though he was a short-tempered, overdignified little Southerner. He was in despair when she died, and he remarried three years later, at the age of seventy-one. In his long life, he lived through a great deal of French history but seemed not to notice it. His first important commission in Paris came from Napoleon Bonaparte himself, as First Consul, whom Ingres painted in scarlet smallclothes and a tight jacket with a picturesque drooping collar. Later, he painted him as Emperor Napoleon I, on the imperial throne, a theatrical work cluttered with every mark of empire from Caesar onward—golden staff of office, embroidered robe, ermine stole and train, and an eagle woven into the carpet beneath the gold-shod feet. The Emperor's face looks gray and pale. The portrait was savagely criticized by Parisians, and has been appreciated in the recent Ingres exhibition mostly as a curiosity after its long years of moldering in the Musée de l'Armée. It is reported that Ingres was painting "La Grande Odalisque" when the Allied troops entered Paris in 1814, and that he painted his "Venus Anadyomene" during the Paris revolution of 1848. Ingres was a painter to whom history, as events of life or death, meant nothing. He was forced, however, to note the fall of the Napoleonic empire after the Hundred Days, because the Napoleonic family in Naples decamped and the French functionaries in Rome fled for Paris, thus depriving Ingres of his richest clients in those two parts of Italy. It was then that M. and Mme. Ingres's hard times began. Later, however, Ingres was weighed down with honors and became well-to-do. He was made director of the Villa Medici in Rome. Back in France, he received the cross of the Legion of Honor from the hand of King Charles X himself, and was afterward raised to the rank of Commander. In the next royal political turnover, King Louis Philippe entertained Ingres at Versailles. He was appointed president of the École des Beaux-Arts, and when Emperor Napoleon III and Empress Eugénie took the throne, they officially called on Ingres in his Paris studio. In 1862, he was made a senator, as a reward for being such a fine painter. And the following year he painted "Le Bain Turc."

The bare-backed odalisque in the 1863 painting was the last of those spectacular females. The third, called "La Petite Baigneuse," or "Interior of a Harem," was painted in 1828, but with the same back. The second bare-backed nude, painted in 1808, was by all odds the most gorgeous—the most beautiful, luxurious torso he ever painted—and, like the third, she sat perched on a white cot. To keep matters straight, she was known as the "Baigneuse de Valpinçon"—the name of a family that at one time owned her. Even the malicious Goncourt brothers said, in praise of her, that "Rembrandt himself would have been proud to have painted that amber-tinted torso." The first of these bare-backed bathing figures (1807) is now known all over France as a big one-franc postage stamp, which was printed last autumn to honor the centenary year of Ingres's death. The original, which is somewhat coarser in line than the three others, is called "Baigneuse à Mi-Corps," or "Half-Length Bather," as she is seen only from the waist up. The original painting was not shown here, being the property of the little Musée Bonnat, in Bayonne, which may not lend its possessions even to the capital of France. These four splendid, satisfying, bare, bent female spinal torsos were major and almost identical works over fifty-six years of Ingres's working life.

The Ingres show has been the major pleasurable event in an early-winter season that has been full of international unpleasantness and money troubles and quarrels.

January 10

This having been the first New Year's Day on which France possessed color TV, Brigitte Bardot, like a national effigy, was chosen as the star of the unique dinner-hour spectacle, casting on the screen the image of her sensual flesh, the long, yellow straight stream of her ochre hair, and the odd, nacrous shading of her personality, with something intimate about it, like the inside of a seashell. The Bardot show was produced, in part, by François Reichenbach (whose remarkable film portrait of "L' Amérique Insolite" you may well recall) and lasted fifty minutes, during which she sang a great many songs, some in articulate English, and repeatedly changed her costumes and wigs. In several of her numbers, she was actually and unexpectedly sensational as a lone, simple performer. She sings on pitch, in a small, steady amateur voice, which sounds confidential. She cannot act, though as a completely trained professional she can be relied on to simulate. But if one were blind she would have little meaning, for it is the proportions of her body that make her such an astonishment today, like a statue on which the sculptor has been suddenly inspired to cease work, to change nothing—not an ounce more marble around the ribs nor a particle less of the marble dust that affords her limbs their vaguely softened thin line. This is her year of physical perfection. Bardot's body has been a familiar Paris spectacle ever since the public's first complete view of her in "Et Dieu Créa la Femme," but now that she has entered her thirties, time has stripped her of a certain cherubic symmetry, and the spirit within is also leaner. Under Reichenbach's inspiration and taste, she also seemed more spare in her movements. In her New Year's Day show, in the opening scene and song among the trees of her Saint-Tropez garden, she stood almost motionless, naked above the waist, with her arms folded over her bare breasts, her only garment being her long brown velvet trousers. In a later number, she was perfectly silent, merely appearing in an astounding costume of stiff dark paper, with a long, full divided skirt and lengthened sleeves, so that when she suddenly spread her limbs and lifted her arms she looked like a totem of a bird readying its wings for flight. This was spectacular, surprising, and very good theatre. In another number, she paraded down London's Carnaby Street in a Guardsman's frogged tunic, with a swagger stick and black trousers (the identical getup she inexplicably chose to wear when invited to the Élysée party by President and Mme. de Gaulle). Dressed in black boots and black leather mini-trousers, she also appeared as one of the Hell's Angels, astride her motorcycle, and in a white leotard—far less becoming than her own skin—she sang a Pop Art song with words limited to the onomatopoeic, monosyllabic vocabulary of the comic strip. The troupe that accompanied her, such as the handsome singer Sacha Distel, and even the eccentric-looking composer Serge Gainsbourg, with whom she sang a mournful ballad he wrote for her about "Bonnie et Clyde"—characters already popular in Paris, although it has not yet laid eyes on the bank-robber film—seemed merely portions of an exceptionally elaborate Paris music-hall show, played slowly enough, *à la française* in tempo, for Bardot to be analyzed and appreciated inch by inch, whisper by whisper. Her best song, sung sitting alone at dusk on a deserted little Saint-Tropez ferryboat, was called "C'est un Jour Comme un Autre." In this, Bardot's simplicity, melancholy, and immobility came close to being those of an artist.

The entertainment most looked forward to by the ordinary public was the release, after almost ten years of talking about it, of Jacques Tati's new film, "Playtime." It has some very funny things in it, including his own long, elastic legs and sagging gait and his perennially flattened hat, and it has a good idea in it, too, though this soon grows thin from not being well enough fed by gags, or even nourished by satire. The plot concerns Tati's search, in a typically ultramodern Paris skyscraper such as now increasingly infests the Montparnasse Railway Station district, for a certain man whom he has never laid eyes on but who works for some high, upper-floor corporation. Both men are such victims of perfected mechanized systems that they never find each other at all—never even wave to each other as they pass and repass in their unidentified proximity, on their air-cooled safaris between glass walls. This should be a plot of genius for Tati, who is the ideal confused, lost, and courteous man of our time, always whipping off that hat politely and bowing to fate itself, and never being recognized. So here he is in "Playtime," getting off on the wrong floors, involving himself with the wrong receptionists—a nineteenth-century-minded, well-educated Frenchman lost in twentieth-century imported architecture and its glassed-in privacies, which he can see through (with apologies) but can never penetrate. The second half of the film is almost slapstick. It depicts the disastrous opening night of the modern building's new restaurant, magically cursed in some way, so that everything goes wrong and the restaurant literally falls to pieces—a fairly funny sight. There is a story going around town that Tati, who is an inveterate practical joker, recently persuaded friends who were giving a small bourgeois dinner party to let him play the butler, whom he mimed to perfection until from the kitchen came the sounds of crashing china—a whole cheap set that Tati had bought for the purpose. Then he dropped some creamed sweetbreads down the front of the main lady guest's dress, draped a bit of spinach on the lapel of a leading political expert, thus hiding his Legion of Honor ribbon, and continued from disaster to disaster until the guests became enraged and Tati sat down gently on the hostess's lap, a happy man. Still beloved since "Mr. Hulot's Holiday," M. Tati in his "Playtime" has, this writer regrets to state, mostly received disappointed private comments, unfavorable comparisons to Chaplin's "Modern Times," and an unenthusiastic general press.

There was one unlooked-for euphoric disturbance in the awarding of the year-end French literary prizes. This was the distribution of *les grands prix* by the Académie Française at its annual public session, held under its famed cupola fronting the Seine, where its prize for French poetry for 1967 was awarded to Georges Brassens. In Paris, he customarily sings his poems at the Olympia music hall following the acrobats or jugglers, the last half of the entire program being his by right of superiority. Of the half-dozen musical poetic males in France who, like middle-aged troubadours, bare their experienced hearts in their verse in public and pluck their guitar strings like cardiac muscles, Brassens is the greatest, worthiest favorite, his songs being the closest to the bodies and emotions of the French common people. He looks like a wrestler, with shoulders big enough to fight for justice, big mustachios, and a big voice—a lonely, morose man who walks onto the stage without greeting his audience, stands on one leg, placing his other foot on a chair to balance his guitar, and then sings his dramas about French life, part tender, part disrespectful, part heartbroken, and mostly concerned with the workers, the poor, and the unfaithful females, such as the *donzelles* who ply the sidewalks at night. He was born in Sète, on the Mediterranean; his father was a mason, and, in preparation for following the family trade, Georges became a chimneysweep. He has read enormously, favoring mythological subjects and the Latin-tinged southern classics. In one of his verses, called "La Complainte des Filles de Joie," he says to man in general, *"Fils de pécore et de minus, ris pas de la pauvre Vénus,"* the rhyming and rhythm being masterly.

Paul Valéry, author of "Cimetière Marin," one of France's great modern poems, was the famed, historic poet of Sète, a scholar and a gentleman. One of Brassens' most ardent verses is "Supplique," in which he asks not to be buried among the marble effigies of that elegant graveyard but to be laid for eternity on the seaside sand. A strophe from "Supplique" was read at the Académie the other day by René Clair, who wrote and recited the allocution saluting Brassens as a poet honored and prized in the eyes of men of learning. Such touching ceremonies and relations in literary France are rare and refreshing.

No French book in our time—or, indeed, in any time—and especially no book that will not be bought by French women, has had the phenomenal rapid success of "Le Défi Américain," by M. Jean-Jacques Servan-Schreiber, founder and editor of the Paris weekly *Express*. Published in October, it is in its twelfth week as France's best-seller, having now reached more than four hundred thousand copies, and is selling all over Europe, including both Germanys and Rumania. What the book is about is America's talent, or genius, perhaps—our built-in gift for organization, like that of ants and bees, those laborious, highly corporated insects. This organizational talent is not native to Continentals, and our possession of it is the main theme of Servan-Schreiber's discovery—or semi-discovery, for it has in fact been noted before, with no special appreciation, by the youthful French political intelligentsia, the Young Turks. President de Gaulle, who naturally refused any public comment, supposedly said confidentially, "The book's analysis is irrefutable, but *ces propositions sont légères*."

What Servan-Schreiber says in "Le Défi" is that if American investments and organization on the Continent increase at the present rate, they will create two Americas—ours at home and the other one abroad. No one before ever spoke of Americans as a people with special gifts, except for pioneering, hard work, plumbing, and immeasurable ambition. Our talent for organization he actually calls an "art"—a high word for a Frenchman to misuse. "The Europe of the Common Market," he says with humor, "has become the American businessman's new Far West frontier." He writes with brilliance and sparkle, as one of the crystal-clear commentators of this hemisphere. His book is more anti-Gaullist than anti-American. "In 1980," he says, "Europe, given over to men who are today twenty years old, will be like a continent emerged from history, without adventure and without aim, in the shadow of American dependence"—unless the French devote themselves to the cult of organization as they have to those other qualities that are instinctive in them and not in us Americans: philosophy, logic, art in churches and in the imagination, an assured belief in educated civilization and refined foods. The best social integration, Servan-Schreiber goes on to say, as well as the rebuilding of Europe, "will move forward together as the result of a new demand for justice and of the modernization of the old values in man himself— the natural heritage that history has designated as the Left."

Servan-Schreiber is a handsome man, with an enchanting smile. He comes from an Alsatian family, entered the École Polytechnique in July, 1943, and fled from France to become a fighter pilot in de Gaulle's Forces Françaises Libres. After the war and the Polytechnique, he served as an editorialist on foreign politics for *Le Monde,* and was a political collaborator with Pierre Mendès-France. Mobilized as a lieutenant of the reserve in the Algerian War, and certainly called up in reprisal for his anti-war attitude in *L'Express,* he wrote a book, "Lieutenant in Algeria," in which he told all—or, at any rate, too much—about the tortures practiced by the French Army, was indicted by the Minister of National Defense for "weakening the morale of the French Army," and was tried and acquitted, as had been expected.

January 24

This has been a strange month of January, as if it were the end of something only too familiar, rather than the start of things new. The weather, at its best, has been like a leftover *été de la St.-Martin,* as the French call our Indian summer—warmish weather, like a winter that has mildewed and, as its only form of energy, has wetted down all of France with tempestuous winds and rains, more appropriate to a too early spring. The Seine is at flood tide, and the costly, picturesque new drives at water level on either side of the stream are now like canals. Over the past week, it has been as if the importance of the international news itself were damped down in Paris by the weather. Even *Le Monde,* the weighty, if small, evening journal that sets the highest reportorial tone and style of all the European newspapers—a journal usually sensitive indeed to whatever happens in Washington—made no major editorial interpretation of President Johnson's State of the Union Message, which it merely paraphrased briefly, mentioning "the deflation of his rhetoric" but adding neither comment nor penetrating opinion, since what he said was, after all, well-known stale important news before he spoke it. There was, however, a general French feeling that he gave no more than "the minimum of the minimum" needed to stiffen confidence in the dollar, and in some quarters surprise was naïvely expressed at the President's silence on how much money American tourists would not spend in Europe this summer—though how on earth could he even guess, let alone hope?

"The week just ended was heavy with events whose historic weight can escape no one," remarked *Les Échos,* the daily paper of the Paris Bourse, in an outspoken editorial. In it, Mr. Wilson's "reduction of Great Britain to an international dimension more suited to its possibilities" was analyzed, along with the latest shock—"the internal disengagement of the dollar vis-à-vis gold," as the paper called it. "Is this a step toward the complete freeing of the dollar from its subjection to metal?" *Les Échos* asked itself. In any case, the paper concluded, "January, 1968, runs the risk of pressing heavily on the destiny of Western economic affairs." Finance Minister Debré, in his own very different way, was also seeing things gloomily when he later said that "the perspectives of 1968 make it look like a difficult year." However, Premier Pompidou, being much more of a pure politician by temperament, was far cheerier at the Friday meeting of the central committee of what we must try to remember is now called L'Union des Démocrates pour la Ve République—the newest official name for the Gaullist Party. M. Pompidou brightly pointed out the following encouraging Party news: "In the past nine months, our parliamentary situation has started moving in a different direction, in which we have demonstrated that even though our majority is feeble"—a majority consisting of exactly one deputy, which, in truth, could hardly be much feebler without turning into a minority—"there is no opposition capable of overthrowing us, much less capable of replacing us." It is such moments of hairbreadth triumph that sometimes make French politics so fascinating. Well, believe it or not, within three days the Ve République Party and its pro-Gaullist but dissenting group headed by Giscard d'Estaing received word that a French deputy named Francis Sanford, who had been elected under the Gaullist banner in French Polynesia, had quit the Gaullist group to become a *non-inscrit,* or unaffiliated, floating deputy. By losing that Polynesian will-o'-the-wisp, the two major Gaullist groups lost their absolute majority in Parliament. Almost equally fascinating are the political reasons that led to Sanford's resignation. It seems that he had earlier announced to the Territorial Assembly in Papeete that he would leave the Gaullist Party if the Paris government did not respond favorably—and it did not—to his demand that six scientists be sent to assess the dangers of the thermonuclear tests soon to be held on Polynesian territory. It is, among other things, such bewildering vagaries as Sanford's resignation at long distance in faroff Polynesia, where no one can conveniently argue with him at the moment, that in multiple ways led President de Gaulle here in Paris to establish his kind of French Fifth Republic, which by political purists is commonly called monocratic.

The Louis Delluc annual cinema prize—rather like the Goncourt Prize—for the best presentation of the previous year has just been given to "Benjamin; ou, Les Mémoires d'un Puceau," filmed by Michel Deville, hitherto no prize-winner of anything. Yet he has here turned out a film that is a kind of delicate masterpiece of voluptuous physical grace and refined libertinage, its story dealing with not one but two young eighteenth-century aristocrats, Benjamin and Anne, both ignorant of the practices of love, who learn their first lesson with each other at the château of Benjamin's countess aunt, where, as a country bumpkin, he has been sent to be socially educated. The scenes, in full color, are like pictures by Watteau, and the story, which is basically daring, has not been weakened by evasions or cluttered with licentious literary frills from Choderlos or Crébillion—the scene where the two innocents disrobe each other is as fresh and charming as a *tableau galant* from some château-bedroom art collection. The equestrian scenes, with Benjamin and the libertine Count, his aunt's faithless lover, riding breakneck in pale silks through the forests, are so handsome that they have been compared to the great galloping in the film "Tom Jones," though never were two films less alike, the French movie possessing its own highly civilized quality, and even its own touch of typical perverse courtly cruelty. For it is the faithless Count whom Anne loves and has determined to marry, although she gives herself first to Benjamin in order to punish the Count's egotistical male pride. The cast is really choice, with Michèle Morgan as the countess aunt and Catherine Deneuve as Anne—the most ravishing feminine sight in any movie now showing. Benjamin is played by young Pierre

Clémenti, who manages the role without prudery, at least. "Benjamin" is already the big hit in Paris, since it offers beauty, sensuality, and perfect taste—rarities in the celluloid world today.

Certainly you will find none of these qualities in "Weekend," the newest of the Jean-Luc Godard films shown here. Godard is the most influential filmmaker in France and the most indifferent to what anyone of any nationality thinks of his films. Certain French film devotees regard each of his new movies as a memorable event, and, what is more, carry all his old films in their memories, like parts of their own private aesthetic experience. He is not so much popular as a fetish with those who evaluate each new production of his as another Godard incarnation. He makes movies with the same haste that brilliant talkers make conversation, some things being hurriedly said and always remaining regrettable. What his films have in common is that they are not like any other movie-makers' films, which gives them their own unique brotherhood. Of all that he has made, "Weekend" is the most fervently disagreeable and alarming. It begins in reality, with the flight of an unmarried French couple, Mireille and Jean, both of a singular lack of charm, who are driving off from Paris for an amorous weekend in the country somewhere, anywhere. Then they get stuck in traffic, and everything gradually turns into a kind of torture scene, beginning with quarrels among the owners of the jammed cars, rising into fistfights, smashed cars, burned cars, and overturned cars, and culminating with the dead being lifted off to the side of the road. As the dead accumulate, they become like commedia-dell'arte figures—fatal figures of grisly waste and humor. The satire and the realism of the scene continue to be mixed without discrimination or differentiation. All the cruelty, envy, and hatred of those who survive for those who have perished come to the surface in a series of bourgeois portraits, which Godard traces with his camera lens as a form of anger, fury, and criticism. In a kind of artist's anarchy, he is like a sculptor of church Last Judgments whose specialty is sculpting not those on the right hand, who are saved, but those on the left hand, who are damned. As the roadside holocaust goes on, the couple's relations with society and nature worsens steadily. So does the film. Cruelty becomes too commonplace, in the clumsy slaughter of a pig by a country butcher, and in the steady robbery of the corpses of their better garments, which Mireille decks herself in. The end of the film is total disorder, with Jean probably eaten in a fit of savagery that seizes first on one and then on the other of the couple—cannibalism supposedly representing modern society, in which man eats man as one country eats another in war. All this offers a total evasion on Godard's part of any sane, constructive solution of a situation that started with a weekend bottleneck of cars on a highroad leading out of Paris. "Weekend" has already been called *"le film le plus dingue,"* or the maddest film, that Godard has ever done. This covers a great many thousands of feet of provocative, interesting, unconventional film made in his relatively brief career, which began with "Breathless," one of the few technically perfect films made in our time, most critics think.

Last Sunday night at ten-thirty, the special weekend TV program called "Un Certain Regard," aimed at careful listeners and at minds with serious curiosities, and backed by the research service of the state radio-and-television company as its most intellectually ambitious broadcast, gave the television public the privilege of a half hour of listening to and looking at the so-called father of structural anthropology—Professor Claude Lévi-Strauss, ethnologist, anthropologist, and professor at the Collège de France. The typical professor in garb, he is gentle and lively, and looks like an intelligent bird, with a voice that is soft but distinct. He began by talking about genes—of trees and fishes, and then of man, with diagrams. He also used photographs of a royal wedding in Westminster Abbey and of tribal marriage ceremonies among primitive South American Indians. (His vast collection of tribal photographs was fascinating.) He spoke of the "ridiculous" variants in genes in cases of incest— reacting one way if the incest was between an uncle and a niece, in another way if it was between a nephew and an aunt. Some time ago, in *Le Nouvel Observateur,* he delivered himself of his definition of structuralism, "which is not a philosophical doctrine but a method." He went on, "It uses social facts that represent certain models, always taking into consideration not the terms but the *relations* between the terms." Among his other propositions is that the human sciences, like ethnology, cannot be called scientific, like biology, because the ethnologist deals with the hand-me-downs of history and geography. "Each of the phenomena we ethnologists wish to study—beliefs, rites, etc.—expresses in a particular language something that is common to each," he said. "This common thing is precisely the structure, or unvarying relation between the terms." So, he declared, such sciences of man as ethnology will be structuralist, this being the only way they can simplify themselves. He also spoke of myths, whose most essential property, perhaps, is that of being beautiful. Of the Greek miracle, he commented that it could not be contested that something took place in a small corner of the world at a certain time, which first made philosophy possible and, through that, certain forms of reflection and scientific knowledge. To an ethnologist, no interpretation of this phenomenon seems possible. "Let us say," he concluded, "that the Greek miracle occurred once, and that, like all unique phenomena, it can only be proved, not explained." Among highly educated French people generally, Jean-Paul Sartre's Existentialism is considered, in retrospect, to have been far easier to grasp—perhaps because it was a philosophy —than the methodical, apolitical manual of Lévi-Strauss's structuralism.

February 20

The city of Grenoble has not yet emerged from the gloom into which it was plunged by the sporting success of the winter Olympic Games last week. The French victories in the ski events were particularly spectacular, popular, and dramatic. But where were the visitors? The crowds of Americans and Italians— even the people from Lyon, usually reliable sports devotees, and the Parisians, too—who had been counted on to gather in the windblown grandstand or on the snowy slopes outside Chamrousse failed to materialize, the Paris papers now state. In hotels, fifteen per cent of the rooms were unoccupied. The townspeople with shops had naturally thought of the games as something of a marketplace. But the visitors who did come bought little, being well dressed against the cold in advance. Instead of serving as a marketplace to tourists, the scene of the games "became an immense TV stage," one reporter wrote. The games had been offered to

Grenoble with the implicit supposition that the sporting world would rally round, as in the past. For the most part, the world stayed home and, without the trouble of having to put on wool underwear and mittens, sat cozily in front of its TV set and saw more of everything going on at Chamrousse, Autrans, and L'Alpe-d'Huez than it could possibly have managed to see at first hand, since the multiple-eyed, farsighted cameras saw literally everything that was visible. For twelve days, there was a veritable avalanche of pictures, which filled French TV screens for a hundred and thirty hours and twenty-five minutes, with sixty hours of it in color (which was magnificent). Competitions like those of the games used to be called spectator sports. This year, by and large, only the contestants had the physique to stand around in the cold and observe what was going on. Maybe spectators now lack the stamina to attempt to do for themselves what their Seeing Eye dog, TV, can do for them.

A kind of insurrection broke out in the world of young and famous movie directors here at the recent news that Henri Langlois, creator and director of the Cinémathèque Française, was no longer directing it. He had been replaced by a government commissioner, who, a few hours after his appointment, visited the Cinémathèque's present main office, in the Rue de Courcelles, requested the departure of the staff, and closed the building's two doors with two new locks, pocketing the keys before leaving himself, as if fearing a counterattack, which did not come until the next day. Then about seventy of the best-known youngish directors, led by Jean-Luc Godard and François Truffaut, started their insurrection against the dismissal of Langlois with speeches and denunciations on the Rue de Courcelles sidewalk, which attracted a crowd, which, in turn, attracted the police. The dismissal of the admirable, inspired (and, doubtless, administratively untidy) Langlois after thirty years' devotion to the conservation of rare or important old films, which he kept in metal boxes, like treasures, turned him, quite justly, into something of a martyr when the story reached the newspapers' and the weekly magazines' editorial pages. Back in the late twenties and early thirties, all of us in the Saint-Germain-des-Prés quarter who were cinema enthusiasts eventually came under the Langlois influence in recognizing that movies made by great directors with great actors or actresses could be ranked as art in celluloid. His Cinémathèque projection room was first in the Rue Messine and later in the Rue d'Ulm, and it was through him that we saw for the first time Eisenstein's "Le Cuirassé Potemkine," which he showed in some little hole-in-the-wall movie house in Montmartre.

Over time, Langlois created here in Paris the biggest of the world's cinema libraries, containing today from fifty to sixty thousand films, as against the fifteen thousand in Moscow and only five thousand in New York's Museum of Modern Art. After the Liberation, in 1945, the Cinémathèque was recognized as having "cultural utility" and received a modest government subsidy. In more recent years the Ministry of Culture built for Langlois a small movie theatre in the Palais de Chaillot and also a storage depot in the suburbs for his films (which in his earliest days he used to store in his bathtub). What makes the whole situation so odd is that these films all belong to him personally, because he had bought them or because they were deposited with him for preservation by their owners, often the directors who had made them. Only the donors have the right to withdraw their films, and only they and he have had the right to lend them. The Cinémathèque is a private association of some seven hundred members, of which a fifth are foreign. The only state control over it comes through an administrative board in the Ministry of Culture. Recently, new members—all in favor of the Cinémathèque's being given a thorough modernization in its methods and bookkeeping like a spring housecleaning—were elected to the board. Of Langlois's lifework, Godard has just written spiritedly that it enabled voices from the past to be heard "on the white sky which is the screen," in the only museum here in which "the real and the imaginary are joined." He adds, "Without him, Lumière, Méliès, Griffith, von Stroheim, Murnau, and others would have died twice. Thanks to him, thousands of spectators have had pleasure, critics have gained culture. *Cinéastes* and actors owe him their vocation and render homage to him." In a solid, energetic article criticizing Langlois's dismissal, the dominant cultural weekly, *Les Nouvelles Littéraires,* asks if "behind *l'affaire Langlois* cannot be seen outlining itself the

French state's progressive takeover of the movies, regarded as too turbulent and too independent." Since the insurrection against his dismissal, an amazing loyalty to him has been demonstrated by the French movie industry generally. A hundred and sixty-five French film directors, as well as dozens of actors and actresses, have signified to the Cinémathèque their intention of allowing only Langlois to use material in which they figured. The important question is: What can now be done with those fifty to sixty thousand films, which are Langlois's personal property or have been left legally in his care, and have an incalculable historic value and meaning? This question will probably be asked of the Gaullist Party in the approaching parliamentary session.

March 6

The strangest production of Shakespeare's "Midsummer Night's Dream" that mortal ever saw has been playing in French, with enormous success, in the old Cirque de Montmartre, half of which, including the ring, has been theatrically metamorphosed into an empty shell with a steep rim and a floor of gray-and-white goatskins, upon which the troupe of the Théâtre du Soleil plays barefooted, runs full tilt, amorously or hatefully brawls, fights and wrestles, or lies dreaming and recumbent. A year ago, this Theatre of the Sun was an obscure drama-student coöperative that played Wesker's "The Kitchen" in the provinces, a production that ranked as one of the best of the year. With this year's Montmartrean Shakespeare, according to certain leading Paris critics, it has taken its place, like a surprising prodigy, among the important, experienced European companies. It has no star actors; it has merely its creative *metteur en scène* and founder, Ariane Mnouchkine, aged twenty-nine, daughter of an English mother and a Russian father, who was studying for her degree in psychology at the Sorbonne before deserting it to found her theatre troupe. According to her statement that accompanied "Midsummer's" opening presentation, "It is the most savage, violent play you could dream of, a fabulous bestiary of the depths, whose subject is the god of fury that slumbers in men's hearts. No fairy-tale marvels but a fantasy made of poison, anguish, and terror, in which our dreams, uncensored, take physical shape." If a woman suddenly desires a man with an ass's head (like Bottom in the play), she added, one does not necd a psychoanalyst to realize that her case is founded not on a fairy tale but on a desire for bestiality. (Mlle. Mnouchkine's authority for her interpretation of the play —or so it can be supposed—may have been taken from that famous speech of Oberon's in Act II that begins, "I know a bank whereon the wild thyme blows" but goes on to declare that with the juice of a flower "I'll streak her eyes,/And make her full of hateful fantasies.")

Certainly the four muddled lovers pursue one another in this Mnouchkine version with true, tragic love-hate fury rather than with farcical mock emotions. Furthermore, the costuming of all the males in the cast when they make their initial entry in single file—for their entrances and exits they use the entryway through which the circus's trained horses used to gallop into the ring—adds to the general confusion, for the men, including the Duke of Athens, are all dressed alike in handsome white Nehru coats and tight trousers, stepping to the rhythm of an enormous drum tapped by a real bearded Hindu. Puck and his friends appear half naked, with red spots on their bare skins, like hennaed leopards, and with Puck bawling his lines at the top of his athletic lungs, running full speed up the arena rim to make his exits, or somersaulting back down to grapple and roll around with his cohorts, who lie about on the goatskins, his sadistic performance being of such relentless muscular energy as to exhaust the seated audience, if only through its eyes. But the scene in itself is exquisite, with Mustardseed, Peaseblossom, and the others garbed in cerise-and-purple robes and carrying sticks and fans surely taken from drawings by Aubrey Beardsley, with Art Nouveau lace panels as the backdrops at the rim's top, and with the soft, hairy gray and white of the goatskins dappling and dressing the arena floor. The sole familiar and comic portion of the performance is the Pyramus-and-Thisbe playlet, enacted by Bottom and his artisan actors, the Wall and the Lion being especially well costumed and played. This is the only scene that Shakespeare might recognize.

Ariane Mnouchkine's stage directions show her indubitable

intuitive, intelligent gift for theatrical action. Each isolated scene in the large circus arena maintains its entirety like a form of choreography, so that, as a compliment, she has been accused of Béjartism—of imitating Béjart's ballet groups, which originally were accused of imitating theatre action. Her troupe possesses an impeccable physical coherence. For the Shakespeare spectacle, it rehearsed for five months. Her "Midsummer Night's Dream" is coming to the close of its run, because someone else has taken over the circus arena. It has been the most talked-of event in the late-winter theatrical season and the only significant novelty.

Last Saturday, *Le Monde,* France's influential and independent newspaper, ran in its "Libres Opinions" column an appeal to French intellectuals by Vercors, who may be remembered as the wartime Resistance writer of the internationally famous short story "The Silence of the Sea." In his appeal he begged French intellectuals to take part, on Saturday, March 23rd, at the Parc des Expositions, in a vast *manifestation de solidarité* with the Democratic Republic of Vietnam. "If there were not a feeling of horror, the bad faith of the White House could be laughed at," Vercors wrote. "But there is horror and carnage. Even when the National Liberation Front, despite the disproportion of forces and resources, inflicts stupefying reverses on the invader, that changes nothing in the odious character of the aggression. This bad faith exasperates the best friends of that America whose past generosities cannot be forgotten. . . . That is why public opinion in the world, and especially in France, begins to feel choked by its very indignation, by its outraged conscience." Vercors made the usual call on all the French intellectuals, like the one that Jean-Paul Sartre made during the hated Algerian War: "Architects, teachers, painters and writers, scientists, technicians, musicians, theatre people—everyone must join in, even those skeptics who do not believe in the efficacy of taking part in this way." French reaction to the horrors of the last fortnight of murderous killing by both sides at Hué and Khe Sanh has hardened against the United States and Americans generally, as if we had become different people. The slaughter of Vietnamese women and children has more than once been compared in the press to the Nazi genocide of European Jews in the

German concentration camps. There is bitterness, especially among more-than-middle-aged French adults, because Washington is unwilling to learn from the humiliating French experience in their defeat at Dien Bien Phu—from their knowledge, there cruelly learned, that a modern, up-to-date army cannot win a guerrilla war against patriotic natives in their forests or villages or caves except by literally exterminating the national population. Pierre Mendès-France, France's most powerful Premier in the Fourth Republic, was the leader who brought the French war in Indo-China to a close in defeat, considered a disgrace to French pride. President de Gaulle (who had changed his mind about Algerian independence in midstream) brought the Algerian War to its end in conditions considered disgraceful to France's European standing. What the French see as stiff-necked provincial Texan pride has made the American President—or so many Parisians frankly state or write—the most unpopular American in power in the close to two hundred years of Franco-American relations.

April 3

On the eight-o'clock Monday-evening state-television news roundup, President Johnson's own Southwestern voice and accent and words were used to announce his decision to retire, having been taken from his speech as he had spoken it over the air in Washington the night before: "I shall not seek and I will not accept the nomination of my party," plus a few more of those surprising final phrases about "the awesome duties of this office." This was apparently the first time that any foreign chief of state or other eminent personage was ever permitted more than a few opening words in his own language on the French TV news, where even the Pope, after some Italian syllables, has always been drowned out by a French translation. So that Mr. Johnson's important statements should not be lost to listeners who did not understand English, a translation of his words was printed across the bottom of the screen while he was speaking. The double news of his decision not to run again and of a curtailment of the bombing of North Vietnam left the French *abasourdi,* or stunned, with satisfaction and suspicion, mixed. "Doubt springs to everyone's mind," the upper-class *Figaro* commented candidly. "Is it all a tremendous trick on the part of this wily Texan? Is he not seeming to efface himself the better to disarm his rivals and prepare the conditions for a kind of plebiscite in his own favor at the Democratic Convention in August? Should we credit Mr. Johnson with such Machiavellianism? It is difficult not to suspect that he must have thought of it. That is no reason, however, to accuse him of a sly maneuver. He is frankly playing poker, having from the start accepted all the risks. He has bet on peace. He is playing his hand like a great player, having taken such obvious care to prepare every detail in order to win that it is difficult to accuse him now of having loaded the dice." As you can see, the Wild West film vocabulary dominated *Figaro*'s editorial style. Aside from that, what *Figaro* wrote was still unusual and scandalous treatment of the United States President, such as this breakfast newspaper had never been guilty of while he was earnestly pursuing the Vietnam war, of which the French press and the French population have, on the whole, profoundly disapproved. He is still a chief of state, even if he is one whose possible presence in power for the next four years was as unpopular a prospect for most of the French as it was for millions of Americans. Yet in the two or three days since he announced before the whole world and his countrymen voters the facts of his conversion to his new, peaceful, private aims he has been more insulted journalistically here than ever he was while respectfully regarded as an unreconstructed villain.

On the other hand, the Gaullist afternoon paper *Paris-Presse-l'Intransigeant* showed a certain temperate sympathy for the President's predicaments and courage. At least, it said, "All America and the world were astounded by the Sunday radio announcements. It is a well-known fact that Mr. Johnson is a specialist in the *coup de théâtre,* but no one expected the magnitude of this one, which has shaken the American nation. Many Americans believe in his sincerity. For many others, however, what he has 'pulled off' is a very slick performance. In some cases, the first reaction of the American man on the street has been to say, 'Johnson has sacrificed himself for the good of his country.' This phrase must be like balm on the heart of this politician who has so often been accused of being a master at maneuvering in the great style of the Radical Socialists." This is, and was meant to be, a damning compliment, because the Radical Socialists were the bourgeois political party that dominated the Third Republic from its founding, in 1871, until the nineteen-thirties, when the party was finally brought so low by its financial scandals and horse tradings that it sank from sight during the war and never was revived. Today, any reference to the old Radical Socialists is made only as a classic reproach.

The Communist reaction to Mr. Johnson's announcement, as summed up in the Party paper *L'Humanité,* was brief and blunt: "A MANEUVER."

As might have been expected, the most brilliant, most carefully measured, yet most stimulating report on Mr. Johnson's announcements—and, indeed, on Mr. Johnson himself—was found in *Le Monde.* Its careful wisdom and caution made a memorable front page out of the critical material contributed by its Washington correspondent, Alain Clément. He began by stating, "Since the beginning of the year, the United States has been barely governed. Today, it no longer has a chief. The virtual abdication of Mr. Johnson, which cannot take effect before the elections of November, is an event that had been rumored among a few rare prophets but that plunged the ordinary electorate into complete astonishment. What could have struck this man, who for thirty-seven years had encrusted himself into the American political system, had manifested all the signs of tireless ambition, and had dreamed only of passing into posterity between Lincoln and Roosevelt, that he suddenly lost hold of everything, swallowed the bitter pill of renunciation, and, in the end—it is the truth—committed hara-kiri? Was it a final upward leap 'to finish in beauty,' as the poet said? Was it the Texas politician's offering up the gift of his private dreams to the good cause—that of universal peace and national reconciliation? Or was it his emergence onto a false path, seeking to arouse the pity of his countrymen by a noble gesture that mixed sincerity with melodrama—the ultimate maneuver to check the free fall of his own popularity and make himself the candidate by tears against opponents who are neither saints nor giants? History will tell whether the President was equal to the height of his responsibilities. It is clear that he never took them lightly. Yet, observing him carefully on the television screen, one was plagued by a feeling of malaise."

The sense of being upset by a break in routine was prefaced for Americans here by the gold rush, which shook the reputation of the dollar. France's Gold Exchange operates in a small basement room in the Paris Bourse, completed in 1825, which looks like an imitation Greek temple, with a peristyle of thirty-foot Corinthian columns—a noble architecture of fraud, constructed on the former site of an old Catholic convent for poor girls. On Friday last, the day the Stockholm ten-power monetary conference opened, a small, quiet-voiced group of gold buyers and sellers was doing business at only three dollars and fifty-nine cents an ounce above the thirty-five-dollar-an-ounce level that Roosevelt had set in 1934—a languid financial scene compared to the pandemonium daily exploding there until a fortnight ago, when the Queen of England, in the middle of the night, graciously closed the London gold market to oblige President Johnson's appeal for a suspension in trading. In that violent initial gold rush, and for some days after, even the staircase leading down to the Gold Room had been so clogged with shouting speculators that the least muscular among them actually risked being crushed into silence. This March gold rush was nothing like the gold rush in November, when the British pound was devaluated. That one seemed merely greedy, to the point of cannibalism—a kind of profiteering hunger in which speculators tried to gobble as much as they could hold and afford. This one was utterly different, was psychological, was political, was more humanly frantic, like people in a mob trying to buy the last ticket to safety before another seismic temblor shakes them and brings down the roof of their world—alarmed people in a panic, buying gold as a form of security or, possibly, of salvation, or so they thought. Foreign exchanges in Europe loyally followed Queen Elizabeth's example and closed, too, except in Brussels and Paris. Michel Debré, de Gaulle's Minister of Finance, had only the following succinct statement to hand to the French press and give to the worried Western world: "The banks, the stock exchanges, and the Gold Exchange of Paris will function today in their habitual conditions." As a result, that day the price of gold in the Gold Room soared like a glittering French Fourteenth of July skyrocket to seventy dollars an ounce. No one had ever heard of such a dangerous price in modern times.

What has given this spring gold rush its hallucinatory quality is the impressive impact it has had on the imagination of very ordinary Parisians, precious few of whom have ever laid eyes on a gold ingot, or even recognized a gold Napoleon seen by chance in a numismatist's shopwindow. But the dramatic excitement in the newspapers' daily reports of the gold fever was like that of a daily serial thriller, with the unfluctuating strong position of the French franc feeding Parisians' pride, and the downgrading of the dollar and President Johnson's position satisfying their acute disapproval of the Vietnam war and of him who was waging it. Furthermore, a sentiment for gold money still flows in the French people's consciousness, deposited there by the royal French history they learned as schoolchildren and by the gold that runs through French fiction, like Balzac's, figuring in a girl's marriage *dot* or in a young man's inheritance from his grandparents. Thus, many Parisians have been sympathetic to President de Gaulle's pro-gold financial views, such as his recent statement to his Conseil des Ministres: "The dollar and sterling crises demonstrate that the present system based on their privilege as reserve currencies is not only inequitable but, from now on, inapplicable. A monetary system based on gold, which alone has an unchangeable character, should be established." Then he added, "It goes without saying that a real and complete settlement of the American balance-of-payments deficit is highly desirable"—to put it mildly. The long-drawn-out Washington delay in alleviating this deficit was first complained of publicly by France last autumn, and is now openly cited here and in the meticulous London banking world as having been the most influential factor in bringing about the present money crisis—the dollar apparently being as almighty in its international influence as many Americans were always bragging it was. On the other hand, the Aladdin-like fortune in gold drawn by de Gaulle from Fort Knox in legitimate, and unavoidable, exchange for his plethora of dollars, which had flowed to France in her recent very prosperous years, is not considered here to be responsible in any way for the monetary crisis, or even for the weakening of the dol-

lar, though it is frankly pointed out, with a certan civilized satisfaction, that so far the dollar has, in truth, been the big loser in
reputation. It seems to be only in the calculations of certain former
American tourists—so far this year almost totally absent—that de
Gaulle's draining of our gold from Fort Knox is what has actually
helped to downgrade the dollar.

According to one French financial expert, writing in a highly
responsible publication, France now holds the world's biggest accumulation of gold, most of which used to be ours. France's present official gold reserves add up to more than five billion dollars'
worth, as against the United States' ten and a half billion, but an
even larger fortune is in private hands, gathered in by the hoard-
ing traditional among the rich in France; since 1934, of course,
nobody in America, rich or poor, has been allowed to possess gold
at all. This little mountain of gold will enable France to play her
cards very close to her chest in the coming arguments over what
monetary reforms are going to take place so that other gold crises
do not form to frighten our civilizations. France, furthermore, will
be backed by both Russia and South Africa, as gold producers,
since they, like France, want to see the price of gold made much
higher. In the last analysis, the world's coming monetary battle
will be fought between the adherents of the two prevailing an-
tagonistic theories about what to do with gold. There are the pro-
Americans, or Atlantists, who want to pry the dollar loose from
gold and attach the value of all currencies to the dollar, a move that
even to many Americans looks risky, though in actual fact this
has been, in major part, the general practice over the immediate
past. Then, there are the pro-French, gold-cult group, who pro-
claim their fidelity to the gold standard as immemorial, classic
financial orthodoxy, and above all because gold as a single standard shows up the position of the dollar and its decline at least in
majesty.

April 16

On Monday afternoon, the day before the funeral
in Atlanta, a memorial service for Dr. Martin Luther King was

held here in the little American Gothic-laced church on the Quai d'Orsay. He had spoken from its pulpit just after receiving the Nobel Prize. On Monday, the church, which was overcrowded by the presence of about a thousand Americans, Negro and white, served as a shelter for the specially troubled emotions that many of us here felt as Americans living outside our own land—our sense of loss and shock mixed with our sentiment of deep shame over the fact that once again our present history had been mutilated by an unforgettable assassination, which had made violent, tragic, American bad news all over Europe and around the world. There was also, of course, our common knowledge that, despite our government's promises, aid and generosity had not—as usual since the Civil War, certainly—been forthcoming in our wealthy cities, and that "the fire next time" had been kindled in Washington itself.

In addition to the addresses and prayers that constituted the memorial program, the choir vigorously sang the "Psalm of Penitence" from Arthur Honegger's "King David" and, as the final hymn, "We Shall Overcome." Besides all of us Americans present, the service was attended by fifteen invited ambassadors, including those from England, Canada, Sweden, Cambodia, and Austria, and several from black Africa. Present also were a dazzling monsignor in pink silk, representing the Cardinal of Paris, and three Knights of Malta, formally garbed in evening clothes and decorations beneath their picturesque scarlet capes, and wearing their great gold Maltese crosses from medieval Christian times. Two telegrams of condolence were read—one from Jacob Kaplan, the Chief Rabbi of Paris, and the other from Baron Alain de Rothschild, representing the Consistory of French Synagogues. Also present was one Black Muslim woman, wearing a white felt hat with the identifying scarlet and green crescents, and some Flower Children of more than adolescent age, one or two carrying wilted flowers as identification. It was a saddening, historic afternoon meeting in this liberal American church on French soil —a meeting to be long remembered, a meeting that was an epitaph.

For international aesthetes, the Continent's outstanding art show of this spring and early summer (until July) is "L'Europe Gothique," from its inception in the twelfth century through its final florescence in the fourteenth, when ecclesiastical fascination with the balanced, airy Gothic arch—that celestial new architectural invention in France—began to cede to the earthly square, princely palaces of the Renaissance, and from there went on into worldly baroque. This exhibition is another of the great postwar international art displays that owe their existence to the initiative of the Conseil de l'Europe. It is on view in the newly reconditioned rooms of the Louvre's recently liberated Pavillon de Flore, which few of us had ever set foot in before—that final riverside west wing, down by the Carrousel. Beginning with the disorders of the Commune in 1871, it was allocated to the Ministry of Finance, which avariciously held on to it, in our time coarsely using it as its National Lottery offices.

This is an art show for adepts and cultivated travellers, who are probably familiar with the famous geographical formula that if one takes a compass and pinpoints it on the Paris Sainte-Chapelle and then opens its other leg to take in a distance of about a hundred kilometres, one will have enclosed the mystically fertile Île-de-France, in which Europe's first and greatest Gothic cathedrals—in that brief temporal space between the years 1180 and 1380—sprang up like high-arching ferns of carved stone, accompanied by the corresponding new grace of humanistic thinking, in one of those simultaneous confluences of genius by which society is mysteriously transformed. Within that hundred-kilometre radius lie the abbey of St. Denis and the cathedrals of Chartres, Noyon, Soissons, Laon, Reims, Amiens, Beauvais, and Notre Dame de Paris itself. For those early, nameless architects and builders, Gothic was a successful, daring tentative of vertical balance in place of walled horizontal mass—a great, precocious modern flight of man's aspiring scientific imagination. Monasticism and feudalism were ended, and French thought was becoming urban, molded by European universities like the Sorbonne, which produced Abélard and Héloïse, and eventually produced us and our Western society of today.

The Pavillon de Flore exhibition illustrates itself by an inclusion of over five hundred religious Gothic art works—statues of the Virgin and Child naturally dominating, plus statues of apostles, annunciatory angels, knights, kings, and saints, and small stained-glass windows, still in perfect condition of color and glaze. There are also church treasures, such as jewelled crosiers and reliquaries, and quantities of sacred paintings, chosen from all over Europe. The Virgins with Child are, of course, the most frequent, and also the most varied, with often a touch of the beginning of realism giving them the true air of individual portraiture, as in the intense, beatified maternal face and the intimate handling of the Christ child, held against the breast, held on high like a little ruler, with the orb of the world in his hand, or posed on his mother's shoulder, in one instance with the child's hand fondling his mother's cheek. There is one hallucinatory statue of the Virgin, almost life-size, that is sheathed in gleaming, smooth silver except for the placid yellow-colored visage, carved from fruitwood. There is a laughing female head with well-curled hair that represents one of the Foolish Virgins who were asleep when the Bridegroom approached. There is one noble male angel wearing on his face what André Malraux, in his "The Voices of Silence," called "the brief and timid Gothic smile." These impressive statues taken from cathedral niches and portals, carved by great artists without signature, supply us at least with the artists' idea of what their Gothic contemporaries looked like, either in reality or as semi-deified into Christian symbols.

The most interesting of the recently accumulating books, and the one that supplies the most stimulating and imaginative reading in full-fledged literary style, is "Vendredi, ou les Limbes du Pacifique"—"Friday, or the Pacific Limbo." It is the first published book of Michel Tournier, an editor in his early forties who works at Plon's publishing house and is the author of two earlier books, which he destroyed in manuscript because he did not like them. His "Friday" is his personal version of the famous, unique one-man English adventure story as lived by Defoe's Robinson Crusoe on his southern isle. It is enriched by Tournier's interpretive use of such modern influences as Freud, Lévi-Strauss, genetic botany, the collapse of imperialism as illustrated by the British Empire, and the rise of democratic, interracial individualism, after Friday's arrival; Crusoe's final triumph is the loss of his bigoted Protestantism through his emancipation into some sort of sun worship, with yogi-like exercises that restore his youth. This summary gives a notion of the book's intellectual ironies, humor, and political and philosophical anachronisms, its terrors and lonely tragedy. The opening of the tale, with the shipwreck on the reef and Crusoe's pillaging of the broken bark, is along the lines we have always known—the hauling onto land of the gunpowder, the Bible, the pistols, the telescope, and also the drowned captain's box of gold coins. In his first, frightening loneliness, Crusoe sleeps, as lunatics do, in his own filth, as instinctive proof he is alive. Then, as he organizes his domain, he passes a law against all abominable follies, with allotted punishments, though there is no one there to obey or to be punished. In the name of King George II, he appoints himself governor of the island, and calls his hut the Residence— though what he governs is a flock of wild goats. In his single-voiced society, he sets up a simulacrum of all he has previously known of British administration as a narrow, pious, provincial Protestant and sailor, whether at sea or at home on land. The awakening of his mind in lonely self-debates on the problems of truth, reality, and logic leads, step by step, to autodidacticism, without books but with increasing meditative enlightenment in his solitary self-study. He even becomes tender toward the beauties of nature in the lyrical Rousseau manner (with botanical names and details furnished by Tournier's careful documentation of island growths in that southern clime). He sets up administrative offices for weights and measures, and a chapel for worship, and from the wheat and barley he has taken from the ship he becomes a prosperous planter, raising more grain each year, like a good English subject, as if he had a growing British community to feed. The arrival, after years, of Friday, brought over from a distant island to be martyrized by Indian cannibals and accidentally saved by Crusoe, is the next step in his human growth. That the newcomer is colored perfectly fulfills Crusoe's conception of how the British Empire works, with an inferior dark native race ruled by the interloping white. "A name had to be found for him," Tournier's Crusoe that night solemnly confides to his logbook. "I did not want to give him a Christian name before he had merited it. A savage is not entirely a complete human being." In a wonderful turn-about of expanding new values, it is Friday who becomes the island's master, through his innocent indifference to power, through his derisive disbelief that God is merciful and kind, and through his pantheistic incomprehension of Crusoe's ingrained capitalism and his own inability to take work seriously, despite the gold sovereign that Crusoe pays him weekly from the captain's cashbox—for why till the land, since it produces more than they can consume? Friday becomes the Apollonian hero—the artist who creates a wind harp in the trees, the expert hunter whose bow and arrow bring down brilliant-feathered birds for them to feast on. There is a marvellous fight with the king of the billy goats, whose skin Friday then turns into leather, using it to make a huge kite, which he employs as a kind of sailplane. When the unexpected British sailboat by chance finally moors at Crusoe's island and he takes a meal aboard with the men, he knows they have arrived thirty years too late for him. He will never go back to England. He has become a new, emancipated island man, and it is Friday who secretly sails off to London. This fascinating book includes the appearance at its end of a new companion, named Thursday.

This has been a recalcitrant spring of vigorous, sunny, inflexible weather, with a constant north wind keeping the sky clear of clouds, so there have been no rains and, in consequence, no fruit trees in bloom in suburban orchards. It has been all that the Tuileries chestnuts could do to burst into mere green leaf, without forming their floral candelabra. On Easter Sunday, the air was finally warmer, but Paris itself was as calm and uncrowded as if it were not the first great church fête and civil holiday of the new season. Midtown Parisians had already motored out of town for the long weekend, and what used to be the start of the foreign-tourist season lacked its impetus this year, owing to the money shift caused by the gold rush across the Channel and a decline in trans-atlantic affections. The English did not come to Paris for Easter because they could not afford to. The Americans did not come because they did not choose to. The new substitute tourist crowd was the young Germans, who were well dressed, well mannered, and well heeled. They came by bus by the thousand, the way New Yorkers and Californians used to come by plane.

May 1

The pandemonium that can mark the French parliamentary system as practiced in this country's modern republic was at its most audible last week during the spring session of the Chamber of Deputies. Premier Georges Pompidou had to fight for the survival of his government against a motion of censure brought by the Federation of the Left, led by François Mitterrand and backed by his Communist allies, all up in arms against the Pompidou project of introducing paid brand advertising (presumably, only of food products to begin with) on the state TV service, O.R.T.F. Actually, in recent years French TV has been giving generalized daily housewifely hints to its listeners, such as "Buy more fish" and "New carrots and beans are today's best bargain," which offended nobody politically. But Pompidou's plan was obviously the inevitable opening crack in the O.R.T.F. through which big-business-sponsored advertising, at high rates, was going to squeeze onto the state-monopoly screen, already richly subsidized by the annual tax that the owners of TV and radio sets have to pay. Freedom of the press also became involved in the noisy Chamber fight, centering on the fatal withering away of small-town newspapers, which would lose their regional advertising, on which they live, once they were faced with competition from national advertising. France is relatively so small a Continental hexagon that, as the Premier shrewdly pointed out, if his TV-advertising scheme was not accepted, the portion of French big business that is modern enough to want to use it would be robbed of *élan* and expansion by Continental neighboring competitors who patronize the peripheral stations around France, like the powerful Monte Carlo and Luxembourg transmitters, which are clearly heard here and have already captured part of French radio advertising. In fact, it was the whole imitative smell of big-business advertising *à l'Américaine,* which individualistic France until recent years had sniffed at contemptuously, that incited the anticapitalist Federation of the Left to bring its motion of censure. Among working-class and modest French citizens, this motion suddenly became the most popular political topic all over France. But it was not quite popular enough when the Chamber votes favoring it were counted, for it missed being passed by eight votes less than the two hundred and forty-four required for a majority. Considering what American TV fans put up with in the way of intrusive advertising day and night, the minimal size of Pompidou's victorious advertising project seems ludicrous. It will consist of exactly six minutes—we repeat, six minutes—per day (probably beginning on the first of October), in three two-minute periods before each of the TV news roundups, at 1, 8, and 11 p.m. But the plaguey principle of using the TV screen as a billboard has been accepted, and next year there will be more advertising, and so on and so on.

In defense of his government, and despite being hoarse with a cold, like a whole population of Parisians in this static, chilly spring, Pompidou spoke on Wednesday afternoon for an hour and forty minutes without pause, except to exchange rebukes and semi-insults with opposition deputies who tried to interrupt or to drag red herrings across the path of his concentration. It was one of his longest performances; was read forcefully from his typed manuscript, which lay on the speaker's rostrum; in manner was rather like the report of a banker—which he has been—totting up the figures on investments of political policy; contained no poetic or literary quotations, though he has been the editor of an anthology of poetry; and at times, when he was annoyed by the verbal squibs launched at him by the opposition, or by the Communists banging their desk tops, sounded like the lecture of a schoolmaster—which he has also been—aimed, in justified anger, at the worst boys in the class.

But it was not until he came in his speech to the opposition's claim that his project would rob the press and public opinion of lawful liberties that the crisis in noisy bedlam began, with Pompidou pounding his fist on the rostrum and shouting, "I am ready to go into battle! You claim that liberty has been stifled by the government of General de Gaulle—he who has repeatedly preserved the liberties of the French, sometimes with your aid but always for your salvation!" Hearing this, the opposition broke into an explosion of jeers and insulting cries, while the Gaullists themselves waved their arms and shouted their approbation in a swelling volume, like a select crowd cheering their favorite race horse when it has suddenly come up from behind and looks headed for the winning post. From the press box under the Chamber ceiling, we journalists in the front row, by leaning over the balustrade, could look down directly onto the strange figure of the old Socialist Guy Mollet, who had risen to his feet behind his desk and, until his voice gave out, kept screaming, "No! No! No!," apparently in denial of any Gaullist-given liberties—a subject that had long been passed by in the turmoil of unintelligible verbiage, acclamation, and insult. On the tribune behind the speaker's rostrum sat the President of the Chamber, whose duty is to maintain order with the big bell in his hand, which he constantly clanged while shouting what sounded, in fragments, like an appeal to calm. "Silence!" he clearly screamed once or twice, and, lifting his enormous brass handbell, he shook it violently in the air.

The other high points in this session were almost like quiet tête-à-têtes between Pompidou and an opponent. After he claimed that his advertising project could be inaugurated by decree rather than by law, which would demand a special Chamber debate, the old-time intellectual leftist Pierre Cot, who now votes with the Communists rather than with upstart Mitterrand, declared courteously, *"Monsieur le Ministre,* the theory you support is denied by the most eminent specialists of administrative law, including my friend Professor René Capitant, the Paris Gaullist deputy and president of the Parliamentary Legal Commission." By this time, nothing—not even superior Gaullist interpretation—could stop Pompidou.

Despite the battle royal of arguments in the Chamber, no party really wished to see the government fall, since that would mean dissolution and new elections. No one here wants to face new elections. The prospect of our American elections in the autumn already seems a burden of worry to the French, as if we were still close friends. The spasmodic lack of solidarity in the British Government is another worry, as if England were an installed member of the Common Market and politically intimate with France. The exercise of the ballot in general, once a civic stimulant, attracts little enthusiasm in this part of the Western Hemisphere just now, disturbed by rioting youth on both sides of the Atlantic. Furthermore, on May 30th President de Gaulle will have been in uninterrupted power for ten years. Pro or con, few Frenchmen think he should be disturbed.

May 16

May 13th is the date of the military coup d'état of the French colony in Algiers which ten years ago brought down France's Fourth Republic, brought General de Gaulle back from his country retreat into power again, and soon into his own present Fifth Republic. In Paris, that May 13th is still called, in irony, "*le 18 Brumaire du Général de Gaulle*," after the famous illicit military seizure of power by Napoleon on that date during the French Revolution. De Gaulle's Brumaire will certainly never be forgiven by the powerful political French left for its "violent and conspiratorial origins"—the blasting phrase used by the London *Times'* severe editorial on France's recent week of student riots and shaken governmental balance. As a followup on the anti-de-Gaulle-toned student manifestations—in which for the first time on the sidewalks was heard the cry *"De Gaulle assassin!"*—the French left and labor unions, in special celebration of this May 13th, suddenly and cruelly called a national general strike. There was something tragic and comic, mixed, in the ruin that this helped make of the previous chauvinist French image of satisfaction built up by Gaullist official France: that France had been finally chosen as the proper site for the peace talks between our Ambassador-at-Large, Mr. Averell Harriman, and Mr. Xuan Thuy, Paris being the natural choice as the intellectual capital of Europe—Paris, by this time with its Sorbonne already closed for a week, with its students battered by fighting in the streets against the Compagnie Républicaine de Sécurité, the government's brutal shock troops, and with the Latin Quarter still filled with the stench of tear gas and smoke from the dozens of charred automobiles burned on the students' barricades near the famous Boul' Mich'. Certainly all these accumulated unexpected disasters were far from the halcyon picture earlier drawn by the secretary of the Gaullist party, who had said, with patriot satisfaction, "That men of good will should turn to France to find the road to peace is a great reward to those of us who have wished to give our country a certain image before the world." If the Champs-Élysées represented the road to peace last Monday morning, it was almost devoid of transportation for the vast company of journalists and radio broadcasters, come from all over the Western Hemisphere and also from the East, for whom, owing to the general strike, there were few taxis, half the normal number of buses, and only a fourth of the usual Métro trains to serve as a means of reaching the Hôtel Majestic, up near the Arc de Triomphe, where the opening Harriman-Thuy meeting was being held.

There was at least one outspoken dissatisfaction with what Paris offered, immediately made known by the North Vietnamese delegation, who discovered themselves housed in the comfortable, bourgeois Left Bank Hôtel Lutetia. They said that for more privacy they wanted at their disposal a large, remote, out-of-town residence, such as a historic château. The Château de Champs, east of Paris, was mentioned by the French as a possibility, it having been used last year as a temporary residence for President Soglo of Dahomey, but the difficult problem of providing security so far away for all the North Vietnamese delegation apparently made it impractical. One château that was certainly not mentioned as feasible was Fontainebleau. It was there that talks were held between Ho Chi Minh and the French government in 1946, and the breakdown of those talks led directly to the Indo-China war, which, one way or another, has never stopped since, and whose ending in Vietnam is the meaning of the Hôtel Majestic conversations right now.

These official conversations so far, of course, are only in the tentative, cordial earliest opening phase, and consist of statements made by one side and courteous disbelief expressed in response by the other side. Basically and eventually, the talks here will represent a hard, fighting struggle between Eastern and Western points of view, but, as with all peace talks, the opening feinting consists of propaganda. Press veterans of previous peace conferences are candid in saying that the American mind is not as smart at propaganda as the European, let alone the Oriental—that our natural angle is that of a simple seller, a merchant, or, at best, a good trader, whereas the European's propaganda arguments rest on dialectic, or even Cartesian logic, and the Oriental's on subtlety, at which we Americans are known not to shine. It is also said that the American position in propaganda here is very difficult, because our situation in Vietnam has been that of the aggressor, with no matter what noble, democratic intentions, and the position and propaganda of the North Vietnamese here are those of outraged victims, who will not cede an inch, like mourners refusing to give up their dead. South Vietnam's representatives are newly present in Paris, established, at our expense, in the Hôtel Claridge, on the Champs-Élysées. But nearly no members of the American press seem to have called on them. However, the French—or so it appears—have granted radio time to them for a South Vietnamese show of some sort. After the propaganda front on both sides has been established here, and has been contested for several weeks, or even longer, it is hoped that behind-the-scenes contacts, which are the most important developments of these diplomatic struggles, can be gradually arrived at between Mr. Harriman and Mr. Thuy (who is, it seems, a well-known poet at home). It is apparently by these contacts that, little by little, fraction by fraction, phrase by phrase, word by word, agreements of some sort may be balanced and advanced, and—with luck, progress, and patience—peace may be achieved.

Obviously, the peace talks, following as they did on ten days of student riots and manifestations, have been of far less interest to the French than the riots themselves, which in their bloody, dangerous, and alarming violence were like a suddenly matured revolution of youth being fought out in the Latin Quarter. The student revolt began on the afternoon of Friday, May 3rd, in the Sorbonne itself, when Rector Jean Roche, who is its head, in an unpardonable academic error, called in the Paris police—an act that violated the sanctuary of the university, maintained over centuries. He requested that they clear the university courtyard of a small, disputatious student meeting, which Roche feared might lead to some incident of violence that could disturb the approaching spring examinations. This violence, indeed, immediately began when the other students and some of their professors saw the courtyard students being bundled off by the police into their *paniers à salade* and hauled to the police station. By Saturday night, the Sorbonne students, arms linked for strength, were streaming up and down the Latin Quarter sidewalks and streets. There had already been outbreaks at the new suburban university at Nanterre, where a German-born red-headed anarchist and sociology student named Daniel Cohn-Bendit had been organizing susceptible students as what he called *"les enragés."* By Sunday morning, in an unusual Sabbatical sitting of justice, several of the courtyard students had been sentenced to two years in prison, without appeal, at which news the Sorbonne as a whole rose in a sentiment of fury, and the week of riots began, agitating all of Paris and taking over power from the city's adults, and from the nation's government, in a way. With the Sorbonne locked against them, students began roaming the streets, insulting the C.R.S. guards, who were armed, wore steel helmets, and carried long nightsticks. (They had been sent posthaste from the Belgian and Rhineland frontier garrisons to keep order with their clubs.) Violence became the pattern. Street fighting animated the Rue Soufflot, broke out around the Panthéon and the Place Edmond-Rostand, at the corner of the Luxembourg Gardens, and in all the smaller medieval alleyways leading off the lower Boulevard Saint-Michel. Everywhere, the students at first advanced with insults as their only weapon, before fleeing to save their scalps from the attacking police clubs. Wednesday night, as if their energy were uncontrollable, the students embarked by the thousand on a long parading march up and down Paris, mounting the Champs-Élysées to the Arc de Triomphe, where they extinguished the flames over the Unknown Soldier's Tomb, had a sit-in around it, and sang the "Internationale."

By Thursday, the physical tension between the C.R.S. and the students had approached a crisis, which broke late on Friday night and lasted horribly and without interruption until early Saturday morning. Early in the evening, with their indomitable anger and energy, the students had started building barricades throughout the Latin Quarter, because barricades are a historic instinctive accompaniment of French rebellions. They dug up the cube-shaped paving blocks from the streets, piled them as ammunition and protection to a height of five or six feet, and in the Rue Gay-Lussac, just off the Luxembourg Gardens, added all the cars that had been parked there. By this time, the students were in a state of crazed exaltation and wild euphoria, according to the alarmed neighborhood adults who talked with them. *"Nous sommes chez nous,"* the students kept saying, as if that medieval section of old academic Paris were their property to despoil or to defend. The fighting was bitter. The students, who were like young Davids, were armed, if at all, only with lids of garbage pails, while the mature, burly C.R.S. men facing them were equipped with enormous shields of medieval size and were wearing modern anti-tear-gas goggles. Whether from the students' amateur Molotov cocktails or from the C.R.S. variety of chemical gas bombs (oddly enough, Gay-Lussac himself was a nineteenth-century French chemist who studied the action of gases), all the captive automobiles in the Rue Gay-Lussac, which became the Chemin des Dames of that Latin Quarter battle, were set aflame. As the police closed in, the students began running up apartment-house staircases to continue fighting from the roofs, tipping parapet stones onto the enemy below, and finally knocking on apartment doors to beg shelter. Their first protection was to scrub their hands, for if the police came prowling up and found a boy with tar on his dirty fingers, it was proof that he had been using paving blocks as ammunition or in a barricade, and he was hauled off to the police vans below. One mother who lived on the street with her three children was absent on business in the provinces but flew back in terror at radio reports of the riot. On rushing into her flat, she found three unknown exhausted students asleep on the hall floor but the flat and the younger children in perfect order, all under the excellent direction of her nineteen-year-old eldest daughter, although there was not so much as a grain of coffee or a heel of bread left in the kitchen to eat. Red Cross stations had been set up on the Boul' Mich', and after midnight women taxi-drivers banded together to take out the wounded students, mostly with bashed heads. The fire department was on the scene, putting down fires, and there were screams and shouts that could be heard as far off as the Boulevard Saint-Germain. The students fought with unflagging courage until they were knocked down and out by the police. The pugnacity of the French in a riot has to be seen to be recognized as a native strain in their character. Had the young French soldiers fought like rioters against the

Germans in June, 1940, Paris might not have fallen.

Until five o'clock Saturday morning, the Latin Quarter lived an epic of destruction, danger, and bravery. Before Saturday noon, it was like a historic battleground, visited by tourists with cameras to take snapshots of the remnants of the night's history. A cordon of C.R.S., in their black helmets, with the silver trim gleaming in the murky smoke, blocked the entry to the Rue Gay-Lussac, which was a shambles, filled with wrecks of cars, fragments of clothing, an occasional shoe, and the generally strange trash that follows city struggles and accumulates in heaps. Not a paving block was left on its sandy street bed, broken glass shimmered on the sidewalks, curtains blew disconsolately out of smashed windows in the morning breeze. On the Place Edmond-Rostand and leading down onto the Boul' Mich', whole sections of the paving had been ripped up, over which taxis jolted. Half a dozen of the ancient streets had become impassable and were closed to traffic of any sort, and by the iron fence of the Luxembourg Gardens still stood two Red Cross ambulances and their attendants, just in case. But the fight was over. Incredibly, no one had been killed, though hundreds had been injured, with more police than students reported hospitalized.

Late Monday afternoon, the biggest parade of marchers that Paris had ever seen started moving from the Place de la République toward the Place Denfert-Rochereau and the Lion de Belfort statue, which had become the new student meeting place. The marching crowd was a mixture of university students, of teen-age *lycée* students who had prematurely joined the academic revolt, of teachers, and of workers, mostly from the striking C.G.T. union. The social mixture of workers and intellectuals represented the new fraternization. The line of march probably included three-quarters of a million people, but word went round that there were a million of them, and that will remain the legendary figure. At any rate, the throng was so dense that the head of the line had reached its destination, with the first few marchers sitting on the lion's back, before the end of the line, three miles distant on the other side of Paris, had managed to leave the Place de la République. The City of Paris had learned its lesson from the riots, and the streets were empty of police. The parade marched behind a huge banner proclaiming "Solidarity of Teachers, Students, and

Workers," with a forest of small black flags for anarchy and red flags for revolution waving along the line. The students, especially, were jubilant, and derisively chanted *"Bon anniversaire, mon Général!"* in recognition of the tenth anniversary of de Gaulle's Algiers putsch. This they alternated with the slogan *"Dix ans, c'est assez!"* The new cry of *"De Gaulle assassin!"* was also heard, and so was *"De Gaulle, résignation!"*

The students, by their riots, won conclusively, and the government of France, through Premier Pompidou's common sense and tact, backed down in defeat. The students' three demands for peace were the reopening of the Sorbonne, the release of the students from prison, and the withdrawal of the C.R.S. (Another of their Monday marching slogans had been *"C-R-S—S-S!,"* the last two "S"s referring to Hitler's storm troopers.) All these demands were rather hurriedly granted. On the opening of the Sorbonne, students immediately took possession of the courtyard, brought in a piano, and played and sang and spent the night, sleeping in classrooms. At the present writing, Thursday afternoon, students have been occupying the Odéon-Théâtre de France—the theatre home of Jean-Louis Barrault and Mme. Madeleine Renaud, the most gifted avant-garde couple in the theatrical profession here—since last night. The students have stated that they do not want to see any more classic plays, suited to a démodé bourgeois education. They have also stated that they do not believe in university examinations, since they are repressive. Last week, the students fought like young heroes. This week, they are acting like clowns at a *kermesse*. The government is saying nothing. All during the dramatic, riotous week, General de Gaulle kept silent, giving no message or advice or comment to his nation and its troubled capital city. Only when Premier Pompidou returned from Afghanistan did the government, within three hours, make a statement of decision, promise, and principle about the sclerotic educational system in France, which over the years has become the trigger for the students' outbursts. Today, de Gaulle is being applauded in Rumania. After his return, he is slated to speak to his own nation on May 24th. The quantity of applause he will receive from the French is at this moment unpredictable. But it will surely be less than he has been accustomed to. And May 24th seems a long way off, what with things in the turmoil they are still in. His speech will not come a moment too soon.

May 23

Last weekend, there were three million workers of various sorts on strike in France. This coming weekend, there will be ten million. The figure cannot go a great deal higher without social danger. Paris is *paralysé*—without the capacity for municipal movement. Two days this week—Wednesday and Thursday— there was also a taxi strike, the final immobilization. No trains, no planes, no Métro, no buses, except those rare trucks, soldier-manned and free, supplied by the government for occasional travelling from one remote section of the capital of France to another. No letters, no telegrams, no communication between citizens except by local telephone, interurban calls not being permitted except in cases of grave family news, such as a death. (You can telephone a French-man from New York, but he cannot phone you, even to give good news.)

On Wednesday, in the Chamber, the motion of censure against de Gaulle's government failed by eleven votes, so the Pompidou Cabinet is still breathing, stertorously. On Thursday, following that raucous Chamber session, came the fête of the Ascension, the great late-spring church and state holiday, which most Parisians who had any kind of car planned to spend someplace in the country until Sunday night, since, along with its factories, the schools and the University of Paris have been closed. Offices, shops, and depart-ment stores, like the Trois Quartiers, have been shut down, the Banque de France itself is struck, and the engravers at the mint, who make new money, are also out, so banknotes are running short.

Tomorrow comes the speech to his nation by General de Gaulle. This is what France is now waiting for. It will be the cli-max of the most unexpected and disastrous dozen days that the country has known since the Commune, in 1871, which these pres-ent days have in no way resembled, because France had then just fought a war and been defeated, and the new, revolutionary Marxian theories were being applied in blood between the opponents in the new social schism. There has been no blood shed here except for a few cracked heads in street fights. The schism this time is principally between generations familiar with each other—between youth and its elders. Politically, anarchy is now the new applied belief for the students, but its black flag is being flown side by side with the red flag of revolution, though not of the old-fashioned Marxist type. The Communists here, once so menacing and fiery as the French political volcano, have been bypassed, as much as possible, by the well-organized New Left leaders, but it is the labor unions, principally the Communist-led Confédération Générale du Travail, that now have the country in their calloused hands; without their signalling thumbs up, millions of the strikers will not go back to work next week. Insofar as the unions are the masters of the situation, this past week has been a demonstration of a management revolution on the lower, not the upper, stratum. To avoid interference from owners or directors of establishments, workers have in some cases locked them in their offices. All of us here know at least one or two highly paid directors of some kind of enterprise who are well-treated prisoners with their phones cut off. The owner of one big firm, when asked two days ago whether he, too, would be locked in his office, replied, with a fatalistic shrug and an up-to-date smile, "They might do it tomorrow morning—how do I know? But I will keep going to my office until they lock me in or lock me out." According to printed gossip, there are banners in front of the Plaza-Athénée and the Georges V hotels—since hotels are also a business—that say, in English and French, "The Personnel Has Taken Over the Responsibility of Running the Hotel." In one or the other of them a few days ago, Prince Michael of Rumania, on arriving here, was met by a leader of the employees, who informed him that the director of the hotel sent his excuses but was unable to welcome His Highness personally, without adding that the director himself had been locked into his suite. These shifts in management have been carried out with remarkable courtesy. When the C.G.T. and its supporting unions entered the Banque de France on Monday morning, there was a certain fever at first, but then a rendezvous was fixed for later in the day with members of Finance Minister Michel Debré's staff. The Banque governor demanded of the union men that, whatever was done, "the Banque's dignity remain assured," and closed his door on his union visitors. Shortly afterward, the under-governor more wisely came to them and simply asked that "order in the Banque not be exaggeratedly upset," which was considered reasonable indeed until the police came Tuesday, pulling the big bell by the locked front door and demanding that all the pickets posted outside be sent away, which was in an orderly manner refused.

The most important shift in power has been that of the state radio and TV outfit—the O.R.T.F., or Office de Radiodiffusion-Télévision Française. There the personnel, in their "pursuit of objectivity," as they have called it, put on the French air and TV screens the Wednesday session of the Chamber debate on the censuring of the de Gaulle government. It was a debate that contained harsh anti-de Gaulle strictures, and noisy outcries when his name was pronounced. For years, there has been no anti-Gaullist criticism shown or reported on the French networks. Such criticism has been printed in weekly magazines like *Le Nouvel Observateur,* but it has not been shown naked on the screen or poured into the ordinary public's ears. It is common knowledge to what an extent the French TV news programs have each day lined up the personalities most pleasing to the government to be shown and interviewed. The classic example of the bias of French TV remains that of the Socialist mayor, Gaston Defferre, of Marseille, who was shown on TV during his campaign, but only from behind, so the public never saw his face and had no idea of what he actually looked like.

As you doubtless know, the Odéon-Théâtre de France is still occupied by the students. Anyone can walk in and see how they and the theatre are getting on. It is a degrading sight. The words "Ex-Odéon" have been painted on the walls and the metal fire curtain, and on the night this correspondent looked in, the aisles and the entrance were filthy, with students asleep in the boxes or playing their transistors in the front row. Smoking had been forbidden and the toilets were locked, so there was no danger of fire or flood, but the lovely, lovable little eighteenth-century playhouse, in its last refurbishing dressed in red velvet, looked like a gypsy camp.

* * *

The Chamber debate that began on Tuesday on the motion of censure of the de Gaulle government was not brilliant but strident, as if vocal energy and political disagreements could take the place of a sustained flow of give-and-take in political arguments and hopes. Premier Pompidou, hoarse with fatigue, made one remarkable statement, which approached a historic *mea culpa*. Referring to the violences of this past week, with the student riots and the spread of the strikes, he said, "After such events, nothing can be the same as it was before. A certain number of things demand revision." These remarks were listened to in appreciative, attentive silence. François Mitterrand, chief of the Federation of the Left, spoke better than he usually does. "What is wrong with your system is that it relies on the domination of certain economic forces and on the political decisions of one single man," he said openly to Pompidou. This brought a loud vocal outburst of loyalty to him from the left. Old Pierre Cot, affiliated with the left, said, with acumen and long political experience, "Those who do not vote for censure will see themselves once more humiliated by the President of the Republic." Edgard Pisani, a former Gaullist Minister and one of the earliest Gaullists on record, declared that he would vote for censure and then resign as a Gaullist deputy, which he now is. He added with candor, while looking at Pompidou, "I have the feeling that I am more faithful than you, in the circumstances, to the man whom I have upheld since the early Resistance," meaning that he thinks the General, as he first knew and followed him, needs to be checked in his present reckless pride and overweening love of France, as if it were his private hexagonal province. The only speech made by anyone that could be called brilliant and intellectual was the last of all those given, made by Giscard d'Estaing, the ambitious head of the Republican junior party of the Gaullist group. Oddly, his criticism of the Gaullist party was the most acute of that afternoon. "The first reform to make," he said, "is to change the manner in which France is governed. There has already been criticism of what is called the government's 'style.'" Then he added, in his high, cutting, intelligent voice, "However, I shall not vote for censure, because I have no confidence in the opposition to direct the country tomorrow."

France has waited for two weeks, composed mostly of troublesome, worrying days, for de Gaulle to say a word to his nation. He has taken time to prepare his thoughts. They should certainly be worth hearing.

June 2

This has been the decisive week since France's crisis began a fortnight ago, and probably last Wednesday was the decisive day, changing all that had happened before and much that will happen tomorrow and tomorrow, in long-drawn-out consequence. Paris had been physically calm since May 24th and that night's most unusual Latin Quarter student riot, in which the rioters arrived equipped with saws and hatchets, enabling them to cut down a reported seventy-two plane trees, some slender and young, some of a certain age and fine size, along the Boulevards Saint-Michel and Saint-Germain, down near the Cluny Museum, to make monster street barricades. Of all their destructive riots, this was the only one that left a pair of venerable Paris boulevards looking as if they had been cruelly ravaged by a Kansas cyclone—the only one after which French Army engineers had to carry off the debris with bulldozers and cranes. On Wednesday morning, the morale of Paris was at its lowest, with a contagious psychology of depression visible and audible on Parisians' faces in the streets and in their voices on the telephone—citizens who felt abandoned, drifting under a government that, as *Le Monde* trenchantly said, had "lost control." In past crises, de Gaulle more than once officially told his Fifth Republic nation that it could choose between him and chaos. Now, the French noted in increasing alarm, they still had him, yet also had chaos. A dominant public reaction was that this time it was de Gaulle's turn, as President, to make the choice, and that the best choice would be for him to resign, as his final, historic gift to himself and to his *belle France*. Then the noon news broadcast carried the startling announcement that he had failed to attend the Wednesday-morning weekly meeting of the Conseil des Ministres and had disappeared. Paris was alive with rumors, but the greatest credence was given to the rumor that he had bolted—as he had done in 1946, when, because of his disgust with French party politics, he went back to his country house in Colombey-les-Deux-Églises in retirement. This time, it was supposed that he had gone back home to compose his letter of resignation as President. One evening paper carried the headline "FRENCH PRESIDENT LOST FOR SEVEN HOURS," since officially nobody apparently knew where he was, but he finally turned up, in a later edition, at home in the country in time for supper. This semi-comic scenario of mystery baffled the public, and its bold plotting—surely by de Gaulle himself—will not be known in detail until the secret state papers of today become food for biographers fifty years from now. Through intelligent leaks to the press it became known the next day that during the blank hours he had flown to Baden-Baden to consult with his son-in-law, General Alain de Boissieu, and the fierce loyalist General Jacques Massu, along with other *chefs de corps* assembled in special meeting, so that he might solicit their opinion as to whether the French Army could, in the main, be relied on to support the government in case of civil war. So far, the only photographic evidence of this melodramatic journey by helicopter and presidential Caravelle airplane is a picture of Mme. de Gaulle, who accompanied him, in the limousine as they finally entered Colombey, sitting beside her husband in that kind of conjugal destiny that draws a wife into the public tapestry woven by her husband's ambitions, her face like a porcelain mask (beneath her correct toque hat) of perfected, strained wifely patience.

If Wednesday was the day that civil war might well have broken out, it was also the day that the pro-Communist Confédération Générale du Travail, the great French labor union, would have had its hands too full to have attended to it. It was the day that—in misty, pearly warm sunlight, readying for June—the union had arranged for a massive march of more than a hundred thousand of its members from the Bastille to the Gare Saint-Lazare, where no trains had run since the previous Friday. The night before, the C.G.T. had announced on the radio that the march would not be made in the spirit of merely demanding higher wages but would be strictly political. In consequence, the marchers sang the "Internationale," and their main slogan was *"Gouvernement Populaire!,"* meaning a popular-front government with Communist participation. *"De Gaulle, Démission!"* was the next most popular shout, along with *"Unité de la Gauche!"* and *"Adieu, de Gaulle, Adieu!,"* plus an occasional derisive *"Adieu, Charlot!"* Since the C.G.T. had previously honored its understanding with the government that it would try not to further tear down the waning French moral climate, this revolutionary aspect of its march, as *Le Figaro* said the next morning, "added weight to the already oppressive political atmosphere of Paris." All over France that afternoon, similar C.G.T. marches, with slogans and strikers' banners, were held in the big cities and in the towns like a ubiquitous funeral for the de Gaulle regime—which, in fact, was not yet defunct.

Though it was admitted that the student riots were what started the crisis, a resistance movement of the young, indulging in urban guerrilla warfare, was an enemy beyond and below de Gaulle's military respect or comprehension, and the crisis was abetted by his strange, disappointing, meaningless first broadcast, given in Paris after his return from Bucharest and after the first student riot. In puzzlement, both the public and political circles decided that he had suffered a *coup de vieux*—a kind of elderly attack of mental fatigue. In retrospect, that vacuous speech is now being interpreted as part of another artful scenario, intended to draw the Communist feeling out into the open, where it would be unmasked, by its own action, as a weapon sure to alarm the rank and file of the more ordinary non-Communist French, modest or wealthy (though the rich have never trusted de Gaulle), and rally them around their nation's familiar old leader once again. It was a brilliant gambit (if that is what it was) in the spirit of what is now called the psychology of "the party of fear." Like an old Frenchman playing political chess, with his government and, possibly, peace in France at stake, he let the men he considered his enemies fall into their own error of overconfidence, on which they lost. He obtained by his ruse a sudden burst of support, even from unexpected sources. Giscard d'Estaing, who holds the balance of power in the Chamber, stated in a broadcast that he was for de Gaulle but against Pompidou. That lonely, admirable Socialist politician Mendès-France, who could be envisioned as a possible interim government leader, merely laid himself open once more to being forced into an undignified discard. Strength began coming back to the Gaullist party, and perhaps more aural sensitivity, after the too many years in which it had been hard of hearing where the protests of ill-paid workers were concerned, and in which the rebus of what to do with young students, eager for change and new problems and answers, had not been solved in a Sorbonne where the class amphitheatres, crammed with youth, impatience, and angered hopes, were as overcrowded as tenement rooms.

On Thursday afternoon, de Gaulle made an upstanding old rallying-cry speech. It was harsh in its statement that the Communists were seeking an international autocracy—this coming from a man whose monarchical, autocratic methods over the past ten years have been the despair of those who have long known that the true French kings have been long since dead. The speech, which announced the dissolution of Parliament and the holding of new elections on June 23d and 30th, came just before a Place de la Concorde sundown rally in his honor. Until three o'clock in the morning, the Champs-Élysées was filled with what was left of the gigantic march up the avenue, in which French of all classes and ages carried the tricolor, the Union Jack, and even the Stars and Stripes, once more in honor. All that night, people with enough gasoline racketed up and down the avenue, sounding on their horns the rhythmic staccato toots that stood for *"Pour de Gaulle, Avec Nous."*

The end of this crisis in such merry-making was much too simple for the complexities and serious lack of answers that it had provoked. Those who never admired the General now in many cases ardently hate him, as having robbed them of their latest chance for a more modern democratic France. With election preparations starting next Sunday, the strike must perforce be ended at least in the post offices, in trains, and in transportation generally, so letters may be mailed and telegrams sent and received and political agents dispatched on their duties around the countryside for the election three weeks from now. Nobody is willing to prophesy on the election results. France has received a violent shock and setback. As a result of this strike (and of the General's victory, so far), there will be difficult, increasingly envenomed relations between French citizens of the left and those of the right—relations still unsettled and forever troublesome.

June 14

The strikes here, now going into their fourth week, have been best borne by peripatetics—by walkers. In this writer's midtown hotel, our middle-aged, portly fifth-floor waiter has been walking five hours a day, to and fro, between his distant suburban flat and his pantry here. When gasoline began to run dry the week before last, for two days everyone in Paris walked or stayed home. At the end of last week, the Métro and buses started running again, and also the commuter trains—a great relief to people's feet. Taxis were expected on the streets Wednesday but have not yet appeared. In industry, nearly a million metalworkers are still on strike, largely in the big automobile factories—Simca, Peugeot, Citroën, and Renault. As the only nationalized car manufacturer, Renault was the pilot in the strike negotiations, until it met with a tragedy on Monday in connection with its huge campestral modern factories at Flins, twenty-five miles west of Paris, built on what used to be well-known truck gardens beside the Seine. That afternoon, the ubiquitous Paris students managed to journey out there to encourage the Flins strikers. In their skirmish through the fields and woods with the alerted Compagnie Républicaine de Sécurité police, whose men and cars filled the country roads, a young girl and a youth tried to swim across the Seine, which is broad and deep in its curves there. She saved herself by clinging to the pillar of the bridge at Meulan, but the boy, aged seventeen, was drowned. He supplied the students with their first martyr.

To honor him and to avenge themselves on the police for his death, a monster, violent *manif'*, as the manifestations are now curtly called by the students, was organized for Tuesday night. It was the first warm, beautiful Paris June night, too celestial to have its beauty abused by rioting, with a full-faced moon, soon to be the color of a blood orange from the tear-gas bombs and the exploding *grenades offensives,* valued for their alarming noise. The battlefield was the familiar Latin Quarter. However, the tactics were different on both sides. Emerging from their covey of black buses, the C.R.S.

kept the Place de la Sorbonne and the Odéon cleared at first. This fractioned the students' forces and pushed them back up to the square in front of the Panthéon, where they ambitiously tried to capture the Fifth Arrondissement police station, next to the *mairie*. Later, they managed to reduce to a scrap heap the old, small police station on the Place Saint-Germain-des-Prés, next to the former Librairie Divan, that famed center for Stendhalian literature. At one moment, the police even took shelter in the doorway of the Café des Deux Magots, just across the way, whose great plate-glass windows were shattered. There was only one big student barricade, set up in the Rue Jacob, in front of the ugly modern medical center on the corner of the Rue des Saints-Pères. Far up the Rue de Rennes, near the old Montparnasse railway station, now being dismantled, the students set fire to the street itself by filling the gutters with gasoline and oil and lighting them. Flames belched from the sewers. The students' tactics were explicit and martial, after three weeks' rioting practice. They divided into small parties, each with its own *troupe de shock* for the fighting. All the students now live as noctambules. The wretched bourgeoisie housed in expensive old-fashioned apartments on the Boulevard Saint-Germain, near the Cluny, and around the Luxembourg Gardens are unnerved by sleepless nights but dare not leave for fear of what might happen to their homes in their absence.

On Monday, transportation having been restored, thousands of Parisians went back to work as the strikes, except in factories, started running downhill. On Tuesday, people's conversations overheard on the Paris streets had a different tone than before, carrying a sharp note of impatience as office and shop workers on the Left Bank saw the devastation remaining from earlier riots— trees cut down or singed, piles of uncollected debris, with here and there the remains of auto fenders, all of which rubbish had so recently been citizens' or taxpayers' property. At first during the riots, Parisians had with sang-froid scrawled *"Vive la Fête!"* on the walls of Left Bank houses, for the riots seemed like a terrifying fun fair— like a Resistance movie being shot at night al fresco, with full sound effects of screams, curses, and exploding bombs. As for the strike itself, it was like an extra vacation. Paris was titillated and excited by the historic words *"La Révolution,"* which flattered their past and animated their present. But the current had shifted by Tuesday, and by Wednesday morning the evidence on hand, still fresh, of the sadistic, destructive excesses of the previous night's monster riot left Parisians thoughtful, disgusted, and alarmed in their native sense of economy as to what it will all cost and who will have to pay. The political implication of the Tuesday-night long-drawn-out riot was as audible as the sharp gunlike staccato of the exploding *grenades offensives,* which, though being thrown around Saint-Germain-des-Prés, could be heard across the river in the Rue de Rivoli and the Tuileries Gardens until three o'clock in the morning. The rioting is now regarded as part of the students' plan to prevent the coming parliamentary elections from taking place in the calm that de Gaulle demanded as a dignified prerequisite. In this plan, the students—if the students are really the moving force behind it—show their fear that his Fifth Republic, and thus he himself, might even win again. This certainly is one of the French elements they have been rioting against.

The feeling of alarm here grew over the past week like a sense of responsibility belatedly discovered. There was also a feeling of almost naïve surprise among middle- and upper-class French that France was in so dangerously fragile and fatuous a condition that its young generation of malcontents could, by slogans and adolescent nightly public violence, deal a semi-mortal blow to France's present body politic and to its educational system (so démodé as to demand only a nudging to fall over flat, like a row of collapsing, ill-balanced, dusty books), and incite underpaid French workers to a national strike involving ten million strikers, which at the present moment is still not yet quite settled. A sharp, authoritarian, brief front-page editorial on the students appeared in *Le Monde* this Wednesday, signed, as a rarity, by the paper's editor, Hubert Beuve-Méry, under his own name, apparently to show that he was speaking as an outraged private citizen. The editorial aroused enormous interest here. Titled "Oui ou Non," it said, in part, "Yes or no: Is the renovation of our educational system to take place as a form of street fighting? Yes or no: Can a government, no matter what kind, let a Paris neighborhood be filled with barricades? Yes or no: If these occupations [of public buildings like the Sorbonne, the Odéon, and so on] continue, and if these riots multiply, will they not eventually lead to a kind of tribal warfare that, as everyone has every right to fear, could provoke extreme reactionary violence? Certainly the elections will be no panacea, but they offer an opening out of a situation that has become impossible. The leaders of this revolution, currently without any aim, have other preoccupations. The main thing for them—and they do not hide it—is *casser la baraque* [to break up the place]. Any effort at a solution, elections included, is, in their eyes, only 'a betrayal.' Any call to order, even the most elementary, is an unbearable provocation. Their victory would be that of pure nihilism, and no one can predict where the tragedy could lead."

Particular attention was naturally paid to the references to students also made by President de Gaulle in his TV dialogue the other evening with Michel Droit, editor of the weekly *Figaro Littéraire,* who had three times before been the General's vis-à-vis on similar question-and-answer programs. On the screen, they form a remarkably perfect pair of opposites, Droit being youngish, black-haired, and short. The subject of the students came up when Droit —rather putting the General on the spot—asked him why, since he had long ago declared that the university system here had to be changed, he had not started to change it in time to avoid the recent troubles. De Gaulle answered with that ambiguity he uses to win battles he is not prepared at the moment to fight. "Two things made up the recent university crisis," he said. "First, there was the anguish of youth, of the students, which is infinitely natural in today's modern, mechanized consumer society, because it does not offer them what they need—an ideal, *élan,* hope. Then an explosion took place, and, rightly enough, in the milieu where it should have taken place—that is, in the university milieu. It was provoked by certain groups who were in revolt against this modern society, whether Communist from the East or capitalist in the West. These groups have no idea at all what they would replace modern society with, but they are groups that delight in negation, destruction, violence, and anarchy, and they fly the anarchists' black flag." This, of course, was not a very penetrating summing-up of the student problem, which is now called the detonator of the Fifth Republic's crisis, but it was, on the other hand, an assurance to the nation's millions of TV listeners that the dialogue obviously had not been rigged—that de Gaulle was clearly not reciting prepared answers from memory, because he would have remembered more and better things to say—and it was also proof that Droit was not handling him with kid gloves. The most important, extraordinary question he asked de Gaulle came toward the beginning of the dialogue, when he suddenly said, *"Mon Général,* there is one thing that has enormously struck public opinion since the crisis began, and that is how it is possible that the government, any more than people generally, or the government opposition, or the labor unions and political organizations, did not sense this crisis coming. It is a fact that the government, whose task is to see what is coming, did not see the crisis in advance. But this enormous chaos, this enormous shock—how do you explain it, *mon Général,* how did you explain it to yourself?" To Droit's too pertinent question de Gaulle gave no real answer, doubtless because he knew too many answers. Considering that this TV dialogue was supposed to be a helpful preëlection piece of propaganda for the General's party, it was odd to have that party's recent disastrous lack of foresight publicly called to the attention of millions of the French electorate, who a fortnight from now might start thinking twice before risking their fate once again to such haphazard governing.

However, everything underwent a total change this Wednesday, when the government, on decisions made by the Minister of the Interior and approved at the weekly Cabinet meeting presided over by de Gaulle himself, banned all street demonstrations throughout France during the election campaign, and, furthermore, dissolved seven student groups of the extreme left. The riots, and the possible revolution, are now, one hopes, over. The seven dissolved groups are called Jeunesse Communiste Révolutionnaire, La Voix Ouvrière (which favors the Fourth Internationale), Révolte (which is the Trotskyite group and the most solid), Le Comité Liaison des Étudiants Révolutionnaires, La Fédération des Étudiants Révolutionnaires, L'Union des Jeunesses Communistes Marxistes-Léninistes (which is of Maoist inspiration and is the most intellectual, being largely recruited from the École Normale Supérieure and the Paris law faculty; it is said to be of such doctrinal purity that its members "sound like early Christians," one tough Trotskyite comrade reported), and, finally, Le Mouvement de 22 Mars, founded on that date at Nanterre by Daniel Cohn-Bendit, the German star and magnet among all the student groups. The seven groups were described in Thursday's *Journal Officiel* as "having had recourse to violence in attacking the republican form of the government." Those seeking to reconstitute these groups will be liable to from six months to two years in prison, and fines of from sixty to eighteen thousand francs. All the groups will now disappear underground.

The return to France last week, on provisional liberty, of former Premier Georges Bidault, once an early Gaullist leader but in exile for six years for having plotted against the state in Algerian affairs, and the rumored liberation of ex-General Raoul Salan, serving a life sentence for his part in the 1961 French Army uprising in Algiers and for being the chief of the anti-Gaullist terrorist Secret Army Organization, will serve as preëlection gestures to heal de Gaulle's breach with the French right over the loss of Algeria as a colony. The liberation of ex-General Salan will especially please the French Army, as the French Army pleased General de Gaulle ten days ago when it reassured him in Baden-Baden that he could rely on it in case of civil war. What is now taking place here in the Fifth Republic—or is about to—is like a great family reconciliation.

Paris, too, can relax at night now, since, with luck, there will be no more audible and visible fiery, explosive riots. The students, at first seeming inspired, are now running out of their early talent for creating slogans that will probably be salvaged as remnants of insurgent poetry, such as *"La Barricade Bloque la Rue mais Ouvre la Voix," "Plus Qu'on Fait L'Amour, Plus Qu'on Fait la Révolution,"* and that stirring call to power *"L'Imagination au Pouvoir!"*

June 27

"Les Jours de Mai" is what the Paris student revolution is called in retrospect and is the title it will indubitably be given in Fifth Republic French history, where it will become legendary as an epic in violence by the most educated young bourgeois in the capital of France. The Days of May are finally coming to their end in this last week of June through the election of a new National Assembly, which might last only one year and which President de Gaulle did not want at all. But on second thought he wanted even less to resign. As in the classic French theatre, some visible change is often necessary to mark the end of an important dramatic action, so a changed Parliament was slated to mark this evolution here, with the General remaining in place, himself almost utterly unchanged. On the high showing of last Sunday's preliminary vote, the Gaullist Union pour la Défense de la République may once more be the party of election—indeed, of predilection—this coming Sunday as well. If this becomes the case, it is taken for granted that hurried reforms promulgated by Premier Pompidou, containing a modicum of what can be saved from ten years of miraculously successful Gaullism, could create a new type of Gaullism, which would make the pre-revolutionary formula seem a Gaullism *dépassé,* or even defunct. Next Sunday's winner will surely not be the Parti Socialiste Unifié, headed by Pierre Mendès-France, with his tragic solo gift, though he is the unique politician to courageously back the students, who still have a special leftover popularity. Whoever does win will be faced with the gigantic task of putting France together again, to contain what is unsettled, new, and even cyclonic, but is surely part of France's young, post-revolutionary atmosphere today.

What also marks the end of the revolution itself is the termination, only this week, of the tremendous and costly strike in the country's three great auto works—Renault, Peugeot, and Citroën (it seems that Simca never was really struck but merely stopped work for lack of supplies)—which flared like a brush fire from the students' bombs and barricades in the Latin Quarter. Its settlement this week gives the hitherto underpaid workers a wage boost of from ten to fourteen per cent, plus promised half payment for each day of the strike itself, which began May 14th. This automobile strike has been the longest, the most crucial, and the most obstinately fought for of any struggle in modern French industry. The Communist-dominated Confédération Générale du Travail, France's biggest labor union, handled the final thirty-five-hour negotiations with the factory managers and owners, and declared with pride that "the result was an incontestable success." However, the Confédération Française Démocrate du Travail, next in size but superior in social vision, declared that its workers accepted the settlement with "rage in their hearts." What its members had hoped for—along with bigger wages, of course—was a radical transformation of the enterprises themselves, "with new democratic structures substituting for the industrial and bureaucratic monarchy of the auto industries' practices." "Participation" in business management, in running universities, in teaching Greek, or in whatever has become the key word of the new young revolutionary society here. Even during the recent three-week general strike, the strikers themselves treated the stricken (or those whom the strike affected, which was everybody) with exceptional consideration, as if realizing for once that they, too, were participants in a helpless way. Gas and electricity were struck here, but with a minimum service assured and, actually, with normal complete service most of the time. Prices have, of course, started to rise along with wages. A *baguette,* that delicious yardstick of French bread, at once rose five centimes the yard; milk and newspapers rose. The four-day strike just last week of newspaper dealers, most of whom closed their shops or kiosks entirely, put newsboys back on the Paris streets for the first time in years, running about and crying their wares: *"Ici Le Monde!" "Voilà France-Soir!"* Gasoline is going up next week, with a rise of two centimes a litre—one centime going to the pump man, the other to the French state. The state radio and TV strikes are just finished, but without the intellectual rebels, who wanted objective rather than paternalistic pro-de Gaulle news programs, having won.

France has lately been an epicenter for troubles. During the student riots, cheap little Paris hotels, even on the Right Bank, simply locked their front doors. The chic Tour d'Argent restaurant actually shut down temporarily because of lack of clients and absence of American tourists, and Maxim's was open only for lunch. The weather has been wet, cold, and stormy during some part of each day, often with thunder and lightning. Suburban flower gardens have produced lovely roses, but by the next day the rain has rotted them away. Farmers are worried about their grain. The Paris air smells like the seaside, filled with strong wind. Everyone says there will be no more bad troubles until October, when they will begin afresh. People are short of cash, of course, and everyone lost money during the three weeks of the general strike, which was calamitous.

Without transportation or postal service, business was simply suspended. There were, furthermore, the cars burned by the students in the Latin Quarter streets, on which no insurance can be claimed and which are a dead loss. All the automobiles of the recently struck auto works are going up three per cent in price this week. By October, French people are expected to be out of patience with France's ill luck. The great threat in October is going to be that of French unemployment.

The Beaux Arts, since the May revolution renamed the Ex-École des Beaux Arts, has over the past few weeks been flying not one red flag but two red flags in its open courtyard facing the Rue Bonaparte. A red flag dominantly hung in any Paris scholastic institution indicates that the place is no longer under the direction of its professors, appointed by the state, but is operating under what is called "student power." Not only has the Ex-Beaux Arts been flying its pair of red flags but the right-hand wall of the courtyard, just inside the gate—a *pignon* wall ornamented with portions of the elegant original carved façade of the Château of Anet, where Diane de Poitiers dallied with her king—has been flaunting high on its roof a red umbrella, rigged up over the statue of some unidentifiable royal dignitary, and another small figure has been wearing a red handkerchief tied around his neck. The flags, at least, were removed today, shortly after dawn, when the Paris police (not the Compagnie Républicaine de Sécurité shock troops) evacuated the hundred or more Beaux Arts occupants, of whom a dozen or more were sleepy girls who were not students, they said. One young man said he was a tourist who had been in Paris only a couple of days and had wanted to see what was going on in the art world. The premises, unlike the Sorbonne or the Théâtre de l'Odéon, were perfectly tidy and in good order after occupation. The Salle Brianchon, named after a Beaux Arts professor, was the room the police were most interested in, since it was there that the students had been making their brilliant anti-governmental posters, which had been pasted up pretty well all over town. The most popular had been a disrespectful cartoon of de Gaulle—nose protuberant, arms up in the air like semaphores—with the title "Le Chie-en-Lit C'est Lui," a reference to a bit of coarse barracks-room slang that the General had recently used to describe somebody else. The posters were made by the serigraphic process (rubbing color through a nylon frame onto the paper beneath), and were about two feet high. On the day last week that this correspondent was in the printing room, a couple of artists were pulling copies of one of the handsomest of the posters, in which the C.R.S. police were shown marching in hard, serrated ranks, like the tops of mountains. Another popular one concerned the O.R.T.F. (the censored French state radio), which was represented by the body of a policeman, one of his arms labelled "Europe No. 1," the most popular station here for objective news, being non-governmental, and the other labelled "Radio Luxembourg," which is foreign. There was a witty cartoon of Marianne, the young female figure who represents La Belle France, with a kerchief tied over her mouth; a kerchief over the eyes is used on the French TV screen when scenes unsuitable for youthful fans are about to be shown. (The censorship of news by the state radio is still one of the most criticized of all the Fifth Republic practices.) The "Atelier Populaire," as the printing room was renamed, was highly organized and could make close to a thousand posters a day. The subject matter was first discussed in committee, then trials of its presentation and treatment were made until general agreement was reached. There was a tin box near the print table for contributions by visitors; posters sold from ten to fifty francs each and were not signed.

Certain Beaux Arts students had earlier been in communication with André Malraux, Minister of Cultural Affairs, in an effort to inaugurate a modernization of the rigorous, old-fashioned regulations dominating art studies here, and they have just this week announced a further ultimatum. They want the abrogation of the statutes protecting the studio *"patron,"* or chief, whose opinion can make or break a young student's personal style—a tyranny resented by Matisse at the Beaux Arts when he was young. They want the suppression of competitions for admission to the school, and of the famous Prix de Rome, of which they seem to think little. Of all the various "student-powered" institutions since the Days of May, the students at the Ex-Beaux Arts seem the most intelligently, persistently concerned with working out new programs for flexible instruction of the sort they are still young enough to desire or almost old enough to be sure have validity. It will be a pity if being interrupted by the Paris police at dawn this week should call their plans to a halt.

July 11

The official bills for the students' Latin Quarter revolution, legally calculated as having lasted from May 6th to June 15th, have already been totted up. So far, only *Paris-Presse L'Intransigeant,* the minor but pro-Gaullist afternoon newspaper, has printed this very odd and interesting historical data, with its worrying amplifications, one of these being that Parisians' city taxes this year may well be ten per cent higher, so as to include their willy-nilly contribution toward paying for the riot damage their city suffered. The biggest bill will be paid by the Prefecture of Paris, and in diminishing size will come the bills charged to the Prefecture of Police, the Ministry of Cultural Affairs, and the various Paris universities. The over-all Paris bill is reported at a hundred and fifty million francs, or thirty million dollars—no petty extra sum, it being equal to a big fraction of the annual budget for the entire capital city in normal, uncontentious times. The Paris Prefecture's opening bill is for the relaying in and around the Boul' Mich' of one million cube-shaped stone paving blocks, torn up to strengthen the student barricades or to be used as ammunition against the police. (A few hundred grubby cubes were sold to German tourists by neighborhood children as revolutionary souvenirs, just as white stone blocks from the Bastille were sold to French provincials when it was demolished after 1789.) Other items that will have to be replaced and paid for are a hundred trees, six direct-line telephones for calling the police and one for calling firemen, five hundred traffic lights, several thousand of those charming semicircular, lacy-looking iron grilles that are placed around the boulevard trees to protect their roots, hundreds of street trash baskets, and a few rusted *vespasiennes,* which will have to be replaced to placate old, conservative male voters. The Prefecture will also have to pay for more than two hundred incidents of destroyed private property, such as first-floor apartment windows, doors, and even sidewalks. More general, because bigger targets, were broken shop-windows, but in only rare cases was there any looting. The Café Gay-Lussac, whose windowed sidewalk terrace was smashed, was robbed of its glassware, its liqueurs, its cakes, and its telephone tokens. Two local cinemas, the Cluny and the Boul' Mich', were vandalized to the tune of forty thousand francs each, the screen of the latter being slit. The Cluny Métro station was wrecked—another Prefecture bill. Certain owners of damaged property have already been reimbursed. These are the identifiable foreign owners of parked cars that were used as faggots or as logs for the student barricades in the Latin Quarter. The Prefecture of Police will have to pay for restoring nine wrecked police stations.

More costly even than the depredations are the city's bills for substitute services it had to hire because of the stoppage brought on by the general strike, which was triggered by the student riots and thus came second in the legally viewed chain of events. Substitute garbage men and trucks had to be found and hired, and now have to be paid for. The French Army is owed for the use of its small trucks, which took the place of city buses around town. The Prefecture of Paris is paying for delays in underground work on new Métro lines, and also in work on the peripheral boulevards and the highway to Rungis, the new market town that will take the place of Les Halles. As for the Ministry of Cultural Affairs, close to a million francs must be paid to the Odéon-Théâtre de France alone, whose red velvet loge curtains were used as covers by those who were regular sleep-ins there; losses were sustained also by the costume-wardrobe rooms, which were pillaged for all purposes. When, after nearly a month, the police finally evacuated the theatre at dawn, three young children, with a mother or so, were discovered among the residents—not one of whom had anything to do with the theatre, except for living in it free, in discomfort. The Sorbonne, which became a combination pamphlet shop, propaganda center, debating hall, jazz-concert headquarters, and general all-night, all-purpose student wayside station, had the biggest cleanup bill to hand on to the Ministry of Education. It took a special sanitary squad four days to disinfect it. The most costly damage took place in the Bourse, when it was briefly set on fire. The destruction of its elaborate electrical apparatus for carrying the stock-market quotations made the highest repair bill for any single building—reportedly close to fifty million francs. That France's symbolic center of capitalism should be the costliest wreck to repair after the riots by the bourgeois students must be a very satisfying bit of political irony to the French Communist Party.

Several extremely interesting books, booklets, and special editions of magazines dealing with the riots have been published here. Two or three merit the attention of serious collectors of historic oddities. France's biggest afternoon paper, *France-Soir,* at once published a stunning paperback tricolor-bound album of its most exciting nocturnal and action photographs, called "Les Journées de Mai." They are superb illustrations of that terrible disequilibrium between the professional and the amateur fighters—the great, tilting charge of the helmeted, strong-bodied, and booted police, their shields angled like those of ancient gladiators, against the students in their sweaters and tennis shoes, perhaps with their garbage-pail lids held defensively aloft. Also shown are the students lying in groups in the streets, their hands clasped behind their necks on police orders, their legs drawn up tight to their bellies, as if to protect their very manhood or to keep their feet from being further trampled on—pathetic but spirited young castaways on the cobblestones in a true ballet of poses of distorted limbs and inexperienced despair. Unfortunately, "Les Journées de Mai" was issued in only one edition, which was immediately sold out and is now out of print. Tchou, the Sino-French de-luxe publisher of Kafka, has brought out the perfect little book for everyone who can read French and is interested in the revolution. It is inexpensive; is pocket-size, with a bright-red cover; is nearly two hundred pages long; is called "Les Murs Ont la Parole, Mai, '68;" and consists of the best of the graffiti and slogans scribbled on walls by the students, mostly in the universities but also in the occupied Odéon theatre—a choice collection of anger, cynicism, hope, hatred, and black, anarchistic, brooding comments, mostly Surrealistic in their intellectual style. Because all the walls were afterward cleaned, these graffiti are like original insurgent commentaries, which would have been lost under the cleaners' mops if the student-action committees had not had the sense to copy and save them. (Even as it is, though, they seem, in a way, like statements by ghosts.) Following each contribution is the name of the university and the part of its building where the slogan was found, such as "The Wall of the Sorbonne Staircase," so that for the reader each thought seems to have had at least a brief physical habitat.

Alain Buhlers' "Petit Dictionnaire de la Révolution Étudiante" is invaluable for defining briefly who and what every segment of the Days of May was, with lists of leaders' names, titles, ages, education, and backgrounds—even for the leaders of the minorities. "La Révolte Étudiante," published by Le Seuil, features statements and arguments by Jacques Sauvageot, vice-president of the Students' Union at the Sorbonne—twenty-five years old, with degrees in law and art history—and Alain Geismar, four years his senior, who is an assistant at the Faculté des Sciences de Paris. The book's major contribution is a remarkable dialogue between Jean-Paul Sartre, benign and enthusiastic, and Daniel Cohn-Bendit, twenty-three years old, born in France of German parents, brilliant, precise, magnetic in mind and laughing face and red, curly hair, without whom the Paris revolution would not have taken place. At present, he is the leading speaker for his generation in Europe. He has now disappeared back over the border into Germany—whether under French Foreign Office pressure is not clear, although his absence from France must officially be considered a salient relief here. It is noteworthy that this dialogue with the German student (who is in his second year of sociology at the new suburban University of Nanterre) has restored Sartre for the first time in several years to contemporary participation in Paris intellectual life, withdrawing him from the moldy immortality that isolated him. A sample of the subtle clarity of Cohn-Bendit's thinking is contained in the following statement he made to Sartre: "The defense of students' interests is, in any case, very problematic. What are their so-called interests? The students don't constitute a class. The workers, the peasants form a social class and have objective interests. Their demands are clear and are addressed to the owner hierarchy—to the representatives of the bourgeoisie. But the students? Who are their 'oppressors,' if not the entire system . . . of French society today?"

Much has been changed in France in the past six weeks, with victories and defeats that no one could predict or see in his imagination or hopes, or even in his hatreds. France itself seems changed by the very perpetuity of the same power figure it has so long known—that of General de Gaulle, whose party was reëlected last week in a victory like a landslide, and in a way as destructive, sweeping everything before it into a new politicized limbo and leaving familiar French political thinking and definitions temporarily homeless, denuded, and unrecognizable. For instance, the Communist share of the votes was pitiable in quantity and in significance, considering that the Party represented the workers of France. The French Socialists, who, under Léon Blum in the mid-thirties, initiated the forty-hour working week and the first paid vacations, were this time lost in the trashy leftovers that constituted the Federation of the Left or were smothered in the little Unified Socialist Party by the ill luck that in these late years has attended the efforts of Pierre Mendès-France, once the Star of David for certain intellectual reformist minds. It was said here that there were no new political figures or groups in this month's elections. Yet was not the so-called Party of Fear—the citizens who, fearing chaos, ignored party lines and voted for de Gaulle—a new dominating group, and were not the revolutionary students the new Paris political figures, discovered by all of France in the newspaper headlines about the riots? In the suddenly upside-down situations that former leaders found themselves in, President de Gaulle, for instance, gained the odd position of a supremely upper-class leftist—the political leader whose old theory of profit-sharing participation between capital and labor many years ago taught the capitalists their original distrust of him. Now he is being hailed by them (and for the first time) as their temporary savior, after having so long merely saved France. The exaggeration of the Gaullist party's victory has turned the election into a kind of national political rebus, whose solution (especially after the disappearance of Georges Pompidou) no one can even guess at until autumn.

September 12

This has been a long, agitated summer season, which seems to stretch as far back as the first days of May, when the student riots broke over the city like nocturnal storms, with the distant rumble of thunder furnished by Left Bank grenades and the false lightning by the flash of tear-gas shells fired by the regimented police. In June came the month-long general strike and its endless parades across paralyzed Paris, with the marchers waving their black anarchist flags like cynical signs of mourning, as if the Fifth Republic had died and they were glad of it. In July came the usual vacation hegira from the city, this summer with a depressingly limited number of workers and shopkeepers who could afford to go, since the strikers had been paid only half-time wages, and shopkeepers, big and little, from the Galeries Lafayette to the neighborhood lingerie emporiums, had simply closed their doors and swallowed their losses. In August, Nature herself disobligingly furnished the storms, with rare, chilly winds and violent rain squalls. In anticipation of a bad grain crop, French farmers began moaning about their wheat fields (now just harvested, with only a moderately subnormal yield). Then, during the night of August 20th, the Warsaw Pact troops and the Russian soldiers drove their tanks into Czechoslovakia. As is his habit lately in non-French crises, the sometimes remarkably vocal General de Gaulle remained silent. A couple of days later, the special Ministerial Council, after a meeting, issued a statement that was headlined in the Paris press as "LE GÉNÉRAL DIT," which said only that his government expressed the hope "that the Soviet troops would retire from Czechoslovakia and leave it to determine its own destiny." Afterward, Foreign Minister Debré, commenting before Parliament's Foreign Affairs Committee, ineptly illustrated France's attitude toward the occupation with what was regarded in diplomatic circles as a historically clumsy metaphor. He referred to the events in Prague as "a highway accident" that did not imply that the highway itself had to be closed, since France's policy of détente with Moscow would continue (presumably once the temporary wreckage was cleared away).

Actually, the most unexpected, spirited anti-Soviet French protest on the occupation of Prague was published two days later in the Paris Communist newspaper *L'Humanité,* which blazoned in big black headlines, "Five Socialist Countries—Russia, Poland, the German Democratic Republic, Hungary, and Bulgaria—Have Militarily Intervened in Czechoslovakia. The French Communist Party Expresses Its Surprise and Reprobation." This was tantamount to a French Communist Party rebellion against Moscow's imperialist *diktat*. In 1956, when the Russians bloodily invaded Budapest, the French Communist Party obediently cheered. This time, *L'Humanité* added to its headline of displeasure an editorial declaring that lately the French Party's Central Committee considered that "Communist problems between different national Parties should be settled by the sovereignty of each country in free determination and in the spirit of international proletarianism," which means in local liberty. To experts on the developments of the European Communist line, this radical change toward self-determination in French Communism marked the second historic change in the European ideological apparatus. The first great change, of course, was Khrushchev's daring denunciation of Stalin and the personality cult at the Twentieth Party Congress, of which this new French breakaway is considered the latest descendant. It has featured the first open derision of the cult of infallibility in which the Moscow Party has from earliest days swathed itself, and which it has repeatedly proclaimed, as if it were Communism's permanent Pope.

This new, liberated Communism, christened Le Socialisme Humaniste, was illustrated by Louis Aragon, the literary *chef de file* of the Communists, in their weekly *Lettres Françaises,* of which he is editor. In a pungent front-page paragraph, he has just declared, apropos of the Prague tragedy and in reproof of Moscow, "In an old colonial country like France, for too many years faced with our war against Vietnam and then against Algeria, we lived through the words of Marx: 'A people which oppresses another people is itself not a free people.'" Aragon being a member of the ruling Comité Central du Parti Communiste Français, he was immediately attacked for this at long distance from Moscow in the *Literaturnaya Gazeta,* which accused him of being "politically myopic" and of having already erred in the past—probably in having been one of the few Party individuals who protested against the Budapest invasion. "Must he continue to make the same error?" the *Gazeta* inquired, as if bewildered, although its national Russian leaders had made the same mistake twice in twelve years. What bewildered the general French public was how the notorious Russian intelligence service could have made such an immense miscalculation about the temper of the French Party (described in more than one Paris newspaper commentary as now temporarily cut in two, with the majority pro-Czech rather than pro-Moscow), plus running the further danger of bringing about a "deterioration of the Soviet image" in the eyes of the Western world generally—an image that already, at least in cartoons, appears that of a Slav Colossus as tyrant.

In another mistake in planning, Moscow had earlier called for a meeting in November of an international conference of Communist Parties. The Italian Party—the West's largest group, and by tradition the most intellectual—has now announced its refusal to attend until the Czech situation reaches "definite and satisfactory normalization." The Italian Party secretary, Luigi Longo, seems confident that he does not have in mind the same normalization that Moscow is thinking about. Longo has demanded that the Russian troops be withdrawn and that the Dubček government be allowed to get on with its work. The Italian Party's break with Moscow over what Longo calls "the tragic mistake in Czechoslovakia" has been even more defiant than the one in France. The conference was supposed to restore the badly fractured unity of the world's non-Russian Communists. Almost all except the pro-Peking parties had agreed to attend. Now it appears that the conference will be cancelled, or, if not, that nobody will come. The end of the year 1968 is doubtless just the perfect wrong time to plan to hold it, especially in Moscow.

Nine years ago, as Minister of Cultural Affairs, M. André Malraux, with his unerring instinct for perfection, appointed Jean-Louis Barrault and Madeleine Renaud, conjugal stars of their unique, celebrated, inspired theatre troupe, to play in the state's Odéon-Théâtre de France. Last week, Barrault announced that they (or, rather, he) had been dismissed, causing a shock and a scandal in Paris. It all goes back to the spring riots, when, because of the Odéon's proximity, an overflow of students picnicking in the Sorbonne surged in on May 15th and settled down as free lodgers. According to Barrault, while he was talking to a packed student house from the stage on May 17th he was extemporaneously addressed by the student firebrand Daniel Cohn-Bendit, who told him that the kind of theatre needed today was "an instrument of combat against the bourgeoisie." Barrault himself says he replied (it has all been printed in the Paris papers, like excerpts from a new theatrical playlet), "At the risk of disappointing you, I shall say that I completely agree with you." Then, in what others present described as a kind of "dramatic panic," he suddenly added, "Barrault is no longer director of this theatre. He is a comedian like all the others. Barrault is dead!" Now, three months later, he has been discharged by Malraux for "various declarations that seemed far removed from the mission entrusted to him." *Le Monde,* being the least transcendent Paris journal, seems the most reliable to quote on this melodramatic contretemps: "Let no one regard with indignation the time when the Church refused Christian burial to actors! The Fifth Republic is now giving to one of its best an affront of far less quality. . . . These men who are always reminding us of the virtues of Euripides, Shakespeare, and Molière become very annoying. The greater some individuals are—and Barrault is and remains great— the more they have to be pulled down."

Monday's press conference by General de Gaulle was held, as usual, in the Élysée's Salle des Fêtes, on a suddenly sultry afternoon, with the elegant Empire room additionally heated by its eight magnificent crystal chandeliers ablaze with light for the convenience of the news and cinema photographers, plus the solar spotlight in the cornice directed onto the table where the General was to be seated. The table was covered with a yellow cloth, and behind him there was a yellow curtain, instead of the familiar scarlet, since the films were to be made in color, in which the royal red photographs merely black. The room was packed with seven or eight hundred journalists from all over the world, many of whom freely fanned themselves with the large, formal, pale-gray numbered invitation cards, marked "La Présidence de la République." Present also were de Gaulle's full Cabinet, foreign diplomats and embassy secretaries, and other listeners and observers. As time goes on, the changing quality of de Gaulle's face and voice is scrupulously noted at each of these press meetings, like a kind of dated facial and vocal calendar of his years. This time, his face had thinned around the temples and his voice had less timbre than before. At this conference, unlike previous ones, he gave no dazzling demonstration of his showmanship by reciting his discourse by heart, all in one piece. Instead, he asked for questions from chosen journalists, received eleven, and avoided three of them, answering ad lib from that fabulous collection of facts and ambiguities secreted in his tall, narrow skull. He chose to talk about France's interior problems for nearly an hour, with the May crisis given sixteen minutes, the demotion of loyal Premier Pompidou only four minutes, Senate reforms and regionalization plans (both dull for foreigners) eight minutes, the financial participation of workers in industry (his old, revived theme of profit-sharing, which the French labor unions are against) seven minutes, and the uncompleted university reforms seven minutes, with twelve minutes given to Czechoslovakia and its drama and four minutes to projected French aid to Biafra, as exemplifying today's worst world tragedies, political and physical. He half circled the globe with his opinions.

On the May events, he poured forth a nearly endless tumultuous sentence, his first real spoken report on the climate of the student riots that almost unseated his Fifth Republic. In part, he mentioned "the kind of vertigo found here in the rapid and profound transformation of our country, with all its faults and backwardnesses and egoisms . . . brought to light in the major newspapers." Then he interpolated, with a malicious smile, "Isn't that true, *Messieurs les journalistes?*" Like most semi-supreme rulers, he has no love for the Fourth Estate, which, along with the radio, he said, noted only what was scandalous, violent, and destructive, plus "the state of mind of certain intellectual milieus, irritated by realities and adopting in all realms—literary, artistic, philosophic— the formula of contradiction." To this problem, "morbid in many ways," he continued with the next breath, "I agree that my government did not at once find the solutions." In this long harangue, he did not once mention French youth itself as one of the causes of the May explosion against French bureaucracy in schools, in government, and in the historic national soul.

In answer to the question why Pompidou had not been continued in his post of Prime Minister after the June elections, de Gaulle said genially, "I am now on my third Prime Minister," indicating Premier Couve de Murville, publicly sitting for the first time in the Cabinet's front row of ministers nearby. As for Pompidou, "After all he did in his six and a half years of office—the longest stretch in four generations—and after he showed such exemplary strength during the upheavals of May and June, it appeared that he should not go on until exhausted. So it seemed right that he should be placed in reserve for the Republic, as he himself wished. This was what I decided, thus inviting him to be prepared for, whatever *mandat* the nation might entrust him with." Obviously, this *mandat* is supposed to be his sometime election as President of the Republic, since he still seems to be de Gaulle's dauphin, now merely taking a preparatory long vacation.

Of Czechoslovakia de Gaulle said, alertly lifting his head, in which his eyes were suddenly animated and flashing, "The French people and all Europe expected something different and much better from the great Russian people than to see them lock up and put into chains their satellites, within the enclosure of crushing totalitarianism."

These were the exceptional, vivifying excursions in the press conference. There was nothing new in the state of his own country or of the world that de Gaulle could mention with pride, so his imagination and his sense of history were not aroused. Impressive as ever in speech and presence as he sat there in his Élysée, he seemed like a great performer saying much of what he has said before, as an encore.

September 26

It is rare that the President of the Republic, in a reflex of disapproval, says anything even faintly humorous. Last week, when several of his hard-shell conservative ministers agreed that it would be folly to vote for Minister Edgar Faure's historic education-reform bill, de Gaulle, sharp as a knife, said, "If Minister Faure had been out of his mind, everybody would have been aware of it, and if he starts going out of it now, there will still be time to take steps." The last straw in Faure's reform bill for de Gaulle's pro-Establishment ministers was the inclusion of permission to discuss politics in special campus lecture rooms—politics having been, in theory, banished as dangerous ever since the educational system was reorganized by Napoleon, in 1808. The system's aim, the Emperor said frankly at the time, was to have "the means of directing public opinion and morals," with education to be used as intellectual support for the government, just as the Army was for physical support. It was these hundred and sixty years of early-nineteenth-century practices and atmosphere that brought the students out onto the streets in the May riots against what they called "educational sclerosis." Other key words in the education rebellion have turned out to be *"l'autonomie,"* or the independence of France's twenty-odd provincial universities, instead of their all being under the centralizing octopus head of Paris; *"co-gestion,"* or the co-management of universities by faculty and students; the right of *"contestation,"* or argument; and the holding of *"le dialogue"* between students and their professors on matters of pedagogy, historical interpretation, and so on. All these are included in Faure's reform bill, if only by implication. What is brand-new is a rule that the faculty must live in the vicinity of the university, so as to provide a teacher-student relationship that has probably not been provided here since the time of the great medieval teacher Abelard. Another new ruling is that professors who stand high in official popularity—they are known as mandarins—are to be restricted from holding their university chairs practically for life. Order in each university will supposedly be maintained by the state-appointed rector. A university president (a new, American-model French functionary) will be elected by the faculty and by students who have finished their first year and passed its examinations—a real revolutionary change. The conservative cream of the official Gaullist party would, if it dared, doubtless vote en bloc against Faure's bill, which (it is known) de Gaulle himself is determined must be passed, as the only calming piece of legislation appropriate to the impending opening of the universities. Faure has already threatened to resign if his bill is not passed in the session of Parliament that opens this week, or if its salient features are watered down into compromises to obtain an assenting vote on it. His opus, if it goes through fairly intact, by French standards, will constitute a revolutionary, iconoclastic, long-overdue modernization of French university education, from which springs the French ruling class in business and government. The bill is perhaps the unique good result of the spring riots, and the only appeasement to have been offered since then that may discourage the students from rioting again this autumn. If Faure's reform becomes law, it will begin functioning this coming February.

Faure's political importance has grown enormously since his impressive, brilliant labor on and creation of his bill. He is now described as the most intelligent—almost too intelligent—minister in the Cabinet. Because of him, this has been an unusual fortnight in Paris, marked by middle- and upper-class concentration on his complex educational reforms, which have involved many parents and their student sons and daughters in bitter dissension. Discussion of the final draft of Faure's bill in the press has covered many pages and has been heavy going. It was probably the only reading matter that the two generations perused together this year.

October 23

Marcel Duchamp, who died at eighty-one this month in his suburban Neuilly home, was the youngest of three remarkable brothers in the bourgeois Duchamp-Villon family, long established near Rouen. They all had the vocational gift for being artists, but what Marcel Duchamp saw, as if by an enriching error in his creative vision, was always the contrary of what was visible to others, which afforded him the invaluable defect for making discoveries in contemporary art. A member in 1912 of the Paris Section d'Or group that included Juan Gris and his closest friend, Francis Picabia, he had a style that was a combination of Italian Futurism and French Cubism. Both were visible in "Nu Descendant un Escalier," the picture that Duchamp sent to the famous 1913 Armory show of contemporary art in New York, where it instantly became the dominant canvas and the greatest scandal, because Americans found it the least comprehensible. Actually, this painting was a rare, highly perfected example of kinetic art, depicting a de-composition of motion, amalgamated through Cubism into a simultaneous form. In 1915, arriving for the first time in New York, where he spent the remaining war years, he found he had already become famous while *in absentia*. Some few fervid appreciators considered his descending nude more important than Picasso's "Les Demoiselles d'Avignon." Duchamp himself later said of it, "What shocked the public was the title," adding, "A nude should be respected. It should not descend a staircase, because that is ridiculous." He said that he had found the violent reception accorded it "very agreeable," and went on, "After all, my aim was not to please a general public. I was paid two hundred and forty dollars for the canvas—also very pleasant." Today, it is in the Louise and Walter Arensberg Collection of the Philadelphia Museum of Art, which values it at a quarter of a million dollars. The Arensbergs, then of New York, and the wealthy Katherine Dreier, of Connecticut, were Duchamp's first American patrons. In 1917, Duchamp provoked a special scandal by sending to New York's first Salon des Indépendants a porcelain urinal with the title "The Fountain," signing it "R. Mutt," a firm of sanitary engineers. This Gallicism was not appreciated; the salon rejected the entry, which Duchamp said proved that it was not independent, and he resigned, amid publicity, from its jury.

Considering the extraordinary influence that Duchamp had on appreciators of contemporary art on both sides of the Atlantic, it is remarkable that he talked about art so rarely, and then only impersonally. A witty conversationalist, he could define his views by paradoxes. He talked in a low, elegant voice, and laughed almost silently. Among his dicta was "Bad taste is the greatest enemy of art." He was a moralist of art, not a philosopher. He also shocked New York by his agnostic views on painting. "When you start to sell your paintings, everything is spoiled," he said. "To create is not to start the same picture once a month, changing the left-hand corner and replacing the blue with red. Most great painters have discovered four or five important aesthetic propositions; the rest—the filling in —is merely to earn a living." In his mid-thirties, he ceased painting entirely and became a kind of influential art myth. Credited by the Surrealists with being, in a way, the father of Surrealism, he developed an interest in manufactured objects, to which he gave a contemporary art value by his appreciation—a bicycle wheel, a bottle rack. By this time, his aesthetic decisions ranked as creations. Today, he is considered the father of Pop Art and of Op Art—a paternity that took more time to develop.

The last years of his life were devoted to chess, at which he became an expert. (*Figaro* mentioned his death in its chess column.) He also taught his wife—she had formerly been married to Matisse's son Pierre—to play. Duchamp seldom entered tournaments, lacking the needed physical stamina. According to Man Ray, the artist-photographer, who first played chess with him above the Pepper Pot Restaurant back in the old Greenwich Village days, chess to Duchamp was a form of conversation, in which one's character emerged as one exposed oneself to the opponent, the conversation being rather like an argument—except that in chess the argument reaches a decision. Man Ray, a third-rate player himself, was a great chessboard and chess-piece designer, his sets becoming famous for their simple modern design—pyramids, cones, and little balls for pawns. Man Ray made for Duchamp a magnetic chess board with magnetic pieces, which remained in place when the board was hung on the wall, like a picture of the previous game.

Duchamp was a unique, brilliant constructive and destructive artist, and the only painter who became internationally famous for painting one canvas. At his death, Picasso said, like an epitaph, *"Il avait tort"*—"He made a mistake," meaning he should not have died.

French leftist politics are in a state of disarray not known here in the last fifty years. Socialist François Mitterrand, leader of the Federation of the Left, which he founded three years ago as a first step toward a united non-Communist left, has announced that he will seek no further political office as a representative of the Convention of Republican Institutions, the Conventionists being supposedly the liveliest of the Federation's three components. The trio also included the traditional Socialists and the Radical Socialists, a party founded in 1901 and now known simply as the Radicals. Their precarious unity was so direly shaken in the elections last June that Mitterrand found himself at the head of a political nonentity. In his speech, he warned that there was no chance for Socialism in France if Gaullism really took root, and that de Gaulle was now creating structures that could permit his system to live after him.

In 1965, Mitterrand won an unexpectedly large vote against de Gaulle in the Presidential elections, and it was after this big, personal Socialist push that he optimistically founded the Federation. Last year, in the National Assembly elections, Mitterrand led an important new population of young faces into the Parliament. All of them and everything he had organized in three years were swept away in June in the elections that de Gaulle called for after the student riots of May. In his recent speech, Mitterrand bitterly blamed "the infantile anarchist student leaders" who had put the French middle class into a panic of fear of some kind of revolution, thus leading to the left's being completely swamped by the Gaullist tidal wave. Then came the Russian occupation of Prague and a storm of unpopularity breaking over the French left. It is now reported that Guy Mollet, chief of the traditional Socialists, is also in some sort of factional trouble—an elderly, doctrinaire reactionary who fought the Federation as newfangled. The Federation was obviously politically weak, because its three brands of Socialists could not agree on how to run the French industrial society, in case they ever were briefly given the chance. Mitterrand is a rather handsome, overambitious man, now only fifty-one years old, so with a long political career still ahead of him. He naturally wants to see founded a brand-new Socialist Party, of which he would stand the best chance of being the leader—at first. Faith in him always wears thin very soon. In his resignation speech, he pointed out that recent events, local and Slav, had weighed against his leadership. But public opinion shrewdly surmised that he was the man who had really lost the election for the left, and it went so far as to feel he had been a villain who, as one paper said, "wanted to lead honest French radicals into the Kremlin."

The struggles that have been going on this week in the inner sanctum of the French Communist Party have clearly been more grave and weighty, nationally and internationally. French Socialists, in a pinch, can be dismissed as political intellectuals. But the Communist Party, which gets about a fifth of all the votes cast in France, represents the majority of the French workers, and its difficulties or major decisions can be significant in the political life of the nation —once it finally hears about them, since the Communists still tend to be secretive. This week, Mme. Jeannette Thorez-Vermeersch, the leader of the pro-Kremlin wing of the Party, officially resigned her long-held functions, as the finale of her protest against the French Party's condemnation of the Soviet invasion of Czechoslovakia. She

is a white-haired Party veteran, now fifty-seven years old, and the
widow of Maurice Thorez, who for thirty-four years, as the French
Party's secretary-general, directed it with such vigor that he was
called *"le petit Staline."* He was a miner's son; she was a textile
weaver in the north. Their liaison produced three sons, the eldest
born in the middle nineteen-thirties. The couple were officially married in 1947, after Stalin himself decreed that there should be "no
more concubinage"—free unions having at first been regarded as
admirable domestic manifestations of the Russian Revolution. She
had never accepted the report of Stalin's crimes in that Russia where
she lived during the Second World War. In the recent Prague crisis,
she represented the strange, mixed, semi-heretical view of those
French Communists who failed to approve completely of the Czech
occupation but were also unable to repudiate definitely their ultimate belief in Soviet infallibility—torturing questions of faith as
illogically enigmatic to outsiders as must have been those of the
medieval Christians. Her opponent on the Czech situation was the
Party's top ideologist, Roger Garaudy, graduate in philosophy and
Doctor of Letters, author of several Marxist books, and latterly the
most outspoken pro-Czech liberal leader. Going further than the
French Party's immediate condemnation of the Soviet invasion, he
had demanded that the Soviet leaders resign, as a sign of their error.
With the backing of the Moscow Embassy in Paris, Mme. Thorez-
Vermeersch at the same time had been campaigning against the
pro-Czech position of Waldeck Rochet, secretary-general of the
Party. The showdown this week demonstrated the depth of the
turbulent passions inside the Party and the schisms caused by the
Prague occupation. Perhaps a third of the active Party ranks agreed
with Mme. Thorez-Vermeersch, and the others backed Garaudy,
with the unfortunate Rochet trying to arrive at a balance in order
to heal the quarrel. The Central Committee would not have
dreamed of taking steps against the widow of its former secretary-
general, but it finally accepted her repeated demands to permit
her to resign from the hierarchy and from the Politburo, at the
same time reproaching her for her refusal to accept "the decisions on the Czech situation democratically arrived at by the
French Party." Garaudy emerged in still better shape, as a member of both the Committee and the Politburo, but at the price of

promising to conform to Party decisions in the future—in other words, accepting a muzzle. He also failed to obtain what he most desired—that *L'Humanité* print his explanation of why he had not renounced any of his personal opinions. To settle the whole affair, Rochet is choosing a delegation of French Communists to go to Moscow next week to discuss their schism with the Soviet Party. What will happen after this meeting—apparently the first of its kind in Soviet *apparatus* history—will depend on whether the French Communist Party pushes on with its Western modernizing of what is now called "democratic Socialism" or whether it obediently returns to Moscow's stricter *diktats.*

An exposé of all these tumultuous recent troubles and power struggles was given to the Paris papers in a Party press communiqué, which has generated columns of newspaper comment—especially in *Le Monde,* which has treated it all with the gravity given to an important state paper. This has been a *crise de conscience* in French Communist circles such as has never before been reported here to the public.

1969

March 12

Through memory, the violent climate and the hopes and events of May last year have produced an inverted, depressant atmosphere here—a kind of slump or chill in the present new spring month of March. The sensitive social barometer in Paris shops and streets has seemed heavy, with no breeze animating commerce or talk. "Behind the basic projects of the labor unions can be discerned concomitant signs of serious trouble in the French economic family," it was pointed out last week by *France-Soir,* the popular afternoon news voice for all France, with its more than a million circulation over the length and breadth of the country. "Salaried workers, peasants, little storekeepers, and artisans are all discontented and, what is more, are worried—rightly or wrongly, and despite a satisfactory industrial output. Workers of every kind are prey to a latent pessimism, and in this they are joined by the owner class. The workers demand an immediate rise in pay, the little shopkeepers want fiscal relief, the rich owning class believe in the possibility of the devaluation of the franc and, to shore up their fortunes, buy gold, apartments, and furnished mansions." Yesterday's one-day national general strike was almost looked forward to as a brief idle breathing space amid the psychological smog—a day off from complaining to contemplate the good luck that had just been announced the day before. On Monday, the Fifth Republic's Finance Minister, M. François-Xavier Ortoli, announced the government's long-promised, elaborate income-tax cuts, especially for modest and middling bourgeois earners (though not for the rich), which he had just placed before the Economic and Social Council, and which, if approved and voted in the upcoming spring Parliamentary session, will become law by 1970—too far off to arouse immediate cheers but welcome as a future reform and relief.

Closer at hand is the citizens' prospect of having to vote again, at the end of April, on another de Gaulle referendum of the kind by which he has legally enabled himself to change France, in successive stages, simply with his demand for a national vote of "Yes" or "No," without changing his own unaltered status as France's continuing, astonishing, inventive elderly leader. This new change will actually reshape the provincial map of France, in order (it is hoped) to increase commercial and administrative efficiency and to fight the age-old paralyzing centralization of the country on and around Paris. If the new regional pattern is accepted, it will divide France into twenty-one new geographical pieces, like parts of a new puzzle but in their names following the old regional titles of Burgundy, Auvergne, Brittany, and so on. Ever since 1790, when France was divided into eighty-three departments, repeated efforts have been made to reassemble it—one even by the philosopher August Comte, in 1854, who wanted to realign it into only nineteen regions. With this new projected map will go a resurrection of the old Senate, which de Gaulle, in his quarrel with its Negro president, Gaston Monnerville, put out to grass several years back. It will have its consultative power restored in relation to Parliament's passage of new laws and, above all, will function through the new regional parliaments. Some Gaullists would like as many as forty regions on the new map; Pierre Mendès-France favors ten regions only, each with enough big provincial towns to assure equilibrium. In a recent vociferous national meeting of big-town mayors, few of them wanted any regional changes at all, and said so loudly. De Gaulle refrained from tying the success of his new referendum to any threat of what he would do if its results were negative, but it is accepted as a foregone conclusion that a "No" vote would let loose a political crisis without precedent.

Just as he did last spring in his televised speech to the nation at the height of the May riots, when he offered his French citizens a choice between him and chaos, so in last night's speech he said that he was offering a choice "between progress and upheaval." Because, unfortunately, he never changes his mind, he accused those who called yesterday's strike of being "the same accomplices, utilizing the same means and threatening once more to bring down the franc, the economy, and the Republic" as the mixture of revolutionaries and anarchists who sparked the May riots. In reproof, *Le Monde* severely remarked, "The unions were right in wishing that what they had gained" in the post-riot Grenelle wage accord "should not be taken from them now" by high prices and inadequate wages. It is true that the long march yesterday afternoon—it took over three hours for the strikers' parade to walk from the Place de la République to the Bastille—was led by a member of the biggest labor union, the Communist-dominated Confédération Générale du Travail, who was carrying a red silk flag bearing the union's initials in gold. But the two other unions—the Catholic and the Socialist— also walked in the parade and participated in the strike. Students who tried to join the march were pushed away by the parade marshals, who wanted no capers or antics, for it was a serious demonstration by serious workers running short of pay. There were repeated shouts of *"À bas de Gaulle!"* and some black flags were waved, both being parts of today's Fifth Republic norm. All day yesterday, the electricity cut in households and offices was absolute, unless they were on a line also serving a hospital.

Not in recent years has de Gaulle himself looked so vigorous and confident as he did on television during his speech, though the professionally majestic voice is, with time, wearing out and becoming increasingly vibrato. And never in the last turbulent year has he in what he said—recited, as usual, from memory—expressed so awesome and mystifying a disregard for the deep reasons that underlie his *belle France*'s persistent social unrest.

It has been many seasons since a theatre here has supplied a play that shocked its audience in the way that a choice range of productions can shock theatregoers in New York and London. The Théâtre de Paris, in the Rue Blanche, is now shocking its listeners and viewers with "Le Concile d'Amour," but it shocks principally in a way generally untitillating to Anglo-Saxons—by a kind of giddy blasphemy, as well as, perhaps, by the fastuous beauty of Léonor Fini's cloth-of-gold costumes for the fifteenth-century papal court

of the unholy Borgia Pope Alexander VI. After all, Paris is blasé
after long-repeated seasons of nude Folies-Bergère spectacles, so
popular with French children at Saturday matinées. In fact, with
all the wickednesses here on earth Paris has long been surfeited,
which leaves merely Heaven and its Trinity as a locality and personages that can arouse certain contemporary Parisians to a state of
shock today—shock through theatricalization of agnosticism as an
idea, since shock through ideas is perhaps the only remaining shock
source that modern Parisians still possess. In France, the Catholic
faith and religion are still regarded as unwieldy, solemn material
for lengthy consideration of immortality, rather than as the source
of a diverting night out, especially to hear a very thin-scripted play.
"The Council of Love" is a translation of a short opus written in
1895 by a Bavarian doctor, Oscar Panizza, who later died in a mad-
house, suffering from a persecution complex about popes engendered
by his widowed mother's having been prosecuted at law for bringing up her children as Protestants and anti-papists rather than in
Catholicism, the local state religion. The Surrealist André Breton
first discovered the Panizza work. As a play, its varied effects on
Paris theatre critics have furnished considerable diversion to Parisians who have not bothered to see the performance, which the *bien-
pensants* consider to be surely in handsome bad taste. Jean-Jacques
Gautier, critic for the bourgeois *Figaro,* having been accused by another critic of being better at dealing with simple good acting than
with abstruse texts that enrage him, exploded in a violent, tautologi-
cal, single-sentence damnation of "The Council of Love," declaring
that it was "stupid, boring, incongruous, obscene, repugnant, ab-
ject, ignoble, revolting, outrageous, offensive, filthy, vile, scandalous,
and deplorable." Robert Kanters, the scholarly and witty critic for
the weekly *Express,* suavely wrote, "It is the golden legend of
syphilis." And, indeed, in the play this malady of infectious love,
like a scourge for the lubricious, is the punishment suggested and
invented by the Devil himself, called up for counsel with God in
Heaven on how to poison at its very source mankind's too flagrant
practice of physical love, yet not wipe out the human race. The long
soliloquy by the Devil, dressed like a fusty church sexton, with a
clubbed instead of a hoofed foot, would have been more entertaining if written by G. B. Shaw. To build up the play's minimum

action, a Borgia dinner entertainment includes wrestling acts by magnificent musclemen, one a Negro; pavanes danced by virgins completely clothed except for their small, naked bosoms, like round ornaments on their bodices; and ancient musicks of the period. God is presented as a rachitic, cross old man on crutches, the Virgin looks like a yellow-frizzle-haired valentine as imagined by some early Italian painter, and the Saviour is presented as an invalid, still suffering from his tortures at Calvary. As a series of magnificent golden-dressed and -hatted characters, viewed almost speechless and in pantomime, the production can at least dazzle the eyes of the beholder, whether French or foreign, though few foreigners are now in this city.

An interesting usual and unusual exhibition on Charles Baudelaire as art critic is soon closing at the Petit Palais. What are shown are vital family papers, such as his widowed mother's certificate uniting her in second marriage to the military person of General Aupick. There are also, of course, early and late editions of "Les Fleurs du Mal," published first in 1857. There is family correspondence about Charles Baudelaire as an industrious schoolboy, soon to become a dissipated, overdressed dandy and ne'er-do-well, whose stepfather, to discipline him, sent him on a voyage to India, which the future poet cut short to return to Paris, to his poetry writing, and eventually to his début in art criticism. He was France's first aesthetician, reporting in his articles on the various salons, beginning with that of 1845, where he started off at once on the wrong foot by admiring "The Fountain of Youth," by the painter Haussoullier, a pretentious mixture of nudes and a medieval garden party around a meagre fountain—a work that was openly laughed at by salon visitors, which, in part, may have determined Baudelaire to praise it. It must be explained that this odd exhibition contains a mixture of pictures by artists whom Baudelaire admired and wrote about, and pictures he should never have written about at all, the mélange giving a startling insight into the workings of his mind and the maturing of his tastes. It contains one splendid early, brutal Manet—a portrait of the hoopskirted Jeanne Duval, now dying and in poverty, and formerly Baudelaire's mistress—to which he did not give any comment at all, Manet never being one of his favorites.

It must be said at once that Baudelaire's great aesthetic sensibility was seeing art with his emotions rather than philosophically, as was then the mode. His aim was to write about what he called modern art in a modern way. He admired Delacroix to the point of exaltation for his perfect drawing, his "incomparable science of coloring." He proclaimed Corot "at the head of modern landscape painting," recognized the quality of Daumier and Ingres, noted that Courbet was an important painter, and had a special fondness for the delicate drawings of Constantin Guys. (Works by all are on the Petit Palais walls, and a pleasure to see again.) He was also very much struck by the portraits of American redskins by the American painter George Catlin, shown here long ago at the Louvre on the invitation of Louis Philippe, the Citizen King. Baudelaire compared Catlin to Delacroix in the quality of his portraits, such as that of Chief Buffalo Fat—one of those savages "who make one comprehend antique sculpture," he said of this striking redskin, now on the Petit Palais wall. In 1846, Baudelaire met Edgar Allan Poe—on the printed page. "The first time I opened one of his books, I saw with shock and delight not only the same subjects I myself had dreamed of but phrases that had been thought of by me and he had written twenty years before," he wrote a friend. And so began his translations of Poe and his investigation of that Baudelairean American, for they looked not unalike. The cover of the Petit Palais catalogue is a self-portrait by Baudelaire in heavy inkstrokes, which, indeed, could be almost a likeness of Poe. The exhibition was preceded by one on Poe organized by the Cultural Services of the United States Embassy and displayed in the American cultural center on the Left Bank, in the Rue du Dragon. Besides its rich material on Poe from the University of Virginia, it displayed six lithographs by Odilon Redon, to whom J. K. Huysmans once said, "Your masters are Poe and Baudelaire."

March 25

Paris is changing fast in certain quarters, almost always at the price of an aesthetic loss of familiar charm or of some modicum of architectural beauty, and invariably with a gain in planned progress that is usually relatively repugnant to look at. The

latest progressive improvement is the desertion this month of Les
Halles, the famous, picturesque medieval city marketplace adjacent
to the Gothic church of St. Eustache, set up around the year 1183
by King Philippe-Auguste for the sale to his Paris people of edibles
of all sorts. In our time, it has developed into the market for everything vegetal and fresh from the local French fields and farmyards,
with trussed fowl ready for the Paris roasting pans; every sort of
feathered and four-legged game in season; dozens of differing
cheeses, succulent and odorous, from the farmwives' butteries;
bleeding carcasses of beef, pigs, and lambs for fine dining; and also
fresh flowers in nosegays and big bouquets. After talking unwillingly for a quarter-century about the possible necessity of exiling the
market and its nocturnal traffic jams from the crowded heart of
Paris, the municipality finally made it new and suburban by situat-
ing it on the Paris side of Orly Airport, in the town of Rungis and
in new market buildings of sanitary cement cubicles that look rather
like a vast one-story prison complex. Back in the early nineteen-
twenties, when a small colony of us unrich Americans began living
in Paris on the Left Bank, those of us close to the river would be
wakened around one or two o'clock in the morning by the rumble
on the *quais* of the farmers' great two-wheeled carts, their wheels
as tall as the farmers themselves, all headed for Les Halles to the
accompanying clip-clop of the hooves of the huge Norman stallions
that pulled the loads of cauliflowers as white as porcelain, or the
huge bundles of leeks as refined, in green and white, as if blown in
glass. Because the markets were open all night for the restaurateurs
buying something fresh for their menus that day, and for the green-
grocers stocking up for their daily housewives' trade, Les Halles
over time developed their own modest nocturnal pleasure spots, set
up around the high heaps of vegetables nightly covering the center
of the market square. Au Chien Qui Fume was a popular favorite
for its rich, brunette onion soup, as traditional a snack for marketmen as the lamb trotters with Paulette cream sauce served at the
more ambitious Grand Comptoir restaurant. At daylight, Au
Chien's bar was crowded with the thirsty *forts des Halles*—the
strongest of the marketmen, who carried the animal carcasses balanced lengthwise on their heads, on top of their special hats with
broad brims that prevented the blood from dripping onto their
shoulders. For our modest purses, the Halles were better for a night

out than the champagne purlieus of Montmartre. At the animated Halles bistros, we drank white wine and Calvados and danced to an accordion, and at dawn we would walk back to our small hotels across the river carrying flowers, for we were all rather young and foreigners, and Paris was gay.

Edibles for feeding Paris are, of course, no longer brought to the old Halles, but the square still smells reminiscently of good cheeses, and the restaurants of the old lively nights still do business and are more crowded than ever, since taxis can now penetrate Les Halles's side streets, no longer jammed with produce-filled motor trucks. In the Rue Montorgueil, L'Escargot, with its rich chocolate-colored walls and gilt ornaments, is the gastronomic mecca for the well-to-do. In the Rue de la Grande Truanderie, the hospitable, picturesque old Pharamond restaurant still flourishes, with its elegant curved staircase, and on the first floor the walls gleam, as formerly, with the intricate Art Nouveau mosaics, encrusted there just before the last century ended. No one seems to know what may be the fate of the Halles's graceful, high-arched iron pavilions, nicknamed *les parasols* by the marketmen, since they protected the food stands underneath from the rains. All but two of them were set up between 1851 and 1868 as the first iron architecture created in France, and at night they look as if made of metal lace. Art historians think they should be saved. When and if the entire Halles neighborhood, with its unsalubrious little medieval shop buildings leaning tight against one another for support, is razed so as to drive out the colony of millions of rats that has battened there on market scraps for eight hundred years, the cleared expanse will have the unbelievable area of some seventy acres, which presents the biggest problem to French urban planning since Baron Haussmann cut through the Paris slums to extend the Rue de Rivoli in the Second Empire.

The best description of the old Halles at daybreak is still that written by Émile Zola in the most popular of all his realistic novels, "Le Ventre de Paris" ("The Belly of Paris"). An unofficial and free translation would read: "At the corner of St. Eustache, the dawn smelled of balsam from the herb market. Along the length of the tripe stalls you would have thought there were fields of thyme, garlic, and little spring onions, and the merchants had wrapped branches of laurel, like green decorations, around the young sycamores on the sidewalk. It was the powerful odor of laurel that dominated. As day began dawning, a sea of vegetables stretched between the two groups of pavilions like a flood, drowning the sidewalks. It was a river of verdure that seemed to flow, taking on delicate violet shadows and milky rose colors, with greens awash in yellows, and all the colors that make the sky seeming like changing silk as day broke. As the fire of morning grew, the salads and lettuces, still heavy with earth, showed their opening centers. The bundles of spinach, the bouquets of artichokes, the piles of beans and peas chorused all the shades of green, which died in the bunches of celery. But the high note, which sang loudest of all, was always the lively stain of color from the carrots."

The first anniversary of the real inception of last year's May riots did not pass unnoticed here. There was a long editorial in *Figaro,* oddly titled "March 22, 1968, at Nanterre: One Year Ago, the Detonator." This lengthy article related the original incidents, which barely received five lines, on an inner page, in the press a year ago. It seems that on Monday, March 18th, last year, just before dawn, a little left-wing commando of two young men, one a university student, and three high-school boys, who all belonged to an anti-Vietnam-war organization, used small explosives to blow out the windows of the office of the Chase Manhattan Bank, and also of the Bank of America, Trans World Airlines, and the American Express Company. As they later affirmed to the police who arrested them, theirs had been a militant act of disapproval against America and its Vietnam war—a war they considered a "scandalous sign of the genocidal aggression of a society that claims to be the creator of prosperity and equality." Late that Friday night, at the suburban University of Nanterre, west of Paris, Daniel Cohn-Bendit, Nanterre's extraordinary German-born red-haired student spokesman, called a meeting to protest the arrest of the commando youths and at the same time founded what was called the Movement of March 22nd. It was this movement that popularized the phrase *"les enragés,"* which the Paris rioters later called themselves in honor of a certain Revolutionary cleric, Jacques Roux, the original *enragé,* known in 1789 as the priest of the sans-culottes. It was the Movement of March 22nd that, almost without precise aim, set off the opening of the student riots on May 3rd.

Little has happened in the universities since then except for in-

termittent and fairly scanty student voting on the Law of Orientation, which was one of Minister of Education Edgar Faure's brilliant reforms for giving the students the power (to be held jointly
with the professors) to control their studies and how these should
be chosen, implemented, and taught. French university students are
now more than halfway through what has been so far a completely
lost year in their education. Classes at the Sorbonne, for instance,
are irregular or ill-attended or practically nonexistent. The old system of elegant, almost effete scholasticism, practiced in French education for several hundred years, has definitely broken down, and
the new system that was so much desired—connecting learning with
the living of one's life, rather than with high grades based on an
obedient memory, all restricted to specially chosen middle- or upper-
class students—has thus far not been put in force. As for examinations, they have been dismissed by many Sorbonne students, who
have declared that "to swim, you must risk trying to do it in water"—that, in truth, examinations as they have been practiced here
until now have been "like lying on a piano bench and going through
the muscular motions of a swimmer," which proves nothing except
physical memory.

There has been great French public impatience with the lack
of discipline still generally shown by the French students. Also, certain members of the Gaullist party's political bureau are becoming
impatient with Minister Faure, and recently came close to demanding his departure from Prime Minister Couve de Murville's Cabinet, a move that former Prime Minister Pompidou would not agree
to. In the end, the Gaullist political leaders glumly decided that the
crisis among students is a quasi-universal phenomenon of the student generation today, after which the politicos simply resigned
themselves to the total sacrifice of this past scholastic year, which
will end in early summer and during which French university students, for the most part, have learned absolutely nothing at all.

April 9

At the age of eighty-three, François Mauriac is
still a phenomenal French writer and national figure. During a two-

hour TV interview last week, he said, "On my eightieth birthday, I said to myself, 'Since I seem to be a long way from dying, why not write another novel?'" This new one is his first in fifteen years, the twenty-third in his long literary career. It was published a fortnight ago, is already at the top of the best-seller list, and is accurately titled "Un Adolescent d'Autrefois." Its protagonist is seventeen years old on page 1 and twenty-two on the last page, which means five years recalled out of the life of young Mauriac himself, between 1902 and 1907, so as to give the correct immaturity to the intimidated, intelligent youth whom he calls in print Alain Gajac. The new novel uses all the old familiar Mauriac themes and influences for the twenty-third time—God, the city of Bordeaux, the rigorous tyranny of French bourgeois family life, and the puritanical religiosity and pressure of provincial Catholicism, these elements together breeding among the young their secretive hunger for pleasure and their appreciation of sin. All mingled in with this is the adjacent countryside, where Mauriac passed his youthful summers amid the slightly festering perfume of resin from the family's vast domain of pine forests, which constitute the region's wealth.

There has always been a disquieting covert, morbid sensualism in Mauriac's fiction. It was finally criticized unfavorably in terms of the more modern psychology that set in before the Second World War. Like a man caught up short in his tracks, Mauriac suddenly stopped writing novels. This did not save him in the winter of 1939 from a blistering excoriation by Jean-Paul Sartre, just coming into full view in the powerful *Nouvelle Revue Française,* in an article called "Mauriac and Liberty," which denounced Mauriac for his unhealthy theocratic relation with the fictional characters he created, over whom he wielded the privilege of omniscience. "What he says about his characters is like Holy Writ," Sartre declared indignantly. "He explains them, he classifies them, he condemns them against any appeal. He has the point of view of God Himself." The French, who like to regard their important writers as one of France's natural glories and enjoy every insult exchanged in their occasional feuds, were highly diverted by this battle royal, so important that it was reported in the press and is still looked back on as a celebrated *scandale littéraire.* After the war, Mauriac followed his new, highly successful careers as playwright and journalist, becoming an editorialist on the important bourgeois morning paper *Le Figaro*. After de Gaulle founded his Fifth Republic and Mauriac had lifted the General to practically a hagiographic height, to judge by the book of praise he later consecrated to him, Mauriac founded his *Table Ronde* review, where he began publishing his own brilliant, frequently malicious "Bloc-Notes," which became, and still are, the most famous, assiduously followed, appreciated, intelligent, and wonderfully written weekly commentaries in all France. (They were transferred first to the weekly *Express* and now to *Figaro Littéraire,* which contained a "Bloc-Notes" last week.) Seventeen years ago, Mauriac was given the Nobel Prize for literature, probably based in part on these "Bloc-Notes," which are mostly in high literary style. In his recent TV interview, he declared that in his opinion he is not more malicious than many other writers but that he writes better than they do, so that his shafts carry farther—"*Ce que j'écris porte mieux,*" he explained before the microphone in a burst of extra-witty maliciousness.

On the whole, the critics treated "Un Adolescent d'Autrefois" rather like wine waiters judging a new bottle in comparison with past years' vintages, with the new wine considered potable and good enough to be consumed with curiosity and a certain satisfaction but not in any way comparable to the great years—for instance, the Mauriac year of 1927, when he published "Thérèse Desqueyroux," in his opinion the most successful female character he ever created, who was a poisoner. Then, in 1932, he published "Knot of Vipers," such a terrifying novel of French family life and its cruelties and hypocrisies that it is considered his chef-d'œuvre and, in France, has outsold any other book he has ever written. "An Adolescent from a Time Gone By" is a relatively simple Mauriac melodrama of concupiscence, maternal tyranny, cupidity, and unacknowledged guilt. Alain's widowed mother is the tyrant, who, suddenly having lost her eldest son to what Mauriac calls "galloping consumption," concentrates on Alain in her scheme to annex the adjoining forest domain by marrying him to the ugly little neighbor girl who will eventually inherit it, and whom the inexperienced Alain so disdains that he calls her *"le pou"*—"the louse." Insulted, jealous, the girl spies on Alain in his mother's empty country house during the night when he has his first experience of love, with an emancipated young woman who works in a Bordeaux bookshop and so is not of his own class. A few days later, with pleasure, he stares at *le pou* standing naked for a swim beside a forest pool. Within the hour, she is raped and drowned by a sadistic woodsman. It was her flight through the forest that attracted the brute's pursuit, Alain says, in order to avoid his own responsibility in frightening her from the stream. Nothing in the novel is tight enough or harsh enough to give it inescapable strength. It turns out that Alain's mother loved the little girl much more than she loved the idea of more land. In any case, the child was only twelve years old, so any imminent marriage with her was no threat to Alain's dream of going to Paris in liberty to become a writer. As for the young woman in the bookshop, he abandons her without remorse; after all, she has sinned before, with other men she has loved. This novel of adolescence leaves Alain in Paris, where he knows no one and nothing, except his certainty of one day becoming a writer.

Mauriac in his novels represents the end of a literary epoch, of which he is the only working survivor. He has always written the French language with perfection and nuance. This was his literary greatness, as he recently said, now that he is no longer the contemporary of his own books.

The great spring art exhibition here this year is under the joint patronage of the Minister of Foreign Affairs of the Federal Republic of Germany, Willy Brandt, and the Cultural Wing of Youth and Sports of the City of Paris, which seems an eccentric coupling of art backers. It is being presented in two neighboring museums on the Avenue Wilson—the Musée National d'Art Moderne and the Musée Municipal d'Art Moderne. It is the first enormous ensemble relating to the famous Bauhaus of Weimar (eventually removed to Dessau and then to Berlin) that has ever been seen in Paris, and it opened here on the fiftieth anniversary of the original Bauhaus's foundation, in the spring of 1919. It is under the blessing of the famous old founder himself, Walter Gropius. From here the exhibition goes to Chicago. The most illuminating, important collection of original Bauhaus art ever shown outside Germany, it clarifies the inception, theories, and pedagogy of the Bauhaus, from which much of modern architecture has developed, principally under the influences and stimulation of Dadaism, Cubism, Abstractionism, Expressionism, and Constructivism, then all being practiced in European painting, since painting served as a kind of handmaiden to modern architecture in the latter's more difficult birth. The exhibition's richly illustrated catalogue contains some three hundred and fifty photographs, plus pages of essays, manifestos, and history, translated from the German. The original fantastic ink drawings and engravings saved from the Bauhaus classrooms give exceptional ocular interest and pleasure to the show. There is a certain miraculous side to it all—the fact that from the Bauhaus school's original simple geometric basis of the cube, the cone, and the circle, and the three primary colors of blue, yellow, and red, the Bauhaus artists and theorists extended their work to the creation of what was new and social and liberated in the first quarter of the twentieth century.

Of the Bauhaus professors, the two who became—posthumously —the most famous painters were Wassily Kandinsky and Paul Klee. The exhibition shows twenty-four original Kandinskys, of enriched, lovely imagination and vitality, most of them unknown to us here because they belong to the private collection of Felix Klee, the painter's son, in Bern. At the outset of the Russian Revolution, Kandinsky was an art professor in the Moscow state studios. Later, he taught mural painting for eleven years at the Bauhaus, and also gave a course in analytical design and a seminar on color. His favorite form in design was the circle, with which he was in love. Among his originals now displayed, one of the finest depicts a dozen or more circles, large and small, rising from the composition like solar blisters. In the mid-thirties, after the dissolution of the Bauhaus, he settled in Neuilly, outside Paris, whose art critics denounced his painting as degenerate. He died near the end of the war, still in his Paris suburb. Klee, born outside Bern, was much slower than his Russian colleague to be accepted by the postwar German state museums—long after his death, of course. For eleven years, he was the director of the Bauhaus stained-glass work. A couple of years before the Bauhaus was closed down, he became an art teacher at the academy in Düsseldorf. Then he was impoverished by the Nazis, and in 1940, already broken by the war, he died in a sanitarium near Locarno. Two dozen original Klees—mostly, of course, from the Felix

Klee collection—are in the show here, of which "Windstorm of Roses" and "Variable Weather," the latter containing a large black arrow such as one might see on a signpost, are the most characteristic.

The architect Ludwig Mies van der Rohe is the third world-famous luminary from the Bauhaus faculty, to which he came late. A participant in the celebrated 1927 housing exposition in Stuttgart, in company with architects from five European countries, he contributed to what was called "the first international style." For three years, ending in 1933, he was the Bauhaus director of architecture, the Bauhaus by then being at Dessau. One of the projects he set for his class was the construction of a garden habitation built around an atrium with movable walls. He was the first of the European architects to envision skyscrapers of glass. The exhibition here features a magnificent blown-up photograph of his and Philip Johnson's Seagram Building viewed in its entirety, from the two small fountains on its Park Avenue plaza to the top of its thirty-ninth story—a construction regarded by Europeans as the supreme example of the American skyscraper.

By 1924, a Berlin campaign against the Bauhaus had begun to be waged by the new nationalist political elements in Germany. In 1928, Gropius announced his retirement from it. In 1930, the Bauhaus finances were greatly aided by the sale of wallpapers made in the Bauhaus studios. But the end was in sight, and handsome wallpaper could not stave it off. On the advice of Gropius, Mies van der Rohe was named director of the entire Bauhaus. In 1931, the Nazis obtained a majority in the local government elections. In 1932, the Dessau Municipal Council decided that the Bauhaus should be suppressed. In April, 1933, the Bauhaus building was searched and its thirty-two students were questioned by the Gestapo. In July, Mies van der Rohe, with the consent of his colleagues, voluntarily dissolved the Bauhaus, the demands of the Gestapo being unacceptable to them all. In August, a circular letter informed the students that the Bauhaus no longer existed. It was founded on freedom in art. Now, thirty-six years and a world war later, it has just provided Paris with one of the most interesting, informative, and historic modern-art exhibitions ever given here in our time.

* * *

On Thursday evening, President de Gaulle participated in a question-and-answer program with Michel Droit, who has appeared with him in such dialogues before, on the coming referendum. This one was carried only on TV, which cut off many modest French who own only radios and are more accustomed to listening than to looking, especially when de Gaulle is on. According to opinion polls taken in advance, fewer than fifty per cent of the French are interested in voting in the referendum at all, and of them about forty-eight per cent have decided in advance to vote no. The Communist Party has made a big thing of telling its members to vote against the General, who wants a yes vote. It might have been more logical if the referendum had been fixed so that citizens could give half a vote to each of its questions—(1) Do you favor the regionalization program? (2) Do you favor the transformation of the Senate into a purely consultative assembly?—which are two entirely different kettles of fish. It is this double-headed inquiry that may well push the French into not answering at all.

May 1

Although it had been deduced early during the week preceding the referendum-plebiscite that President de Gaulle would doubtless lose, nevertheless his immediate resignation a few minutes past midnight on Sunday from his high office as President of France was as unexpected by the French people, and nearly as great a shock, as if he had suddenly and almost voluntarily died at that hour. The fatal side of politics in his complete disappearance from public life after eleven years of dominance, struggle, and power supplied more tension and melodrama than the narrow majority of those who had gladly voted against him had imagined in advance. There was also a sense of complexity, and even of mystery, in what had happened with such relative ease to such an ascendantly intelligent and experienced political personage, spreading the feeling that only he could explain it all, as if in some way he had been an accomplice.

In fact, it all started nearly three weeks earlier, in de Gaulle's

April 10th television dialogue with his official television interviewer, Michel Droit, when the President suddenly declared that if his referendum on France's regionalization and the renovation of the Senate (both unpopular marginal reforms) failed to be passed, he himself ought not to continue as Chief of State. For if the French people showed themselves in majority opposed to his referendum, "what kind of man would I be if I did not without delay take the consequences of such a profound rupture between us but absurdly persisted in maintaining myself in my present functions?" he asked on the air, as if consulting an invisible portent. Already his party advisers had dared to suggest that the regionalization project, which ran to ten full, documented pages in its complications, should more properly be shifted to Parliament, to be publicly debated and voted upon. But when de Gaulle, over the microphone, suddenly included his own person to be retained or discarded along with regionalization, which is principally a question of geography, he turned the dull referendum into a dangerous plebiscite. Actually, the French at first paid little attention to his televised threat of resignation, being accustomed to his histrionic prophecies on the chaos that would attend his departure for whatever reason. But the English listeners to his broadcast took his threat as seriously as gospel and reported it gravely in the London papers, from which it was, in turn, repeated in Paris (in one or two cases as examples of British humor), and thus what may have started as one more of his coercive myths hardened into a crisis of fact. There is nothing in the Fifth Republic's constitution that covers anything as unimaginable or as desperate as the President's handing in his resignation, nor is there anything in French political practice about a lost referendum's being any more critical than a professional sharpshooter's failing in full sight of the nation to hit anywhere near the bull's-eye. In any case, the referendum had almost become irrelevant by last Sunday, when the twenty-nine million French voters—slightly more than half of them women—were asked for the fifth time since the founding of the Fifth Republic to say yes or no as to whether they were for or against de Gaulle himself. Actually, this vital query was omitted from the text of the bill distributed to all the voters, which reduced itself to the question "Do you approve this bill sent to the French people by the President of the French Republic relative to the creation of regions and a renovation of the Senate?"—a bill of several thousand words, published at considerable government expense, which many voters did not receive at all, or not until the last moment (owing to printing delays by the national printing office and to the vagaries of the postal service), and which even more voters did not bother to study fully, as being beyond them in the complications of its detail. Much of the high percentage of hesitations and indecisions reported in the opinion polls came from the voters' increasing, alarmed realization that the plebiscite was forcing them to a decision of destruction or of salvation—of voting to save de Gaulle as head of state or of decapitating him, in a way, by voting him out of office and into the wilderness of exile in his country house and garden at Colombey-les-Deux-Églises. A further paralyzing sense of the irreversibility of this decision was loaded onto the voters' shoulders on Saturday night by the intimidating broadcast statements of the government leaders. Prime Minister Couve de Murville said, "If your vote is yes, there is no scission. The Fifth Republic goes on, and evolution takes place normally. If there is a no vote, there will be a wrench, with the departure of the President of the Republic and a new election—in an atmosphere of crisis, most likely. And no one can tell what might happen. On Monday morning, a period of great uncertainty, and even of outbreaks, would begin." More dramatically, the Minister of Culture, André Malraux, declared, "If the noes win, there will be another Month of May. The whole of Europe is quite certain of that, and it would be a European phenomenon of the first magnitude, with extremely far-reaching consequences"—meaning, without mentioning them, the fall of the franc (which, in turn, would push down the pound), a further slump in French industrial affairs, and a faster rise in French high prices. The brutal, logical simplicity of the prospect of a possible revival of the May riots and of municipal violence—a violence that the French know by heart as one of their irresistible national psychologies, left over from their great Revolution—certainly heightened Sunday's worry, acute interest, fear, and excitement.

If the basis for the referendum-plebiscite had seemed odd in being casually announced in a conversation on the air, the efforts made by certain rare Paris commentators to throw some light on de

Gaulle's mystifying resignation and its background have been explicit, precise, and very positive and interesting indeed. Jean Ferniot, writer of a brilliant column of daily political comment for *France-Soir* (with its circulation of a million readers, it is the largest purveyor of journalistic information in all France), said in his Tuesday column, "In the end, and considering everything, it is General de Gaulle who defeated General de Gaulle. Why did he not submit the regional reform to Parliament? Why, having submitted it to a referendum that was, as his most faithful partisans considered, inopportune and thus dangerous, did the Chief of State stake his Presidential mandate on this vote, which from the first appeared uncertain? These are the General's secrets, which he may answer in a new chapter of his memoirs. One is led to believe that he no longer felt intimate with the French people, and that—leaving to one side the triumphant Gaullist parliamentary elections of last June, because they reflected more the French people's fears, which had been aroused by the student riots, than the people's expressed fidelity to Gaullism and to himself—he wanted to see clearly where he stood. Without doubt, he has preferred to retire rather than to govern a country that has shouted at him, 'Ten years is enough!' The placards that were waved almost a year ago in the student uprising of May 13, 1968, trivially expressed the vote that the majority of the French registered on Sunday—that *'Dix ans, ça suffit!'* The electorate that between 1965 and 1969 changed their vote—passing from yes to not voting at all or to voting no, thus closing behind the grilled gates of his house at Colombey the man who governed them for so long— were not voters of the left. They were the disillusioned Gaullists and the angry center voters of bourgeois France."

The small daily newspaper *Combat,* that ultra-democratic journal founded at the Liberation by Albert Camus and his friends, said on its Monday front page, "Let no one count on us to worsen what has already happened to those who have been defeated. For years, we have struggled against General de Gaulle and the regime that he installed. But our share of triumph in his downfall must be modest, since, in the first place, General de Gaulle fell because he wished to. It would be preferable if he had not been an artisan of his own defeat. It would have been more noble for him and more glorious for his adversaries. In truth, France has shown herself once more to be inconstant and light-minded, changeable and capricious. She throws out General de Gaulle after having acclaimed him, just as she turned against Philippe Pétain after having burned incense to him, just as she deposed Napoleon after having worshipped him. Giving way to an irrational and provisional state of mind, she will now provide herself with new masters out of a simple taste for change. But whoever builds his trust on France's sentiments would be crazy."

Le Monde's enriched commentary on de Gaulle's sudden departure was contained in a Tuesday-afternoon editorial signed Sirius, meaning that it came from the pen of editor Hubert Beuve-Méry, who writes always under this nom de plume and only on especially significant occasions. His editorial was titled "Roulette Russe?" Sirius treated the referendum-plebiscite as a kind of gamble that de Gaulle played with destiny. "Power must come from the people," the General wrote in his memoirs, Sirius noted, so he felt forced to supersede last year's legislative elections with a direct consultation this year with French citizens in a referendum. "A bold gambler who had long been lucky but who now heard the hounds at his heels, did he not deliberately risk a theatrical way out, a kind of political suicide, like a shot in Russian roulette?" Sirius asked. "Did Charles de Gaulle thus mean to mask the feeling of impotence and of being stopped short in his course that arose briefly last May, and that little by little enveloped him? Charles de Gaulle has left, yet no problem has been settled by his departure. One can hope that the somewhat idolatrous piety he always proffered to France will incite the country not to repeat the errors of early Gaullism and to repress the temptations that its ultras will not fail to stir up. Those who remain faithful to him feel a sadness, which is shared, more or less, by those who were against him. For all, the task will be more difficult because, instead of firmly establishing the institutions and customs that the French expected of him as head of state, he too often taught them not to be constrained by rules that had become burdensome, thus creating precedents that others might rally to without setting the same limits. Such is, in their greatness, the weakness of most heroes of history."

By those of us who often saw and heard him, former President de Gaulle will probably be longest remembered as the modern French leader who united France by uniting those who were for him and those who were against him. His fame was as an emotional catalyst.

May 15

The enormous Palais de Chaillot was filled to overflowing on Monday night last week, with standees upright against the back wall of the vast, sloping top balcony. They were assembled, as were the more comfortable listeners filling every seat, to hear the major musical event of the opening spring season—the single concert to be given here this year by Pierre Boulez, leading the visiting B.B.C. Orchestra of London (of which he has recently accepted the conductorship) in one of his most complex compositions, "Pli Selon Pli," a so-called portrait of Mallarmé, since Mallarmé's poem of that name supplied the inspiration for the music and furnishes the lengthy sung text. It had been given its first audition here under Boulez in 1960, at one of his famous Domaine Musical concerts, and was then reworked until 1963, the original version having become almost legendary in Paris because it was heard only once, nine years ago, and had never been recorded. The present reworked version is being recorded by the English as given the other night. As a conductor—something that his Mozart programs amply demonstrated a few years ago—Boulez is superb, dominant, and authoritative. Also, he appears in the highest, stiffest white collar worn by any youngish conductor, and it is never wilted, even at the last note—an implacable circle of blanched starch supporting his round, intelligent, baldish head, exactly centered, when he conducts, between his abrupt, commanding, stiffly gesturing arms, which terminate in delicately waving fingertips. He uses no baton, and his strange arm movements look like those of an automaton—"He conducts like a semaphore," one Paris critic has just remarked. In a way, he operates like a traffic policeman on one of those little private platforms locally called *miradors,* on which the *agent* is mounted amid interlacing streams of vehicles that progress by the sudden signalling of his arm and hand, as if his muscles were their very motors. Tactless in his speech, which is Rabelaisian, Boulez, in a famous article in *Der*

Spiegel a year ago, said that the most elegant solution for German opera houses, which in his estimation were covered with dust and dung, would be to blow them up. As for the Opéra in Paris, he said that opera's future was dead in any case. (Actually, he had lately directed Wagner at Bayreuth, and in Paris created the "Wozzeck" cycle of performances, both hailed as popular triumphs.) He thinks that opera's fatal predicament is the composer's difficulty in finding the perfectly useful librettist. Like Stravinsky, Boulez is determined to be his own master wherever he accepts work, and he feels he can always, on impulse, interrupt his conducting for composing. He has no ambition except to do exactly as he pleases, since he has his dually creative necessities. He is, like Berlioz, the perfect rebel, and is to-day's most controversial European musical figure. For years, he has evaded tying himself down even to the choicest orchestral posts in New York or Paris, all of which have from time to time been offered to him. Instead, until recently he chose to remain unbothered in Baden-Baden as musical director of the West Deutscher Rundfunk, which early specialized in serial-music programs for the young Germans, with whom they were popular.

As for the music of "Pli Selon Pli" at the Chaillot concert, it was at first lengthily entered into by a rich group of brasses, playing unaccompanied. Then came various types of xylophones, wooden or metal, the music being further animated by mechanical sounds, chimes, spurts of piano playing, vibrations emanating from softly struck large sheets of metal—the whole producing what sounded like onomatopoeic serial music. However, the long final section of the opus had its very certain sorcery in a multiple sonority of sound from the whole orchestra, as if all the instruments were engaged in secretively practicing what would later become disengaged for ears intelligent enough to follow and choose from it. The singing of the long Mallarmé text by Halina Lukomska, with its special serially patterned intervals, was (though one could not understand a single word she sang) a positive pleasure. Her voice was high, ripe, exact, and luscious.

Many of the younger standees had come merely to look at Boulez as a revolutionary exile. Many of the intelligent music lovers present, who had come actually to listen, found his Mallarmé opus heavy and tiring, so a few whistles were faithfully intermingled with the hysterical applause that Parisians have of late years given to what is popular or à la mode.

It seems almost like one more sign of disrespect to General de Gaulle that his departure has in no way been followed by chaos, though there is now confusion, because of the multiplicity of candidates preparing to run for his liberated post of President. Only two of them seem valid prospects, and especially one of them, whom few of the French had known even by sight until he became interim President and at least temporary resident of the Élysée—Alain Poher, president of the Senate, a position that, had de Gaulle's referendum been passed (Poher was one who voted against it), would probably have been wiped out, and Poher would never have seen the inside of the Élysée. The other candidate is almost too well known—Georges Pompidou, who until about a year ago had, over the previous six years, assumed that he was de Gaulle's heir apparent, and who next month will try to legitimatize his heritage at the polls. A candidate of the Centrist Party, Poher has already achieved a certain publicity and popularity by being so exactly the opposite of what de Gaulle was. He is grass-roots, educated but not cultured, political-minded but mentally without distinction, and, aside from having an acute sense of morality, of which he has already given proofs and signs, is the acme of *le Français courant*—a run-of-the-mill, ordinary provincial petty-bourgeois decent Frenchman, big-boned and tending toward fat. A mining engineer and a lawyer by schooling, he was *chef de cabinet* of Robert Schuman, was four times elected senator, was State Secretary of the Budget (so is familiar with funds), was president of Schuman's Transport Commission in the coal-and-steel pool (so knows international trade), was president of the Common Market Commission (so is an internationalist), was then elected president of the European Parliament (so is doubly international-minded), and last October was elected president of the French Senate, from which chair, by the Fifth Republic's constitution, he entered history as de Gaulle's interim substitute when the General resigned. After he made his first speech on the state TV, he at once complained to Premier Couve de Murville that (a) the light had temporarily gone out during his TV speech, so that part of the time he was invisible, and (b) his speech was not followed by the customary playing of the official fragment of the "Marseillaise," by protocol supposed to follow the public words spoken by France's President or interim substitute. His criticism was the first official attack against the state radio and TV and their sabotage of any persons not on their preferred list, and, in general, against their careless performance of their duties—the most criticized of all the Fifth Republic's governmental iniquities. With the candidates' lists now just closed, the opinion polls have already given Poher an almost fifty-fifty chance against Pompidou on the first vote, and a little more than fifty per cent of the vote on the second, or run-off, vote, where Poher can count on being automatically sustained by the various kinds of left and leftish voters who regard Pompidou, a former Rothschild banker, as strictly capitalist, rightist, and, over the years, de Gaulle's dauphin, even though he was tossed out in the cold at the end.

Other little-known candidates also have surprising identifications, such as the young Alain Krivine, presented by the Ligue Communiste, which is of Trotskyite persuasion. Krivine, a second-string leader in last May's student riots and now a soldier in the French Army at the Verdun garrison, had to obtain a twenty-four-hour leave so as to collect the signatures of twenty elected functionaries—mostly village mayors and the like—with which a demand for candidacy must be adorned. The Communist Party's candidate for President, which makes everyone laugh even to hear it, is the old Party wheel horse Jacques Duclos, former running mate of the more handsome Maurice Thorez, now dead. No one, least of all the Communists themselves, believes for one instant in the possibility of a Communist French President. But the Party decided it had to be represented, and the portly, elderly Duclos, aged seventy-two, was put on the spot. In his youth, he heard Jaurès, the great Socialist demigod, make his famous speeches, and in his own middle age, each winter, he pinch-hit for Thorez, always the more popular, in making hour-long Party speeches at the old Sports Palace, filled with smoke, cheers, and sleepy, faithful workmen trying to keep awake, and, on the platform, a row of distinguished Party members, which used to include Picasso, with a red scarf wound around his throat and his little black bulls' eyes snapping with interest at the crowd. Michel Rocard is the Presidential candidate for the P.S.U., or Unified Socialist Party, which, like the Communist Party, also has no chance on earth. The regular Socialist candidate, Mayor Gaston Defferre, of Marseille, has announced that if he is elected President he will ask Pierre Mendès-France to be his Prime Minister, but Mendès-France's serious admirers do not want to see him politically crucified and defeated once more as a service to friends who, when the chips are down, do not remember to serve him as his superior intelligence merits.

Beneath all the electioneering activity, there is still the political vacuum once filled by de Gaulle, into which the second-rate and the ambitious will be pushed by nature's law, plus the French passion for political dissension and struggle.

The only really cheering French news is that spring has come at last timidly and with her green leaves protruding well in advance of her flowers, but with agreeable warm half days, each day being divided, as if by some new rule, into halves, with a fine, sunny morning and then black clouds, rain, and chilly evenings. In the suburban countryside there is a shortage of swallows returning from their Egyptian sojourn to last year's familiar nests, and nightingales in the Île-de-France forests have grown few and have not serenaded the stars or the clouded moon.

June 5

A week from Sunday, France will face its second Sabbath of voting in the runoff finale of its Presidential elections to produce a successor to General de Gaulle, now at liberty on the moors of Ireland. His seven-year term would not have ended until 1972. Four days ago, in the first Sunday of balloting, twenty-three million French citizens, utilizing the system of direct Presidential elections that was the General's final managerial endowment to his *belle France,* cast their ballots for seven candidates of differing political coloration in the most confusing, interesting, significant, multi-party heteroclite postwar national election that France has yet seen, and with the most unexpected results in two out of three important cases. The opening surprise was the poor showing made by the centrist candidate, interim President Alain Poher—so modest a fellow that he is all puffed up with humility, one Paris wit has said —who, though a new and thus attracting French public figure, won only a mediocre twenty-three and a half per cent against the extrovert Gaullist ministerial survivor, Georges Pompidou, with his more robust forty-four per cent. The other surprise tended in exactly the opposite direction. This was the successful high-polling campaign pursued by the rotund septuagenarian Jacques Duclos, who was belatedly ordered by his French Communist Party into the Presidential lists because the Party suddenly decided that it had to be represented in the election, like any normal political group. His vigorous, critical, anti-Gaullist, anti-Fifth Republic speeches, delivered with professional vitality and a lifetime of platform experience, brought him a higher rating than had been dreamed of as possible, especially by the Communists—a rating of better than twenty-one per cent, which put him third among the top three candidates. Then, in the eight-o'clock news on Monday evening, with the balloting duly performed and computed and commented upon, there came, like a clap of thunder, the extraordinary announcement from the French Communist Party that its almost five million voters of the day before would be "invited" not to participate in the runoff vote to come. The effect on the non-Communist French listener was at first one of bewilderment and then, on second thought, one of worried suspicion. What was Moscow up to now? As any educated Frenchman of common sense would know, so imperially eccentric a request did not spring from the brains of the leaders of the French Communist Party, a party composed of and run by and for the French working class and operating at a distance and in translation from the hierarchical decisions taken far away to the east.

As this recent election made clear, the French Socialist Party has been acting as if it were on its last legs, and, partnered with candidate Gaston Defferre, of Marseille, even Pierre Mendès-France's ideas scintillated with less precision. Furthermore, over the last few years in France, the Radical Socialist left has moved to the right and into the centrist ground, thus emptying the familiar left-wing scene. It was into this emptied space that the obedient French Communist Party seemed to step last Monday. Its control over its followers permitted its leaders, says Jean Ferniot, the knowledgeable political columnist of *France-Soir,* to risk "recommending" that they refrain from further voting, instead of telling them merely to vote blank ballots. The Party's tactical necessity was, quite simply, to quarantine the votes of the first round, because they contained the Duclos triumph intact (as far as it went)—a triumph precious to Party history as a success such as the Party has never known before in capitalist France. Ferniot further believes that the Communist Party, by abandoning its customary battlefield, where the ballot was its regular weapon, will now move with aggressiveness into other theatres of operation, where the Comrades can develop their *action revendicative,* or social agitation.

The only touching incident so far in the whole election was old Duclos' being charged by the Party's Central Committee to meet the press in the Communists' main building, on the Rue Le Peletier, and give the assembled journalists the official oral announcement of the strange "suspension request." Part of the announcement contained a note of homage to Duclos for his part in the electoral campaign. This he spoke without adding one syllable of commentary, merely reading very rapidly the Central Committee's reference to the candidate's personality and qualities, "which played an important role." Then Duclos added the Central Committee's final words, as if they explained, to a degree, why the Party did not think it worthwhile to have anything to do with the runoff between a pair of candidates—Pompidou and Poher—neither of whom was worth a kopeck in the Party's political opinion. "Neither of them," the Committee said, "brings anything to the problems of our workers, of our people, of our nation. Their entire political policy aim for tomorrow, like yesterday, is to satisfy the demands of high finance and of big industry."

If Poher had followed the advice repeatedly given him by the most important political men in France—Antoine Pinay, Valéry Giscard d'Estaing, and Jacques Duhamel—he would have dropped out last week. Had he made at the beginning the sort of energetic good speeches, full of reforms and ideas, that he made at the end, France would be less concerned at still having him on her hands. Actually, the Germans are also interested in his continuing the struggle, and even hope that he will win it in the final vote, since he is an Atlanticist in his international policies, which means pro-

American, and so are they, in Bonn and West Berlin. The Russians, on the contrary, hope that Pompidou will win, because of de Gaulle's favoring Moscow over Washington as a commercial influence—one of the few Gaullisms that Pompidou has retained from his six years with the General. It seems incredible that, in its thoroughness, the electoral system demands that these two lone political rivals, whose attitudes are really quite closely allied, should continue the routine of radio discourses, television interviews, and speeches in country capitals, and that, furthermore, their friends should continue similar services in their behalf, with nightly speeches in Bordeaux or Lyon or Gisors—all this to be followed by the final vote a week from Sunday, for which many earnest French people will take long train rides home to their provinces to participate. This direct-election system must be, as de Gaulle was confident, the fairest mankind has invented, yet it is certainly hard on the voters.

Direct voting was first tried out in France in the Presidential election of December 10, 1848, in which Prince Louis Napoleon was the winning candidate. In that 1848 campaign, there was a great deal of lofty social idealism warmly expressed by the literary avant-garde, who were deep in politics and for whom Victor Hugo founded a new daily paper, called *L'Événement*. It ran an editorial backing the new Napoleon, with references to his more famous warrior relative. This was presumably written by Hugo himself, because of the flamboyance of the style, and it said, in part, "Today there is a *Grande Armée* that demands a general, but it is the Army of Ideas. The enemies to be conquered are no longer the barbarians but wretchedness. The Mameluke today is called Poverty. The Cossack of the present is called Hunger. The frontiers that must be widened are no longer those of France but those of well-being. It is no longer Europe that is on the horizon, it is the Promised Land. The bank of the Rhine to be conquered is that of Happiness. The Louis XIV of modern civilization should no longer say 'There are no longer any Pyrenees,' he should say 'There is no longer any misery.' " The poet Lamartine, who was also an enthusiastic Presidential candidate (he did not receive many votes), put out street placards saying, "The new principle of the Republic is universal suffrage. . . . May God bless the Constitution! May it begin and end with His holy name, may it be full of Him!" Flaubert, the other literary figure of the avant-garde, was not in their midst, being by principle apolitical. But he devoted a chapter in his famous comic novel "Bouvard et Pécuchet" (those inimitable ragamuffins of the mind) to the 1848 election and to the principle of the vote, about which Pécuchet accuses his friend of "horrifying skepticism," while Bouvard says, "Progress—what a joke! Politics—what a mess!"

June 18

This is the end of President de Gaulle's regime—the end of the most historic personal modern governmental experiment that France has known since Napoleon Bonaparte hastily crowned himself Emperor in Notre Dame. It is the end of Gaullism as inspirationally created by General de Gaulle, who, when a young man, had fallen passionately in love with the civilized country he was born in—a strange, Freudian mirror relationship between an exalted citizen, with a professorial genius for history, and a hexagon-shaped section of Europe that supplied the rich geography of his mind. With last Sunday's victorious election of his former Prime Minister, Georges Pompidou, as France's new President, it is evident that Gaullism of some sort will continue here without de Gaulle, but what will its remnants consist of? There was never any doubt over what the heritage of Napoleon would contain, even after his exile and death on St. Helena. The essence of him still functions today in his Napoleonic Code, the solid skeleton of every French government since and a shaping influence on the bodies of its citizens, since the Code furnishes the apparatus for French existence—for being born, getting married, educating your children, making your living, staying out of prison, and, eventually, being buried. Gaullism, taken purely as an ideal, was impersonal and strictly national, and probably has rested all these years on de Gaulle's own brief words, finally printed in the first volume of his memoirs: "I always had a certain idea of France," meaning something undefined but so high as to be nearly mythical.

Right now, with de Gaulle's reign at its official termination, it is invariably mentioned in the casting up of accounts that he restored France's prestige, forcing her once more to be the diplomatic dowager of Europe, as she had been, off and on, since St. Louis and the early Crusades. By his political astuteness, he wiped out the multi-party competitions by which Fourth Republic governments were knocked over like ninepins, as if governing France were a kind of indoor game. He gave his country a strong regime without falling into the brutality of professional Fascism. He showed the egotistical mark of his greatness in his decision to put his strongly centralized government into the trustworthy hands of a born leader with a sense of vision and of history—himself, Charles de Gaulle (as he always spoke of himself). In an illuminating analytical article published recently in *Le Monde,* Professor Maurice Duverger points out that "like Napoleon proclaiming himself Emperor 'by the grace of God and the volition of the French people,'" de Gaulle, as the leader of the Resistance, became the President of France by the grace of his "historic legitimacy," with the people's votes coming considerably later. Right now, after three weeks given to the Presidential campaign, and after voting not once but thrice (counting the final run-off vote this Sunday just passed), the French are understandably surfeited even with talk about balloting. Nevertheless, the old-fashioned election of their President made the people feel down-to-earth, realistic, and normal, as if they had turned over an old leaf that seemed as good as new again. Duverger regards the election as an important outpouring of the native French libertarian spirit. "The need for liberty," he says, "is stronger than ever after all these years of partial submission to the wishes of a hero."

Even in retrospect, the election, with its mixed hopes and unexpected warnings, is interesting, possibly more so than while it was going on piecemeal. In the end, the utility of the Centrist candidate, Alain Poher, was very great to everybody, except possibly to himself. He based his campaign less on what he would do if elected (his most concise promise was that he would follow a policy of "anti-grandeur") than on listing all the errors he thought de Gaulle and Pompidou had committed while in power over those long years. This freshened the public's memory of everything that it, too, had deplored and could protest against during the campaign by means of the newly influential opinion polls or its own presence and voice raised at party rallies—and above all by the way the public first voted one way and then sometimes another, since it had three chances at self-expression, each change being as important to the wretched candidates as a new reading on a fever chart. As a result, no incoming government leader ever faced with more clarity than does Pompidou the knowledge at least of what a large part of the country's population does *not* want him to do, such as permit the national radio and TV news to continue as a sycophant propagandist for the Establishment's favored personalities. French TV listeners know perfectly what they want—exactly the same sort of truthful news and personality reports that the English receive from the B.B.C. All this will demand complete reorganization and change in personnel in the handsome circular Maison de la Radio beside the Seine, across from the Tour Eiffel. The other much criticized Fifth Republic service that was a strong campaign issue was France's appalling, antiquated telephone system, by which it can take longer to obtain a communication with someone in a suburb twenty kilometres from Paris than for you to telephone your sister in California.

The grave new warning note in the election was that of the suddenly increased importance of the Communists as a returned reality on the French political scene—Communism in the new guise of "advanced democracy," as candidate Jacques Duclos genially called it. The Communist Party's resuscitation here in the election and the Party's obedience to discipline have been especially disquieting to certain Paris observers, considering what goes on once more in Prague and Rumania. As one looks back in the strictest spirit of post-election analysis, it seems clear that the two dominant personalities involved in the struggle were Pompidou and Duclos and their two opposing cults of capitalism and Communism.

The oddest novelty in the election was the significantly increased reliance on opinion polls. There are two French poll services, both known by their acronyms, since their full titles are jawbreakers —the Institut Français d'Opinion Publique and the Société Française d'Enquêtes par Sondage. Polls came into prominence when IFOP, on December 2nd, predicted de Gaulle's probable vote as forty-three per cent, which on December 5th turned out to be 43.97 per cent—close enough for the polls to be accepted as a new decisive element of French political electoral life. Each of the two polling organizations declares that what it offers is not prophecy but "a mirror, reflecting figures." Each questions fifteen hundred people to determine the opinion of thirty million French voters at a certain moment. The persons questioned are given a sheet on which they write down their answers to the questions asked. *Figaro,* the main morning newspaper here, used both polls during the election, publishing its first one on May 27th, when the personality of interim President Poher was new and unknown. The poll presented a list of twenty adjectives that could reasonably describe Poher as a new political phenomenon, which he seemed then to be, and asked that five be chosen, from which emerged the following composite character study: "Inspires confidence," forty-six per cent; "Intelligent," forty-five per cent; "Sympathetic," forty-three per cent; "Honest," thirty-five per cent; "Sincere," thirty-four per cent. As a kind of footnote, he received fourteen per cent as "a man of action"—a quality that by the end of the election he certainly seemed weak in. As the final day of voting approached, SOFRES took a poll on "the firmness of intention on how you will vote," in which the main question was "Is your mind made up, or do you think you might change it between now and June 15?," with fifteen per cent confessing that, in truth, they might shilly-shally again. One of the later polls pertinently addressed this leading question to the people being polled: "Are you interested in the electoral campaign?," to which twenty-seven per cent answered "Greatly," forty-two per cent answered "A little," sixteen per cent said "Not much," and fifteen per cent said, candidly, "Not at all."

September 24

The presence of General de Gaulle in recollection still inhabits Paris, despite his unrelenting physical absence from it since last spring, and even under the new Presidential regime bearing Georges Pompidou's name. Pompidou's Monday press conference at the Palais de l'Élysée—which largely consisted of advice to the entire nation, since France last month had suffered an unavoidable devaluation and recently a week's bout of transportation strikes of all kinds that paralyzed the country's capital and put its citizens on their feet in the city streets—naturally brought Pompidou onto the TV screen, and also into an inspired Jacques Faizant cartoon in *Figaro*. It showed de Gaulle in his country study and in his housecoat, watching Pompidou at the microphone, and Mme. de Gaulle in the doorway with her knitting, having come in response to her husband's call: "Yvonne! Come see our President of my Republic!"

Toward the close of his speech to the press (and, by extension, to the listening French nation), Pompidou suddenly and surprisingly said, "I have been reproached for lacking the epic style," which had been so resoundingly and satisfactorily proffered in that same Elysian palatial gilded ballroom over the years by the General in his biannual addresses to journalists come from all over the world—for one reason because he always included what he called a *"tour d'horizon,"* bringing in aspects of history possibly being made on the other side of the globe, which he treated at such moments as if it were a planet of crystal, through which he could peer and almost prophesy. "I have voluntarily avoided the lyric style," Pompidou went on, "because I am dealing with grave affairs"—a reminder, perhaps, to his listeners that although he had mostly been talking about the sad state of French finances and had lately been a banker, he was, at any rate, also something of an authority on French poetry, of which several years ago he edited an anthology. Furthermore, he ended his Monday press talk with a quotation, drawn from his prodigious memory, of part of a fine modern poem on grief by Paul Éluard. These Gallic touches distinguished his official summing-up of France's trouble from those being emitted at the same time by Rome concerning Italy's inflationary difficulties and accompanying strikes, and by Bonn, whose money troubles consist of fiscal constipation because of the overrich, undeflated German mark, yet are accompanied by industrial strikes, too.

Pompidou's first press conference, held some time back, was not an impressive success. But this time he gave as much satisfaction to his listeners as was possible, considering that he was talking about bad French news, about what had caused it, and about what he planned to do to remedy it, which will be austere and therefore disagreeable to the pleasure-loving French. The images he employed in his speech were neither epic nor lyric but trenchant and commonplace, of the kind that stick usefully in a listener's mind. Part of France's trouble, he said, was that she had suffered "the brutal shock" of the student riots in the spring of 1968, which, in a month's destruction of Sorbonne classrooms, Latin Quarter street pavements, and the Odéon Theatre, plus the city's closed factories and shops, netted France a loss, he said, of between two and three *billion* dollars. Then followed the loss of a billion more in the public speculation on the German mark, after which there was the rise in wages, welcome to the workers but always a financial shock to those who have to pay. Since the riots, he said, France has suffered like someone who has been through a bad accident and emerged with "a slow hemorrhage," located in her finances—at first nearly painless but, if not stopped, likely to prove mortal. For the state of France's currency he used an image from the sporting page. He said that the runner who dopes himself at the beginning of a long race may do several impressive laps but will end by collapsing. "Our franc was doped," Pompidou said. "Thus, devaluation was necessary to set its real value." He said that for twenty years the French had been spending all they earned, and sometimes a little more. Now everybody, including municipalities, must save, including each French citizen, and especially "the mothers of families." He went on, "If a woman wants to change her washing machine, she may say, 'Let's do it now.' Generalized, this leads to inflation. I am speaking to everybody when I say that every time a mother argues about prices, protests unjustified increases, or delays purchasing what is not indispensable, she defends the franc. And when she puts a little money into the savings bank, she is working for the good of her country and her children's future." He said that at the end of the last century France had been one of Europe's great industrial powers. After the Second World War, France owed her revival in large part to American aid. What France now needs to move ahead is to modernize her industries and to change her business mentality. "Our economic apparatus needs to develop a mentality that I dare to call aggressiveness, which leads to conquering outside markets, to fighting for business on the territory of others, as nowadays they come to fight us on ours," he said. (This was a blow that was not below the belt, being obviously aimed at the enormous recent purchases by American capital of French resources, which the French eagerly sold for dollars instead of developing for themselves and for their franc.) As an example of the wide range of his mind, Pompidou said that he had lately "entertained himself by giving the following problem to a computer to solve: Supposing that all France's social-welfare expenses began to increase at the same rate as the current increase in spending for the care of the sick, how long would it take before the social-welfare budget of the nation absorbed the totality of the nation's resources?" He added, "The answer was nineteen years and two months." It was such extensions of his mind and imagination that made his hour-and-a-half press conference stimulating, if not epic.

A week before, Pompidou's Prime Minister, Jacques Chaban-Delmas, had spoken vigorously in Parliament on what he called "the new society of France," which contained enough novelties of reform and social goodness to constitute a benign sort of new French Revolution—if the present government stays in power long enough to set it in motion. At Pompidou's press conference, a long question about the new society was put to the President by the editor of the famous Catholic daily called *La Croix,* who added, as if in encouragement, "You are now in the Élysée for seven years, if God so wills that you live." To this the new President of the Republic answered, with a broad, Voltairean smile, "You are better placed than I am to ask Him."

For fair weather and sunshine, the summer now ending seems to have been one of the finest in local Paris recollections. Roses in suburban front yards and on estates in the Île-de-France bloomed as if under orders for a flower show, with top-heavy pink roses on stalks four feet tall. In the Beauce, France's wheat bin, near the Gothic landmark of Chartres Cathedral, the harvest weather and the crop satisfied even the French farmers, usually prone to complaint about everything, as their basic agricultural principle. Fruits and vegetables are, naturally, dearer than last year. What is grievous about the vegetables and fruits this year is that, with the Paris central market moved away from the picturesque, pestiferous old Halles—where small restaurateurs often taxied down at daybreak to buy stuff culled the afternoon before on the outlying farms—everything is changed. With the Paris market now removed to the new cement barracks at suburban Rungis, few little restaurant keepers can afford the trek, and they buy their vegetables and salads from some local Paris supermarket or from a wholesaler. Thus, time is lost in the life of fresh vegetables themselves, and, with it, that delicate modicum of superiority in their taste at French tables. Choice Paris cooking in small, famous bistros is doomed to head downhill as a manifestation of so-called progress in municipal planning, now that "the belly of Paris," as Zola called his horrifying, realistic novel on Les Halles, has been moved outside the city limits.

Whenever you leave Paris for a few months, you invariably find on your return that it has been brutally improved here and there, with the modernizing of some old façade or with an entire edifice replaced by a huge hole, indicating one more skyscraper to come or an altitudinous new apartment house of the type the French call *"de grand standing,"* meaning luxury flats. It is said that the useless old Gare d'Orsay, which apparently belongs to the City of Paris, is scheduled to come down. Increasingly, tree-filled squares of the city are being undermined by new public garages. Even though we don't see the automobiles, there is the knowledge that viscerally they are there, inside the body of the city as well as rushing or crawling on the asphalt skin of its streets above. Because of the frequent *chantiers,* or work sites, for the continuing suburban Métros, Paris has become so choked on its own traffic that seven new "toboggans," as the French call these temporary bridges, are reportedly being built this autumn over certain congested key Paris streets and intersections. These toboggans always look tempting and perilous. There is already one on top of the stone bridge at Saint-Cloud—a bridge on top of a bridge—to handle the weekend country-going traffic heading for the Autoroute.

Paris is still full of tourists, and the hotels of all grades are still packed. This summer saw more American tourists here than for many years. Many of them came because General de Gaulle had finally departed.

As has often been privately said in musical circles, concert pianists are generally embryo actors. At one period, Liszt even dressed for his appearances in his *abbé's* soutane. Chopin's long hair and the waving of his beautiful white hands, plus his famous love affair with the cigar-smoking lady novelist Georges Sand, added to the popular attraction of his Frenchly composed waltzes when

played in Paris. In our time, de Pachmann, in his New York concerts, used to lean down after a passage he had particularly relished
and converse with the front row of his auditors about how well he
had played it. Wanda Landowska used a regular theatrical business
with her small white handkerchief when she sat down before her
harpsichord. First, she would place it on the right side of the instrument, then remove it to wipe her strong, bony fingers, then
place it again at her right. She always bowed her head for a moment before lifting it and her hands to bring life and sound to the
plucked, delicate music she was the mistress of. Today, the greatest
actor of them all is Artur Rubinstein. The proof is in "L'Amour de
la Vie," a cinematographic profile of his life and his more than
seventy years on the world's concert stages, acted and spoken by
him in what is an unusual and important kind of autobiographical
format. It was directed by its creator, the Parisian cinematographer
François Reichenbach, who made the very special "L'Amérique
Insolite" some years back. The Rubinstein film was made in two
versions and languages—French and Spanish, both spoken by the
pianist, who relates the elements of his life story from his birth in
Lodz, Poland, through his musical education in Berlin, his concert
début at the age of six in Warsaw, and his arrival in Paris at sixteen,
where he met Debussy. While he talks, he is walking amid the
ruins of Persepolis, or across the empty Israeli desert, or climbing
with his wife, Niela, up the Montmartre slope of Paris to the house
where they lived for years. When he travels, we travel with him,
listening and looking, and again listening, when he plays parts of
the "Appassionata Sonata" and the Polonaise in A-Flat Major,
parts of two Beethoven concertos, Liszt's "Liebestraum," some
Brahms and some Villa-Lobos, both solo and with the Orchestre
de Paris and the Israel Philharmonic. These, of course, are the
magic portions of the film and the greatest privilege it offers—that
of watching him at close range, rehearsing in a worn old sweater
with short sleeves. As the orchestra starts up, a strange look comes
over his face, which seems to swell as if with some physical feeling
of re-creation. His eyes become the agate eyes of an amazing old
man who is seeing nothing but is remembering the report of his
memory on the music he will play—a very great pianist. By moving
back and forth across Rubinstein's life and memories and familiar

countries, Reichenbach has composed a chef-d'œuvre of a profile, in which the camera writes the report with its lens and, by further mechanics, supplies the conversation. In his casual talking moments, Rubinstein mentions a Prince Lubomirski, one of the great Warsaw nobles, of generous musical culture, who heard Rubinstein play as a boy and offered to finance his career. (The Warsaw Philharmonic was founded and at first directed by Niela's father, who later directed the Warsaw opera.) The television biography of Rubinstein that recently appeared on TV in New York used some of Reichenbach's footage but was otherwise distinct. The French version of "L'Amour de la Vie," now playing here in five movie houses, was a triumph at the Cannes spring film festival. This month, it has substituted here for the opening of the musical season in the pleasure it has given to musicians and also to filmgoers—the pleasure of meeting the joyous, civilized genius of Rubinstein himself, in his eighty-second year of a happy life.

October 8

This year is the bicentenary of the birth of the Corsican Napoleone Buonaparte, who, until he set fire to Moscow, held Europe conquered in his hand. Now a new historicity has been given both to him and to the French Revolution by Jean Chatelain, Directeur des Musées de France, in his brilliant preface to the catalogue for the extraordinary Napoleonic exhibition that opened in June at the Grand Palais and will close in December. There he states that "the French Revolution was not the extinction of a bloodless, exhausted society but the bursting of a dam in France, at that time the most populous, richest, most cultivated nation in the Occidental world," letting loose a flood of exceptional men, ideas, and forces—and fresh theatres of death on the guillotine and battlefields. All of this Napoleon (by adding together what remained of old France, what he revivified, and what he created anew) "synthesized by his genius into a coherent and at first fragile ensemble on which he founded modern France," with his touch still discernible "once the tears were dried and the dead forgotten"—for with his enormous armies he was the first man in modern times to turn Europe into a graveyard. He organized the administrative structures of France, all still standing—the Conseil d'État, the *départements,* the prefects, the Cour des Comptes for its finances, and all the fundamental rules for its social and family life as contained in the Code Civil. Perhaps this last was his greatest creation. He also unified the French university system, established the Banque de France, reëstablished the Comédie-Française, and regenerated France's museums.

The rich, often intimate Napoleonic exhibition at the Grand Palais owes much of its éclat to the rarely shown treasures lent by His Imperial Highness Prince Napoleon, present head of the family, who is descended from Jérôme, the inadequate brother whom Napoleon rashly made King of Westphalia. Also shown in the exhibition are belongings of the descendants of the countryside stalwarts whom Napoleon enrolled and ennobled, such as the innkeeper's son Murat, represented today by the Murat princes. There are also objects lent by the Queen of England, by Prince Rainier of Monaco, by the present Duke of Wellington, and by Hermès, the Paris shop famed for its historic collection of leather artifacts, and also historic jewels from Van Cleef & Arpels. At the threshold of the Grand Palais stands an astonishing introductory thirty-panel panorama of nineteenth-century printed wallpaper depicting the Battle of Austerlitz, one of Napoleon's greatest victories, fought between the French, Austrian, and Russian emperors and armies, the panorama being accompanied by life-size standing figures dressed in miraculously preserved uniforms of the French grenadiers on that great bloody day.

The garments worn by Napoleon for his coronation at Notre-Dame, where he not only crowned himself with his own hands (though he had summoned the Pope from Rome to do it) but also crowned his wife—"the incomparable Josephine," as he always called her—have attracted the greatest curiosity of all the regalia shown at the Grand Palais. Displayed in a glass case is his long coronation robe of white satin, with palm leaves and oak branches embroidered lavishly in real gold thread on its sleeves, and with real gold fringe at the bottom. His white silk shoes are of antique classical design, embroidered with gold paillettes, with a palm leaf embroidered just above the heel, and with cork soles. He must have had large feet, because the shoes look lengthy for so short a military man. His coronation ring is of gold, with golden eagle talons holding its twenty-carat emerald, cut in intaglio with his imperial arms, which contain, almost as an irony, an olive branch held in the beak of an eagle. He also wore a gold collar of the Légion d'Honneur, also displayed. Actually, no official text was issued during the Empire to explain the significance of this decoration, which he had invented, and he was the only one to wear it at the coronation—or probably even to possess it. Later, he gave the Legion of Honor to his brothers, and also to Talleyrand (but it was not popular, and was a commonplace until the late nineteenth century). Josephine's coronation ring was a large ruby, and she also wore the famous diamond diadem that Napoleon had given her, and that he utilized at Notre-Dame for her crowning. This tremendous headpiece was set with a thousand and forty diamonds of various sizes and shapes, in all weighing two hundred and sixty carats, arranged in an ornate design that jewellers call *fleurons et rosaces découpées*. Josephine willed it to her daughter Hortense, later Queen of Holland, through whom it came down to Napoleon III. After the disastrous war of 1870, when he and his ex-Empress Eugénie were in exile in England, she sold it. The diadem, which still glitters sumptuously, was eventually bought by Van Cleef & Arpels, to whom this unique relic still belongs.

Of the famous portraits depicting Napoleon, the most popular (as it has always been) is David's "The Emperor in His Study in the Tuileries," which now belongs to Prince Napoleon. (After the Second World War, he was permitted—by special indulgence, since he is, in theory, a pretender to Napoleon's throne—to live obscurely in France.) One great reason the David likeness is so popular is that it shows Napoleon standing in white breeches with his right hand tucked into his white vest—a pose invented by some German artist and repeated by David. David himself liked this portrait so much that he kept it in his studio until he died. It is a fine psychological portrayal, showing the imperial oval face thoughtful and handsome. The other popular portrait is by Gros—far less fine as a painter—showing Napoleon at the Battle of Arcole, his long youthful hair flying, his features acute with the stress of conflict. Gros was himself a witness of this battle, in which he took part as a soldier, and his is one of the few battle pictures that show carnage, tension, and realism. All in all, however, the picture that is the most pleasing to the public is the portrait by Géricault of Tamerlan, Napoleon's famous white battle stallion—a magnificent equine action painting, with the saddle empty and the great creature rearing idly in the air. The exhibition naturally contains a couple of Napoleon's famed eccentric black felt hats, one of them probably being the hat that he wore through the terrible Russian campaign of 1812.

There are a few more than six hundred Napoleonic items that the curators considered worthy of inclusion in this exhibition—china, silver, gold trinket boxes, gold tableware, gold snuffboxes bearing his likeness, and so on. To honor his bicentenary, French collectors, and even the state itself, took advantage of what may be their last chance for centuries to show off this treasured iconography. There is a first edition of the Code Civil, but in so superb and overworked a binding—rather like a box—that one sees nothing of its printed text. There is no lovable portrait of Josephine, but there is a touching, sweet one, probably by Greuze, of Madame Mère, and an affluent one of the imperial second wife, the Austrian Marie-Louise, and several of their male infant, the tragic small blond King of Rome.

The Napoleonic exhibition at the Bibliothèque Nationale, which is devoted to "La Légende Napoléonienne," bares the fact that his legend was not created only by *les images d'Épinal,* those cheap, popular color prints, but was controlled and assiduously furthered by Napoleon himself. He created his own legends because he was a great *metteur en scène* and orchestrator of all events concerning him. He controlled the French political press, of which the official paper, *Le Moniteur Universel,* set the tone and dealt out the national themes. Books and plays were censored. He had a representative in the Beaux-Arts, because, as far as his taste went, he enjoyed the arts. From 1800 to 1812, more than eighty portraits of him were hung in the annual Paris Salon. He disliked journalists but recognized their new power, which he said nothing could resist. One newspaper versifier, hard pressed but meaning no harm, conveniently rhymed "Napoleon" with "chameleon" and was put in prison at Charenton. In the rush of his many labors, including his presence in battle astride Tamerlan, he was so hurried that his signature on official papers shrank. It had started as "Bonaparte," then became an almost illegible "Ier Consul Bonaparte." By 1807, it had become a flourishing underlined "Napoléon." Then, as time pressed heavier, his signature became, in succession, "BP," "Napol," "Nap," and merely "N." He took to dictating his letters. On St. Helena, with a prodigious effort, he wrote his entire last will and testament by hand, though he was already weak from the cancer that was consuming him in the equatorial island heat. He penned it because he wanted his own handwriting to give his will "ultimate authentic proof of its validity to posterity." Part of the accumulating publicity that built Napoleon's cult came from the great European men of letters who wrote of him in their novels and poems, among them Balzac, Victor Hugo (an ardent admirer), Heine, and Tolstoy. "If my material power was great, my power over opinion was greater," he himself stated with candor. "It went as far as magic." But to some petty person whose excessive flattery offended him he said, as late as 1808, *"Je vous dispense de me comparer à Dieu."* In Dresden in 1812, standing beneath a representation of the sun bearing the inscription "It Is Less Great and Less Beauteous than He," he said angrily, "These people here must think me very stupid."

As a finale to the Grand Palais exhibition, there are placed in a section apart, as if withdrawn into their own isolation, Napoleon's two small travelling campaign beds, which always accompanied him, and which he demanded go with him on his last journey, to St. Helena. The larger bed could be folded only lengthwise and probably had to be carried in one of the carriages in which he often travelled from battle to battle. It is displayed complete with its original feather mattress and its pillowcase and sheets of fine batiste, bearing his embroidered imperial crown. Its faded green silk travelling case is pulled up to shelter it, like a tent top. The smaller camp bed, capable of being folded both lengthwise and crosswise, was carried on muleback; it is also shown fully made up with its monogrammed sheets, and is traditionally supposed to be the pallet on which he drew his last breath. The two small beds, both tented over by their faded greenish silk travelling cases, look like fragile, funereal monuments.

October 22

The rather rollicking theatre hit of the autumn Paris season is so old that it seems new. "La Périchole" is precisely one hundred and one years of age and sounds perfectly fresh, because no one here has heard its score in the past seventy-four years, since its last performance. As a revival, it celebrates the hundred-and-fiftieth birthday anniversary of the Cologne-born composer of its tunes, that light German genius Jacques Offenbach, whose *opéras bouffes* were so celebrated in the last century's Second Empire that today the French regard his music as purely French and are patriotically proud of it.

At the Théâtre de Paris, in Montmartre, the stage curtain depicts an enormous enlargement of the famous Nadar photograph of the bald-pated composer, fashionably démodé in his fur pelisse, excessive sideburns, and dwarf mustache, smiling hospitably through his ribboned pince-nez at the Paris audience as if still its living entertainer. With Lima the operetta's Peruvian locale, gaudy parrot-colored costumes were concocted for the chorus, which so over-crowds the stage that it cannot dance, and is so vocally insufficient for *opéra bouffe* that a loudspeaker system is used to bolster the singing and to aid the inexplicably scanty orchestra. In the title role, the mezzo Jane Rhodes, who several years ago was the new Carmen at the Opéra, belts out her gypsy songs vigorously. The unfamiliar tenor Michel Caron offers a fine light voice as her gypsy street-singing swain, and Jean Le Poulain, a favorite French comedian, in the role of the amorous Viceroy of Peru who has a predilection for La Périchole herself and also for making puns (all funny, because they are all terrible), is a lifesaver throughout, with his superior comic qualities. The entire spectacle, unfortunately, misses the artistry and the high, mocking historical tone of Jean-Louis Barrault's entrancing 1962 Odéon production of Offenbach's "La Vie Parisienne," with Madeleine Renaud achieving, by dignified effort and always to applause, one high kick per evening, which brought on the dancers of the cancan—the supreme Offenbach French music that is almost as well known in France as the "Marseillaise." There was also recently a so-so Marigny production of

"La Grande-Duchesse de Gérolstein," which, with "La Vie Parisienne" and "La Périchole," formed the rich triptych of new Offenbach *opéras bouffes* for the Paris seasons of 1866–68, just before the Franco-Prussian War.

What makes La Périchole a considerably more interesting historical character than she appears to be on the Paris stage right now is the fact that in real life she was a female of charm, loose morals, and dramatic piety, who entered into literature through Prosper Mérimée. Born in the late eighteenth century, she was a half-breed gypsy singer in Lima whose name was Micaela de Villegas. She was picked up starving on the streets by Viceroy Manuel Amat, who, in a lovers' quarrel, called her "a Creole bitch"—in Spanish *"una perra chola,"* which became La Périchole. He furnished her with fine horses, which she rode dressed as a man, and a grand carriage with servants in livery, in which she drove through Lima as its most elegant whore, adored by the poor as much as she was despised by the rich. Driving through Lima one day in her elegant vehicle, she saw a shabby priest on foot, carrying the Last Sacrament to some dying parishioner. She descended to the street so he could use her carriage to transport the sacred articles, while she walked humbly behind. On this incident, which he heard of, Prosper Mérimée wrote his great popular story "Le Carrosse du Saint-Sacrement," which Anna Magnani utilized in her film "Le Carrosse d'Or." The operetta here naturally makes no use of this pious material, though it ends virtuously, with the Viceroy resigning in favor of the young gypsy tenor, and with the two lovers reunited in joy.

Shortly after the operetta opened here last month, the Peruvian ambassador to UNESCO placed a bronze plaque in the reception hall of the Théâtre de Paris commemorating 1969 as the hundred-and-fiftieth anniversary both of the death of Micaela de Villegas and of the birth of her composer.

Rarely does a middle-aged European woman artist receive the homage of a retrospective of her paintings in a French state museum, and even more rarely does the public here see fine post-Cubist Portuguese art. Both exceptions are realized at the Musée National d'Art Moderne in the close to one hundred oils and gouaches displayed there representing a major selection of outstanding works by Maria Elena Vieira da Silva. Born into a wealthy, cosmopolitan, humanistic-minded Portuguese family, she passed her impressionable childhood surrounded by the tiles and pavements of Lisbon, balanced between sky and linear estuary plains laid down by nature as if for Cubism's eventual solution. She was taken to see the world early, by the age of five already a traveller with her family in France, Switzerland, and England. At the age of twenty, she fixed her center in Paris, studied sculpture with Bourdelle, and even studied medical-school anatomy, but finally, in 1929, settled on the École de Paris painting school, which then could accommodate a synthesis of the earlier discovery of Cubism and the imagination of a painter like her, who, knowing the world was round, still redistributed it with geometric appreciation into the cubes that had become a permanent fixture in a certain analytic, aesthetic vision. In 1930, she was married, apparently happily, to the eccentric Hungarian painter Árpád Szenes.

Mme. da Silva is the most famous woman painter of Europe. There is a felicity in her compositions shown here—all non-representational—which actually communicates a spiritual well-being that is vigorous, salutary, and unique. As if in meticulous analysis, she often reduces her cubes to the small proportions of mosaics, such as those pieced together by the ancient Latins in her native part of the world, so that what may be the portrait of a city seems laid down for the beholder's eye to walk upon—an architectural pavement that gives liberty of movement to the senses. Her compositions have directions of ebb and flow; they never appear to be stationary, and sometimes they seem to float on their moderate, unbrilliant colors. Many of her canvases being shown here are from famed private and museum collections, such as the Galerie Beyeler in Basel, the Rotterdam museum, the Walker Art Center in Minneapolis (her picture "La Gare Montparnasse"), the Düsseldorf Kunstsammlung (both "Flags" and "Airborne Subway"), and New York's Guggenheim Museum ("Aix-en-Provence"). The French poet René Char wrote that "this painter possesses the sense of labyrinths." It is difficult to determine the period of her various paintings, since they have no epoch but proceed in arbitrary, often contradictory developments. She is hypersensitive to pleasure in light itself. She has a passion for Corot's paintings, and none for the great, violent-colored baroque creators like Veronese, because her preferred color is gray. A fairly recent picture in her present exhibition (it is dated 1966 and is already in the possession of a private collector here) is her large Cubist painting called "La Bibliothèque." It depicts upright rows of brown-backed books with red-tinged title labels, and to one side, as if in generous inclusion, are painted what seem to be the stacked white pages hidden within the volumes.

The Paris newspaper *Le Monde* is like no other paper on earth. It is considered by its entire staff and by most of its readers to be the most faultlessly edited, the most authoritatively compiled, and indubitably the best-written newspaper in Europe. Since April, it has been branching out. It has been publishing an eight-page "Weekly Selection" of its news in English translation (mostly done by British translators), which, if at first it smacked occasionally of Franglais, has now settled down into an acceptable cross-Channel vocabulary that adequately conveys almost everything except *Le Monde*'s magical and moral superior tone, perfectly audible only in the original French. In format, this little weekly *Demi-Monde*— as the English magazine *Encounter* dubbed it wittily—exactly resembles its daily parent, except that it contains eight instead of thirty-odd pages. Since it is composed only of what has already appeared in the daily *Monde,* it passes on to its readers the opinions of Pierre Viansson-Ponté, *Le Monde*'s chief political interpreter and writer, plus the contributions of Jacques Sauvageot and Jacques Fauvet. These three are the paper's key writers, all brought up in the severe school of Hubert Beuve-Méry, *Le Monde*'s over-all director, before whom the staff lines up, standing, at eight o'clock every morning to receive and discuss the plans for that afternoon's paper. *Le Monde*'s salaries used to be heroically small but are somewhat better now that the paper operates as a profit-sharing organization for all employees, from Beuve-Méry down through pressmen and typesetters. The paper's unchanging tradition is to be absolutely and completely accurate about facts, to argue political theories in a logical manner, according to the French view, and to try to place every question in its proper context. Over the years, it has kept conscientiously in mind its raison d'être as the leading French newspaper: to regard facts as of predominant importance in news, and to maintain its own special tone, by which the manner of treating a topic achieves editorial comment—a tone that its editors and writers regard as essential and theirs alone. In the past few years, the paper's circulation has risen from a quarter of a million to nearly half a million copies, read by the choicest readers in France.

In the rigorous effort that Pompidou's government has made to urge saving and austerity upon French citizens ever since the midsummer devaluation of the franc—which now looks like a possible candidate for a late-autumn redevaluation—a handsome pictorial advertisement for the franc itself has been running in the French press. It is presented by the Ministère de l'Économie et des Finances and bears the warning *"La Défense du Franc Est l'Affaire de Tous les Français,"* printed in elegant typography. At the left is a simple line drawing of an oversized franc, with its familiar figure of *La Semeuse,* the sower, who appears on most small-denomination French stamps—a barefoot agricultural goddess in flowing robes and carrying a sack of grain, her right arm still lifted from tossing the seed out. Behind her is the optimistic rising sun spreading its rays. Just inside the coin's rim is printed the national identification: "RÉPUBLIQUE FRANÇAISE." At first glance, this publicity announcement resembles a high-class invitation with a decorative crest, and an invitation is what it really is—an invitation to all the French to protect their money from further misadventure by holding on to it. France is passing through a period of malaise. In Parliament, the Gaullist majority is so large that the chamber seems bogged down. At the moment, there appears little coherence in the government or in those being governed. The Communist trade union, the C.G.T. (the other unions do not count), will certainly demand higher wages presently to meet its fear of an even higher cost of living. It is strange that many of the French are still attempting to decide whether General de Gaulle's resignation was political suicide or a political assassination. The disappearance from public life of a leader who by his exceptional capacities made himself temporarily incomparable leaves a nation with no set standards to measure its immediate life by.

November 5

The award of the Nobel Prize to Samuel Beckett was, with few exceptions, very popular among the French, who had been instantly attracted to "En Attendant Godot" without understanding it any more than anyone else did, and without having heard of the author before. In 1930, Beckett's first writing ever to appear in English was published in Paris by Nancy Cunard's Hours Press, then operating across from the Mint, in the Rue Guénégaud. In her posthumous, recently published memoirs, called "These Were the Hours," she tells how, in collaboration with Richard Aldington, she decided "to offer a prize for the best poem on a certain subject," adding, "In that way new talent might be discovered and it would get the press even better known." So a card was printed and sent out to literary reviews in England and elsewhere which read, "Nancy Cunard, Hours Press, in collaboration with Richard Aldington, offers £10 for the best poem up to 100 lines, in English or American, on Time (for or against). Entries up to June 15, 1930." It was not a large prize, but the poem could be short—maybe four perfect lines. All the entries that arrived at the press were mediocre, when not bad, and none by anyone who could be remotely regarded as a poet. On the morning after the close of the contest, she found under her door, where it had been slipped the night before, a small folder marked "Whoroscope" and bearing the name Samuel Beckett. His unrhymed poem of ninety-eight lines—mysterious, intricate, and obscure—was centered on Descartes. "Immediately sent for," Beckett arrived and told of "Whoroscope's" having been written the afternoon before, when he had first heard of the competition. Half of it was done before dinner. Then came "a guzzle of salad and Chambertin at the Cochon de Lait," after which he went back to the École Normale Supérieure to finish it, later walking down to the Rue Guénégaud to put it under her door. In describing her first sight of him that day, she wrote, years later, "He is a man of stone, you think, until he speaks, and then all is warmth if he be with someone sympathetic to him. He is fair, with a direct gaze, at times coming to pinpoint precision, in his light-blue eyes. . . . He is very self-assured in a deep, quiet way, unassuming in manner, and interested in mankind, despite all the despair in his plays, which, to me, are imbued with the strange paradox of compassion-contempt." She added, " 'Whoroscope' was quickly set by hand and printed in Caslon eleven point." It was bound in dull scarlet covers with black lettering, "had good reviews, and sold well," including the five-shilling signed edition. A copy of this edition was sold recently in London at Sotheby's for the equivalent of four hundred dollars.

November 18

Those Americans here who last Friday wished to observe in advance the recent second moratorium against the Vietnam war—the regular moratorium day had long been scheduled for Saturday, with a march from the Halles to the Bastille by thousands of French leftists drawn from among the Communists, the General Labor Confederation, the National French Students' Union, and the United Socialists—were a lonely lot as they gathered matinally in the pleasant, leaf-strewn garden of the American Embassy before going in to sign their peace petitions. On the garden path, an Embassy official informed them that they could neither enter nor remain in the garden in groups of more than ten citizens. Asked why, he said that because Paris was still host to the weekly peace conferences at the Hotel Majestic, any sizable peace-minded group on Embassy property was considered "not appropriate." Certainly the Embassy garden had been overrun during President Nixon's visit here last March, when the center of Paris was turned into a regular Franco-American anti-Nixon peace rally. On Friday, about thirty American men, mostly young, standing on the sidewalk outside the Embassy were suddenly hustled into police vans and taken to the station house for identification, some of them not being liberated until dawn the next day. Such raids on sedentary human beings or passersby have become so multiple in Paris that *Le Monde* on Tuesday printed a sharp reprimand titled, in irony, *"Grandes Manœuvres,"* saying, in part, "The government had the right to forbid demonstrations for peace in Vietnam"—and

a lot of good it did, since the leftist parades were held anyway—
"just as the government has the right to keep order in the streets of
Paris. But even a legitimate end does not justify all the means." It
went on, "Is so-called 'preventive questioning,' such as demanding
identification without cause, even legal? The questioning of women
for the simple reason that they are wives (though themselves not
engaged politically) of militants, even of leftists, is, in any case,
unworthy of a democratic regime. It brings back many unpleasant
memories"—meaning of the German Occupation here. The article
continued, "The police pickups of young, perfectly peaceful passersby of both sexes, which happened in certain Paris districts even
though the parades were long since finished, are no less inadmissible. Even more scandalous were the police insults, the conditions
of incarceration, and the liberation of detained persons in the
middle of the night and in the middle of the forest of Vincennes.
One or two more operations of this sort and the police will forfeit
any understanding they may have regained among the Paris population since last year"—meaning since police brutalities in the
student riots had begun to fade from people's memories. In New
York, the citizens on the streets are in danger from the criminals.
Here, of late, the citizens on the streets are in a kind of possible
danger from the French police.

It is the beautiful long, clinging, voluptuous 1913 Paris gowns
worn in the first act of Jean Anouilh's "Cher Antoine," at the
Comédie des Champs-Élysées, that furnish the play's dramatic
frisson—such as the black satin costume whose floor-length skirt
traces, en route, the sculptural line of the grieving widow's thighs,
to fall in devotion and perfect dressmaking at her feet, shod in
delicate patent-leather high shoes, while atop her blond head she
wears a large, emotional black picture hat. Surrounded by her
almost equally chic Paris friends, all of them in the past, if only
from time to time, as intimate with her late husband as she herself
was, she is oddly gathered together with them in a small Bavarian
castle where Antoine, a supposed former prince of Paris dramatists,
had several years previously hidden himself, without excuse, in retirement, and where he has just died while mishandling his favorite
hunting gun—a writer, as one Paris critic succinctly stated, who had

been "adulated like Rostand, now dead in a dubious accident like Hemingway." They are all there in answer to a posthumous invitation sent by Antoine himself to attend the reading of his will, which is spoken aloud, in his own voice, on an old-fashioned wax roll issuing from a démodé gramophone horn (a dramatic device borrowed from Sartre's play "Les Séquestrés d'Altona"). Nor do they learn anything from his testament except what they already knew and are already busy discussing: how much they will miss him, his charm, his infidelities, his various conceits and egotisms—all the persistent verdancies of his person and life on which they have vicariously fed over the years, like locusts. Actually, the whole import of the play is contained in this first act, though it is repeated twice in the second act's two scenes, and is also contained in the play's subtitle, "L'Amour Raté" ("The Failure of Love"). From the chorused conversation of his posthumous guests, it becomes clear that they realize they have been summoned to concentrate on him for one last, dramatic time, as a way of extending by a few hours the essences of his life, and as an oblation to his monumental ego—all of them who had once loved him. But, as they remark, whom did he ever truly love? Present in this château résumé are the youngish second wife, now the official widow, who scrupulously adored him and bored him; his divorced first wife, an actress coeval with Bernhardt (of whom Françoise Rosay does a ripe, wonderful takeoff, played with rich spite and simulated rheumatic pains); a shadowy love from his Latin Quarter days (played by Madeleine Ozeray), accompanied by a glum youth who is certainly his son; and a young Bavarian girl whom age had prevented him from adding to his list. As for the men, there is mainly a Sorbonne professor who perhaps acted as a mentor—so scantly plumbed a part that is thrown away in chatter by the great Pierre Bertin, finest character actor in France. This scene is very interesting, representing that first human reaction of candor and truth, like a funeral wreath of words, about the departed.

In Act II's two scenes, Antoine has come back to life disguised as himself (Anouilh is known for his fascination with disguises), but in a Pirandellian state that confuses many of the Comédie des Champs-Élysées listeners until they realize that everything sounds, if it does not look, fairly familiar. In a magnificent full-skirted plaid silk dressing gown, and as a former expert dramatist, dear Antoine is now listening to his assembled friends awkwardly ad-libbing (at his request) what they have to say about him, for truth is what he thinks he wants. Discouraged, in the second scene he feeds them, often in a whisper, his rewritten lines, including his cynical asides on playwrights generally (among them Shakespeare and Molière) after the dangerous age of fifty (Anouilh himself is fifty-nine) and his unprofound comments on man's ignorance of himself and on man's embittering final loneliness. It is a summing-up of professional bitterness, and probably of envy, from the dead playwright, who feels himself ignorant of the important emotionalism of life, which he has been able to skimp by condensing it into three successful acts of upper-class Paris plays. This seems to be Anouilh's major, melancholy thesis in this play-within-a-play-within-a-play—suavely written, excellently acted, peculiar, on the whole psychologically interesting, and, because of his professional importance here, considered the play not to be missed in the Paris season.

A far stranger entertainment is the Spaniard Fernando Arrabal's production called "Le Jardin des Délices," the title of the carnal, elaborate painting by Hieronymus Bosch in Madrid's Prado. Without scholarship but with his Iberian flair for exploiting the present taste in sin, eroticism, and masochism, he has created a very strange spectacle, which supposedly springs from the unconscious of a worldly-wise actress who, as if interviewing her past to create the present, evokes what she chooses of what she has known—early childhood, phantasmagorias of friendship and anguish, later monsters of imagination, the delights and terrors of passion—which, as she thinks of them, economically appear in real form or as actions on the stage. There, in a Surrealistic set of refreshing plastic airiness, Delphine Seyrig, in pallid striped fleshings and with that elegant detachment of manner that is her characteristic, deals with the implausibility that is the focus of events. From her childhood memories emerges the figure of a rival she may have tortured or loved (played with animal grace by Marpessa Dawn). In a mixed love-hate relationship, the two women embrace in an erotic lesbic revelation while overhead in a cage swings the watchful figure of a great furrily dressed man-monkey, whom the actress has already hailed, in a confused form of Darwinism, as her father and mother, making her obvious tenderness for him doubly incestuous. And, finally, there is the conquering human male, the civilized brute, who by Act II, in punishment, perhaps, for his cruelties, has been reduced to a one-legged cripple, cracking a whip like imitation gunfire. In the interstices of these Christian and pagan elements, with bits of black magic, Arrabal has added his own particular taste for minor blasphemies. As an audible background, pleasant gongs and faint cymbals give the sense of a world in mechanical suspension, soon to come to its end. At the finale, the man-monkey and the actress-enchantress, curled together inside a plastic globe, start their unholy ascension together to some sort of eccentric paradise. The Arrabal fantasy, playing at the Antoine Theatre, has attracted a certain type of prurient boulevard audience that has certainly never before heard of Hieronymus Bosch.

December 4

In the magnetic, scholarly, and intimate exhibition at the Bibliothèque Nationale of the poems, manuscripts, drawings, photos, personal letters of love or of mere inspiration, and other memorabilia of Guillaume Apollinaire, there is, hung in a corner, a peculiar black-and-white painting of a door—ugly, unvarnished-looking, shabby, and precisely the size of a very common door—which is the perfect portrait of a door in the famous Montmartre Bateau Lavoir studios, where most of Apollinaire's closest friends lived in the first splendidly gifted years of the early nineteen-hundreds, and in the poverty that still distinguished them, as proof that their superiority had not yet been recognized. It could not have been a portrait of Picasso's door, because on his he had painted "Rendez-vous des Poètes." In any case, the door portrait has an added historical interest this week, because the Bateau Lavoir was sold at public auction a few days ago and was then rebought by the City of Paris, to be preserved as a sentimental *monument historique* to the memory of those gifted creators of, and believers in, the bizarre, bewildering novelty that was French Cubist art.

The exhibition offers an ideal climate for staring and browsing; there are no crowds, and the visitor has time and space to peer, to consult the catalogue notes, and to remember, if he is old enough, the advent of Cubism—the greatest new aesthetic excitement in

344   *(Paris Journal 1969)*

Paris in the first quarter of this century. It is the people around
Apollinaire at that time who make the exhibition seem today still
intimate and satisfying to Parisians. Repeatedly drawn toward
women, he began his literary career when one quite reasonably refused to elope with him and he wrote what is still his most celebrated and popular poem, "La Chanson du Mal-Aimé"—a phrase
that entered the French language. Absorbing the material in the
showcases, the visitor follows Apollinaire's career step by step—how,
when penniless, he found a job in a bank, became intimate with
Picasso and Max Jacob in the Bateau Lavoir, and, under their influence, began writing his first articles on Cubist art, of which he
came to be the theorist. There is on view the handwritten original
of a love poem to Marie Laurencin, the dominant love of his life,
since his passion lasted at a white heat of suffering and joy for five
whole years. The poem starts, "Mon destin, Ô Marie, est de vivre à
vos pieds" and is written on the back of a credit slip of some provincial bank, for which he must have been working here in Paris.
There is Marie's famous self-portrait—oval-faced and expressionless,
like a swan's egg—which she gave Apollinaire, and which remained
in his collection of memorabilia, the source of so much of this exhibition. In 1913, *Le Mercure de France* published "Alcools," a collection of his most recent poems, which established the first of his
modern styles in poetry—styles that made his fame for their audac-
ity, the titles of his books alone being like private headlines. His
career in the First World War is now a familiar classic: a foreigner
(he was born in Rome), he volunteered into the French Army as a
front-line infantryman, and was given the rank of second lieutenant
as recompense. In 1916, this led to his suddenly being naturalized a
Frenchman—he who had always considered himself merely an internationalist, with Paris as his homeland. At this point in the exhibition, there is displayed the pleasing, unfamiliar photograph of
his attractive unwed, lighthearted mother, who passed her nights
and, indeed, her life at the gambling tables of Monte Carlo—the
wayward Angelica de Kostrowitzky, daughter of an excellent, if
modest, old noble Polish family. Her son was sired, it is supposed,
by a well-born Italian follower of the Neapolitan Bourbons.

It was in March, 1916, now serving as an artillery officer, that
Apollinaire was wounded in the temple by a shell fragment
that pierced his helmet (shown in the Bibliothèque exhibition)—

wounded to his surprise, because, according to the gossip André Billy, "he had believed in his own legend of invulnerability." With haste, his publishers brought out a book with another of his amazing titles, "Le Poète Assassiné," which was not poetry but a collection of mostly autobiographical short stories he had written earlier. He was now the mastermind of the whole Montparnasse collection of writers, as a letter from young André Breton testifies: "I would give up Verlaine for you. I know most of the 'Alcool' poems by heart." Apollinaire wrote the program notes for the opening Ballet Russe performance of "Parade," at the Châtelet, and Picasso had long since made the famous portrait drawing of him in the hospital —head bandaged as though with a turban, and, only faintly visible, his Croix de Guerre pinned to his sickbed jacket. To celebrate the publication of "Poète Assassiné," his coterie gave him a banquet, at which the quarrelsome speeches by the Futurists against the Cubists deafened both groups. In June, 1917, a Montmartre theatre put on, with unimportant music, his anti-war playlet "Les Mamelles de Tirésias," a youthful satire that prefigured Surrealism. On its cover, it was subtitled "A Surrealist Drama"—the word being employed here for the first time. These "Tirésias" relicts are among the most carefully scrutinized by the bibliophiles who have attended the Apollinaire exhibition, for Apollinaire's time was running out. He had met a red-haired French girl named Jacqueline Kolb, who, like many other French girls, had become a war nurse. She had lost her fiancé in the same battle in which Apollinaire was wounded. She and Apollinaire were married in May, 1918, and Picasso was one of the bridegroom's witnesses. But that autumn the poet sickened with the new scourge of Spanish influenza. On his deathbed, he cried, "I want to live! I have so many things to say!" He died two days before the war ended. Behind him he left, like a new colony in literacy, an extension of modern emotion and expression in remarkable French poetry.

December 17

Paris today ranks third on the international art market, which has two firsts: New York, for its big prices and its huge appetite for art, and London, as the place where most of the great salable art now turns up either to begin with or to end with—temporarily, in exchange for the buyer's check. But Paris is still first as an art exhibitor, owing to the natural French talent for display and the ingrown French habit of conservation, induced by France's repeated wars, from which a special watchful, scholarly attitude toward art values in general has emerged that is typically French, bourgeois, and, in practice, admirable. At the Paris Musée National d'Art Moderne, the current exhibition (to be on view until mid-February) of works by the Blue Rider Paul Klee, formerly a teacher at the Gropius Bauhaus in Weimar, furnishes a rarely perfect example of this French gift for studiousness and conclusions about art. The Klee exhibition consists of only a hundred and ninety-nine items, of which a hundred and fifty-five were not exhibited in Manhattan's Klee show at the Guggenheim Museum two years ago, and of which a dozen or more have never been exhibited anywhere at all. The informative quality of the pictures shown, and their ability to give what almost amounts to original pleasure to the French, comes from the fact that though it is really the second big Klee show staged in Paris, the first one (at the same museum in 1948) was practically submerged by an outburst of strikes, so that relatively few of the French managed to see it and become familiar with its treasures, all of which came exclusively from Bern—presumably from the Klee Foundation created by the artist's son Felix.

Klee is so unlike any other artist of his or our time (including his close Bauhaus friend Kandinsky), and his paintings are so unlike rationalized reality as we, with our less gifted senses, know it, that even to indicate the superior sort of joy he lends us when we view certain of his small, ineffable compositions in this exhibition can be done only in his words, not ours. He early said, "Art does not reproduce the visible, it makes visible." As a Swiss-born European impelled by imagination toward warm, bright lands, on his first visit to Kairouan, in Tunisia, he wrote in his diary, "Here is the meaning of this happy moment: Color and I are one. I am a painter." As for his pictures' colors, as varied as rainbows, he often used them with the violence of lightning. Among the exhibition's paintings considered famous is "Clocher Vert en Centre," basically a magnificent mathematical creation in multiple colors, with a green shaft in the middle like a tree trunk. There is also "Graduation de

Cristal," an extraordinary celebration of the genesis of part of the world (genesis having always interested him more than its product). And there is the seductive "Fruits Suspendus," a fugue in red that is part of a series of rhythmic variations by which he wished to realize in form and color Bach's "Art of the Fugue," Bach being to him the musician who was "more modern than the twentieth century." It must be recalled that Klee was brought up from childhood as a violinist, as a boy played Mozart's trios with his parents, and continued to play the rest of his life. Some of his paintings are deliberately comical, which is a relief. "Saltimbanque," of 1930, never shown in New York, ranks as one of the greatest miniature posters of our time—one of the most carefully elucidated triumphs in balanced line: a mountebank reduced to his merest elements for eternal preservation. Klee was a gentle genius—scholarly and a great reader, especially of the classic French playwright Racine, whose sense of order gave him satisfaction. He was also a talented cook, who cooked for pleasure for his wife and small son. He died in 1940, aged only sixty, of a strange malady called scleroderma.

The Klee exhibition, assembled under the supervision of the museum's *conservateur en chef,* M. Jean Leymarie, is regarded in European museum circles as an exceptional success, considering the limited popular appeal of Klee's work in France. The pictures were selected, mostly in Switzerland, by the museum's new young assistant curator, Mme. Françoise Cachin-Nora. She is the granddaughter of the Pointillist painter Paul Signac and also of Marcel Cachin, the left-wing leader who, after the famous Congrès de Tours, in 1920, split Léon Blum's Socialists, the receding portion becoming the official French Communist Party, where Cachin established himself. There are few young female curators in France, and the training is heavy. After art studies at the École du Louvre or at the Sorbonne (usually under André Chastel, art critic of *Le Monde* and the most noted French art professor), there is a stiff competitive examination. If you pass, you then have three years of practical experience in different museums. Under Chastel, Mme. Cachin-Nora specialized in Post-Impressionism and prehistoric art, and also in religious problems in art, such as Jansenism. This is the extensive French way—including the religious-art problem—of trying out and choosing young people of highly responsive, broad intelligences for museum posts. The most vigorous training period Mme. Cachin-Nora underwent was in the Louvre's painting section. She worked on the Ingres exhibition team, she did a year at the Orangerie Museum in its Impressionist section, and then finally was sent to the Musée d'Art Moderne. Between times, during her studies, she wrote a book on Gauguin. The most famous French woman curator was Mme. Rose Valland, of the Jeu de Paume, who, during the Nazi occupation of her museum, secretly and patriotically kept track of where in Germany the Nazis were sending the French art, which made possible its postwar recovery.

At this season, art shows proliferate, though of such high quality that their prices would preclude their having any ordinary relationship with *le Père Noël*. Many of these displays are simply a superior Parisian form of organized Christmas gaiety. As is usual every other year, the art collector Alex Maguy is offering for view in his Rue du Faubourg-St.-Honoré gallery his choice of seven—never more, never less—rigorously French canvases that rank as modern masterpieces, each rare because technically impeccable or perfected in some manner of color or line. There is a Manet portrait of a woman's auburn head and blue-coated shoulders, seen almost from behind as she stands on a beach below the scant red-roofed elements of some Atlantic town—a female portrait of touching intimacy and isolation, a portrait of a Frenchwoman whose family seems all of France itself. There is a Vuillard of exceptional rich parlor colors, with a kneeling female figure on the Persian carpet; a Sisley of tall poplars in spring-yellow leaf beside the river Loing; a gorgeous van Dongen of civilized savage colors, depicting a fake bouquet; a tubist Léger of what looks like acrobats on what looks like a horse; and a rich, impressive de Staël of large blue-and-white cubes on a red background—a great young picture by a great young painter who died before his time. And, finally, there are two van Goghs—one of a worker beside a clumsy weaving loom, and, most rare of them all, on its back a charcoal-and-paint sketch that is a self-portrait of van Gogh, sad-faced, already reminiscent of failure, seated by a little potbellied stove, his bearded visage like that of one of the Apostles.

The Picasso sold the other night at the Palais Galliéra auction rooms in the most notable art event of the season was the most important canvas sold in Paris in this now ending year. The event opened at four hundred thousand francs, and the international dealers present at once lifted the price by two hundred thousand—and then the melee began, with the upward thrust of prices and the clanking foreign voices of the bidders sounding like swordplay, for, after all, a fortune was at stake and would be fought for. As the offers passed to and beyond a million francs, a small silence seized the bystanders, as if the old-fashioned weight of the word "million" had squeezed the breath out of the French. When the gavel finally rapped on the table of the *commissaire-priseur,* the selling price of Picasso's "Bottle of Rum," painted in 1911, had reached one million one hundred and thirty thousand francs, or a bit over two hundred thousand dollars. Not a large picture, it is an interesting, if not beauteous, example of hermetic Cubism, developed by Picasso and Braque just prior to the summer of 1911, which they spent with their models, Fernande Olivier and Marcelle Lapré (whom Braque soon married), in the village of Céret, in the Pyrenees. Braque had taken his accordion along, and Picasso painted a handsome hermetic Cubist portrait of him playing, called "Accordionist." But, as was Picasso's habit, he merely wrote the name of the town on the back of the canvas, so a subsequent owner enjoyed it for years under the misapprehension that it was a Cubist landscape near Céret. "Bottle of Rum"—of a lovely, rich general brown color—could be taken to represent anything or nothing, its only identifiable realities being two large letters, "E" and "T," and, below them, a small, faint "R." In a way, it is a tragic picture, because of its sad early history. It was bought by Le Corbusier in November, 1921, at the second sale of pictures seized by the French government from the German-born Paris art merchant Daniel-Henry Kahnweiler during the First World War. The great Cubist pictures were knocked down, under government auspices, at pitiful prices, with small Braques going at the equivalent of seventeen dollars each. After Le Corbusier's purchase, his picture was never shown until it was displayed the other night in the Galliéra auction room, where it was carried around held high for general inspection. In its years of isolation, it seems to have achieved a certain elderly virginity, which doubtless made its price higher. It was one of the last examples of purely hermetic Cubism that Picasso painted, though both he and Braque (Braque especially) moved from there on into synthetic Cubism, led by Juan Gris, as the final example of the space-time continuum that the original Cubism had let to—or so Kahnweiler said a quarter of a century later, after that sad picture sale.

It is rare in France that the Christmas season does not bring some sort of political event. This year-end, President Pompidou gave his first televised message to the country, delivered on Monday night, December 15th—the half-year anniversary of his assuming the Presidency of the Republic. He looked calm, was dignified, and spoke with precision. It was an adept political speech without unacceptable surprises, having the clear aim of healing splits in the Gaullist party and hoping, with determination, to hold it together, since it represents the Parliamentary majority. Above all, Pompidou spoke of himself for the first important time as *"Je,"* thus personalizing his power and making clear that he is the *patron,* or boss, of France and of its government. This was seen by many of his listeners as a *rappel à l'ordre* to the Fifth Republic. The President spoke very openly to the student population and mentioned the enormous cost of the university system, which must be "the center of study and of work, not of disorder and of infantile jabber." This was popular with adult listeners. He also boldly gave a warning to the labor unions, saying that public services must function, that no one has the right to paralyze the entire country with strikes whose methods are unbearable and lie heavy on the lives of French citizens. (He will hear from the unions about this later.) As cover to his criticisms, he said that the owner class should not resist the present indispensable evolution, and should understand the need of reforming France's industrial organization "to permit a concentration of method, so as to produce better and more at less cost." For many of his listeners, the most important thing he said—if he does something about following it up, for they have heard some of it before—was that he accepted the reform of the O.R.T.F. (Office de Radiodiffusion Télévision Française), so long criticized as being simply a propaganda arm of the government. "I understand that news should not be deflected from its true meaning," he said, "and that our television and national radio should be truly impartial and worthy of our country, of which they are, and should be, the expression." Well, these are grand words. What the French want to hear is the proof of them when they start listening in 1970 to the French news programs.

There is an enormous crystal-beaded globe on top of the Printemps department store, with an occasional block of pale color in it, like a peaceful and pretty continent. It is something so lovely that children may remember it as a Christmas sight for many years in their coming lives. On the Champs-Élysées, the trees are strung with gold lights, which do not twinkle but glow steadily. They are beautiful to see.

1970

February 10

       The new Italian-language film "Medea," directed by Pier Paolo Pasolini and starring Maria Callas as merely a great dramatic actress, was recently given its gala world première at the Paris Opéra, where, in her former opulent vocal days, her extraordinary thespian gift was generously included like an obbligato to any major aria she sang. Because movies mostly still rank aesthetically as vulgarian upstarts compared to grand opera, the relief and surprise among Miss Callas's faithful followers was breathtaking when her cinematic "Medea" turned out to contain the greatest acting performance of her career—being, moreover, immovably set in its perfections by the camera, so that the grandeur of her accomplishment cannot alter or diminish from one showing to another, as did her singing performances, until they at last became only tragic infidelities of what one's memory retained. To her physical artistry Pasolini not only has supplied the melodramatic sweep and scope of the ancient classic tragedy but has placed it in terrains so little known to us as to seem truly the antique Mediterranean world, which we have just discovered for the first time. For instance, he used the unoccupied high plateaus of Anatolia for Colchis, the land where Medea's father was king and she was schooled in magic—the land of the legendary Golden Fleece. In the opening screened silence of the film (nearly half of it is without sound, except for some pentatonic music), she speaks as if unheard except by history, amid majestic yellow stretching landscapes suited to the remote dawn of Greek life still peopled by mythological figures, struggling to become an early barbarian race of heroes. Furthermore, Callas as Medea is visibly turned, by a facial miracle, into an inhabitant of her ancestral Greek country—a restored member of her own Greek people, with her pointed, strong-jawed archaic visage like a profile on some matriarchal primitive Greek coin, so early as to be dateless.

From among the various versions of "Medea" left over the centuries since Euripides—from Seneca down through Corneille into semi-modern French literature—Pasolini felt free to choose what apparently most interests him in humanity. That is its destructive, dark psyche, which contains its instinct for bloodshed, crime, and cruelty as an eternal balance and as part of its civilizations' struggles over time and under different gods. Thus, his new film begins with the flight of Medea and her lover Jason after his theft, aided by his Argonauts, of the Golden Fleece, and with his and Medea's escape in an archaic high-walled cart carrying murder within it, as she tosses overboard the head and dismembered fragments of her own brother, so as to retard the pursuers, who must pause to honor the princely remains. Only the stolen Golden Fleece itself is a disappointment—at least to modern eyes—in these opening scenes, for it looks merely like a large, brownish billy goat's head-and-shoulder pelt, instead of some fantasy monster as big of skull as a bison. Jason disappoints one, looking less Olympian than Olympic, and being, in truth, too handsomely played by the former professional athlete Giuseppe Gentile, chosen for the role because of his great shoulders and his well-poised, small, blank-looking classic head. Not until the latter half of the film, with the couple now ensconced in Corinth with their two little sons, do Medea's emotional tortures begin, when Jason breaks his sworn oath of faithfulness to her. He has fallen in love with Glauce, daughter of Corinth's king, and in order to marry her he plans to have Medea banished. Her love for him turns to vengeful hate, which she at first artfully conceals. These scenes of mixed artifice and agony are, by calculation, the high point in the great acting that Callas brings to the tragic role. Attired in a long, clinging embroidered robe, decked with ropes of barbaric ornaments falling to her feet, she abandons her body to its own grief, flinging herself to the ground, grovelling with anguish and fury in contortions of pain accented by extraordinary grace—a hypnotic performance such as one rarely sees even attempted nowa-

days, and endowed with true magnetic power. It is a virtuoso corporeal and psychological triumph. By sorcery, Medea contrives to
set Glauce aflame as she takes the air alone on the palace roof. Then
Medea turns to the destruction of her own two little sons, stabbing
them, naked and trusting, in their bath. (Only the knife itself is
shown; the act of double infanticide is not made visible.) Finally,
she sets fire to the palace and, presumably, perishes in its flames.

In its basic elements, "Medea" ranks as the bloodiest theatre
piece inherited from antiquity—the bloodiest horror story of the
early Hellenic dramatists' imaginations. Owing to the presence of
Maria Callas—along with all the ennuis for the spectators that are
inevitably in the revival of any drama already two thousand years
old (and complicated by Pasolini)—it can be said that in this new
"Medea" there is contained acting of a supreme dramatic achievement, which will rank the film as a rare work of cinematographic
art.

A minor intellectual rebellion in the Communist Party, which
could have favored members' being free to think for themselves
about at least one new Communist idea, has just failed here—of
course. But unusually dispassionate discussion of it has filled the
bourgeois newspapers, and it has been the bone of conversation at
Paris businessmen's lunch tables. The rebellion, sparked by its in-
ventor and loser, came from middle-aged Roger Garaudy—intellectual, political philosopher, and for twenty years or more the so-
called ideological adviser to the Party's Central Committee, from
which he has just been ousted in disgrace. The Party had accepted
his earlier protest against the Russians' takeover of Prague, since at
first this was the Party's own attitude, from which it soon timidly
backtracked. The Soviet occupation of Prague is unpopular with all
the French, who see in it a denial of the libertarian principles enun-
ciated by their own French Revolution. Actually, the only leading
French Communist with the privilege of immunity in matters of
criticism is the elderly poet Louis Aragon, editor of the Communist
literary weekly *Les Lettres Françaises*. In it he has just run a criticism of what he calls Soviet anti-Semitism in the Daniel trial and a
protest against Soviet treatment of the novelist Solzhenitsyn. But
Garaudy's rebellion consisted of an intelligent new theory he had

invented, which he called "the new historic bloc." This was a remarkably sensible idea to the effect that the traditional Communist
manual workers should be united with the new educated technical
and scientific workers in modern French industry, the result being
that Party membership, which had lately been lagging dangerously,
would be greatly increased. The Communist Party is the largest political party in France, and can always count on a regular twenty
per cent of all the votes in a national election. But as manual workers decrease in number, and as all workmen are increasingly educated, the over-all Party membership has lessened in proportion to
the growing French population. This ratio Garaudy wanted to re-
balance with his "historic bloc." And this is where he ran afoul of
the Communist Party, which denounced his bloc as "intellectual
revisionism"—a dangerous charge for any Party man to face. Last
week, at one of the meetings of the five-day national Party Congress,
held in the huge municipal gymnasium at Nanterre, he was given
exactly one hour to refute it. Between the boos of his listeners,
mixed with their glacial silence, Garaudy failed. His position was
like that of Galileo centuries ago, when he said *"E pur si muove,"*
Garaudy himself being sure that the modern industrial political
world had indeed moved, whether his Party colleagues had noticed
or not. And if they had not, his historic-bloc theory would sooner
or later still have to be accepted as one way of saving European
Communism. Two springs ago, in the Paris student riots, the Communist Party cravenly refused to take over the direction of the
revolutionary possibilities that the riots offered, so this direction was
taken over by young Georges Seguy, chief of the Communist-backed
Confédération Général du Travail, France's biggest, most powerful
labor union, where the real working-class Communist strength is
still concentrated today, rather than in the Party apparatus. But at
least Garaudy's explanations of his historic bloc were heard and
valued from afar by the Paris industrialists, who recognized, if unhappily, the truth of his prophecies, which would certainly further
weaken their control of their own businesses and profits. This is
why the Garaudy Affair, as it is called, has been so repeatedly discussed in the bourgeois French press. It is ironic that, like all small
French political upheavals, this year's Party Congress at Nanterre
had as its specific aim the increase of the Party's effectiveness against

the Gaullist-centrist, essentially bourgeois government coalition now operating under President Pompidou. If the rebel Garaudy failed to save his skin at Nanterre, so did the Communists themselves, who can be reckoned to have lost even more of their prestige.

February 25

A quarter of a million people and one baby elephant—it had something to do with publicity, which the occasion hardly needed—were present at the public inauguration of the grandiose, ultramodern Métro station named La Défense, the first new subway station to come into use on the just opened regional express line, which starts at the Étoile and will supposedly terminate in 1973 at the sedate suburban twelfth-century town of Saint-Germain-en-Laye, where Louis XIV was born. La Défense, which is slightly less than five kilometres from the Arc de Triomphe, was so named because at that spot, west of Paris, the French troops made their last stand in 1870 to defend their city against the oncoming Germans in the Bismarckian war that overthrew the third Napoleon's empire and brought on the bloody Commune.

The Défense subway station is itself making a kind of history, in municipal construction here. Its gigantic upstairs concourse and waiting room give the key—an impeccable modernism, in every line and detail, carried out in satin-finished stainless steel, so that every surface gleams, heightening the sense of up-to-date speed by the power implicit in the style itself and its visible mechanisms, which are part of the show, such as the waiting room's multiple animated staircases, hoisting or lowering human beings standing in unbroken lines, as if posed, without moving through space yet participating in motion. Time, too, is polished into new fractions in this new station, so your ticket, as you slip it, to be cancelled, into a slot in the handrail by the stairhead, almost instantly pops up at you from a slot a few centimetres farther on, as if inviting you to hurry. In general, the station's waiting-room walls, when not infested with shops, are decorated on their steel surfaces with a semi-sculptured pattern of large cubes. The effect is impressive and obtrusively decorative.

We have all heard a great deal about Moscow's luxurious sub-way stations, and seen photographs of them, with their columns carved from marble, but in elegance, tone, and style the Soviet sub-way stations can't hold a candle to La Défense, where the décor's material is nothing rarer than the common metal of machinery and commerce—mere steel. The style of the Défense subway station can be summed up as Fifth Republic and Now. In the long, curved corridors, the white tiled surface (mostly shiny, so as to defeat graffiti writers) has at the turns painted waves of pleasant Japanese-like colors (blue, green, or reddish), which are directional signals giving you news of where you are and how close you are to where you want to be, so you can catch the next train back to Paris. The new, quiet cars are scheduled to do the run from La Défense back to the Arc de Triomphe during rush hours in four minutes, at a speed of seventy kilometres an hour. A second-class ticket costs one franc seventy centimes; first class—superior because the car is a little more comfortable and much less crowded—is two francs sixty. As for the many main-floor shops, those French who have been to Hollywood praise them, saying that the assemblage reminds them, with delight, of the Century City Shopping Center in Los Angeles. It is a remarkably complete and overreplete agora. Everything you cannot think of is there to remind you of what you had forgotten that you need, with florists and banks dominating, so you can carry flowers while you draw out more money, plus a post office, and on sale around you everything, from miniskirts and maxicoats, motorcycle boots, airplane tickets and the rental of private airplanes to delicatessen foods of the highest quality at supermarket prices and Félix Potin wines at the same prices as in the Paris shops. And, of course, the inevitable "drugstore"—a term that in France has come to mean a snack bar or smallish restaurant. At the Défense, the drugstore is operated by Hachette, which yesterday was merely one of France's biggest book publishers but now, by owning a drugstore, has obviously diversified, or amalgamated—or whatever the new business processes are called that wipe out old-fashioned shops and small tradesmen. There is one Défense shop that is special. It is called Le Stand de Bricolage, and turns out to be a do-it-yourself shop, with a section for housewives in distress who bring in something to be repaired. The shop sells carpenter's tools and supplies, such as nails and small saws, and is one of the biggest shops operating there.

It took four years to dig the new Métro tunnel and build the Défense station. Around the Opéra, especially, with the Rue Scribe blocked by fences closing off half the traffic, the swarms of Algerian workers in red or white or yellow helmets, to protect them from their underground dangers, the chugging machinery, and the other impediments to the old familiar pleasant scene gave the entire center part of the city the appearance and sound of being what the French call *un chantier,* or work yard.

The French radio has just said that the Défense station goes down thirty metres, which is about the equivalent of eight stories. No one who is claustrophobic should go all the way down. The station is a triumphant example of work well performed, and Métro travellers there will be perfectly supplied with fresh air, bright light, and all comforts—including shiny little red chairs, rather like mushrooms, to sit upon—and probably companionable crowds. But as one strolls about in restless curiosity one feels one already knows the answer to the inquiry that the body itself reflexively poses: Isn't one indeed really very deep underground?

Simone de Beauvoir is an admirable, invaluable bluestocking. Throughout her literary life, she has been writing about what Shakespeare called the ages of man, which she, being of the feminine sex and also a feminist, has pursued with her French pen as the ages of women. She began with "Mémoires d'une Jeune Fille Rangée," the book on her own carefully brought-up adolescence, because she herself is always part of her source material in these matters. She had already written her great work of interpretation of France's generalities and particularities about French women, called, with asperity, "Le Deuxième Sexe"; that is to say, the lesser and secondary sex in the eyes of French history, law, and social consideration. This is the work she will be known by, into which she put the creative personal quality of her never helpless anger at the minimal degree of appreciation woman has been granted, and made a major contribution to raising it by her own scholarship and wisdom. As the ages of women were what she was herself living through, she wrote "Une Mort Très Douce"—a comment on the relation between mother and daughter, and a study of the long-drawn-out death by cancer of her mother, a formally Christian Frenchwoman of the old school, with whom she, since she was a modern agnostic, had always been on bad terms. She noticed, to her shock, that her mother's Christian reliances fell away and, like any unbeliever, she believed at the end only in living one more hour on earth, because "whether you think of it as heavenly or earthly, if you love life, immortality is no consolation for death." This is a bitter, important, analytical short book of verities. Her most recent work, now just published, is "La Vieillesse"—the fate of both sexes. In it she traces from antiquity to the present day the thoughts on old age that make up the book's first half. It is dry, incontestable, and without her customary personal enrichment of observation—in other words, not very interesting. The second half of the book is *engagé,* as the French say, meaning that it has political implications, which in her case are always toward the left and against bourgeois society. She sees old age as being endured unwillingly by old French people, for the most part poor, as a dreadful punishment inflicted by the employer class on those who can no longer earn their bread. She quotes Hemingway as saying, "Whether one chooses to retire or is forced to, to be retired and abandon one's occupation is equal to going into the tomb." All she can do with her energy is protest the treatment of impoverished old age in French institutions, where only lately, and in exceptional instances, have old couples, who in fact rarely survive together, been given the privilege of remaining with each other at the end of their days. The only fortifying section of her volume comes when she cites the cases of famous old people, largely French, who are renowned for refusing to bend the knee before old age, keeping themselves upright by their words, their expressed thoughts. She quotes Chateaubriand, who said, "Old age is a shipwreck," which is what de Gaulle later said, almost with kindness, of Marshal Pétain in his *déchéance.* Her fifth chapter is a compendium of statements made by exceptional human beings over the centuries, and is especially to be read by those interested in eventual consolation, if that is possible—to be read, in any case, for the fortitude, or sometimes the strangeness, of the elderly reaction. To begin with, she quotes the poet Aragon. *"Que s'est-il donc passé? La vie, et je suis vieux,"* he wrote. She herself, at the age of forty, stood incredulous before a mirror and told herself her age. "Old age," she writes, intelligently defining it for herself, "is a new state of biological equilibrium. If the operation takes place without shocks, the aging person does not notice the changes." She quotes Mme. de Sévigné, who in 1689, having received from Mme. de La Fayette a letter that said, "You are old," wrote to her daughter, "I don't feel any decay that I can recall. However, I often think about it, and I find the conditions of life hard enough. It seems to me that in spite of myself I have pulled along to the fatal point where one has to suffer old age. As I see it, there I am, and I would like at least to manage to go no further, would like not to advance on this road of infirmities, sufferings, the losses of memory. . . . There, however, lies the fate of all those who go a little too far in life." At sixty-eight, Casanova said spiritedly to someone who called him "a venerable old man," which, in the light of his ebullient past, he rightly resented, "I have not yet arrived at that miserable age at which one can no longer pretend to be alive." Mme. de Beauvoir quotes Baudelaire, still young, writing with disgust, "I have more recollections than if I were a thousand years old." At the age of fifty-four, Flaubert, to whom being alive always seemed an exhausting undertaking, was desperate: "Life is not gay. . . ." "I regard myself as a dead man." "I wish to die as quickly as possible, for I am finished, emptied and older than if I were a hundred." Gide was made of sterner stuff. At the age of sixty-five, he wrote, "I can hardly convince myself of the fact and certainly hardly feel it. The space is narrow where my desires and my joy, my virtues and my will can still hope to spread themselves. They have never been more demanding." Later, he added, "I hardly feel my age, and without managing to convince myself I say to myself every hour of the day, 'My poor old fellow, you are seventy-three and a bit more.'" "I have never met a woman, either in literature or in life," Mme. de Beauvoir interrupts her quotations to say for herself, "who considered her old age with complacence. . . . I know only one self-portrait of an old man that is truthfully gay—that which the artist Monet painted of himself for Clemenceau. Though a certain part of his eyesight was blurred and he could no longer see the colors clearly, he never stopped painting. He used his memory to make up for his loss in perceptions. Then, later, his sight returned intact, and in his old age he produced his most astonishing chefs-d'œuvre. . . . Gifted with a surprising energy for work and with good health, fond of life, that is how he pictures himself in his portrait in the exuberance of old age—erect, laughing, with a vigorous complexion, with a crinkled beard, his glance full of fire and gaiety."

Toward the end of her book, Mme. de Beauvoir discusses eroticism in the later years of the age cycle, discusses Freud, discusses Churchill, and even discusses Hitler. She is never Mme. de Sévigné in her glancing ripe comments on life, nor is she, in truth, Mme. de Beauvoir at her best. Her tome, which is published by Gallimard, is oddly dressed for such a serious, unpopular work—the volume is a rich lavender from the top of the binding nearly to the bottom, where the color becomes an affectionate sort of rose.

March 11

For the past fortnight, this capital city has oscillated between two sorts of press announcements, both unpleasant reading for adults. Almost every day, the news has dealt with snow, usually announcing more to come or else chronicling the results of the latest blizzard. Last week's prize blizzard result was a thirty-mile-long traffic jam on the Autoroute de l'Oueste, leading out of Paris. The jam was of such proportions that it included accumulating car accidents as well as the snowblocked automobiles themselves, unequipped with snow tires, which are not part of the normal gadgetry of Paris motorists. Parisians are complaining that this has been the snowiest, longest, rainiest, and nastiest winter they have put up with for some time. This past week, the radio newscasts cheerfully mentioned the northbound flights of the wild ducks that have been wintering in the south—usually the harbingers of spring on the way. Parisians now suspect that either the newscasters or the ducks were out of touch.

The other disagreeable, even alarming, news to grownups concerns the continuing brutal student violence and fights at the suburban university at Nanterre, where the 1968 student riots had their inception. Student riots in France always have the same base. It is always the same fight the students' ancestors thought they settled in the French Revolution—the struggle between rightists and leftists. As near as one can make out from the daily Paris press, this month's exacerbation sprang from the Nanterre classroom of Professor Paul Ricœur, dean of the faculty of literature and social science, in which latter department he expounded the Existentialist philosophy of Husserl and Jaspers. In 1968, he regarded the student revolt as a promising dream of greater social-scholastic reforms, and enthusiastically accepted the new "law of orientation," or free choice for the students in selecting their studies, as laid down by Edgar Faure when Minister of Education and accepted by the French government. After the 1968 riots, a certain indiscipline reigned in Ricœur's classes, but there was no real trouble until January of this year, when some of his students locked him in his classroom for two hours. Later, some inflammatory troublemakers stopped him in the corridor, spat in his face, and stuck a wastebasket, with its contents, on his head. Why his leftist students turned against this liberal professor has not been understood by or explained to the Paris public. In any case, Ricœur's dream has become a nightmare. Recognizing that Nanterre had become an armed camp for opposing leftists and rightists, the unhappy philosopher, as a dean, last week officially requested the Minister of the Interior, who in France is in charge of the police, "to consider the university grounds as property open to the public." This was tantamount to abrogating the inviolable privacy from municipal or paramilitary interference enjoyed by European universities since their founding in the Middle Ages. He also demanded "the elimination of violent university groups," because "at any moment a murder might be committed." How to eliminate violent young Frenchmen without closing the university and also encouraging homicide he did not explain. At the entry of the police onto the Nanterre campus last week, the violence automatically increased by one-third. The student leftists and rightists continued their ferocious fights against each other, and both sides fought the police—all students' hereditary enemies. The week's Paris headlines have included "VIOLENT INCIDENTS BETWEEN NANTERRE EXTREMIST STUDENTS," "VIOLENCE STILL DOMINATES NANTERRE," and then "FOUR HOURS OF SEVERE FIGHTING WITH POLICE," who used their rifle butts to club students, with sickening resulting photographs. Headlines also reported that sixty police had been injured by the students. In the hand-to-hand campus fighting, the students used rocks and tear-gas grenades, thrown down at the police, who were legally forbidden to enter the campus buildings, which the students fought from as if from fortresses. The destruction inside the buildings was awful and costly—books, chairs, tables, and everything big and movable were heaved onto the police outside or broken up to be used as clubs. On Saturday, Minister of Education Olivier Guichard announced that "the situation on the campus has not changed." In the midst of all the ruckus, some diehard professors clamored for the continuation of teaching, "with dignity and calm" on the part of the faculty. The Napoleonic tradition of professorial imperturbability—one of the attitudes that the students were rebelling against two years ago, and one that was slated for some humanization—has been given nothing but a façade of change, the students declare. On Thursday of last week, *Figaro* announced that the day before some students had interfered with the *Figaro* photographer's "liberty to work," had taken his films away from him, and also his press badge, and had threatened to beat him up besides. Also on Thursday, Minister Guichard closed the Nanterre faculties of law and letters for two days. The crisis also aroused some French politicians to inquire into the validity of the university franchises, which under the old regimes have always included the idea of a university's being "an asylum of safety." Indeed, the decree of 1811 reaffirmed this for the modern universities, so as to "assure the intellectual independence of professors and students as regards political power"—meaning their right to think for themselves.

There was a very funny, apt newspaper cartoon that showed Minister Guichard in his office receiving two students, one a long-haired, bearded hippie, the other a militant type wearing a combat helmet, accompanied by three younger students with placards. One placard stated, "Study Is the Opium of the People." The second said, *"Vive Rien."* The third said, *"À Bas l'Instruction."* The caption of the drawing read, "And furthermore, we demand that tobacco shops be given to the veteran fighters of May–June," meaning the rioters of 1968. In France, the privilege of owning a tobacco shop—always a gold mine—is a perquisite given by the government to the widows or the immediate families of brave soldiers. To the adult French, the cartoon and commentary were slashingly comic, which is just the way they like them.

* * *

It is not often that *Figaro*'s illustrious music critic, who writes under the pseudonym of Clarendon, indulges in gaiety as a form of praise. This he did for Leonard Bernstein's first-night conducting here of Gustav Mahler's two-hour-long Third Symphony, which he repeated twice, the third time at ten o'clock Saturday morning at the Théâtre des Champs-Élysées. At the Saturday-morning performance, one saw the tiny little grilled boxes, tucked just under the theatre ceiling, filled for the first time, perhaps, since they used to be filled in the old days for Diaghilev's Russian Ballets. As *Le Monde*'s critic said, with customary solemnity, in choosing that particular opus Bernstein was not offering himself an easy success, since it was practically unknown to the Orchestre de Paris, which he was leading, and to its public. But Clarendon, in his review, went all out with bright pleasure in teasing Bernstein for his antics. He wrote, "Leonard Bernstein danced the Third Symphony superbly. Certainly the Orchestre de Paris was also superb, transported, lyric, and even impassioned. In the language of the dance, Bernstein gave us everything—*jetés-battus,* the undulations of a dervish, the swoonings of an Egyptian dancing girl, the leaping flight of a bayadere, the strut of a boxer, the tilt of a pigeon's wing, vertical leaps into the air. You think I am joking? On the contrary, it took all that to animate that Cyclopean symphony. Bernstein was right to do too much in order to get enough. His interpretation was precisely irresistible." Rarely does one hear such unrestrained French enthusiasm as at that preprandial Saturday-morning concert—enthusiasm from the members of the orchestra itself, standing and whacking their violins on the back with their bows, then putting their violins on their chairs and clapping their hands, as if music were not their regular profession, as if they, too, had received the joy of listening like an audience. Bernstein warmly embraced and kissed the concertmaster, finally kissed the leader of the second violins, and waved in greeting to the four trumpeters close to the back row, who had so valiant a series of loud entries to play and never snuffled them once. The audience would have been pleased had he gone on to kiss handsome Josephine Veasey, who sang her alto solo excellently, on rich and perfect pitch. Used as Bernstein is to public appreciation, what he received that morning was like a great bouquet of French applause that kept on flowering and blooming.

A most unlikely new French film has attained popularity in midtown movie houses here, where the French queue up to see it. It is called "L'Enfant Sauvage," is directed by François Truffaut, and Truffaut himself plays in it. He has dedicated the film to Jean-Pierre Léaud, who played the runaway boy in Truffaut's first great success, "The 400 Blows." This new one is a film about a wild boy who was discovered (which is true) in the Aveyron district of France in the eighteenth century—a kind of alarming pre-Mowgli who was a mute and lived like a naked beast in the forests. Truffaut plays the part of a young scientist who, aided by his housekeeper, is determined to attempt the civilizing of this strange creature. The film is the story of their semi-successful effort. Step by step, it is fascinating to watch. The viewer becomes involved with the hope inherent in the whole humane project. It is flawlessly directed, without sentiment, by Truffaut, a handsome figure in his tall top hat; nor is there any sentimental nonsense in his relation with the housekeeper. The eighteenth-century house in which the experiment takes place is a model of fine sobriety. The film is one of human kindness, important enough to be of interest two centuries later. The savage child, at the end, can at least wear clothes, and becomes attached to the house where he is sheltered. It is like a Jean-Jacques Rousseau incident related on celluloid instead of in print. The savage boy is frighteningly well played by young Jean-Pierre Cargol, nephew of the Spanish guitarist Manitas de Plata.

March 25

No one could have dreamed that the recent television debate between France's Minister of Finance, M. Valéry Giscard d'Estaing, and M. Jean-Jacques Servan-Schreiber, founder of the non-pro-government weekly magazine *L'Express* and recently self-appointed chief of the old, once powerful Radical Socialist Party, with which he proposes to reform and modernize France, would provide the most interesting, popular, and nationally followed TV night program of the present year. All that it featured, for nearly two solid hours, was two highly educated, diametrically opposed Frenchmen arguing about *l'égalité des chances dans la vie,* or equality of opportunity in life in France today—an increasingly political social question of bitter wonderment or of hope for millions in this elderly country. A kind of sharp, sporting tension was furnished in the debate by the likelihood that the two debaters will be opposing candidates for the Presidency of the Republic in the election of 1976. To begin with, each debater presented a very brief, rather clumsy movie of how he saw the possibilities of equal opportunity in France. Servan-Schreiber showed two naked plump boy babies. One, born in poverty, would by the age of two (he said) have already lost a percentage of his chance of equality, and by the age of ten would be definitely headed for the working class; the more favored, boosted, and educated infant could hope to end up as the manager of some big business—an odd notion of earthly paradise for such a sincere radical reformer as Servan-Schreiber, except that he is mesmerized by power as a form of proof. Giscard's movie script was narrated by a young woman with a black braid of hair who had her back to her listeners until the end, when she turned around to reveal her intelligent, handsome dark face—a Creole, or a French girl from one of the French islands, Giscard's tactful evidence that nature itself also furnishes impediments to equal chances. The debate was part of a series titled "À Armes Égales" ("On an Equal Footing"), but this proved to be not quite the case. As a political free lance, Servan-Schreiber, formidable in his gift for argument, was able to indulge at times in a certain wolflike demagoguery in some of his attacks on the Minister of Finance, who at one point was pushed to protest, with a tight smile, "You can hardly expect me to dissociate myself from the government I represent." At another moment, in reply to his opponent's statement that French chances for a better life were not increasing, the Minister—who had all his answers inside his head, with its tall cranial formation, whereas Servan-Schreiber had backed himself up with a pile of memos in case he needed help—said, "When you and I were in school together, in

1935, the secondary schools contained only two hundred and forty-five thousand pupils. Today, there are four million two hundred thousand. The scholarship students then numbered twenty-seven thousand. Today, they number one million six hundred and seventy thousand." Though the Minister, with his overrefined studious Gallic face, looks older than Servan-Schreiber, he is two years younger, now aged forty-four. Both men were educated at the Polytechnique, regarded as the most eminent of all of France's famous great schools, entered only by competitive examination, specializing in higher mathematics, and producing the highest grade of French technologists, at their top rank known as "Les X," of whom Giscard was one. He was also an *Énarque,* or graduate of L'École Nationale d'Administration. This was founded after the last war with the aim of creating what de Gaulle called *les grands commis de l'état,* or great trained servants of the French state. Giscard d'Estaing is doubtless unique in Europe as the most highly educated member of any functioning government. His speech on TV reflected his mature, civilized mentality and his carefully filled and upholstered brain. There was only one interruption of the two debaters' arguments, made by one of the young intellectual referees seated in a wide circle around them. The question raised by this young woman referee was "Would not this debate have been more fruitful if one of the two men had not come from a privileged family?" Most of the other young referees nodded in affirmation. In this writer's opinion, this would have ruined the ideally subtle, balanced relation between the two debaters, equal in past privileges but not in present political opinion—Servan-Schreiber a natural radical, and Giscard a native liberal. Both men richly inherited, in a professional way, from their families. Jean-Jacques stepped easily into the footprints of his journalist father, director of the Paris financial paper *Les Échos.* Giscard's inheritance was somewhat more complex. He entered politics under the guidance of his grandfather Jacques Bardoux, whose parliamentary seat he took as deputy from Puy-de-Dôme. His own father was an *inspecteur des finances*—one of France's high technological titles. The son earned the same title by his dazzling career at L'École Nationale d'Administration. Together, Servan-Schreiber and Giscard d'Estaing, as a pair of spectacular, educated talkers, gave us, the *polloi,* a TV performance of high political and, indeed, patriotic thinking and talk, which we shall not soon forget.

Last week, France had a sitdown strike of trucks and truck drivers on the national highways and autoroutes all over the country, with Paris completely blocked off. Outside the city, the local villagers walked across the fields to stand and stare at the strange spectacle of inert mastodons cluttering the highway as far as they could see. The trouble arose from an intelligent, kindly conceived government project to clear the national routes of all trucks on Easter Sunday and Monday (and on certain other holiday weekends), so that motoring French vacationers, speeding to and from their holy holiday, could scoot down unimpeded thoroughfares. But the plan miscarried, because somebody forgot to consult the truck drivers, who argued that they would be halted far from home on a holiday, without pay, and in some cases with their cargoes starting to rot. So they struck. Inspired to an imitation, *petits commerçants*, or little shopkeepers, also began blocking the roads all over France—especially around Bordeaux—with their family cars lined up by the kilometre in protest against the unpopular *taxe sur valeur ajoutée,* passed about two years ago but still rankling. (It is a kind of super sales tax that loads the petty shopkeeper with paperwork.) The whole notion of striking on the roads against what you don't like elsewhere has, in a way, spread all over France. One newspaper has run a cartoon of a blocked road with a weedy-looking truck driver and his truck at its head; he is carrying a sign saying, "My wife is unfaithful! Comrades, solidarity!" There was no humor in the recent four-day strike at Orly of the *aiguilleurs du ciel,* or air-traffic controllers, who regulate the descent and takeoff of the planes. Twenty-five thousand would-be passengers jammed the airport, whose six bars and restaurants were also on strike, so that there was neither food nor drink except tap water for that vast angry gathering. Transatlantic planes arriving from New York landed two hours late, and luggage was unearthed only after delays of three hours or more.

There has even been a threatened strike by the ballet dancers at the Paris Opéra. The rumor had spread among them that the recently appointed *directeur* of the ballet, Roland Petit, would demand that the dancers all take special examinations on their technical competence, with the privilege on his part of dismissing those he found lacking—a highly unlikely tale, since once a performer is a member of a French state theatre, he is protected by his contract and is as difficult to dislodge as a limpet. Calm has been restored with Petit's announcement that the ballet section is actually to be augmented and separated into two sections, one to be used this coming season as the dancing chorus that customarily accompanies some operas, such as the waltz number in "Faust." The other is to function only as a proper, classic corps de ballet.

The constant invisible rebuilding of Paris for the sake of several thousand automobiles, and never for the sake of a few hundred thousand citizens, goes on apace. The Place Vendôme, beneath which a four-floor garage for almost nine hundred cars has been constructed, is almost completely resurfaced. It will be covered with gravel, to scare off motorists from parking their cars there, parking on that square in the future being strictly illegal. New digs have already been started under the Louvre, on the Rue de Rivoli side, down by the little church of Saint-Germain l'Auxerrois, where another fine subterranean parking lot will be dredged beneath all those fabulous art collections stored overhead. At the Maine-Montparnasse Railway station site, digging is going on for what may be the tallest tower in Europe—six hundred and sixty feet high—for use as business offices. Another tower, only half as tall, for the use of the Sorbonne faculty, is projected for the Halle aux Vins, only a block or so distant from Notre-Dame. The proposed tower would be taller than the towers of Notre-Dame, and two Paris deputies have finally risen in wrath to protest. They asked, "Is it a good plan to massacre forever the site of Notre-Dame? Such a tower would irremediably ruin the central landscape of Paris," and expressed their surprise at the contradiction that exists between the state policy of university decentralization, the preserving of art sites, and such a project. At this rate, *Le Monde* has just prophesied gloomily, it would seem that "the bowl of Paris" will soon be full of skyscrapers, "to its aesthetic detriment." In the meantime, according to indignant articles in several other Paris papers, the Place des Vosges—most harmonious, shabbiest, and most historic residential square of all Paris—is slowly eroding away, house by house. That would seem a good place for the Paris city architects to vent some of their energy on.

April 9

The Salon des Indépendants, now showing at the Grand Palais, was once, back toward the end of the last century, the great pugnacious art event of the Paris painting year. It was founded as a successor to the Salon des Refusés of Napoleon III and was the first Paris salon ever organized by those who were still considered the "outs" and were just becoming the "ins." Its founders, in 1884, were the big new young artists, like Signac, Odilon Redon, and Seurat, in revolt against the mossbacks in the Salon des Artistes Français, still devoted to anything that was old hat or else politely nude. Unable to push in anywhere else, the rebels made the Indépendants their own stamping ground, their free-for-all club, because of the then astonishing liberty it afforded by having neither jury to pass on the entries nor prizes to placate public opinion. As has since often been found a melancholy political truism, too much freedom eventually weakens standards and then performance. But before it lost all meaning, the Indépendants made invaluable art history. It showed the Neo-Impressionists, the Nabis, the Fauves, and the Cubists, and it has intelligently made it a custom ever since to borrow whatever good examples of these styles it can lay its hands on and include them in its exhibitions of the ever-declining painting performances of the year, which this year, 1970, have struck bottom. As one Paris art critic wrote, "Despite the new works of twenty-six hundred artists, the Salon des Indépendants is dead on its feet." Among the new art shown, there is nothing that catches the eye sufficiently even to sneer at, cruelly. The truth is that the young new Paris painters worth their salt can all be seen today in the front windows of the multiple art shops behind the Institut and up into Saint-Germain-des-Prés, and that at the moment there is no new French art tendency of any special savor anyhow. Even the retrospectives shown in the *cours d'honneur* of the Grand Palais, this year devoted to the late Cubists and their friends, around 1914, seem a little tepid, a little warmed over, because they are not necessarily examples of their creators at their moment of creative heat, such as today are found in a private collection or in a tightfisted commercial gallery, neither of which likes to loan things out. The last private dictum this writer ever heard from Miss Alice B. Toklas was "Paintings are nothing like people. They do not like to travel, and it does not do them any good. They always come back home the worse for wear. So I shall never lend any more of Gertrude's paintings as long as I live"— which was, alas, to be only a short time.

Among the Cubist period's honored relics at the Grand Palais are a Léger called "Femme en Rouge et Vert," too typical to be interesting; a good Gleizes canvas of "Clowns," fresher and with more meat in it than his more theoretical subsequent performances; a lovely La Fresnaye, whose poetry emerges in a woodland scene, painted, like all his works, too early in Cubism to give full value to the style as reflected in his short career; a good still-life by de Waroquier; and a lovely Dufy, always in his early days an excellent student of the theories being practiced, such as Cubism, at that time marking his regattas and horse races—topics in motion, which always fascinated Parisian eyes. There is an exquisite, voluptuous Modigliani nude, contorted and rosy; a rare Louise Hervieu architectural painting of a carved doorway; a third-rate Pascin; a Max Jacob; a Theo van Rysselberghe; and a lovely self-portrait by Marie Laurencin, which she must have painted about the time Apollinaire was so much in love with her. This past week, owing to the many strikes among state employees, which have extended from employees in the national gunpowder works to Paris museum guardians, the Grand Palais guards on Monday afternoon consisted of a group of old chaps who at three o'clock were too tired to stand up any longer, so squatted on and around a large table, where they sat smoking a supply of strong, slender stogie cigars, giving the severe museum scene a rare atmosphere of jolly sociability and the fumes of a bistro.

April 23

The two most formal journals in this part of the hemisphere—*Le Monde,* of Paris, and the London *Times*—both burst forth with "O.K., Joe," dictated directly from the skies, to headline their front pages bearing Friday's great good news of the approaching salvational descent to water and earth of the Apollo 13 astronauts. "As memorable as, and perhaps even more than, the solemn 'one small step for a man, one giant leap for mankind' pronounced by Armstrong on first setting foot in the Sea of Tranquillity was Swigert's 'O.K., Joe,'" *Le Monde* declared with satisfaction, and went on to say, "On the moon, the astronauts had been supermen, ready to perform all the tasks demanded of them and to say what was appropriate. Become refugees in their fragile cabined shelter, pierced with cold, mending one thing and concocting another, the Apollo 13's crewmen were cut down to the size of our petty world. With Apollo 11, the astronaut took his place as the best product of American civilization. With Apollo 13, he once more put on his human face. . . . Paradoxical as it may seem, the voyage of Apollo 13, far from raising any question about the American space program, will doubtless reinforce it. In the United States, nobody imagines that the moon flights will be abandoned. The habit has been established. Especially now, with the rescue having been effected, confidence will be stimulated, and the man in the street will feel closer to the man in space. It was to compete against Russia that the United States threw itself aloft into the conquest of the cosmos. Everything now leads one to believe that, even with the present slack in the Soviet efforts, the Americans' activity will go on. In accepting their space program from its start, and at whatever the cost of proclaiming it and displaying it in full, the Americans entered into a great risk, and it is only fair that now they have been rewarded"—in the meticulous rescue, and the miraculous good luck on top of bad, of this past week.

In Paris on Tuesday, which seemed the blackest day for hope, it was like the day when Roosevelt died and Parisians stopped Americans on the street to express their sympathy. On Tuesday, a pious old Frenchwoman on the Rue de Castiglione said to this correspondent, "I have just been to church praying for your men." In the newspaper shop, the young clerk said earnestly, "We are thinking of them constantly. We won't let them go. We will bring them back, you'll see." Public sympathy so acute that it becomes private in its expression is touching and rare in a conventional civilization like that of France. If it is to take shape in spoken words between strangers on the sidewalk and between generations in shops, it demands an event that causes pain.

The melodramatic return to earth of Apollo 13 was followed fairly closely by the radio stations audible here, although only one —Europe No. 1—was a permanent contact with NASA. Radio-Monte-Carlo followed the news in bulletins from 6 p.m. to midnight; France-Inter, which is a French national station, had a crew in Houston and brought in special speakers of interest to French listeners. And the Luxembourg station ran what it called a nonstop Apollo program as its afternoon news. On the two French national TV chains, a flash about the astronauts was given every hour on the hour. The children's daily evening program was cancelled, but not the Liège-Bastogne bicycle race, which was carried every afternoon at four-thirty. However, the five daily news roundups on the first and second national TV chains ran overtime with excitement and joy when the good news started coming in. Previously, there had been one peculiarly French element in the universal reaction of fear that the men might be lost in space. This French reaction was so positive that it was mentioned on the first national TV chain as a news item. By the end of the week, it had been summed up editorially by the *Nouvel Observateur,* which said that the public had indeed wanted to know every detail about the space drama "not because there are three men in danger of death but because there are three men in space who risk dying without ever being *interred,*" adding, "Faced with their situation, every man feels the anguish of the earthling."

During the week of the Apollo drama, France itself was suffering a national tragedy. On the Plateau d'Assy of the Savoy Alps, which is studded with sanatoriums because of its benevolent high air, the Sanatorium du Roc-des-Fiz was submerged by an avalanche that swept it away and down into the valley, and with it the lives of over seventy people, mostly children. The village of Assy is famous in the art world. Its remote modern church, which certainly few art lovers have ever journeyed up to see, is noted for its decoration by a complex of modern artists, each working independently in his own style—Matisse, Léger, Chagall, Rouault,

Lurçat, and the sculptress Germaine Richier, whose Christ in a chapel is particularly renowned. The church, which is the most spectacular, if the least familiar, result of the project to revitalize church decorations conceived by the late noted Dominican Père Couturier, was not harmed. There have been other avalanches, such as that at the popular ski center of Val d'Isère, which was also tragic, with forty dead. Nature in France, beginning with the delayed, winter-bound spring, has been brutal, and even dangerous, at its worst, and, at its best, unkind, sunless, and melancholy, with rain or the threat of it daily, except for one perfect sunny poetic primaveral day out of the last thirty. The bad weather is part of a discouraging social climate that only higher temperatures and frankly higher wages in some sectors seem likely to relieve. Various spring strikes have already begun, with the garbage collectors now following the postmen. Today, there is a strike of high-school teachers in southern France, and tomorrow there will be the same strike in the north, demanding larger educational appropriations for next year, and also more scholarships and grants, all sharply refused by the Ministry of Education. Last Sunday in Paris, the big master bakers struck, because the government refused to let them boost the price of their bread by five centimes a loaf. The smaller master bakers and three bakers' unions disagreed about raising the price at all, it being their opinion that price-raising merely irritates the customer and increases taxes—and so it does. The strike threatened for yesterday of half a million civil servants, which would have paralyzed France, including its airports, was called off at the last minute because the government put up a mollifying ante of a five-and-three-quarters-per-cent raise in salaries, which is cheap at the price, especially since the civil servants had demanded a six-per-cent boost. Unlike spendthrift Washington, European governments all pay their people poorly, except their Presidents. The French civil servants are, in their way, almost more valuable, because when a French government falls the civil servants keep right on working, carrying the government on their backs.

A body blow was dealt to the age-old supreme authority of the French husband in family affairs by a new law, passed last Thursday, which expels him from his superior position in the Code Civil, founded by Napoleon, and legally replaces him with a new principle—that of the moral and material direction of the French family by *both* parents. The wife has now become her husband's equal in civil rights *"au sein de la famille"* ("in the bosom of the family"), in the phrase of the Law of Parental Authority, which is what this new domestic equalizer is called. It was first proposed by a former Minister of Justice, M. Jean Foyer, who, as the project was being debated in Parliament, made a few highly pertinent, extremely progressive remarks on how the times have changed. "The notion of paternal power as consecrated by the Code Civil is absolutely out of date now, and can have no more meaning for the young generation," he said. "If the new text is on many points innovational, it is because the new definition that it brings to the role of the parents in relation to their children, and especially to their children's education, corresponds to what is already practiced in the great majority of families, and represents the young people's views. In today's society, the family is in reality a conjugal community in which father and mother co-operate closely, and is not a relationship based on the dominant—one might even say domineering—authority of the father."

The difference between the new French domesticity and the way Napoleon saw and codified its sexual and social elements can be seen at a glance by merely quoting three or four of the old Code Civil dicta, which will continue to have legal force until January, 1971, when the new parental-authority text goes into effect. Most of them are enough to set any American or British feminist's teeth on edge. Dictum No. 1, on parental authority, declared simply, "Authority is exercised by the father alone, in his position as head of the family." By deduction, this led to the father's necessary signature on all important family papers, including a wife's demand for a passport, or even for opening her own bank account. Under the new legal setup, the wife will have the right to participate in certain important family procedures. For instance, she will be able to demand a passport for her child, enroll her child in school, send it to a summer camp, and so on. In cases of disagreement between the parents, the father's decision was always sovereign under the Code Civil. In the new domesticity, if the parents cannot agree on some point, either of them may take the case to a *juge d'instance* (roughly approximate to our justice of the peace, with ameliorations), who, if both remain obdurate, will make the decision for them—a celerity of procedure that would have cut thousands of words from the endless reports of lawsuits and marital quarrels such as were chronicled by Balzac. The only disagreement in which the husband will still automatically dominate the outcome is the decision on where the family is to live—provided that what he selects does not present "physical or moral danger." Napoleon having chosen to ignore the question of grandparents, of which his Code Civil therefore made no mention, it was necessary in the new family laws to give some protection to both the old and the new generations. So neither father nor mother, by these new laws, can interfere in the normal relations between the child and its granny or granddad, with visits and letters between old and young being fully protected. Where illegitimate children were concerned in Napoleon's time (and quite a problem they were, even in Napoleon's own family), the Code was very explicit. It said that parental authority was exercised over the little by-blow by whichever parent first acknowledged the child's existence; if both parents acknowledged the child, the father's claim took precedence. By the new law, if both parents acknowledge the infant, it is the woman who exercises the parental authority. Finally comes the responsibility of payment for damage caused by children—no small item today, when even minor children who wreck school property are threatened with having to pay for it. According to Napoleon, the mother did not have to pay a centime unless she was a widow. Now everything is to be tinged with real justice. Thus, under the new law both parents are responsible for whatever destruction is caused, at least by their minor children still living at home. How the university students who smash things will be treated seems not to have been determined in Parliament last Thursday. However, in paying for student damage, if the father's funds give out, the mother (provided she is a woman of property) is supposed to continue to pay up. "By acquiring the same parental rights as her husband, the wife acquires the same duties" is the final comment being made on these admirable new French social-reform laws, which next year will start altering many of the old difficulties of being a female here in France. And high time, too.

May 5

French concern over President Nixon's sudden dispatch of American troops into Cambodia is so great that reference to it is not limited to portentous editorials in *Le Monde* and *Figaro* but has moved into a new channel of public expression, as proved by the long, unexpected commentary on Tuesday night in *France-Soir,* the afternoon Paris paper usually given over merely to *les informations,* or the latest news, but with the largest circulation and readership of any newspaper in France. On Tuesday, it stated, "By intervening in Cambodia, President Nixon has taken the decision to extend the war over the entire territory that formerly constituted French Indo-China," in which the French people, left with realistic memories of their painful defeat in Dien Bien Phu, still take a special acute familial interest. "The United States, the Soviet Union, and China are now involved in a situation that is extremely complicated and dangerous, on which the life or death of humanity may depend. . . . A few months ago, M. Georges Pompidou, President of the French Republic, M. Harold Wilson, Prime Minister of Great Britain, and M. Willy Brandt, Chancellor of the German Federal Republic, one after another visited President Nixon, who formally assured them that no grave decision would be taken by the United States without consulting its allies. Yet at no moment has Paris, London, or Bonn been even informed of the American intervention in Cambodia. The President of the United States could not make clearer what slight importance he attaches to Europe. It is as if Europe did not exist."

May Day, on which a certain public effervescence can always be feared, passed off quietly here, perhaps owing to an extraordinary and peculiar new French law. It is a law against the French public's practice of destructive violence, and it had just been passed by the National Assembly. It was introduced by the government apparently as a consequence of the violent student riots at the suburban university of Nanterre in March. However, truck drivers, small shopowners, and various labor groups have also staged strikes and demonstrations, which, if only because they interfered with traffic, invariably turned into angry confrontations with the police. To these have been added outbreaks by youthful extremist political groups, ranging from Fascists to anarchists, who often acted exactly alike. In recent weeks, among them, they have sacked two of Nanterre's university buildings, invaded a suburban city hall, vandalized the little Lenin Museum in Paris, burning some of the books that Lenin had owned when in exile here, and attacked a Paris police station, which is most unusual. Prime Minister Chaban-Delmas had earlier pledged his government to mitigate the unrest that provided a constantly worrying atmosphere for the French citizenry, and especially for the Gaullist right-wing Parliamentary majority. Then, in a TV interview, he suddenly announced the decision to make the *casseurs*—the smashers—foot the bill for what they destroyed. This appealed to Frenchmen's national sense of logic, and also to their regard for their pocketbooks, since it indicated that somebody might get some money back sometime, if only for repairs. Parliament's spring session thus undertook a lengthy afternoon preliminary discussion of the *anti-casseur* law, which, in order to maintain public order according to the republican tradition, demanded a choice between "the law and the street"—a law that achieved its weary, semi-tumultuous passage at 5 a.m. the next day, long after most of us correspondents had abandoned the Parliament and gone home to bed. The drafting of the law required some elaborate tinkering, so as not to alarm the French people to an even greater degree than the recent sessions of violence had done. A pair of consultant experts from the Paris law faculty had warned that the *anti-casseur* law "shifted the penal code from the principle of personal responsibility into the limitless sphere of collective responsibility," or something as vague and uncontrollable as air pollution. In this state of detachment, the idle members of a *casseur* group could be more easily arrested on the street for what they had not done than the actively guilty, usually on the run and out of sight by the time the police arrive. The political left, *in toto,* was against the law, because the left always suspects strong democratic governments, and the general public, after its opening enthusiasm, also soured somewhat on the project upon discovering that the Chaban-Delmas government had slipped into the law a proviso designed to give the authorities control of all street demonstrations

—those little or large parades, usually to celebrate dissatisfaction, that are a precious inherited Revolutionary French privilege for the neighborhood politicians. The trade unions, which supply a driving power that the weakened Communist Party has lacked ever since the 1968 student riots, when it dodged the responsibility of leading the pack, were intelligently organized to propagandize against the *anti-casseur* law, if only because it is the trade-union delegates who call French strikes, and in case of explosive trouble later the leaders could, by the new law, be arrested and imprisoned as the organizers. By the time the *anti-casseur* law was passed last week, it had been thoroughly identified as "a repressive law against individual liberty" and dubbed *"une loi scélerate,"* or "an iniquitous law," meaning a law worse in its repression than what it seeks to repress. The infamous original *lois scélérates* were passed in the eighteen-nineties against some anarchist manifestations led by a man named Vaillant, and they have remained like historical wayside warnings to French reformers ever since. Because the *anti-casseur* law is as complex as a spider web, the penalty it can inflict on whoever tangles with it, and for whatever specific cause, has already been simplified to a maximum two years in prison for persons participating in violent attacks on property and for those actively taking part in violent demonstrations. As a matter of fact, the penalty can rise to five years in prison for the organizers of a legally forbidden meeting that intends to use *force ouverte,* and it can bring three years in prison to the leader alone if he fails to warn his followers to cease and desist when violence begins—as if he had eyes in the back of his head. In presenting to Parliament the finally approved law, Minister of Justice René Pleven was oddly begged by the government to "use it only with the greatest discernment," since its chances of engendering injustice are obviously multiple. Even now, the problem of identifying the *casseurs* will be difficult, unless they are caught with rocks in their hands in front of broken windows. At first, there was talk of identifying campus troublemakers by photography—an idea given up after one or two tests, because the young miscreants' faces were so distorted by rage, pleasure, and excitement during riots that their own mothers failed to recognize them except by their clothing. Despite its unpopularity, the passing of the *anti-casseur* law may be of extreme importance to the French social scene and to the collegiate youth who animate it. As for the trade-union men and the Communists in any future parades, they will know how to take care of themselves.

"Beginning to End," a selection from the works of Mr. Samuel Beckett, edited and performed as a one-man recitative by the Irish character comedian Jack MacGowran, formerly of the Dublin Abbey Theatre, had its Paris première last week at the Théâtre Édouard VII. Mr. Beckett, a friend of MacGowran's of long years' standing, supervised his adaptation. The Édouard VII's opening night was visibly a Paris cultural event, with Salvador Dali arriving early, his mustachios akimbo, followed by certain of the bilingual literary Parisians and by most of the remnants of the American Joyce circle here, now as attached to Mr. Beckett as this isolated man of great gifts allows. The performance, which runs two hours, with an intermission, consists of the actor-spokesman (presumably Lucky, from "Waiting for Godot") making a cohesive running report of the troubles and the exasperated wisdom he has accumulated in his long Dublin life—a monologue amalgamated from the Nobel Prize-winning Mr. Beckett's works, including "Malone Dies," "Molloy," "Krapp's Last Tape," "Watt," something called "An Abandoned Work," and "The Unnameable," which is part of a trilogy, and also from "Embers," which was written for the B.B.C. What are recounted are the commonplaces of poverty and of being a tramp. On a stage that is bare except for a small rock that represents the cliff by the sea over which he hopes his mortal dust will soon float out on some tide, Lucky stands or shuffles about and occasionally scratches himself, precariously garbed in a remarkable all-weather long, elderly, raddled overcoat, held together by a pair of safety pins—a man of memory abandoning himself to what he can recall, most of it vexatious. He mentions his early memory of his senile mother standing in the window in her nightdress, who dies and leaves him homeless. He even drags up some reference to his father, nearly unknown to him. He recalls the talk of Bolton and Holloway, two old fellows chatting by the fireside one night. He recalls his early habit of dreaming pleasantly of animals, as against the realities he has since known—being chased by stoats and being driven nearly out of his mind by finding himself helpless in a farmyard filled with chickens and ducks. He expounds on his attempt to systematize the problem of stowing away sixteen "sucking stones" in the various pockets of his greatcoat and trousers, so that by rotating them he may be sure to suck a fresh one each time—a dither of confused mathematics and careful planning that is inordinately comic to listen to. He engages in a long genealogical tirade about his mother's mother's mother and his father's fathers, over generations, that is insanely funny. His is a strayed mind, occasionally directing itself onto paths of memory, only to fall by his own wayside through elderly lack of interest. There are patches of lovely poetic language about the sea sands and the seasons, ending in a bitter, wise complaint that spring's return will start the whole senseless process once more in motion, as the continuum of life. Suddenly he announces, "That's enough," and shuffles offstage with the same abruptness he had shown at the beginning, when he announced, almost with satisfaction, "I shall soon be quite dead, at last."

MacGowran gives a performance of perfected balance and cross-grained comedy, mixed with melancholy explosive anger at the unbearable burden of the surprises of life on earth for a man who has lived on its lonely roads and has seen and recorded them in his memory. It is an artist's acutely intelligent interpretation of Beckett's humor and pith and creativity. By his voice and his rambling gait, MacGowran animates and brings to life, merely with words, the existence of people we have never seen but listen to when he speaks.

May 21

Henri Matisse is more than ever regarded here as the greatest modern French painter of his time. Never before has there been seen in Paris—nor is it likely to be assembled soon again—such an overinclusive, enormous exhibition of his colors and canvases as has just been put on view at the Grand Palais. It was conceived by André Malraux, while still the Gaullist Minister of Culture, as the nation's centenary tribute to the energetic Fauve genius, born on the last day of 1869, his lifework being suddenly interrupted by death at the age of eighty-five. This spring-to-autumn five-month retrospective show of his creations, from April 21st to September 21st, is the major summer art event not only of France but also of Europe. The organization of the collection was aided by his sons and especially by his daughter, Mme. Marguerite Duthuit (usually called Margot on her father's portraits of her). Her private *catalogue raisonné* of his works has, through her youthful remembrances and careful research, clarified and fixed dates and travels connected with his career and pictures. His youngest son, Pierre, the picture merchant of New York, was of particular utility in tracing the whereabouts of early canvases of Matisse, whose first works, though laughed at loudly by the French, were purchased by a quartet of Americans living in Paris or visiting there from California, and were thereafter repeatedly passed from one of the four art-loving Steins to another, beginning with Gertrude and Leo, and continuing with Michael and his wife, Sarah (the couple that ended up with the larger quantity of these increasingly valuable canvases after Gertrude traded off her share of them to Michael for some Renoirs she fancied). The elder son, Jean Matisse, who had often helped his father hang his canvases and well knew the old man's fanatical habit of measuring off the procedure by centimetres, was instrumental in hanging parts of the Grand Palais show, especially the opening section, which he hung as he thought his father would have done it. It has been widely criticized by the public as looking disorderly. The truth is that it is simply too crammed. The exhibition was not chosen, collected, and organized by the staff of official museum art curators trained for such special tasks. Instead, like a palace revolution, it was, at Malraux's insistence, organized by a gifted outsider of his choice, M. Pierre Schneider, foremost among the younger Paris art critics and the regular art commentator for the weekly magazine *Express*. Since Schneider was already writing a definitive book on Matisse, he wrote the Grand Palais catalogue. It is intimate, authoritative, and extremely stimulating to read. Almost every page of text contains inserted quotations from Matisse's conversations with other painters on the troubles of painting, or from his correspondence with them, or from his 1908 document "Notes d'un Peintre," which ranked over time as analytical canon. Among artist friends he corresponded with was Bonnard, whom he always wrote to and wanted to see when troubled about how a new picture was or was not turning out. Another consultant was his elderly neighbor in the South of France, Pierre Auguste Renoir. He also corresponded with a newer friend, Juan Gris. For a painter whose expressed aim in painting was to give joy, Matisse gave himself recurrent bouts of pain in conscientious self-analysis concerning his work. After his temporary entry into Neo-Impressionism (during which he painted "Luxe, Calme, et Volupté," present in this exhibition), he wrote to an easier-going, less important painter friend, Camoin, "I now know better what I am. I know that Seurat is completely the contrary of a romantic, and that I am a romantic with a good half of me scientist and rationalist, which creates the struggle that I emerge from a winner but breathless." Among the most important of these catalogue excerpts of Matisse's own words is one in which he says, "The choice of my colors does not rest upon any scientific theory; it is based on observation, on sentiment, and on the experience of my own sensibilities."

The Matisse exhibition fills three floors of the Grand Palais. It contains two hundred and forty-nine paintings, drawings, and sculptures. One Paris art commentator wrote, with a kind of justice, and perhaps fatigue, that "one dozen of them could sum up Matisse's artistic career," whereupon he chose and named his significant twelve. This correspondent would settle for six. Ranking No. 1 is "Woman with Hat," a portrait of Mme. Matisse painted in 1905. It has major historical meaning because it ranks as the first Fauve painting; from the greens and blues and purples of the hat a new aesthetic style emerged. It is the only sad portrait Matisse ever painted. The Grand Palais catalogue note on it says, "It is known that both Gertrude and Leo Stein claimed to have discovered and acquired this picture at the Salon d'Automne. Leo Stein is supposed to have said, 'It is what I was waiting for without knowing it.' According to Mme. Thérèse Jelenko, who was living at that time with M. and Mme. Michael Stein, and who accompanied them to the salon, 'They fell in love with the woman wearing a hat. . . . I remember that everybody stopped in front of it. The young [French] painters were in paroxysms of laughter. And there stood Leo, Michael, and Sarah Stein, very impressed and very solemn about it. They talked about who ought to buy it, and I think that my side of the Stein family did not have enough money. It cost four hundred dollars, and it was decided that Leo should buy it. It hung on his walls for a few years, and was finally transferred to Michael in exchange for those Renoir paintings' "—really desired by Gertrude, always Leo's partner in the family deals. "According to Sarah Stein, Mme. Matisse posed for the portrait dressed in black and wearing a black hat. . . . Her only note of color was an orange ribbon around her throat." The confusions about the fate and the possession of the portrait only add a sort of lurid charm to its strange Fauve coloring. It is now the property of Mr. and Mrs. Walter Haas, of San Francisco—fervid Matisse collectors and followers in the Steins' path.

Choice No. 2 is "Blue Nude," painted in 1907. It is a great composition in Matisse's style of "rhythmic expression," Orientalized by background palm trees, which had become native to his imagination. This was bought by Gertrude and Leo Stein, then sold to John Quinn, then to the Cone sisters, of Baltimore—distant Stein relatives by marriage. Baltimore is still its permanent museum home. Choice No. 3 is "Still-Life with Oranges," painted in Tangier, bought in Paris during the Second World War by Picasso, who had long coveted it and who was always Matisse's devoted friendly rival. It is a solid composition illustrating what Matisse believed to be most significant in modern painting—that it advanced toward the beholder instead of retreating from him, as the vistalike paintings of Renaissance artists did, owing to their discovery of perspective. No. 4 is another portrait of Mme. Matisse, painted in 1912, bought by Serge Shchukin, now owned by the Hermitage Museum, in Leningrad. It is an elegant trick, painted by Matisse as a counterpart to a Cézanne portrait he admired of a chic-looking hatted woman in a blue *tailleur,* called "Woman in Blue"—this being a chic woman in a green *tailleur.* Both portraits are today in Russian museums. The Matisse work is remarkable as an example of the permanence of his linear style, like a signature on a check. No. 5 is "Portrait of Sarah Stein," painted in 1916, and a stunning, eccentric portrait, unlike Matisse's normal manner, in which the Stein face comes so far forward as to seem to explode with significance—a rare melodramatic Matisse. No. 6 would be any one of

Matisse's famous semi-nude houris, of which the exhibition contains half a dozen, all examples of the semi-Orientalism that became Matisse's artistic citizenship after his first voyages to the North African sun.

The public favorites in the exhibition are the two great decorative panels, "Dance" and "Music," never before seen in Western Europe, that Matisse painted for Serge Shchukin's mansion. In them Matisse carried to violent simplification his belief in color as a delegate for composition—with, in one, the scarlet nude bodies of the dancers prancing in a saraband circle against the azure sky and, in the other, the nude male musicians with pipes and viol on a greensward, some of them singing with mouths pursed, like whistlers. The other great exhibition inclusions are "Le Luxe I," which almost caused a riot of disapproval when shown at an early Paris salon ("Le Luxe II," when shown in Chicago as part of the Armory Show of 1913, caused an investigation by the State Vice Commission into the "four-flushing" foreign painters and their "distorted art"); "La Desserte Rouge," a great arbitrary red composition of a buffet table set with dishes and leaned over by a servant; and his succession of studies of the Pont Saint-Michel, which he painted over the years by looking out the window of his cramped little studio beside the Seine, where the entire family lived and where his wife helped out the family income by making and selling hats. The final extraordinary compositions are the panels of leafy designs cut by his scissors out of colored paper, used almost heroically as a means for the thinnest possible sculpture decorations, to which Matisse was reduced during the long last years when he was confined to his bed after a grave operation. As the famous master of hedonism or joy, he was indeed modern French art's greatest stoic.

June 3

This has been a feverish fortnight in France, preceded by a series of alarming, mysterious bombings in the handsome city of Grenoble, the reduction to cinders of a huge new supermarket outside Lyon, and sporadic outbursts of dynamiting here and there, plus a rising background of *attentats,* or aggressions, against individuals, with public and private violence in the very atmosphere, like a special pollution. And last week saw the temporary resurrection in Paris of the May, 1968, Left Bank student riots, but in better-organized and more warlike form. On Wednesday night, the Latin Quarter and Saint-Germain-des-Prés had their opening night of the new turbulence. It was a mass demonstration ordered by La Gauche Prolétarienne, a militant Maoist group made up of amalgamated *gauchistes,* in protest against that day's trial of the two editors of the Maoists' small, virulent tabloid *La Cause du Peuple,* of which M. Jean-Paul Sartre is now the editor. It began at sundown on the Rue Bonaparte with a set-to between Beaux-Arts students and the special riot police, and ended sometime before dawn on Thursday with the two sides throwing teargas bombs and paving stones at each other down by the Sorbonne's off-campus Faculté des Sciences, in the old Halle aux Vins, and it left the familiar savage, insane path of destruction behind it all the way back to the Place Saint-Germain-des-Prés. Decades ago, this correspondent lived for twenty-one pleasant years a few steps away from the Place, and last week lacked the heart—or perhaps had too much—to go over the next morning to stare at the familiar scene and its fresh marks of abuse. Of four barricades built near the Boulevard Saint-Germain—or so the Thursday-morning newspapers reported—one, on the Place Saint-Germain-des-Prés itself, between the Deux-Magots and the church, had been set on fire. As a consequence, the Café de Flore lost its windows, and the modern chichi snack bar called Le Drugstore, on the corner next to Lipp's, was badly damaged, with its interior partly burned. Near the post office on the Rue de Rennes, the famous old men's-shirt store called Cent Mille Chemises was broken into and looted. It seems that the Wednesday-night riot served as popular entertainment for the Paris nighthawks and a crowd of tourists, who trailed it faithfully, following its convulsions with the devotion of movie-gang-war experts for once seeing it like it is—except for no deaths, *mirabile dictu.*

The riot was not the spontaneous amateur affair the riots of two years ago were. It had a precise plan of organization, and it did not consist only of young students. This time, the students were subalterns in commando units of fifteen or twenty that were led by older men, whose tactics were to alert them by a war cry (for one group, behind the Boulevard Saint-Germain, the cry was the name "Patrick") and send them rushing out at the police in a violent offensive foray, then to withdraw them suddenly, so that they seemed to disappear underground, like real guerrillas—a tactic that at first mystified the police. This year, too, the young rioters were better prepared; many wore crash helmets, goggles, and, often, a bandanna tied over the nose. At the same time on Wednesday night, also on orders from the Gauche Prolétarienne, the Paris riot was being repeated in Grenoble, where it began at the Law School; in Rouen; and, with the fiercest fighting of all, in Marseille. In Paris, the students were considered to be winning the battle until past midnight, when the police began pulling themselves together and adjusting to the new form of battle. The Thursday-night Paris riot was minor in violence.

For the Paris riots, a new population of police flooded the Latin Quarter in a quantity never seen before: tough country *flics* and hard-bitten former Army sergeants enrolled in the national riot police—men from all over France ordered flown to Paris. The students were outnumbered. Furthermore, the police used some new equipment: small motorcycles, on which they could pursue isolated students fleeing down side streets, and small jeeps, which they drove on the sidewalks, leaning out with special long clubs to batter, *en passant,* anyone within reach—bystanders, tourists, lone young men merely trying to go home, swains with girls on their arms, trying to find their parked cars. Another new element consisted of police disguised as civilians, whose role was simply that of surprise aggressors, suddenly attacking a young man—any young man—on the edge of a crowd.

On Wednesday night, the second French TV channel ran a propaganda feature that must have outraged those Left Bank viewers who could hear what was going on in the streets below. It was called "Le Portrait d'un C.R.S."—meaning the Compagnies Républicaines de Sécurité, the full title of the riot police. It was, in a way, like a striptease portrait, first displaying a uniformed policeman, who looked like the Commendatore in "Don Giovanni," and then showing him unaccoutred and identifying all he wore or carried in the way of arms when at work: his plastic helmet, with its attached face shield; his circular plastic body shield, carried over the left arm, like a medieval warrior's; his belt, with hooks for carrying tear-gas bombs and a pistol; his splendid boots and gloves; and his flexible nightstick. When he had been reduced to his mere police uniform, he became a different fellow—a smiling, affable, and even vulnerable-looking man, who, in his twenty-minute talk, explained how he loved his family and his two children, and how he had always had a political preference for order and public service, though he advised his young son never to become a cop. It was one of those mistaken bits of official propaganda that probably should never have been made at all, and certainly should not have been shown on Wednesday night, when the Left Bank streets were filled with police-hating students, with their parents hanging out of the apartment windows above watching the fray and betting on their sons to win.

At the request of the Minister of the Interior, the Gauche Prolétarienne movement had been officially outlawed at the Wednesday-morning meeting of government Ministers, just in time to make *La Cause du Peuple* vulnerable, along with its editors, at their trial that afternoon. One editor, the Beaux-Arts professor Jean-Pierre Le Dantec, read aloud in court an endless, politically slanted defense, filled with anti-Trotskyite slogans but at least delivered with energetic conviction—more than was heard from his colleague, the weak-voiced Michel Le Bris. Both were accused of "provocation of crimes against the security of the state, and incitement to robbery, pillage, arson, and murder." (Their sentences, pronounced the next day, were one year in prison for Le Dantec and eight months for Le Bris—mild penalties just after the Gauche Prolétarienne riot.) But no one in the courtroom, crammed with black-robed lawyers come merely to see the show, cared what was said by anyone except Sartre, the star defense witness and public figure. Loyally accompanied into court by Mme. Simone de Beauvoir, he complained in his opening statement that on taking over the editorship after the two others had been arrested—for their personal political opinions, he claimed, rather than for what they printed (the two sets of opinions actually seemed identical)—he had not been arrested, this being a publicity gift that the government was, naturally, too smart to make. The Paris newspaper reporters even described what Sartre wore (such recognition being the height of masculine fame in the Paris press)—a beige polo coat over a suède jacket. No report was given of Mme. de Beauvoir's pretty flowered jerkin, which photographed nicely. In the May 1st number of *La Cause du Peuple,* a bottom line in small type on the back page declared, *"Directeur de Publication: Jean-Paul Sartre."* Since then, the judge has spoken of a "person unknown." *"X— c'est moi,"* Sartre said indignantly to an interviewer, and, later, "Why have I been treated differently from the way they were?"— as if he did not know. *Figaro's* trial portrait of Sartre was touching and rather merciless. "It is difficult to grow old well," *Figaro* said. "A defrocked professor, a philosopher who no longer incites enthusiasm but only respect, a famed writer who on his pedestal no longer feels himself to be on the same level as the times, he retains his nostalgia for the young. The novelist of decay, of the absurd act, heroic and desperate, the theorist of engagement in revolutionary causes and of the spontaneity of the masses, he sees widening around him the abyss that his years create in separating him from the new generation, its personages, and its reality, its dreams, and the revolution that never arrives. For him, May, 1968, and its riots were [or so he said] *'une divine surprise.'* "

After the noisy, explosive modernity of contemporary Paris these last weeks, and its riotous cacophonies, theatregoers here had the good fortune to be able to drop back three centuries, if they succeeded in obtaining seats to what was a brief but rarefied and elegant production. This was "Bérénice," which has been traditionally regarded as the most beautiful love drama ever written in French, and which is the creation of Jean Racine, the great seventeenth-century master of rhymed alexandrines. Certainly it was also the most exquisitely artificial formalized stage production one has seen in modern times, and it is this that gave it its peculiar fascination. It was acted at the Théâtre Montparnasse by Roger Planchon's famous Théâtre de la Cité troupe, from Villeurbanne, outside Lyon. Planchon directed the poetic tragedy about Titus, Emperor of Rome, and Bérénice, Queen of Palestine. It is the French classic before which generations of literate French have wept in their suffering over its love story, and in which, a generation ago, it was even considered permissible for the actor playing Titus to weep visibly on the stage—provided he was a really great star—during those emotional rhymes that demand the lovers' separation because his true love, frankly, is not the Queen but the City of Rome, with its imperial power. To enlarge the Montparnasse stage, it was built out in front in a peak, like a ship's prow, and the right-hand side was widened and carpeted with white fur to simulate an entryway to the Queen's temporary palace. The cast was dressed in various shades of white, the males wearing white broadcloth Louis XIII straight trousers, subtly rich short jackets, and exquisite white kid boots to their thighs. In its romanticism, the play is a long, interrupted poetic farewell. At the rear of stage right there was a succession of tall mirrors, as narrow as pilasters, one behind another, which reflected slices of every motion that the actors made, and also served as a magical porch of exit—an extraordinary stage invention, and perhaps a unique one, by Planchon's gifted scenic artist and costumer, René Allio. But it was Planchon's geometry of physical movement, which he has created as a new classic stage style, that was the most strikingly visible innovation in his "Bérénice." In his program notes, he said, "The characters in the play move or walk in straight lines and right angles. This movement was chosen to give an equivalent of the constraint imposed by the text, which is in verse containing twelve syllables per line. Following a straight line on the stage seems right for tragedy. It affords style to the actors' movements, and in the search for naturalness the movements back and forth are justified by the psychic pulse of the characters within a geometric frame of such delicacy that it gains increased interest. Furthermore, this angular stage method permits certain isolated curved movements by the actors, which thus become all the more significant. This favoring of the angular style can be questioned. But in the end the rigor it forced seemed seductive." Apropos of the stage set, he added, "The spectator of the seventeenth century, for whom the play was written, dreamed—Racine was clearly the first dreamer—of an ideal society in which the princes were equally remarkable as politicians, valorous warriors, and sublime lovers. The scene shown is an evocation of a palace in such an ideal society. This society is not of Rome or of the

Versailles of Louis XV. It is a Louis XIII court, in a dream that borrows the armorial decorations of Rome and the mirrors of Versailles. This box of mirrors seems to me to afford a poetic connection with the way in which the characters question themselves and one another. They are reflected in it in their monologues and are written in the glass. It is a form of reality created backward, by mirrors. The mirrors multiply their unsure world. Titus believes he still loves Bérénice, doesn't know that he no longer loves her. Perhaps mirrors are sometimes necessities for recognizing one's likeness even as a costly illusion." Francine Bergé was the beauteous blond Bérénice, whom Planchon drilled to shout her lines occasionally. Simi Frey was a meditative, sombre Titus, the symbolic man of state and power, who finally banishes love from his idea of government as if it could be an opening form of rebellion. "Bérénice" was as close to unforgettable as a three-hundred-year-old French classic can be today.

June 17

According to travel agents, Europe—and France especially—is enjoying, as well as suffering from, the greatest visitation of tourists in the last half-dozen years. Through the rest of June and all of July, there will not be an unbooked or empty hotel bed anywhere from the North Sea down to the Mediterranean. The present week's Grande Semaine de Paris, ordinarily given over to special public entertainments, inappropriately opened on Monday with a strike of the Métro and the bus lines, during which the city's workers walked to work and walked back home, and the city's visitors walked to their evenings out under a handsome, hazy half moon, while central Paris underwent a phenomenal traffic tieup. The strike is supposedly to be repeated soon, to enable the strikers to win their two demands—a wage hike plus a sixth week added to their paid summer holiday.

Unfortunately, this week's most enticing public entertainment will be enjoyed by very few, owing to lack of space arranged for the public to see it and cheer it. The three nocturnal military tattoos on the east side of the Place Vendôme (the first one is tonight) have been supplied with only two small grandstands. However, last night an unannounced dry run was enjoyed by a few hundred of us neighborhood locals, attracted by the horses parked in the Rue de Castiglione, the promising exploratory toots of an Army brass band, and the presence on the Castiglione sidewalk of the Army's young, haughty Saumur cavalry officers, probably the smartest and most elegant of any left in Europe today—young, aristocratically slender, and impeccably tailored, casting a roving eye on all the prettier demoiselles, while idly slapping their long, tasselled whips against their spurred, shining boots. Then, to the squeal of trumpets and the thumping of kettledrums carried on the white lead horses, the Place Vendôme for two hours turned into the scene of a spirited horse show, ironically honoring, in part, the completion, beneath the big façaded square, of the city's newest underground automobile garage. This being only a rehearsal, we bystanders had the benefit of repetitions of certain exercises, such as *la courbette, la croupade,* and *la capriole,* to assure perfection of unity between the riders and their mounts. In one maneuver, at the touch of a whip the animals all reared up absolutely vertically at the same moment, holding their stance for an instant like profiled equestrian statues, and in another they all suddenly kicked up their hindquarters in unison—while the band, installed in front of the Morgan Guaranty Trust doorway, soothingly played over and over the same dulcet musical theme. The horses were performing under spotlights on one of the sanded halves of the Place, while on the other half, un-illuminated even by the branched sidewalk lanterns in front of the Ritz, which had been turned off, the horses that had completed their performance were being quietly cantered around in the dark, they and their riders both barely visible, like a circle of night raiders; to the astonishment of Napoleon's devotees, his statue atop the famed verdigris bronze Austerlitz column was not illuminated. For the three formal performances, the élite Cadre Noir de Saumur will be joined by the Cavaliers de la Garde Républicaine, dressed in Napoleonic uniforms. For historical-costume value, the most unexpected example will be a small marching contingent in tatterdemalion uniforms, representing the *grognards*—the famous foot-slogging grumblers of Napoleon's army. The Garde ought to be a fine sight and aurally a treat, with its famous trotting brass band.

The Jardin des Tuileries is putting on a more explicitly popular cultural show than ever before for the Grande Semaine. The garden fountains are illuminated, and loudspeakers under the trees carry music from the Paris Radio Orchestra, including Handel's "Water Music." The Jeu de Paume museum is open, free to the public, until midnight. And along the broad garden *allées* nine enormous screens have been set up to carry what is called a *cybarnama,* or huge documentary illustrations of the history of the Tuileries, such as a photograph of the Florentine tapestry illustrating Catherine de Médicis' reception of the Polish ambassadors. The displays are apparently highly satisfactory to the Parisians, who gather in such masses in the Tuileries *allées* that nobody less than giant size can see anything much. The *cybarnama* also shows some of the Jeu de Paume's Impressionist pictures, like large illustrations hanging outdoors beside the trees. Among the pictures is Degas's noted "Absinthe," and it is shown along with an old photograph of the poet Verlaine seated before his café glass of absinthe, a drink that since his time has become illegal. If the good weather only holds—already it has started being interrupted by recurrent showers—the unusual al-fresco June entertainment this year will have given highly civilized enjoyment.

Thursday of this week is the thirtieth anniversary of General de Gaulle's speech over the London B.B.C. in which he said, three times over, *"La France n'est pas seule,"* adding, *"Cette guerre est une guerre mondiale."* This year's June 18th is the second consecutive one on which he will have been willfully absent, in a foreign land, from the scene of the Paris remembrance of his words, which still have their vibrational echo in the recollections of unnumbered French citizens.

July 1

It is now just one year and one week since the present French government settled into place under Jacques Chaban-Delmas as President Pompidou's Prime Minister. His first unpleasant task was to devalue the franc, which President de Gaulle had refused to do, calling it "the worst absurdity." The Premier's end-of-June unpleasantness this year has consisted of keeping his head during what has been a minor rebellion against the post-de Gaulle majority Parliamentary party, the Union des Démocrates pour la République. Quantitatively, there was almost as much criticism from inside the party as there was from the outside—specifically, from a slice of the population in the eastern city of Nancy, in southern Lorraine. This corrective small provincial rebellion shook France's government almost as thoroughly as if it had been national and had taken place in Paris itself. The damage came to an end this past Sunday in a by-election for the recently vacated seat of the Nancy deputy—an election won, according to certain embittered losers, by "American-type huckster publicity," as practiced by the victorious newly arrived Parisian outsider M. Jean-Jacques Servan-Schreiber, founder of *L'Express,* France's most successful weekly news magazine, and author of the influential best-seller all over Europe that was published three years ago under the provocative title "Le Défi Américain." It was in praise of American business management as a necessary replacement for France's rich confusion in such matters, inherited from her long aristo-bourgeois owner-class history. As a débutant politician in Nancy, Servan-Schreiber ran without a political label except for his affiliation with the old Radical Socialist Party, which he joined last year, resuscitating it from France's long-past Third Republic and modernizing it beyond recognition to suit the surprises that constituted his inventive Nancy campaign.

The revolt was essentially against the U.D.R.'s slothful sinking into Parisian centralization, leaving France's provinces like a civilized Gallic wilderness. The unusual, impassioned electoral events at Nancy centered the eyes and the press of Paris on the historic region where Gaullism sprang into bloom, only to wither away last year with de Gaulle's angry, impulsive resignation from public life after he was defeated, ironically enough, in his referendum for increased political regionalization. Nancy's rebellion began in a local squabble about a new highway from Paris to the eastern border, for years served only by an old two-lane road that runs through Nancy. Government ministers in Paris decided that the new road to the east would be a costly four-lane freeway that would run through Metz, Nancy's more industrialized and more prosperous Lorraine rival, thus leaving Nancy deeper than ever in the shade. The project was vainly protested by Nancy's U.D.R. deputy, M. Roger Souchal, who finally resigned his seat in sheer frustration, confident that in the by-election he had thus provoked the Nancy voters would gratefully reëlect him for his stand against the Metz highway. The Nancy saga began taking on the quality of a Balzac short story of French provincial life with the entry on the scene of the free-handed, well-to-do, ambitious Servan-Schreiber (soon reduced to his initials as a simplified form of nomenclature even in Nancy's most popular newspaper, *L'Est Républicain,* which first called him "J.-J. S.-S." and finally reduced him merely to "J.-J."). He had been searching for an opening for his increasingly impatient political ambition, and on Souchal's resignation found Nancy made to his order. "It was like putting the cat among the pigeons," the London *Times* remarked, referring to the carnage among his Gaullist, centrist, and mixed-leftist opponents in the by-election's first balloting, in which he won almost half the votes. He proved a dynamic, inventive campaigner, determined to promulgate reforms; his campaign style was not only new but candid, as part of its novelty. "Truth is always concrete" was reportedly his favorite remark. In an extraordinary, creative effort to aid southern Lorraine's depressed industrial conditions, he hurriedly obtained promises from twenty-one important French and foreign industrialists and bankers to found branches of their businesses in the area of Nancy.

The U.D.R. chiefs in Paris at first thought that J.-J.'s political progress in Nancy was worrying but could not be fatal, but they soon became sufficiently alarmed to send five Cabinet members to Nancy to pinch-hit against him (including their Minister of Finance, Giscard d'Estaing), but their presence merely irritated the Nancéiens, who considered them presumptuous and belated. Hasty party self-criticisms were collected at a meeting of the National Council of the U.D.R. in Versailles and from Paris political circles; indeed, all France suffered more shocks and temblors than at any time since de Gaulle quit the Presidency. Politicians of all parties as well as the public itself were driven to serious consideration of fundamental French policies: of national habits in governing, such as the centralization in Paris, which has been going on since the time of Richelieu; of the role of political parties in relation to Parliament; and of the basic merits and weaknesses of the entire French political system. Never in the memory of French newspaper chronicles has a minor local provincial election caused such a stir. One explanation offered was that it was a sign of the growing personalization of politics today, and the accompanying weakening of the role that political parties themselves play in arousing public interest in their generalized ideas. What the public on both sides of the Channel and both sides of the Atlantic has seemed hungry for recently is a report from a politician's own brains and mouth. Another interpretation of the Nancy rebellion was that it was the result of insufficient authority at the government's top—that yesterday, in de Gaulle's time, the Gaullist deputy Souchal would never have dared resign his seat merely because he disagreed with the government on the question of a local highway; that Servan-Schreiber would never have dared challenge the government in what was normally a safe Gaullist constituency; and that the electors of Lorraine would never have dared vote for him heavily in defiance of de Gaulle's disapproval (which last was taken for granted). In the second, and final, Nancy ballot, Servan-Schreiber triumphantly won 55.28 per cent of the votes cast, and the rest of the candidates were nowhere or lost in the abstentions. Deputy Servan-Schreiber has announced that he will sit in Parliament on the Socialist bench.

The two internationally best-known literary couples of our time have been Elsa Triolet and Louis Aragon, and Simone de Beauvoir and Jean-Paul Sartre. In the United States, Elsa Triolet was less well known as a writer than Simone de Beauvoir, but in France their ranking was equal, if different. Elsa Triolet died unexpectedly two weeks ago after strolling with her husband in the garden of their little property in Saint-Arnoult-en-Yvelines, not far from Paris. Feeling a malaise while still out-of-doors, she sank down on a rustic bench and suddenly died, aged seventy-three. Even knowing her fame, one is astonished at the quality of intimate public reaction that her death aroused among the French. A Russian ornamented by nature and by race, she was unique in appearance, and during much of her life she was ranked by herself and by others as a beauty. She was a nearly perfect intellectual—a bold and critical-tongued Communist who was never afraid to speak her mind on the errors of conduct that the U.S.S.R. often enough committed, such as the tank invasion of Budapest and, more recently, the second occupation of Prague. She was a natural, practicing egotist. She had startlingly beautiful eyes, as Aragon never tired of saying in his poetry—"eyes the color of rain." She was the first woman ever to be given the Prix Goncourt, bestowed on her shortly after the Second World War. Her short story "Mille Regrets" was her first success and is perfection. Written during the last war, it is the story of a Russian refugee in the Midi who has nothing left of her past life but her old fur coat. It is a story that brings tears to the mind and heart. Of her novels, which at first she still had to write in Russian and then translate into French under the eyes of her schoolmaster, Aragon, this correspondent's favorite was "L'Inspecteur des Ruines," the story of a Frenchman after the last war whose municipal post was simply inspecting war-caused ruins. Physically (and one always came back to the subject of her appearance, to which she led one), she perfectly illustrated herself—a rare, small-bodied, foreign-looking Slav, a nineteenth-century Muscovite *petite grande dame*, carried forward over the years by her own sense of self-preservation into our modern times and hers.

When she and Aragon were young and became unbearably penniless, she took to creating fancy, odd pearl necklaces, which she sold to smart Paris dressmaking shops, while he went to work as a cub reporter for *L'Humanité,* the Communist daily paper, for a poor wage. They survived in a rich atmosphere of the luxury of love. Both of them were extremely vain. They could be a little embarrassing in a restaurant because of the ocular attention they centered on themselves; they enjoyed seeing themselves eating well, as reflected in the restaurant's mirrors. Three days after Elsa's death, almost as if it were a final form of public reception, she lay in state on her bier on the ground floor of *L'Humanité*'s office, surrounded by a throng of Parisians filing past and by an opulence of flowers such as might be offered by the people to a female head of state. She had made a broadcast in January that was replayed here the day after her death. In the broadcast, she talked about her sister Lili's great friend, the poet Mayakovski, who killed himself. She related that at a certain time in her life she had repeatedly been visited by a dream about him—a dream that was always the same. In it she would beg him not to take his life, and he would answer, "But I have already done it and I cannot come back and change that now." She added in the broadcast, "Mayakovski could not live in Russia if he were to come back today. He was incapable of lying."

Of all the letters of condolence sent to Aragon and given by him to the press as a matter of public interest, one of the most unexpected and impressive was that from the President of the Republic, Georges Pompidou. He specialized in literature at the university, and is the editor of a well-chosen anthology of poetry. To Aragon he wrote, "Monsieur: Even though we have never met, I am too great an admirer of your poetry not to express to you my condolences at this moment when you have lost the one who was the summary of your existence, its inspiration, and, at the same time, the companion of your life. Do not see in this letter anything but a testimony from one of your readers and the expression of special sympathy for the emotions that you have admirably translated into your poetry. *Croyez, Monsieur, je vous prie, à mes sentiments de haute considération.* Georges Pompidou."

July 15

There has been such a slump of late in first-rate French fiction that even the last Prix Goncourt was simply a murder story, suitable for light August-vacation reading some morning when it rains. However, for ideal holiday reading, to last a full fortnight, there is a new, enormous, calm, interesting volume of memoirs just off the press by France's best-known, best-selling author, the Belgian-born Georges Simenon, famous mystery-story writer and creator of Commissaire Maigret of the Quai des Orfèvres Criminal Brigade. The memoirs will doubtless not be a bestseller, since they are not fiction but Simenon's own inquiry into and recounting of several years from the middle of his life, under the enigmatic title of "Quand J'Étais Vieux." They are preceded by a baffling seven-line preface, which states, "In 1960, 1961, and 1962, for personal reasons or for reasons I do not know, I began feeling old, and I began keeping notebooks. I was nearing the age of sixty. I shall soon be sixty-seven and have not felt old for a long time. I no longer have need to write in the notebooks, and those that I did not use I have given to my children. Epalinges, December 24, 1969." Epalinges is the Swiss village, near Lausanne, where Simenon lives, in indubitable domestic felicity with his second wife, Denise—born Canadian and a tearing beauty—and his four children, three of them boys, the oldest by his first marriage, to a painter. In his memoirs he says that when he first came from Liège to Paris, he frequented Montparnasse and knew Vlaminck, Foujita, Derain, and Kisling, who for the most part became his friends. "Each week, I visited the art shows. Matisse was one of my gods. I saw life through these painters, or, at any rate, I loved its surface that they showed. Today, I find myself facing abstract art, which throws me off my stride. Some of the canvases delight me, but I admit that I don't understand them, that I don't trust them, and that I get the scent of something that smells of a trick. Seen logically, the abstract painters appear to be right. At this moment when we begin to discover the mechanics of the universe—the atom, genes, and anti-matter—it is probably normal that painters should be interested in a decomposed world. The new novel, which contains no plot and which people talk about (I haven't read any of them)—isn't that the same thing in literature as abstraction in painting? I should like to understand, to become enthusiastic, not become a reactionary, but I can't manage it. I have doubts. I hunt reasons. The parallelism between my writing, between my life, and painting has suddenly stopped. Is abstract painting wrong, or am I?"

This is more sustained than most of his discussions with himself, but it sets the tone of his new book, whose aim seems to have been to put his general ideas in order, so that he could see what he thinks and knows and understands. An omnivorous reader, he is also such a self-disciplined writer that he is constantly rewriting in order to assuage his own grumbling dissatisfactions, to a point where he acts like Flaubert. Actually, he is considered a phenomenon, a freak of organization in the French writing and publishing world. Once he has found his idea for a novel (of which he has published two or three hundred), he can sit down before his typewriter at ten o'clock of a Monday morning and finish, without skimping, by Friday afternoon. (He wrote his memoirs by hand, which makes them a self-identifying production.) In these novels he has created a certain style of written French that sounds like spoken French in its easy security, fluency, and capacity for communication—a style that is *sui generis* and that apparently comes from his belief that in writing even of a criminal he must write as if from inside the character's skin. André Gide, who became a fan of his and carried on a long correspondence with him, thought him, for style, perhaps the best novelist in France.

Whatever it was he was worrying about in those troubling years he never divulges, though it may have been a faulty diagnosis by a doctor who assured him he would soon be dead. It certainly did not affect his extracurricular sexual activities, candidly mentioned in the memoirs as a form of truthfulness that he thinks basic to civilized, successful domestic love. What Simenon has written in his long memoirs, running to four hundred pages in octavo format, is like the chronicles that countrified Englishmen wrote a couple of hundred years ago as a form of their national instinct for writing down history, no matter how small its field—a record of their local events and wonderments and crops and family and animals such as made up a complete normal life and was consequently called "a commonplace book," because that was what it was. For anyone who likes to read lengthily in French and at the same time to read intimately of the ideas of a veracious memoirist, Simenon's volume will be a palpable pleasure, like one tall, straight exotic tree that has achieved full growth in a crowded *jardin à la française*.

The real gardens of France—the rose gardens of the Paris suburbs, and their fences—have never been so fully draped in pink buds and blossoms as during this past fortnight, having been first well watered by night rains and then pampered by ten days of rare Seine Valley sun, which shone unflickering from dawn until a cloudless, lemon-tinted dusk set in, with the new crescent moon swelling to the shape of a golden melon cut precisely in half. To the terror of the Tuileries pigeons, on Bastille Day, July 14th, the annual morning flypast of the Fouga-Magister planes of the Air Patrol of France, followed by sixty-six Mirages and seventy-two other planes, plus a gaggle of helicopters, took their noisy flight through the Paris sky. July 14th is France's greatest annual fête day, still celebrating the fall of the Bastille and the resurgence of republican man in full governing power. As if government by the people were always bound to set off sparks, the evening of the Fourteenth is traditionally given over to a superb display of fire-works. The most beautiful, elaborate, costly, and fanciful of any in any city of Europe throughout the year, they are a magnificent celestial display, fired off in its full artificiality from various high points in the capital city—from the hill of Montmartre, from the Buttes-Chaumont in the northeast, from over near Vincennes in the east, from down by the Parc Montsouris in the south—with the richest display this year being sent up from the prominence of the Palais de Chaillot. The best viewing point, allowing one to see all of them in turn with a roving eye, is the roof of one's hotel, if it is near the Tuileries. This year, the skyrockets were, if anything, more elaborate than ever before. As usual, they were manufactured according to the old Chinese art by the house of Ruggieri, with gunpowder supplied in part by the French government, which jealously controls its production. From year to year, pyrotechnic styles change a little, like women's evening clothes, but are now perfected to the point of being able to resist rainfall, such as Paris underwent at 10 P.M., drenching all the crowds. The rockets from the Chaillot hill had rare new lavender colorations Tuesday night, and were elaborately involuted in their packing, so that after the first fallout of effervescent colors, like a great, spreading parasol patterned against the sky, littler umbrellas of solid colors emerged, to float away or to be reinforced by large cerise pear-shaped forms, holding their shape as they drifted off in the style of parachutes, bent on their own brief airy destiny. They were all gorgeous and exquisite, no matter in what direction one looked—all luxurious, civilized, and useless, giving joy and delight and pleasure to the eye for the length of a long breath and the cry of "Aaah-a-ah!" Each pyrotechnic center in the city ended with the same classic finale, always called *le bouquet*—a great rocket that explodes in the sky into what looks like a snowfall of silver-and-gold sparklers. Each of these detonates with a loud bang, creating in its explosion smaller sparklers and bombs, until the last and smallest of all give off their minimum final report. By the time *les bouquets* were all finished, the rain had stopped, and the crowds and the tired children went home.

July 30

There is usually an appreciable news vacuum at this time of year—the opening of the holiday month of August, which has become so hide-bound in practice that it produces a kind of thirty-one-day paralysis of almost everything in France. This time, as an exception, it brought Parisians news of very considerable importance because it was such bad news. On Wednesday, the Paris Opéra finished its annual season with its scheduled "Tosca," but it had been preceded the week before by the Opéra's surprise press announcement that, owing to unspecified *travaux,* or repairs, the opera house would be closed after Wednesday night for the next year and two months—until October, 1971—which was big and bad news indeed. This press release had been followed by another, somewhat more illuminating, from the artists, technicians, and staff of the Opéra, who, with the support of their unions, "requested an interview with the President of the Republic and the Prime Minister, since they wished to make it known to the highest government level that the closing of the state opera house for so long a period would be a serious event, injurious to French lyrical and musical art." Paris gossip added that the Opéra personnel were saying that the talk of repairs was a bluff to hide the insufficient budget of the Ministry of Cultural Affairs since the departure of André Malraux from his post as chief, and that in the necessary cheeseparing the Opéra was trying to force the ballet dancers and chorus singers, already ill paid, to accept diminished working conditions, with no guarantee of their jobs. The reaction of the French public, and especially of its operagoers, has been to say with indignation that this lengthy obliteration of the Paris Opéra in flourishing France is an absolute scandal, and to point out that last year it was also closed for so long that the Opéra ballet had to dance, pro tem, in the enormous Palais des Sports, which only dancers from the Moscow Bolshoi could fill with French balletomanes, and that the opera company sang its operas for a while at the strictly run Théâtre National Populaire, where the lack of discipline among the members of the Opéra troupe made them unpopular both with the T.N.P. audiences and with visiting opera stars—being late for rehearsals and late in ringing up the curtain, having chorus strikes, undergoing labor trouble with their scene shifters, and so on. These were all inheritances from and proofs of the fact that over the last years the Paris Opéra has been running downhill at sixes and sevens. What it needs, according to competent, unprejudiced international critics, is to be completely reorganized, with new blood, new important, gifted, permanent conductors, new administrators, new money from the Minister of Finance, and, above all, with new, strict opera-house discipline. What it will be like after it has been put out to grass until October, 1971, one fears to imagine.

France and its provincial towns and cloisters are increasingly under the spell of the summer festival this year—*le festival estival,* as it is rhythmically called. Some of the August magazines contain maps of France with nothing on them but the festival towns and their programs. It seems that the first provincial festival of our time was organized in 1947 by Jean Vilar in Avignon, in its Palais des Papes. This week, Pirandello's "Ce Soir On Improvise" played there. In the little antique southern hill town of Vaison-la-Romaine, formerly (as this traveller recalls) a haven for silkworms, with cages of them sitting in the main-street café chewing their mulberry leaves, the Aristophanes drama "The Birds" is to be given this week. At Collioure, a little Mediterranean fishing village near the Spanish border, popular with Surrealist painters in the mid-twenties, Giraudoux's "La Guerre de Troie N'Aura Pas Lieu" is to be given in the first week in August. In the theatre of the archbishop's palace in Aix-en-Provence, ambitious music will be given, such as concerts by the Bartók Quartet and by the Orchestre de Paris with the Prague Choir. Off the French maps, in North Africa, festivals will be presented at Hammamet and at Carthage, amid its ancient ruins.

Here in Paris, there have been and will be festival musical offerings in places where music is rarely heard and the place itself rarely frequented, such as the Chapelle Royale of the suburban Château de Vincennes; and the Sainte-Chapelle, behind the Palais de Justice, where the Musica Polyphonica of Brussels will give Scarlatti's "Passion According to St. John"; and even the church of Notre-Dame des Blancs-Manteaux, over in the Marais, where there were heavy organ concerts. The most utilized of the small city churches has been the famous little Gothic gem Saint-Séverin, near Notre-Dame de Paris, where the internationally famed Russian cellist Mstislav Rostropovitch gave the Paris festival's signally great performance when he played Bach's "Suites pour Violoncelle Seul." On the whole, the provincial programs have been more contemporary than those of Paris, which have tended toward ancient or medieval revivals. Certainly the exhilarating influence of American jazz and rock has been more frequent in the south. One or two of the festival towns situated near the inflammable big pine forests above the Mediterranean, where the annual plague of forest fires was already raging, cancelled the rock portions of some of their programs as a literal fire prevention—or so the village mayors said, fearful that their young listeners would get out of hand in careless joy.

Of the theatre performances, the most eccentric one in all France seems to be the one most criticized. Obstinately presented here in Paris every day except Sunday from mid-July through the first week in August, it is Racine's "Andromaque," played in the underground Salle Saint-Louis in the Conciergerie—the old revolutionary prison beside the Seine, on the Quai de l'Horloge, with the gigantic colored clock in its tower. The ceiling is arched, and behind the makeshift stage the spectator sees, like a backdrop, the underside of a stone staircase leading to the street above. On the stage, Andromaque, Hermione, Oreste, and Pyrrhus are carried on encased in plaster statue forms, with apertures at the sides for the arms to protrude with tragic, helpless gestures, and with smaller apertures in the statue faces to speak through. They are carried about by their servitors, dressed in black trousers and jackets, so what the spectator sees and hears is not very well-articulated alexandrine verse in this drama of spiritual conscience in the struggle between the archaic Greek and Trojan civilization and the new Christian sentiments of love, as expressed by Pyrrhus. The servitors for the most part stand immobile and in perfect discipline, while at stage left a tomtom player accompanies, or sometimes even interrupts, the dialogue by tapping and scanning the twelve-syllable lines of the alexandrine verses. The performance lasts a solid two and a half hours, through which this correspondent sat with unbroken interest, with the ears straining but with the imagination stirred, as seemed to be true of the fifty or sixty other listeners, all presumably French and all seemingly unacquainted with one another, knowing only Racine. It is possible that a production with such calculated museological touches as encasing the leading actors in plaster might, in the case of a Shakespeare play given somewhere in England, offend the British listeners to the same extent that it would captivate foreigners, whose ignorance would furnish them with special stimulation at the sight of the bizarre. The Paris critics disliked or ignored this odd "Andromaque." The most damning of them briefly declared that no idea could justify such a ridiculous presentation, nor could any sentiment explain it "except the desire of somebody stupid to do something original," come what might. What was original was the limitless concentration it permitted to the handful of listeners and watchers there in the Conciergerie's ancient hall.

An exhibition of "L'Expressionnisme Européen" was recently on view here at the Musée National d'Art Moderne, and it aroused greater attendance and interest than one would have thought likely, for Expressionist art occupied only a narrow fraction of time in this century, dominated by the German painters and their heavy psychology, though relieved by the French painters' remaining Fauvism. Expressionism usually defies strict definition except as a form of a certain strong feeling for life itself and the entry of certain painting men into a certain state of the soul, as it was then candidly called. The most important of these artists were unhappy to the point of desperate melancholy—artists whose tragedy was the dark mainspring of their art and who have aroused a cult of public love that still surrounds them: van Gogh, Gauguin, Ensor, Emil Nolde, Pascin, Munch, Soutine. In their super-emotionality they were—no matter what their dates or painting styles—ranking Expressionists. In this recent exhibition, there were some extraordinary paintings by them, which some of us had never seen before and are now not able to forget. The honor of the catalogue's colored frontispiece went to Oskar Kokoschka, a junior of Expressionism, in a double portrait of himself and the famous Alma Mahler, widow of the composer and Circe to how many other men and husbands, including Gropius. In the technical brilliance of its painting, this canvas, which comes from a private collection, is a modern rarity. Kokoschka shows the two standing with their hands almost but not quite touching, like tentative lovers—she in a reddish gown, he in a yellow-and-brown jacket. The other master canvas was a 1907 Picasso, a "Demoiselle" of the so-called proto-Cubist series—a dish-faced female creature of even more intense style than the half dozen that Gertrude Stein had hanging beside her salon mirror. The No. 1 portrait was van Gogh's of the narrow-jawed, kindly-faced Belgian painter Eugène Boch, which belongs to the Jeu de Paume Museum of Paris. There was an unfamiliar Gauguin portrait of van Gogh himself—his cheeks showing a red stubble of whisker, his body crouched in a chair, with vague sunflowers growing in the air around him—which belongs to the Vincent van Gogh Foundation in Amsterdam. There were several gay Pascins, in some cases signed "Pincus," which was his real name. Pascin was the most important Expressionist suicide; he killed himself at the height of his fame, in 1930, on the eve of the day his great exhibition opened at the Georges Petit Gallery. As for the suicide of van Gogh at Auvers-sur-Oise, it is so well known that the recent disappearance of the small café and its billiard table, on which he was stretched, seems an underlining of the loss. The wretchedness of Chaim Soutine until his death here, in 1943, from lack of medical care, is almost equally well known. His horrible self-portrait, with hanging lower lip, was hung in this exhibition, along with the sprightly little red-suited "Chasseur de Chez Maxim's." Of the German Blaue Reiter group there were pictures by the Russian Alexei von Jawlensky, as well as by Kandinsky, Klee, and the American Lyonel Feininger. Of the Belgian James Ensor there was shown a self-portrait surrounded by masks of humanity. The Munch pictures showed that Germanic woe which so soon palls on everyone except the German painters themselves. It was an interesting exhibition, and even exciting, because of the portrait by van Gogh.

August 12

Between the first of July and the last of August, the twenty million French who work for a living the rest of the year take their annual paid holiday of one month. This year, even the government is giving itself a three-week August vacation from governing, with President Pompidou at leisure down in the Midi. In July, it vainly tried to influence Parisians, especially, to do what it was not doing itself—to take a holiday then, rather than wait for the warmer, more popular, and more crowded month of August. A fortnight ago, on the opening weekend of August, the hegira of vacation-bound cars on the highways out of Paris was more than ever like the intense, inexorable migration of lemmings headed for the sea. However, fatalities took a dramatic drop on the almost ten thousand miles of French toll roads, where the usually unlimited speed was controlled by signs and policing to the equivalent of sixty miles an hour. Over that first August weekend, there were only 170 dead and 2,245 injured in all France—an increase of a mere twenty-five per cent over last year's road-accident figures for the same event and thus regarded as almost encouraging, since it might have been worse. On roads leading south to the Mediterranean, the bottlenecks lasted five or six hours at a stretch, with a seventeen-mile queue of cars waiting to cross the border into Spain.

There has, however, been one welcome amelioration for the French citizen leaving on holiday travel abroad, provided the citizen is at least ten years old. Owing to the strong condition of the French franc since its devaluation a year ago—the eighth since 1944—Finance Minister Giscard d'Estaing announced that the restrictions of the *carnet de change* would be lifted, and that French citizens would now be allowed to take two thousand francs (something under four hundred dollars) out of the country. Since the two wars, only the citizens whose national money is the almighty dollar have not known what it means to be unable to buy all the foreign money one wants, though now the dollar doesn't buy as much of anything foreign as it used to. *Sic transit.*

Of the seasonal art robberies that rather regularly accompany the quiescent holiday month in Paris, where owners have too economically left their richly ornamented apartments totally un-inhabited, the most sensational in a decade has been that of the remains of what is still called in art circles the Caillebotte Collection. It was the property of the eighty-year-old Geneviève Chardeau, who had often sat to Renoir for her portrait—indeed, one was included among the stolen canvases—and was herself a niece of the Gustave Caillebotte who, as a rich young man (if a poorly endowed would-be painter), assembled his famous collection of Impressionist works by his artist friends in the nearby river village of Argenteuil, where he even built a fine big house to hold his art. Through his friendships, initially with Monet and Renoir, the youthful Maecenas began particularly to buy those canvases that the Argenteuil artists could not sell to anyone else, which meant that he kindly took off their hands the most advanced paintings in the new and generally despised Impressionist style. Later, of course, they became the most significant and also the most valuable in his collection. Among the seventeen just stolen were Renoir's "Young Girls Playing Ball"; a Manet, "The Croquet Game"; two Monets, one of them the famous picture of the Gothic-like open-arched roof of the Gare St.-Lazare; a Corot; three Pissarros; and two Sisleys. It was the harmonious ensemble of the Renoirs that made Mme. Chardeau's small collection so invaluable. According to the French police, all her major stolen paintings are so well known internationally that they could be sold by the thieves only to "a rich maniac" who would be happy merely to gloat over them in secrecy. The police also said that the Chardeau apartment's security system had been neutralized by the robbers' injecting mercury into the door locks and cutting the electrical system that, in case of disturbance, would have rung alarm bells.

Caillebotte's effort—when he was twenty-eight years old, in delicate health, and convinced he would not live long—to will his collection of sixty-five Impressionist paintings in such a way that they would eventually reach the Louvre, to the glory of Impressionism, resulted in such an uproar, principally by the bigoted state Académie des Beaux-Arts, that Impressionist art received its first enormous dose of publicity. Even the French Senate held a solemn, worried discussion of it. A leading Beaux-Arts professor threatened to resign if the Caillebotte legacy was accepted, saying patriotically, "We are in a century of decline and imbecility. The legacy contains pictures by M. Manet and M. Pissarro, doesn't it? For the state to accept such filth would indicate moral blight. Anarchists and madmen! It would be the end of the nation, the end of France." After three years of bitter public argument, which included several newspaper campaigns for and against, forty of Caillebotte's collection were finally accepted by the French state and, in the end, reached the Louvre. (The seventeen recently stolen paintings were a small family remainder of the twenty-five refused canvases.) In an effort to set a value on all this art that the state was getting for nothing, the canvases were given an official financial appraisal upon acceptance. All the Renoirs were given the same value, equivalent at that time to a thousand dollars apiece. (Of the eight great Renoirs in the collection, only six were accepted, including what is now regarded as his most entrancing dance-hall masterpiece, "Le Moulin de la Galette.") The eight Monets were priced a little higher, equal to an additional hundred and fifty dollars a painting. There were also two stray Cézannes among Caillebotte's pictures; so great was the ignorance of the state art officials that they did not even know that Cézanne was not an Impressionist. Indeed, they knew nothing about him, and so gave him the lowest monetary valuation of all—equal to a hundred and fifty dollars a canvas. One expert, glancing at the pair of Cézannes, was recorded as saying, "There's a fellow that will never know how to paint," thus anonymously immortalizing himself.

A de-luxe and definitive volume, called "Diaghilev and the Ballets Russes," which fully portrays Diaghilev himself and sixty of his ballets (it includes several hundred photographs in black and white and seventy in color), will be published in New York this autumn. Written over the years, it was finally compiled and completed here in Paris by its author, Boris Kochno, the most scholarly, meticulous-minded eccentric remaining of all the once-young Russian intellectuals who were early attached to the great ballet impresario. Kochno was born in Moscow and educated at the Lycée Impérial. He first met Diaghilev in Paris in 1921, seven days later became his permanent secretary and artistic counsellor, and remained with him until Diaghilev's death in Venice in 1929. Kochno has written his opus from his enormous private library of correspondence, which he assembled over his years with Diaghilev and all those who worked with him—musicians, writers, painters, and poets. Kochno's collection of memorabilia and documents is vast, unique, and incomparable as source material on this historic foreign dance troupe, which swept Europe and then the Americas with its leaping choreography, its silken colors, and its sensuous aesthetic influences. Some of its décors, such as in "Parade," with its setting designed by Picasso to look like New York skyscrapers, strengthened the position of modern art, and some of its scores solidified the new, violent tonalities of the great music of Stravinsky, as in the carnival tragedy of "Petrouchka." Kochno's particular literary task was to create what are called *les arguments,* or librettos, on which the ballet's action is built, and of which he wrote ten. When Diaghilev, tired of borrowing familiar plots from classics or fairy tales, told him that, as a change, he wanted an *argument* that would be a story everyone on earth knew but that no writer had ever signed his name to, Kochno suggested "The Prodigal Son." It was Lifar's greatest ballet success.

November 11

Upon the death of General de Gaulle in his rural retreat last week, President Pompidou stated, "France is a widow," thus announcing the country's new historical condition with the loss of the single elderly citizen who had husbanded the nation's failing strength in the war in 1940 and from then on had given himself, in devoted obstinacy, to saving France whether in war or in peace, whether in office as its President or in retirement as its critic. He created France's modern history, and wrote it in his "Mémoires de Guerre" and "Mémoires d'Espoir," the latest volume of which appeared only last month. As a people, the French have a special, civilized gift for words suited to their larger events, which seems to enlarge them further, as if the lucid French language were a magnifying glass, presenting selections from French history in bold, big type, easy to read and difficult to ignore. It was by his words that de Gaulle took control of France. To be sure, as a soldier he won a battle at Abbeville, in Picardy, in 1940—possibly the only battle that France did win in those sad days—but it was a victory so obscure that the French public, and even the French Army, practically ignored it. It was by his words, then, that he conquered his people and united them around his person, for or against him, whether in detestation or in devotion—at some moments it seemed to make little difference. Both attitudes were recognitions of a national fact: that he was the polarizing figure of France, imprinting his name on three of its Republics—the waning Third, the disastrous Fourth, and his particular creation, the Fifth. His press conferences, held in the glittering ballroom of the Presidential palace, and attended (on invitation only) by journalists assembled from all over the world, consisted of long, faultless recitations, committed to memory and spoken in his peculiar buglelike voice. His pronunciamentory style was better suited to listening to than to reading. He coincided with the advent of the radio, which served him to perfection, and without which his career, fame, and power would all have been less, muffled by printer's ink and interrupted by punctuation. The grandeur of France was his salvational theme. He altered the invisible map of Europe, the geography of power. He changed the relations between his country and her inherited enemy, Germany, by concluding a pact of friendship watered by the Rhine—a pacific invention that no other Gallic or Germanic chief of state had ever thought of. He interrupted the bitter war of repression against the Algerians to force upon them the freedom they had been fighting for. Though it was Mendès-France who ended France's endless bloodshed in her Indo-Chinese war, thus freeing the region to become a mantrap for American participation, de Gaulle successfully stood off the Communist influence in France itself, which had one of the largest and most powerful Communist Parties of any democracy in Europe, one of his methods being to call the Communists the separatists.

A jealous Frenchman, de Gaulle worried about the seductive

strength of America as France's richest neighbor—indeed, as everybody's richest neighbor—and, with cupidity and ingratitude, tapped our gold reserves in Fort Knox in a system of skillful, legal exchanges that restored the fallen franc, in part at our expense, we being, in his opinion, the only country that could afford to put France back on her feet. His strange political invention of the referendum, which served as a popularity contest for the French voters, in the end led him to retirement, because, as a proud man, his popularity was integral with his pride, and the lost referendum in the spring of last year was a refusal he could not accept. It is a pity that the French themselves could not accept the referendum's aim, which was for a reformed regionalization of France, by which Paris would have lost many of its isolating privileges.

By 1958, de Gaulle discovered that he was further in the lead than the dominant bourgeois political class was able to follow. He radically transformed France's political structure with a new constitution, which was, in a way, a step backward, in that it weakened Parliament by making government an emanation of the Presidency rather than of the National Assembly's deputies, in whose elected strength and wisdom de Gaulle felt that France could no longer completely trust. In obliterating the antiquated Fourth Republic, he dismantled France's remnants of empire, such as the vast territories of sub-Saharan Africa, and gave freedom to Algeria, which many French regarded as a physical part of the nation. In the angry political heat in France over the loss of Algeria, de Gaulle narrowly escaped assassination when a band of malcontents tried to ambush his car on the road from Paris back to Colombey. Their bullets passed behind his head and in front of the head of his wife, Yvonne; de Gaulle criticized them as bad shots. He never lost his sang-froid on any occasion.

Because France had dismantled her own empire, he became a kind of spokesman for the little nations. At the same time, he denounced the splitting of the world into two hegemonies, the American and the Russian—to which, of course, he added a third: France herself, in her new position in the front rank of the Western nations, where he had placed her. He built up France's atomic power as the only military force that had contemporary meaning. At peace with the world, France had a philosophical and foreign policy that seemed close to ideal, in which de Gaulle alone was criticized, for his authoritarianism, his overweening patriotism. He was, indeed, an international figure of first-rank importance whose patriotism was his main blemish.

It was on de Gaulle's trips to the provincial centers of France—to the great wine hills of Burgundy, to the industrial steel centers, to the agricultural southwest—that most of his fellow-citizens saw him in his towering person. These were stately visits, achieved all too often in driving rain, which he would weather without a hat, with a muffler around his throat, and generally with a bad cold, as he sang the "Marseillaise" even more off key than usual at the big factory or vineyard rallies. Once, near the Burgundy cathedral town of Tournus, he made a special visit to a nearby village chapel to see the tomb of an early-eighteenth-century ancestor of his, the de Gaulles having originally been Burgundian, starting with a certain Gaspard de Gaulle, given special privileges by the king in 1581. De Gaulle's father was a professor at Lille; his lineage was ancient. He was a member of the powerful French bourgeois upper middle class to his dying day. The foremost man of Europe and a great French eccentric for more than a decade of personal power, he remained a profound believer in a better, civilizing world. His voice on the air was that of the French leader of his epoch, reciting his convictions.

INDEX:
PARIS JOURNAL

Index

Janet Flanner

Janet Flanner was born in Indianapolis and attended the University of Chicago. Between 1921 and 1974 she lived in Paris. She signed "Genêt" to her first Paris letter for *The New Yorker* on October 10, 1925, the year of the magazine's founding, and her "Letter from Paris" has continued to be one of its regular features. The first volume of her *Paris Journal,* spanning the years 1944–1965, won the National Book Award. Miss Flanner is also the author of *The Cubical City, An American in Paris, Pétain: The Old Man of France,* and *Men and Monuments,* and she has translated books from the French, including two by Colette. A member of the National Institute of Arts and Letters, Miss Flanner has been decorated with the Legion of Honor. She now divides her time between Paris and New York.